Houses
of
Worship

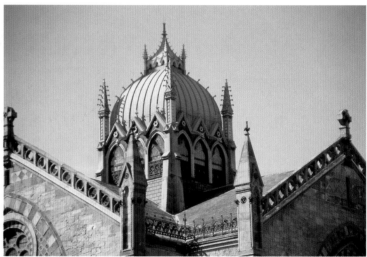

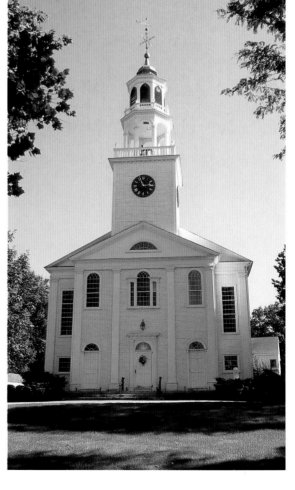

Houses
of
Worship

*An Identification Guide to the
History and Styles of American
Religious Architecture*

Jeffery Howe

THUNDER BAY
P·R·E·S·S

San Diego, California

Thunder Bay Press

An imprint of the Advantage Publishers Group

5880 Oberlin Drive, San Diego, CA 92121-4794

www.thunderbaybooks.com

Produced by PRC Publishing Limited,

The Chrysalis Building

Bramley Road, London W10 6SP

An imprint of **Chrysalis** Books Group plc

ISBN: 1-57145-970-7

Library of Congress Cataloging-in-Publication Data available upon request.

Printed and bound in Hong Kong

1 2 3 4 5 07 06 05 04 03

Contents

115183

There's a church in the valley by the wildwood,
No lovelier spot in the dale;
No place is so dear to my childhood,
As the little brown church in the vale.

—Hymn written by Dr. William S. Pitts, 1857

Religion has been a defining factor of the American experience since the very first humans walked on these shores. The history of our churches, temples, and shrines—the houses of worship—is the history of America. These walls can talk, if we only stop to listen.

The building of churches and temples has always been one of the highest purposes of architecture, and throughout history many of the finest buildings have been created for religious purposes. The architecture of houses of worship reflects the highest values of our culture, and distinct forms have evolved for use by specific groups. These styles have been shaped by national origins, religious history, and symbolic and liturgical requirements. The history of American houses of wor-

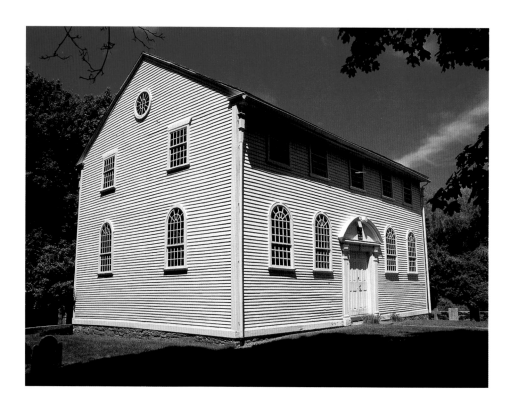

Right: St. Paul's Church (Old Narragansett Church), Wickford, RI, 1707. A meetinghouse built for an early Anglican congregation.

Left: Robert Twelves, designer; Joshua Blanchard, builder: Old South Meeting House, Boston, MA, 1729–30.

ship is the story of America. This book presents an overview of the historical development of religious architecture in America, connecting the buildings to the historical evolution of religions in this country. A range of stylistic sources and meanings is outlined, as well as the changing role of the architect. The evolving relationship to European and world architecture is considered in light of the concept of an American national identity and multiculturalism.

Although the building of churches and temples has often been associated with lavish monuments, Americans have frequently worshiped in structures that were originally built for other purposes. In the colonial era, religious meet-

Left: Richard Upjohn:
Trinity Church, New York,
NY, 1839–46. Side view.

Right: Volney Pierce:
First Congregational
Church, 26 Meetinghouse
Lane, Madison, CT, 1838.
One of the finest Greek
Revival porticos.

ings were often held in houses, and in modern times nearly any type of building has been converted for religious use. Vernacular, or folk style, as well as high style buildings are surveyed in this book. The role of style as an index to social values and historical developments is also explored. These themes recur in many of the specialized subsections.

As a survey of American sacred architecture, this book is intended to serve several purposes: firstly, a history of the development of American churches and temples, and, by implication, American social history and building technology; secondly, a guidebook to assist in the identification of the style of individual buildings, based on historical examples of typical buildings; thirdly, a travel guide to regional monuments of interesting architecture; and finally, a guide to the possibilities of architecture. A distinctive feature of American history is the wide range of religions that have either been brought here by immigrants, or which have arisen from within the culture. Although Christian churches are prominent in this book, the distinctive styles of Jewish, Buddhist, Hindu, and Islamic sacred architecture are also featured. The primary goal for this book is to show examples that illustrate the range and development of styles in American religious architecture. Buildings have been chosen on the basis of their historic significance, architectural merit—whether designed by an architect or not—and representation of ethnic or religious diversity. They have been found by searching the National Register of Historic Places, numerous architectural surveys, a wide variety of guidebooks, and serendipity. Every town and county in the United States has noteworthy churches and temples; a comprehensive survey would be impossible, so this study aims for representative samples.

This book contains nearly 700 photographs, the majority of which were taken by the author. Many were photographed specifically for this project, while others were gathered over a twenty-year period. The book is enhanced by an equal number of drawings. Ground plans are provided for many buildings to show the layout of interior spaces. This extraordinary wealth of images, illustrating different periods and varieties of American churches and temples, is intended to give a detailed portrayal of as wide a spectrum of American building as possible. Clusters of drawings illustrate key features, which help to identify the different housing styles and constructions. An illustrated glossary at the end explains technical terms, and there are brief biographies of many of the important figures in the history of American religious architecture.

Above: On-I-Set Wigwam Spiritualist Camp, 9 Crescent Place at Thirteenth Street, Onset, MA, 1894. A twelve-sided wigwam capable of seating a large number of people. The wigwam shape was chosen to honor the Indian "spirit guide" of the Boston medium Mary Weston.

Above: Eero Saarinen: Chapel, MIT, Cambridge, MA, 1954. The round church countered the prevailing International Style boxes.

Organization of the Book

A general introduction will sketch the overall history of American houses of worship and the forces that shaped them. Subsequent chapters will examine the development of American religious architecture in greater detail, from the earliest shrines and sacred monuments of Native American peoples in Chapter 1 to the most recent contemporary experiments in Chapter 6.

In addition to surveying sacred Native American architecture, the first chapter will examine the development of colonial churches in the seventeenth century. The development of colonial meetinghouses and churches in the eighteenth century will be presented in Chapter 2, including English, Dutch, Scandinavian, German, and Spanish traditions. The third chapter will investigate the first European Revival styles of the early nineteenth century, from Classical to Medieval Revivals. This era introduced the attitude that style was a matter of conscious choice and brought a new eclecticism with revivals of classical and Gothic styles. This attitude came to full development later in the century; the panoply of Victorian Revivalism will be the subject of Chapter 4. Besides the full range of historic revivals, new styles from the Near East and Asia are imported and new homegrown religions spring up, including millenarian and spiritualist groups. Chapter 5 explores the new range of eclectic revivals in the late nineteenth and early twentieth centuries. This was also the period of pioneering modernist experiments in the work of Frank Lloyd Wright and the experiments of Art Deco and Art Moderne.

The final chapter will survey the range of religious architecture created in the modern age, from recycled movie theaters and other commercial buildings to the bold experiments of postmodernism and beyond. The modern age brought the tensions between the traditionalists in church design and the inventiveness of modern architects to the fore. Following the shocks to traditional faith posed by world wars, the Holocaust, and the revolutions of modern science and technology, architects and congregations tried to find a new symbolic language of form for their churches and temples.

Above: Marcel Breuer: St. John's Abbey, Collegeville, MN, 1961. One of the most expressive modernist church designs.

Above: God's Compassionate Center, Chicago Avenue, Chicago, IL. A storefront converted into a church.

The Significance of Style

Architectural style is the primary focus of this book, since it is one of the most visible signs of historical and cultural values. The term "style" refers to the consistent qualities and features that link different works together into groups. The history of style in American architecture is as complex and rich as the history of the nation and its people. There is no single American style of architecture, nor has there ever been. Different immigrant groups and individuals have adapted their own national traditions, and many have borrowed or combined stylistic traditions to create hybrid designs that may confound the architectural historian. In the heyday of eclecticism, about 1865–1930, the entire gamut of historical styles was revived at one point or another. In many cases, the style chosen was meant to signify the allegiances or aspirations of the worshipers. In some cases, however, styles were freely combined, and it can be very challenging to identify which style a particular church represents.

Above: Hindu Temple of Chicago, 10915 Lemont Avenue, Lemont, IL, 1985. The architectural setting reinforces the cultural identity of the immigrant group.

Above: Temple of Eck, 7450 Powers Boulevard, Chanhassen, MN, 1990. A postmodern building for a new religion.

Stylistic labels are frequently associated with value judgments. When making a conscious choice, Americans have tended to pick revival styles on the basis of the moral values attributed to them. Thomas Jefferson felt that classical architecture promoted clear thinking and civic virtues, and so was the most suited for the new republic. Exotic styles appealed to a spirit of adventure and discovery, reminding world travelers of favorite places and stimulating the imaginations of those who had not been to these far-off lands. However, borrowing styles from European sources was increasingly viewed as inauthentic by more avant-garde architects and clients. Champions of twentieth-century modernism argued that the new style marked a complete break with the past and signified a return to the fundamental principles of architecture. The very concept of style was thought to be obsolete, since the method of modernism was thought to be as true and as inescapable as the scientific method. In the latter part of the twentieth century, postmodernism challenged that idea, and the various forms of modernism have taken their place among the historical development of styles.

New and evermore creative houses of worship are being introduced today. Old-fashioned tent revivals still thrive, and bold new cathedrals and temples are being built by architects such as Philip Johnson and José Rafael Moneo. Historic churches and temples are prized for their beauty and symbolism. The cultural landscape has been enriched by the houses of worship of new immigrant groups from Asia and the Indian subcontinent, and New Age worshipers try to find the deeper meaning of ancient rituals. To explore these is to explore our American heritage and the history that shaped it.

The History of Religious Architecture in the United States

I'm but a stranger here, heav'n is my home;
Earth is a desert drear, heav'n is my home.

—Hymn by Thomas R. Taylor, 1836

Themes of exile and the return to a safe home are deeply ingrained in American culture. Again and again in hymns, popular tales, and movies, it is the church or temple that provides a safe haven or comforting home for the errant pilgrim. The experience of living on a frontier was shared by many different groups at different times, from the early Puritans in New England to the Spanish Catholics in the Southwest and the Mormons in Utah. Living in a new

Right: St. Luke's Old Brick Church, Smithfield, Isle of Wight County, VA, 1632–75. A church that is more "Gothic survival" than Gothic Revival.

world was a journey of discovery but also exile. In many religions, earthly existence itself is considered a kind of exile, with the soul temporarily banished to earth. The frontier experience thus mirrored the theological doctrine. Churches and temples served as havens, fortresses, and visions of this lost paradise. Colonies sought to create a "shining city on a hill" wherever they were established, and one of their main goals was to create a house of worship that would bring them together and remind them of their shared identity.

The quest to find meaning in life and the need to honor that meaning through ritual or prayer is one of the fundamental human needs. It is a defining characteristic that is found in the evidence of people's earliest cultural activities. Religion profoundly affects the most primitive and the most sophisticated cultures.

In its widest sense, architecture consists of the entire built environment—anything constructed or shaped to define space or serve as a spur to reflection or memory. In this, it is similar to religion, which takes the whole realm of human experience as its subject. From ancient times, the essential qualities of architecture have been defined as the art of providing shelter, security, and visual stimulation.

Below: Old Ship Meeting House, 107 Main Street, Hingham, MA, 1681, with additions in 1731, 1755. The oldest meetinghouse in New England.

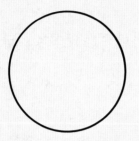

Above: Central planned church; the circular shape denotes eternity, infinity, and perfection.

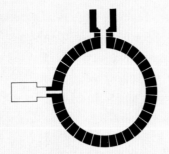

Above: Plan of the Treasury of Atreus, circular beehive tomb, Mycenae, Greece. The axial plan leads into the tomb.

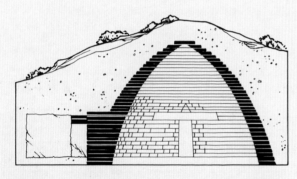

Above: Section of the Treasury of Atreus, circular beehive tomb, Mycenae, Greece. An early corbeled vault, where the successive courses of stone lean progressively further inward.

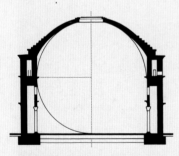

Above: Cross-section of the Pantheon, Rome, A.D. 125. The spherical shape of the dome reflects the heavens.

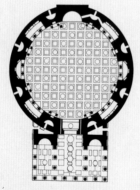

Above: Plan of the Pantheon, Rome, A.D. 125.

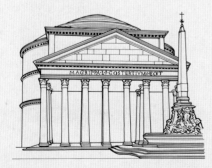

Left: Pantheon, Rome, A.D. 125. This Roman temple was dedicated to all the gods and combines the geometry of spherical, rectangular, and triangular shapes.

The ancient Roman architect Vitruvius (*c.* 20 B.C.) used the terms "commodity, firmness, and delight" to describe these qualities. Compared to houses, religious architecture places more emphasis on the aesthetic dimension. Great architecture is an expressive art as well as being merely utilitarian; it touches our lives in many ways and conveys meaning through both physical and psychological effects. Religious architecture carries a heavier burden than merely functional buildings in that it is also presumed to symbolize or express deeply felt spiritual or philosophical meanings through its form, decorative ornaments, and even materials. The architecture built for worship is enriched with many layers of meaning, stemming from the origins of the group that built it to the evolution of their beliefs. Generally speaking, houses express the values of the individual; churches and temples reflect the values and history of the group that created them.

To make architecture "speak," architects and builders have relied upon natural metaphors of paths, reflective of the pilgrimage of life—either straight and narrow, winding, or even labyrinthine. The association of verticality with the heavens has also been predominant, reflected in the wide usage of steeples and domes to remind one of heaven. High vaulted naves or brightly colored stained glass similarly transport one into a special realm. Inscriptions, sculptures, and paintings often help to further clarify the particular religious faith. There is frequently a tension between the demands of construction practicalities and the desire for symbolic meaning. In fact, tensions run through the history of American religious buildings. Many groups have been torn between the wish to replicate the traditional buildings of their ethnic or religious group and the desire to create a new framework for their new American identity. Religious architecture serves as a marker of cultural identity.

Different groups in America have held widely varying concepts of God and nature; there has never been a country with such religious diversity. It is estimated that there are over 2,600 different religious groups in North America today. The composition and even the beliefs of many of these groups have changed dramatically in the last two hundred years. For some Native American worshipers, the sacred landscape was primary and the purpose of the ritual architecture was to point to that natural dimension. The modern world strongly challenged communities of faith to find symbolic forms that would preserve the fundamentals of traditional belief and yet respond to the challenges of

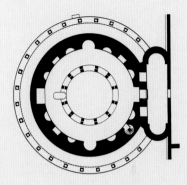

Above: Plan of Sta. Constanza, Rome, c. A.D. 350. The circular plan was adapted from pagan temples and mausoleums.

Above: Axial planned church; the longitudinal plan reflects the journey of life. These are longer than they are wide and are typically entered from the narrow side. The focus is on the altar or pulpit.

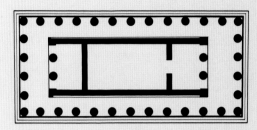

Above: Plan of typical Greek temple. The outer row of columns surrounds the inner temple, a shrine reserved for the temple god and high priests.

modern science and history. This is most strikingly seen in the range of creative expression found in churches and synagogues after the two world wars, which confronted all with the crisis of faith caused by the Holocaust. Although sometimes awkward, many of the new houses of worship are vital expressions of the tenacity of community and of faith.

The techniques and tools available to the builders of American houses of worship have spanned the range from stone-age to space-age technologies. Concepts of beauty have undergone equally radical changes. With new materials and technologies have come the possibilities of new shapes; after centuries of building in traditional wood, brick, and stone, strikingly new expressive shapes have been created by architects such as Frank Lloyd Wright and Philip Johnson, to name only two of the most well known. Architecture brings order out of chaos; geometry and natu-

ral irregularity are the two poles that frame architectural design. In religious contexts, geometry frequently stands for perfection and the divine principle, while irregularity and variety correspond to the changeable qualities of human life and the vagaries of fate. Entire sermons can be constructed from the analysis of these qualities in religious architecture.

The expectations and understanding of the public have changed dramatically in America over the years, from its founding to the present. In both early New England and New Spain, the pragmatic constructions of the first period colonists answered a need for basic functionalism and a comforting image of their European home, and little more was expected of them. The eighteenth century brought a new consciousness of style and demands to keep up with the latest European trends. A new awareness of history was

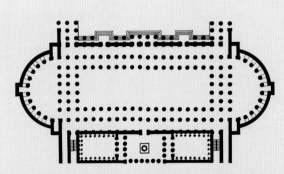

Above: Plan of the Basilica of Trajan, Rome. A stately audience hall for a pagan emperor; the throne was at one end, ensuring a longitudinal approach.

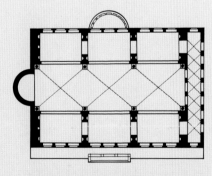

Above: Basilica of Constantine, Rome, A.D. 310–20. A basilica for the first Christian emperor.

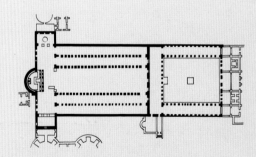

Above: Plan of old St. Peter's, Rome. The first Christian churches adapted the basilica plan, with the altar at one end.

Spatial Plans—Historic Origins

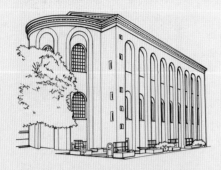

Above: Aula Palatina, Early Christian Basilica at Trier, Germany, early fourth century.

Above: Interior of Aula Palatina.

Above: S. Apollinare in Classe, Ravenna, A.D. 533–49. The Roman basilica plan adapted to an early Christian church.

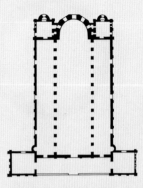

Above: Plan of S. Apollinare in Classe.

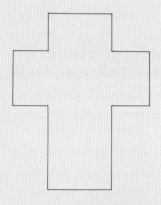

Above: Medieval church plan; transepts gave a cruciform shape to the earlier basilica plan, adding Christian symbolism to the structure.

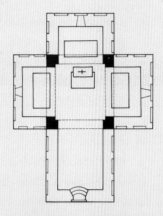

Above: Plan of the Mausoleum of Galla Placidia, Ravenna, Italy, c. A.D. 425. Cruciform plan.

Above: Labyrinth, Chartres Cathedral, France. Medieval labyrinths provided models for the soul's pilgrimage to heaven. The spiral leads inexorably to the center.

Above: Labyrinth on a coin from Knossos, Crete, c. 1400 B.C. Labyrinths are found in the earliest architecture.

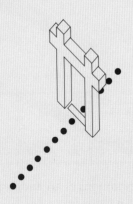

Above: Paths of approach: linear. Ritual processions often follow prescribed paths.

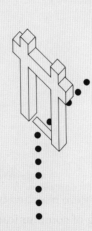

Above: At times the prescribed approach is oblique.

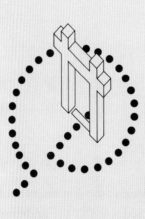

Above: At other times the prescribed approach is a spiral.

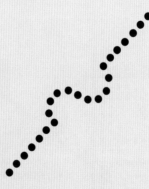

Above: Processional path; the direct linear approach is sometimes preferred.

Above: The spiral path adds dimension to the procession.

Right: Adena Culture, Serpent mound, Adams County, near Locust Grove, OH, *c.* 1000. The mound is over 600 feet long.

developing in the late eighteenth century and bringing with it the conviction that architects could choose from a wider variety of historical precedents. This offered more options for building in the newly independent nation. Only slowly, however, did architects or the public seek an original new style. Andrew Jackson Downing felt that it was simply "absurd for the critics to ask for the *American style* of architecture."[1] The repeated borrowing of European forms, copied from the past and brought to a completely foreign continent and different era became increasingly troubling in the nineteenth century. In 1864, James Jackson Jarves declared:

> Strictly speaking, we have no architecture. If, as has happened to the Egyptians, Ninevites, Etruscans, Pelasgians, Aztecs, and Central American races, our buildings alone should be left, by some cataclysm of nations, to tell of our existence, what would they directly express of us? Absolutely nothing![2]

Yet the ingrained patterns of tradition and ritual invested particular styles and building forms with a nearly sacred quality, which the faithful never considered changing. Ralph Adams Cram avowed that the word "Gothic" "is like an oriflamme, a standard set up by the king for rallying of

loyalty: the fiery cross of Constantine set up with its prophetic legend 'By this sign, conquer!'"[3] The very intensity of this debate reflected the modern concern with style and the relationship between art and culture. The architect Leopold Eidlitz observed in 1881 that:

> The present condition of architecture may be inferred from the question constantly asked, "Will the civilized world, England, America, France, or any other civilized country, ever have a new style of architecture?" There is no evidence that this question was ever asked by the Egyptians, Greeks, and Romans, or by the nations of Europe during the Middle Ages; nor are the Chinese, Japanese, and Persians interested in it at the present day; it is eminently the concern of the so-called civilized world and of the nineteenth century.[4]

Only in the late nineteenth century did Louis Sullivan and Frank Lloyd Wright try to create a new style for the young democratic nation. The revolutions in technology of the twentieth century were matched by revolutions in art and the understanding of communication. Postmodern aesthetic theory grappled with the problem of reconciling the gulf between the avant-garde and popular culture.

Early Architecture in the U.S.

The changing relationship of humans to the environment is inscribed in the history of American architecture. The earliest inhabitants—the Native Americans who lived in the southwestern pueblos, western plains, and the northern and eastern woodlands—used natural materials and preindustrial techniques, which had a minimal impact on nature. Natural and human-made forms were understood to convey

Above: Timothy Palmer (attributed): Rocky Hill Meeting House, 4 Elm Street, Amesbury, MA, c. 1785.

Above: Trinity Episcopal Church (Malbone Church), 7 Providence Road, Brooklyn, CT, 1771. This church was built by Captain Malbone when he refused to pay taxes for the construction of the meetinghouse in Brooklyn.

messages from the spirit worlds; the pantheistic universe reveals itself in sacred places. Native Americans worshiped not just in buildings, but at sacred sites, where the spiritual forces were directly linked to humans. Even domestic architecture incorporated spiritual principles in orientation and structural plans that reflected religious beliefs. Despite limitations of materials and tools, many of these traditions are quite complex and well adapted to the environment. Pueblos possessed remarkable thermal qualities, providing a consistent internal temperature, despite the extremes of climate. The rapidly demountable tepees provided efficient shelter for the Plains peoples. Spiritual and social ideals shaped the structures also; the corbeled dome of the Navajo hogans echoed the shape of the dome of heaven, and the kiva, a sacred ritual chamber, was an essential part of the pueblo. The plank houses of the Northwest tribes were decorated with sacred symbols, generally of natural totems, and the functional layout of their interiors was based on the clan structures of the social group. The rich Native American religious tradition was imbued with a different understanding of symbols and the relationship between humans and nature. The grounds for misunderstanding between their culture and the European immigrants were many. When the European colonists arrived, there were many thriving Native American cultures, with a rich variety of home building traditions; these were soon severely diminished by disease and conquest.

Newly arrived Europeans in America had no thought of creating a new architectural style; they were driven to re-create the church forms they had left behind in the Old World to create a sense of continuity and security. The first European settlers in America were not trained architects, and in many cases their early structures were far inferior to the Native American dwellings. Since both labor and capital were in short supply, the early churches tended to be simple and rather small. Their harsh reality was far removed from later romanticized visions of the first colonial settlements.

The earliest colonial churches were essentially folk-style buildings, made to fulfill functional requirements in the manner of the simple vernacular housing traditions the settlers had known in Britain and Europe. In many cases, they simply worshiped in houses at first. Vernacular architecture is driven by practical needs and shaped by craft traditions, which tend to be conservative. Unlike court-based architecture, which changes style rapidly according to the developments of knowledge or patterns of taste in the court, vernacular architecture evolves very slowly. The postmedieval houses built in New England in the seventeenth century were very much like those built centuries earlier in form and layout. Although it is usually the most common kind of building, vernacular architecture is also the least likely to be preserved and therefore is much less familiar to us than mansions or government buildings. The very first houses of worship were crude, in keeping with the general architecture of the period, and have all disappeared. Reconstructions such as the Fort Church, Jamestown, VA, *c.* 1610, and other archaeological replicas show the character of these primitive buildings. The simplicity and depth of tradition reflected in the houses of this first period, however, made them appealing to later architects such as Frank Lloyd Wright, who sought the roots of American architecture in the first houses built here.

The marked difference between the Puritans in New England and the royal colony in Virginia is clearly shown in the contrast between the Old Ship Meeting House (1681) in Hingham, Massachusetts, a plain, square, wood frame structure, and St. Luke's Old Brick Church (1632–75) in Smithfield, Virginia, which is a very late English Gothic parish church. The square plan and unornamented walls of the Massachusetts meetinghouse reflect the Puritan desire to avoid hierarchical structures and vain ornament in the

Above: San Estevan del Rey Mission Church, Acoma, NM, 1629–42.

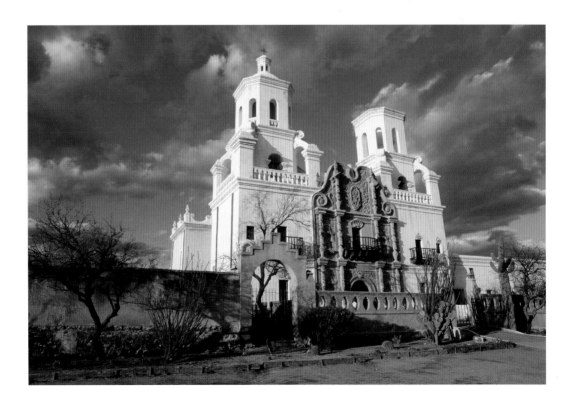

Right: San Xavier del Bac, Tucson, Arizona, 1783–97.

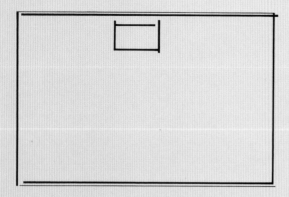

Above: Generic New England seventeenth-century meetinghouse plan; these are square, or nearly so, and typically entered from the long side.

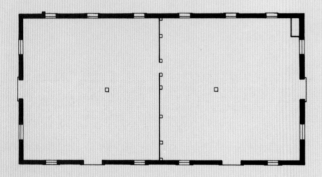

Above: Diagram of early Quaker meetinghouses, divided into separate sections for men and women. Temporary dividers were sometimes used.

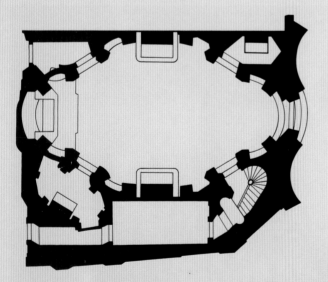

Above: Plan of Francesco Borromini: S. Carlo alle quattro fontane, Rome, 1665–67. Constructed at the same time as early American churches, European Baroque churches displayed a flair for dramatic spatial composition.

approach to God. In contrast, the Virginia church's use of the Gothic style with its traditional oblong nave and long approach to the altar reinforces a sense of hierarchy. The stepped gables, medieval buttresses, and lancet windows advertised the unity of this colonial church with the Church of England.

Greater religious diversity appears among the colonists in the eighteenth century. The first Jewish synagogue in New England dates from this time: the Touro Synagogue (1759–63) in Newport, Rhode Island. It was designed by Peter Harrison, a classically oriented architect. Meetinghouses for the Quakers and Shakers in Pennsylvania and New England reflected their preference for a plain style and lack of ostentation. The eighteenth century brought economic growth, cultural consolidation, and stronger ties to the European courts, with a resulting transformation of the dominant architectural styles. The two main developments were the spread of Wren-type churches in the first part of the eighteenth century, inspired by Sir Christopher Wren's plans for fifty-one new churches for London. Later, the influence of Gibbs's St. Martin-in-the-Fields (1722–26) became more prevalent. The second half of the eighteenth century saw increasing sophistication in terms of style and craftsmanship.

This pattern of crude beginnings rapidly followed by increasing sophistication was repeated in the frontier settlements throughout the nineteenth century, as successive waves of settlers built simple churches and temples of wood, or even sod, in the western prairies, replacing them with more elaborate structures as quickly as they could. Regional differences and the different traditions of the national groups who settled these regions were very important. The coming of the railroad led to a more homogeneous architecture, as materials and designs were more easily transported.

The Colonial Era

Colonial history in the seventeenth century was marked by strong regional differences. There was certainly no unity among the colonies founded by rival nations. They were competing ventures, seeking to establish themselves and to gain primacy over the native inhabitants and each other. Nor did the multicultural settlements of the time lead to mutual cooperation. Each rival group sought a foothold:

Structural Guides

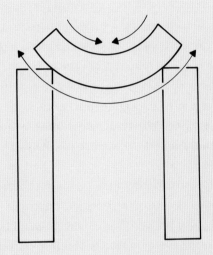

Above: Diagram of post-and-beam, or column-and-lintel, construction.

Left: As a lintel bends, the top is subject to compression forces, while the underside is subject to tension.

Above: Early lintel construction in a religious structure; Stonehenge, Salisbury Plain, England.

Left: Diagram of a cantilever, a projecting element counterbalanced by its own weight or the weight of the wall above it.

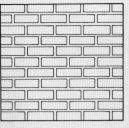

Above: Brickwork—running bond.

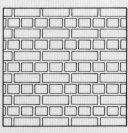

Above: Brickwork—English bond.

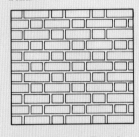

Above: Brickwork—Flemish bond; alternating headers and stretchers.

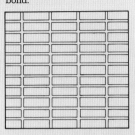

Above: Brickwork—stack bond.

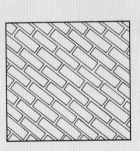

Above: Brickwork—diagonal running bond.

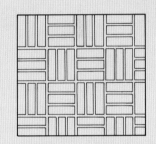

Above: Brickwork—basket weave pattern.

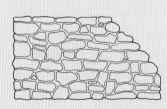

Above: Types of stone masonry: Coursed rubble masonry.

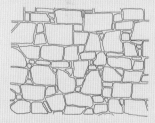

Above: Irregular polygonal masonry.

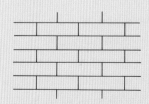

Above: Ashlar masonry. In ashlar masonry, all stones are rectangular, of the same size, and laid in continuous courses.

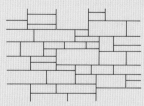

Above: Random ashlar masonry. Stones are rectangular, but not of the same size and not laid in continuous courses.

Above: Asher Benjamin: Meeting House, Route 103, Windsor, VT, 1798 (portico added 1922).

the Spanish in Florida and the Southwest, the British along the eastern seaboard in New England and Virginia, the Dutch in New Amsterdam (now New York) and the Hudson River valley, the French in Canada and Louisiana, and Swedes and Germans in the Delaware valley.[5] The life of the colonists was hard; the importance of the church as a symbol of security and meaning cannot be overestimated. There was little energy for or interest in stylistic innovation, and American building lagged considerably behind the fashions of European architecture.

The eighteenth century brought a greater homogeneity of style on the East Coast, as the classically inspired Georgian style spread across the region. The time lag between the appearance of new European styles and their introduction in America began to shorten, as trained builders and carpenters came to the New World and books on architecture began to be imported. In the absence of trained architects, these books were invaluable to the gentleman builders of the era. They were scarce, however; even

the largest libraries, such as the collection of 4,000 books amassed by William Byrd II in Virginia, had only twenty-three books specifically on architecture. Thomas Jefferson's great library of nearly seven thousand volumes, which he sold to Congress in 1815 to form the core of the Library of Congress, included only forty-three books on architecture.[6] Skills in drawing and architectural design were considered important parts of a gentleman's education, and some of the most notable American buildings were built by such enthusiastic amateurs as George Washington and Thomas Jefferson. Until 1797, when Asher Benjamin published *The Country Builder's Assistant* in Greenfield, Massachusetts, all books on architecture were imported from Europe.[7]

The period of about 1714 to the American Revolution is called Georgian, after the ruling English monarchs. After the reign of Queen Anne (1702–14), George I ascended the throne (ruled 1714–27), followed by George II (1727–60) and George III (1760–1820), who ruled during the American Revolution.

The second half of the eighteenth century saw increasing sophistication in terms of style and craftsmanship. The Georgian style was succeeded by a classical style strongly influenced by the British architect Robert Adam (1728–92). It is often called either the Adam Style or the Federalist Style, after the Federalist period of American government. This period also saw the rise of more professional architects, such as Charles Bulfinch (1763–1844) in Boston. Bulfinch was the first American to attempt to make a living as a professional architect, although he still needed salaries from positions he held with the city government.

At this time, imitation of historical precedents was valued more than personal innovation; it was the era of classical revivals in painting and sculpture as well as architecture. Independence in architecture was to be found not in creating a new style, but in a new choice of models. In the late eighteenth and early nineteenth centuries, a new form of classical architecture arose and quickly spread around the world. Inspired by Enlightenment studies of ancient history and archaeological excavations at Pompeii and Herculaneum, neoclassical architects strove for a higher degree of accuracy in their re-creation of ancient forms. The many newly established academies in Europe encouraged artists and architects in this study of history. One of the most influential proponents of classical art, Johann Joachim Winckelmann, summarized the academic attitude: "There is but one way for the moderns to become

Arches

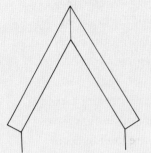

Above: Triangular arch.

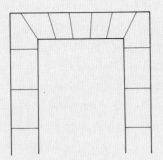

Above: Flat arch.

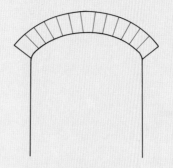

Above: Segmental arch.

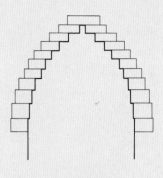

Above: Corbeled arch.

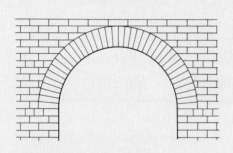

Above: Diagram of a circular arch made of brick. The arch was the basis of Roman architecture and offers more design possibilities.

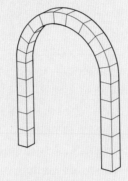

Above: Stone arch diagram—semicircular arch. Vaulting with stone was beyond the capabilities of American architects for many years.

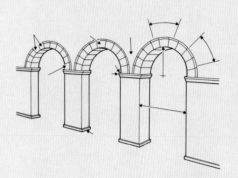

Above: Parts of an arch, shown in an arcade.

Above: Acute arch, or lancet arch.

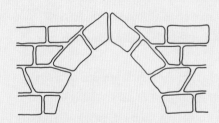

Above: Stone arch diagram—pointed arch. The pointed Gothic arch was introduced in the Middle Ages and became popular in the Gothic Revival of the nineteenth century.

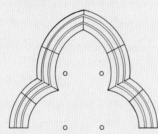

Above: Trefoil arch.

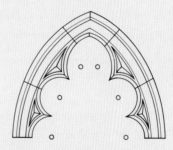

Above: Cinquefoil arch.

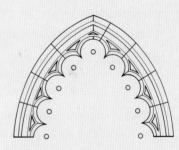

Above: Multifoil arch.

Above: Horseshoe arches; Herter Brothers: Congregation K'hal Adath Jershurun, the Eldredge Street Synagogue, New York, NY, 1887.

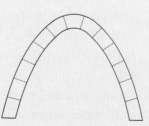

Above: Parabolic arch.

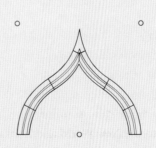

Above: Ogee arch.

Above: Multifoil arch; Schneider & Herter: Park East Synagogue, New York, NY, 1890. The Islamic influence is evident here.

Above: Mohegan Congregational Church, Church Lane, Montville (near Uncasville), CT, 1831. A church built for a Native American congregation in Connecticut in a European-based style.

great, and perhaps unequalled; I mean, by imitating the ancients."[8] This did not mean that they were dispassionate; Thomas Jefferson (1743–1826), the most important neoclassicist in America, described his feelings about a Roman temple he had seen in France as like those of a "lover staring at his mistress." This was a Romantic classicism, motivated by high ideals and passionate yearning for a new and better era.

Although designs were frequently merely copied from ancient Greek and Roman prototypes, another equally important factor, the rationalist admiration for geometry, inspired architects to a style of simplicity and purity of form. Compared to Baroque or eighteenth-century architecture, neoclassical buildings are more severe, with simple colonnades and more planar wall surfaces. Classical architecture was associated with the foundation of learning and law, and hence was frequently used in

libraries and government buildings. The Enlightenment confidence in the rational design of social and political institutions was reflected in the choice of the best examples of classical architecture for their institutional buildings. Eighteenth-century architectural theory focused both on the structural qualities of classicism, and also the expressive significance of the classical forms. According to French theorists known to Jefferson, the goal to find the foundation of architectural symbolism was to create a "speaking architecture" (*architecture parlante*), which communicated meanings. The French Jesuit Abbé Laugier suggested that classical columns derived from tree trunks and thus symbolized both nature and freedom. The column should never be attached to the wall, but left freestanding. Neoclassicism was born of this new analysis of structure, history, and symbolism.

The end of the eighteenth century witnessed the first neoclassical buildings in America, created by Thomas Jefferson. The initial designs for Jefferson's own house, Monticello, were first closely modeled on the villas of Andrea Palladio, but they became increasingly complex as Jefferson transformed the rigid symmetry of the original geometric plan into a series of rooms shaped by functional requirements and his own personal predilections. As a Deist committed to enlightenment values, Jefferson had little interest in building churches. The University of Virginia is centered on the library, not the chapel.

To look at American history through the prism of religion casts new light on small groups of idealists, who tend to get overlooked in the emphasis on larger economic and political issues. Yet they are a fundamental part of the rich texture of American life.

The unique Ephrata Cloister was created for a group of devout separatists, followers of the mystic Conrad Beissel, who was inspired by earlier German Pietists. The imminent return of Christ was fundamental to his doctrine, and earthly life was seen as just a temporary exile from the true heavenly home. The Ephrata Cloister was built in the early 1740s in the manner of earlier German timber architecture in Lancaster County, Pennsylvania. The most striking building is the central Saal, or meeting hall, with steep pitched roofs and many small windows. The members of this community committed themselves to celibacy and a strict regimen of work, simple diet, and prayer. The group was at its height in the mid-eighteenth century, and the community comprised over twenty buildings. Internal dissension in later years led to the dissolution of the group, although it had an important legacy in the Seventh Day Adventist church.

The late eighteenth century brought new groups to America, including the Shakers. Led by the charismatic Ann Lee (1736–84), who left England in the early 1770s to find greater freedom in the colonies, the Shakers were guided by personal visions and a dedication to strict celibacy and a simple lifestyle. Mother Ann had been part of a group of "Shaking Quakers" in England and found many new followers in New York and New England. Rejecting the formal symbolism of the Anglican church, their chapels were deliberately based on domestic architecture. Excellent examples survive at Canterbury, New Hampshire (1792); Sabbathday Lake, near New Gloucester, Maine (1794); and Hancock Village, Massachusetts.

Above: William Rhoades, master builder: Old Round Church, Bridge Street, Richmond, VT, 1812–13. This unusual church was built to serve five denominations.

Below: Ephrata Cloister, Ephrata, PA, 1741/43.

Vaults and Domes

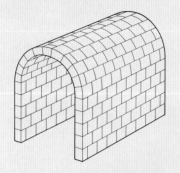

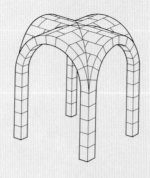

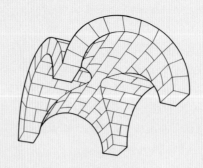

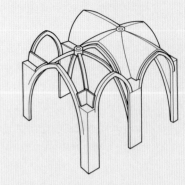

Above: A barrel (or tunnel) vault, which is basically an extended series of semicircular arches.

Above: A groined vault, formed by the intersection of two barrel vaults.

Above: A groin vault seen from below.

Above: A ribbed groin vault structure.

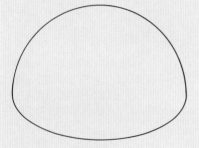

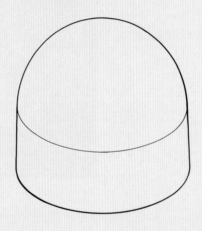

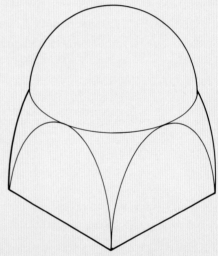

Above: Dome; a hemispherical shape created by an arch rotated in space.

Above: Dome supported on a cylindrical drum for a raised profile.

Above: Dome supported on pendentives, curved shapes bridging the distance between the circular base of the dome and a square foundation.

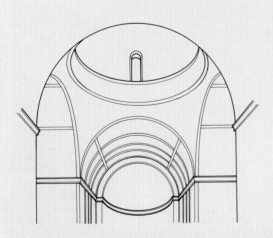

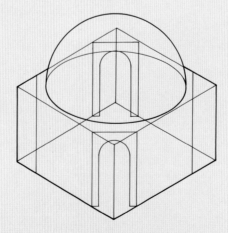

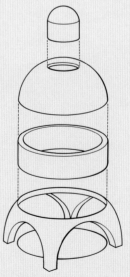

Above: Pendentives—curved, triangular transitions between a round dome and square plan of a Byzantine church.

Above: Dome supported on squinches, arched shapes bridging the distance between the circular base of the dome and a square foundation.

Above: Diagram of a dome.

Roofs

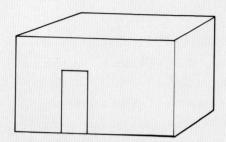

Above: Roof types—flat roof. Flat roofs are common in early architecture, such as adobe houses and pueblos of the Southwest, as well as Mediterranean buildings. They are also a hallmark of the International Style in the 1920s and 1930s.

Above: Steep pitched late medieval gable roof. The steep pitch of gable was related to Gothic design and also helped Northern roofs shed snow and rain efficiently. Many first period meetinghouses in New England had similar roofs.

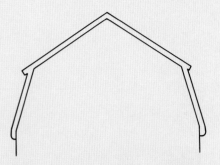

Above: Profile of a Gambrel roof frequently found in Shaker meetinghouses.

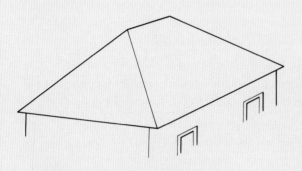

Above: Hipped roof. The hipped roof gave a lower and more unified profile, and was typically used by meetinghouses that strove for a more classical appearance in the eighteenth century

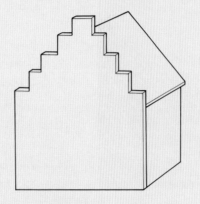

Above: Flemish stepped gable. The stepped gable, which is a false front before a regular steep gable, was characteristic of Dutch and Flemish settlements in the seventeenth and eighteenth centuries, and revived during the eclectic revivals of the nineteenth and twentieth centuries.

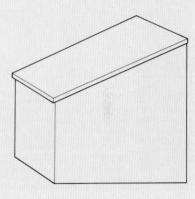

Above: Shed roof. Shed roofs were frequently used in late twentieth century modernist homes, commercial buildings, and some churches.

Above: Simple roof truss with collar beam.

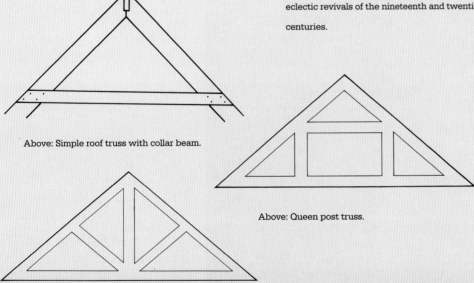

Above: Queen post truss.

Above: King post truss.

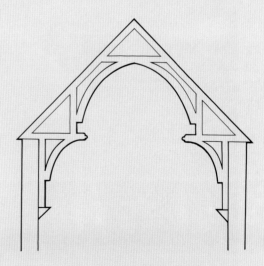

Above: Hammer beam ceiling framing.

Above: Volney Pierce: First Congregational Church, 26 Meetinghouse Lane, Madison, CT, 1838. A perfectly proportioned Greek Doric temple front.

European Revivals of the Early Nineteenth Century

The nineteenth century brought a great increase in historical knowledge and an increasingly sophisticated awareness of the relationship of style and religious and social values. The range of historical reference and stylistic expression expanded dramatically, with styles consciously chosen to reflect specific emotional or ideological associations. These linkages were particularly important for religious buildings. Since there were no direct links to these historical traditions in America, styles were a matter of deliberate choice. In this eclectic century, nearly every historical style that had flourished in Europe was revived at some point.

Traditional meetinghouses continued to be built throughout New England, expressing the continuity of faith. New historic references were found in the first neoclassical churches, which frequently echo the forms of Roman churches, either as a sign of Catholic identity or as a symbol of enlightenment values. Examples include Benjamin Latrobe's Catholic Cathedral (Basilica of the Assumption), Baltimore, Maryland, 1804–18; and the Monumental Church, Richmond, Virginia, 1812, designed by Robert Mills.

The Greek Revival, which flourished from 1818–50, was the first national style in the U.S., spreading across the continent and used in all levels of building, from high style to

Left: William Miller: William Miller Chapel, County Route 1, vicinity of Fairhaven, Low Hampton, NY, 1848. A simple folk-style Greek Revival church for a visionary preacher.

Above: Zoar Moravian Church, County Highway 10, Chaska, MN, 1863. Greek Revival in a frontier setting.

Above: A. W. N. Pugin: Plate from Contrasts, 1836. The foremost polemicist for the Gothic Revival favored Gothic over all the classic churches in London.

folk architecture. The Greek Revival was fostered by such books as *The Antiquities of Athens* by James Stuart and Nicholas Revett (London, 1762), which featured the first measured drawings of ancient Greek architecture.

Greek temples were originally constructed as houses or shrines for the gods, not for the worshipers. The temple interiors contained statues and offerings to the gods, while the public worshiped out of doors. The classical style was associated with prestige and power from the very beginning, and through association with aristocrats and kings has become almost a common language of power, especially in secular architecture.

The Greek temple form was used for both Christian and Jewish houses of worship. Examples of this style include: Alexander Parris's Stone Temple (1828) in Quincy, Massachusetts; St. Peter's Roman Catholic Church (1836) in New York City; and Kahal Kadosh Beth Elohim

Synagogue (1843) in Charleston, South Carolina. Not all neoclassical buildings incorporated elaborate quotations from classical models, however.

The Greek Revival was a flexible style, which could be adapted to many different building types, from houses to commercial buildings. Many small churches were built with just a few small touches to make them seem more classical. The William Miller Chapel, built by the visionary prophet William Miller in 1848 in Low Hampton, New York, near the Vermont border, is one of these. This rural chapel also indicates the growing trend of Americans to create new religions based on their personal experience of the divine. Miller converted many followers to his belief that the second coming of Christ was going to occur on October 22, 1843. When it did not occur as he predicted, this date became known as "the Great Disappointment." Although his prediction was wrong, Miller inspired many later evan-

Left: Richard Upjohn: Church of the Ascension, Episcopal, New York, NY, 1840–41.

Right: Richard Upjohn: St. Luke's Episcopal Church, Main Street, Charlestown, NH, 1863. Addition by Richard M. Upjohn. This church is similar to the designs published in Upjohn's *Rural Architecture* of 1852.

gelicals with a millennial focus. The yearning to return to a heavenly home continued undiminished.

The chief rival to the Greek Revival in the early nineteenth century was the Gothic Revival, which flourished from about 1800–60. This was perhaps the most important style for church building in the nineteenth century. Historical and religious associations made it particularly appealing, and even mandatory for some denominations. The first Gothic Revival churches appear shortly after the turn of the century; one of the earliest is Maximilian Godefroy's St. Mary's Seminary Chapel (1806–8) in Baltimore, Maryland. Even classically oriented architects designed Gothic churches, as seen in Benjamin Latrobe's Christ Church (1808) in Washington, D.C., and William Strickland's St. Stephen's Episcopal Church in Philadelphia of 1822–23. The major figure is Richard Upjohn, whose Trinity Church (1839–46) in New York City is only the most prominent of his many commissions. Upjohn adapted his Gothic style to simple wood frame structures, which could be built for smaller rural congregations in a "Carpenter's Gothic" style. This style was based on medieval precedents, encouraged by popular literary trends. The first Gothic

novels in the eighteenth century presented an exotic and imaginative view of a Romantic medieval past.

The Gothic style had one great advantage in the eyes of many since it was not of pagan origin, as were the Greek and Roman temples. The Gothic style originated in the late twelfth century and was appreciated for its spiritual suggestiveness. In 1858 the architect Leopold Eidlitz noted that the great height of Gothic churches, aided by the use of pointed arches, leads the eye "continually upwards, without a well defined, but rather a suggested conclusion, leading the mind to the infinite *above*, which conveys the idea of God, not only beyond the limits of the building but beyond the limits of space appreciable to the physical sense."[9]

A growing conviction that the irregular and picturesque Gothic architecture was more closely attuned to nature than the abstract classical style also encouraged its popularity in the United States. Nineteenth-century critics such as Ralph Waldo Emerson compared the structures of Gothic churches to natural precedents such as forests, with the pointed arches inspired by intersecting branches or to the fanciful crystalline structures created by frost.[10] Even Frank Lloyd Wright identified the Gothic spirit with a true appre-

Above: Reverend George Stewart: Good Samaritan Episcopal Church, Main Street, Sauk Centre, MN, 1869. English Gothic transplanted to the Midwest.

Turrets

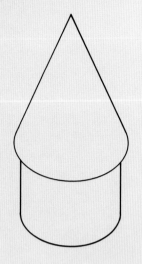

Above: Turret with a conical roof.

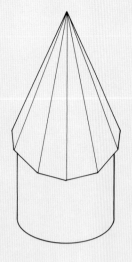

Above: A spired roof.

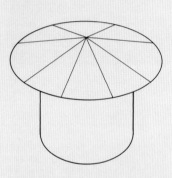

Above: Rotunda; round with a shallow, domed roof.

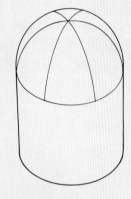

Above: A domed roof.

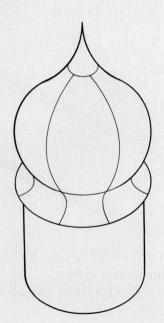

Left: Imperial, with an onion dome roof.

hension of natural principles and harmony with nature, which he calls Organic Architecture; Wright asserted in the introduction to the first German publication of his works (*Ausgeführte Bauten*, 1910) that the feeling for the organic quality of form was more perfectly realized in Gothic architecture than in any other style.

By midcentury, other style options appeared. The lure of Italy was very strong, and the Italianate style flourished from about 1846–1900. This was another style with broad appeal, which was easily adapted to both wood frame structures and stone villas. Pattern books such as those by A. J. Davis and Samuel Sloan played an important role in popularizing this style. The Italianate mode could be more flexible than the Greek Revival, but was less fussy than the Gothic Revival. It was particularly recommended for those with artistic tastes. Churches built in imitation of Italian Renaissance examples were built for urban congregations in Philadelphia, Boston, and New York, and then spread further across the United States. These were frequently built for Roman Catholic congregations.

The nineteenth century was a period of individualism, with a number of experimental revivals of styles remote in history or geography. While exotic styles, such as Egyptian Revival, were more commonly used for cemeteries and public memorials, such as the Washington Monument, there were also a number of houses built with Egyptian columns and other devices reminiscent of the ancient culture. A few churches were built in this style. The most important was built by Minard Lafever, the First Presbyterian Church (Old Whaler's Church), Sag Harbor, New York, 1843–44.

Victorian Styles—Heavenly Mansions

The Civil War marked a transition in American building; after the conflict, a rich variety of highly decorated styles from wider ranges of historical and geographic sources flourished. This was an age of economic and geographic expansion in the United States, which Leland Roth has aptly called an era of energy and enterprise. Although styles were still derived from European precedent, increasing signs of innovation appeared. A new professionalism emerged in architecture at this time, with the first school of architecture founded at the Massachusetts Institute of Technology in 1868. Illustrated journals of architecture also appeared in the 1880s.

Above: Charles A. Cummings and Willard T. Sears:
New Old South Church, Copley Square, Boston, MA, 1874–75.
A splendid example of the High Victorian Gothic.

Above: Alexander R. Esty: Christ the King Presbyterian
Church (Prospect Congregational Church), 99 Prospect Street,
Cambridge, MA, 1851.

These more ornate Victorian styles were used to create churches and temples that seem to embody the phrase "heavenly mansions." The greater economic wealth and sophistication of the congregations was matched by more elaborate houses of worship. A wide variety of historical styles were revived in this period.

The Early Romanesque Revival flourished from about 1844 to 1880, and was related to the German *Rundbogenstil* (round arch style). This style was a revival of pre-Gothic architecture, as created in Europe during the eleventh century. This very substantial style, with its thick walls, narrow windows, and even crenellations, suited the image of the church as a fortress against the challenges of sin and modernism. This was largely replaced by the Richardsonian Romanesque in the 1870s. Leading practitioners included Richard Upjohn and Alexander R. Esty.

The Renaissance Revival was adopted at this same time. The basilica plans of Early Italian Renaissance and Early Christian churches were revived by architects seeking a simple, yet not stripped-down style rooted in the past. The style allowed for both the symbolism of returning to the forms of the earliest Christian churches and also the sophisticated palaces of the Italian Renaissance. Interesting examples were built between about 1845–90, including Patrick C. Keely's Immaculate Conception Church in Boston (1858–61), and McKim Mead and White's Judson Memorial Church, Washington Square South, New York City (1888–93).

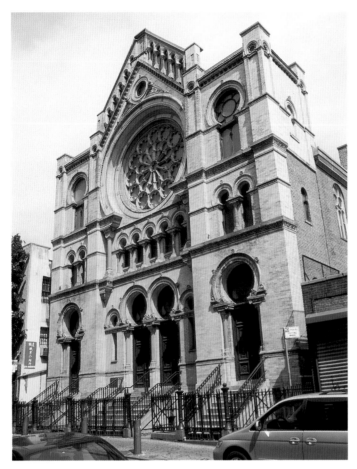

Above: Herter Brothers: Congregation K'hal Adath Jershurun, the Eldridge Street Synagogue, 14 Eldridge Street, New York, NY, 1887. Eclectic mix. This was the first major synagogue established on the Lower East Side by the Orthodox Eastern European Ashkenazi Jews.

Above: Louis Sullivan and Dankmar Adler: Pilgrim Baptist Church, originally built as Kehilath Anshe Ma'ariv Synagogue, 3235 E. Ninety-first Street, Chicago, IL, 1891. Front view.

One of the most vibrant styles to appear at this time was the British-inspired High Victorian Gothic. This modern Gothic style was inspired by the writings of John Ruskin and included an emphasis on polychromy and irregular patterns derived from Venetian and French Gothic buildings. This was one of the dominant styles for public buildings during the period of 1860–80, but the style was also adapted for houses. The variety and irregularity of the High Victorian Gothic style created an image of flux and change, rather than timelessness. It seemed in keeping with the rapidly increasing pace of modern life. David Handlin has argued suggestively that the clashing vibrancy of the most dramatic High Victorian Gothic may have been intended to reflect the "often dissonant nature of life in the latter half of the nineteenth century" and the unsettling dominance of flux and change in modern life.[11] Important examples of High Victorian Gothic churches include: Jacob Wrey Mould's All Soul's Unitarian Church (1853–55) in New York City; the New Old South Church (1874–75) in Boston, designed by Cummings and Sears; and Leopold Eidlitz's Church of the Holy Trinity (1873) in New York City.

Equally decorative and also rooted in complex history was the Moorish/Islamic Revival, which flourished from about 1846 to 1900. It was used for synagogues that sought to emphasize the roots of their tradition in the Near East. The Jewish diaspora created a sense of exile, and the use of Islamic architecture reflected a nostalgia for the period in Spain before 1492, a time and place where Jewish culture had at least temporarily been left to develop in peace. Spanish mosques, such as the great mosque at Cordoba, were used as models. The first Moorish synagogue was the Isaac M. Wise Temple (1863–65) in Cincinnati, Ohio, designed by James Keyes Wilson. In New York City, the Central Synagogue by Henry Fernbach of 1872 and the Park East Synagogue of 1890 by Schneider & Herter are distinguished examples.

Security and stability were qualities exuded by the Richardsonian Romanesque style. One of the most original architects of the late nineteenth century was Henry Hobson Richardson, who introduced a new style based on European Romanesque architecture. Although it was another historical revival, the new style was distinctive enough that it came to be named after him. Richardson adapted the heavy stone construction of French and Spanish Romanesque architecture to new purposes and

Above left: Henry Hobson Richardson: Trinity Church, Boston, MA, 1872–77. Front view.

Above: Notre Dame le Grande, Poitiers, France. A model for Richardson's Romanesque style.

Left: John Lyman Faxon: First Baptist Church, 848 Beacon Street, Newton, MA, 1888. This church is frequently mistaken for one of Richardson's own works.

Above: Religious symbolism—Roman triumphal arch, Rome. The triple arch was adapted for Christian churches as a symbol of the trinity and the triumph over death through salvation.

modernized forms. His churches in Boston launched the style: Brattle Square Church, 1871, and Trinity Church, 1872–77. Richardson's designs were larger than the earlier Romanesque Revival and show the influence of Ruskin in their animated patterns and powerful forms.

Some styles more commonly associated with residential architecture were also used for churches, such as the Second Empire Baroque. This richly ornate style, derived from French models, was the main competitor for stylistic dominance in public buildings and housing in the third quarter of the century. It is called the Second Empire Baroque because it was a Baroque Revival style that appeared during the reign of Napoleon III in France, which was known as the Second Empire (1851–70). The expansion of the Louvre in Paris at this time contributed enormously to the prestige of this style. One of the hallmark features of this style in housing is the use of Mansard roofs, with their distinctive profile. The Second Empire, or Mansard, style was flexible and could be built on a very large and ornate scale in stone or on a much smaller, cottagelike scale using wood, making it possible for different classes to utilize it.

The passion for ornament and individualism combined with the thriving lumber industry to lead to the creation of a less common, but highly decorated style of wooden architecture known as the Stick Style. This style flourished from

the 1850s to 1890 and featured angular and rectilinear patterns of boards used as ornament on the exterior of the house. It was rarely used for church architecture, though a few examples can be found. As with the original Gothic style, ornament is derived from structural elements.

One of the most popular styles ever found in American houses was the Queen Anne style of about 1880–1910. This was a highly elaborate style, with only the loosest connection to the historical Queen Anne, who reigned just before George I. These houses typify the term "Victorian" to the average person and include many of the so-called Painted Ladies. This style may have seemed too domestic for use in religious buildings, however, although a few have been found. The late nineteenth century Baptist Church in Ludlow, Vermont, is one example.

For those seeking an alternative to the busy variety of materials and forms in the Queen Anne and other Victorian styles, the Shingle Style offered greater simplicity. A distinguishing feature is a continuous skin of wooden shingles for the roof (now generally replaced by composition roofing) and wall surfaces. The Shingle Style appeared in the last quarter of the nineteenth century and was one of the first styles to tap into American building history for its sources. Partly inspired by seventeenth-century colonial architecture, when many houses were covered with shingles instead of clapboards, this style also included design elements from Japan and Britain. The centennial exhibition of 1876, commemorating the Declaration of Independence, helped encourage interest in American design precedents. The Unity Chapel in Spring Green, Wisconsin, by J. Lyman Silsbee and Frank Lloyd Wright in 1886, is one example.

Religious revivals and a new prosperity after the Civil War led to much church building. The erection of dignified churches was seen as an extension of missionary activity, as the church was a material symbol of the permanence and security of the religion. An essay published in 1894 by the Church-Extension Society of the United Brethren Church (which became part of the United Methodist Church in 1968) identifies the church building with the true home for the congregation, and the prestige of an appropriate church building is necessary for the practical tasks of fund-raising: "Much money and people have been lost to our own Church, and much will be lost, by not having churches." In a land with freedom of religion and where denominations must compete on the open market for new recruits, a church is a powerful advertisement:

> A church, to make its way in a land populous with churches, must have prestige to succeed the best. A house is necessary to foster the confidence of success in the projectors of the work and to inspire confidence of purpose, ability, and perpetuity in the community where a church enterprise is undertaken. While many have turned away for want of confidence, much has been and will be gained by having a homelike church. Church erection is absolutely essential to permanent church-extension, and most people know it. A church is one of the chief cornerstones of success.

The author of the essay was candid about the need to exercise control over the flock: "As a cage is necessary to hold the canary, and a palace to keep the thrifty hive from flying away, so a church-house is necessary to keep the most thrifty congregation together."[12]

The church thus serves as a home for the congregation, a fundraising tool, and a public advertisement of their prestige.

The multiple roles of religious architecture in providing a badge of identity, shelter, and a vision of heaven is especially notable in the houses of worship built for the Church of the Latter-day Saints, or Mormons. The first Mormon temple at Nauvoo, Illinois, of 1846 was destroyed soon after the murder of Joseph Smith and the migration to Utah. One hundred and fifty years later, this temple has just been reconstructed (2002). Memory and history are reclaimed in this monument.

While descriptions of heaven and the afterlife have long been provided by theologians and biblical texts, these are necessarily speculative. Many hungered for direct knowledge of the life hereafter, and the Spiritualist movement offered a means to do that, by contacting the spirits of dead people through mediums. This movement was at its height in the late nineteenth century, and while never very large, it inspired some unique buildings. The most established

Above: Frank W. Sandford: Shiloh Temple, Durham, ME, 1896–97. Second Empire, plus lighthouse-like tower. Denomination: The Kingdom, a Protestant sect. A style rarely used for religious buildings.

Religious Symbols

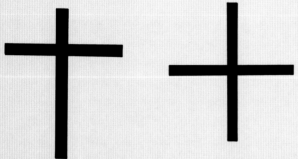

Above: Latin cross. A variety of cruciform shapes can be found in Christian churches.

Above: Greek cross.

Above: Maltese (Crusaders') cross.

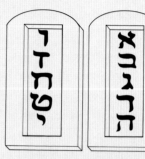

Above: The tablets of the law, as given to Moses. Frequently found on Jewish temples.

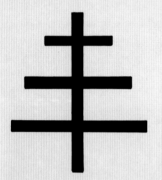

Above: Papal cross.

Above: Russian cross.

Above: Gothic window with a Star of David motif; John Murphy: St. Peter's Church, Hartford, CT, 1865–68.

Above: The Star of David, frequently found on Jewish temples, but also on some Christian churches.

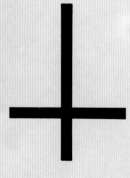

Above: St. Peter's cross.

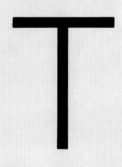

Above: Tau cross; a T-shaped cross.

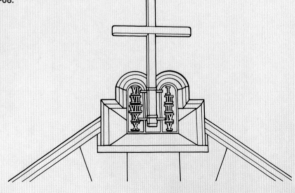

Above: Leonard Asheim: B'nai Israel Synagogue, Bridgeport, CT, 1911. Now the New Hope Missionary Baptist Church: The tablets of the law have been combined with a superimposed cross.

Above: The star and crescent, a key Islamic symbol.

Right: Patrick C. Keely: St. Stanislaus Kostka Roman Catholic Church, 1327 North Noble Street, Chicago, IL, 1876–81; towers 1892 by Adolphus Druiding. Ornate Northern Baroque.

groups of Spiritualists adopted traditional historical styles, such as the Richardsonian Romanesque Spiritualist Temple in Boston (1884). One of the earliest spiritualists was Timothy Brown, who claimed he built his own house in 1855 according to directives from spirit guides. Many spiritualist mediums relied upon the ghosts of dead Indians for their "spirit guides." In 1894 the Boston medium Mary Weston had the On-I-Set Wigwam Spiritualist Camp built in Onset, Massachusetts, in the form of a large tepee in honor of the Native American spirituality. The borrowed form is purely symbolic.

The late nineteenth and early twentieth centuries were marked by large waves of immigration from Europe. Many churches were built by specific ethnic groups who sought to maintain their cultural identity through the symbolism of their traditional religious architecture. The design of their

Above: George Ries: St. Agnes Church, 548 Lafond Avenue, St. Paul, MN, 1909–12. Austrian Baroque.

Above: comparison: Hofkirche, Innsbruck, Austria, 1553–63, with seventeenth-century addition.

Religious Symbols

Above: A symbol of the Evangelists, inspired by the Revelations of St. John: St. John, an eagle.

Above: A symbol of the Evangelists, inspired by the Revelations of St. John: St. Luke, an ox.

Above: A symbol of the Evangelists, inspired by the Revelations of St. John: St. Mark, a lion.

Above: A symbol of the Evangelists, inspired by the Revelations of St. John: St. Matthew, an angel.

houses of worship provides a tangible reminder of their ancestral home, just as it did for the first European colonists in America. It is an architecture of continuity in exile. Revivals associated with specific ethnic groups include the Flemish Revival, Baroque Revival, Russian Orthodox Revival, and Spanish Colonial Revival. It should be noted that these revival styles were also used by academically trained architects, who saw them as an alternative to the classical and Gothic styles. Specific examples will be discussed in Chapter 5.

Late Gothic Revival

At the end of the century, a new wave of Gothic Revival churches was built, influenced by the Arts and Crafts movement and also liturgical considerations. Ralph Adams Cram was the leading architect of this movement. This latest phase of the Gothic Revival presented a more unified appearance, with greater archaeological accuracy in the revival of Gothic forms.

Above: Notre Dame, Paris, *c.* 1163–1250. One of the first Gothic cathedrals.

Left: Ralph Adams Cram: Cathedral Church of St. John the Divine, 1047 Amsterdam Avenue, New York, NY, begun 1893.

Pre-WWII—Eclectic Revivals

The period from 1880 to 1940 saw a wide variety of historical styles utilized in American building. Many architects now had extensive academic training, and the revivals were frequently more historically accurate than in preceding decades. These historical revivals provided a counterpoint to the modernism that was to develop in this period.

There was a revival of American eighteenth-century architecture, the first revival of American buildings. Some impetus for this was given by the renewed interest in American history occasioned by the centennial exhibition in 1876 in Philadelphia. Many examples of the Colonial Revival were built across the United States between about 1880 and 1955.

Although Ralph Adams Cram is generally identified with the later Gothic Revival, he also appreciated the Colonial style for its "simplicity and directness, its honesty, its native refinement and delicacy, its frequent originality." Cram built the Ruggles Street Church, in Boston, in 1913–17.

European revivals were still very important; among the most prominent of these eclectic revivals was the Twentieth Century Gothic. This was an era of ambitious cathedral building, reflecting the new prosperity and confidence. Examples include the Cathedral Church of St. Peter and St. Paul (Washington Cathedral), Washington, D.C., begun in 1907; and the Riverside Church in New York City of 1927–30. The melding of Gothic church and skyscraper is seen in Holabird and Roche's Chicago Temple of 1924, where a church is built atop a 512-foot-high skyscraper.

Although this period also saw the rise of modernist experiments, the vast majority of churches were built in traditional revival styles. Some of the revival styles of the era include the following:

Tudor Revival
This style was popular between 1890–1940; it was inspired by British Tudor and late medieval architecture. The style is characterized by steep pitched sloping roofs, and often with half-timbered façades and asymmetrical towers.

Left: Ralph Adams Cram: Ruggles Street Church, Audubon Circle at 874 Beacon Street, Boston, MA, 1913–17. A Colonial Revival church by the master of the Gothic Revival.

Right: Holabird and Roche:
Chicago Temple, Chicago,
1924. This church is 512 feet
high, perched on top of a
skyscraper.

Beaux-Arts

The Beaux-Arts style flourished between 1885–1930. It was a Renaissance-inspired style made popular by the training of the French Ecole des Beaux-Arts. The style is characterized by formality, symmetry, and lavish ornament. The success of the classical 1893 World's Columbian Exposition in Chicago contributed to the popularity of this style. Because of the expense and high degree of skill required, the style is typically found only in churches and temples for large urban congregations.

Left: Jack Liebenberg: Temple Israel, 2324 Emerson Avenue South, Minneapolis, MN, 1928. A Classical Revival temple.

Below: Maginnis, Walsh & Sullivan: St. Catherine of Genoa, Catholic Church, 170 Summer Street, Somerville, MA, *c.* 1915. Front view.

Italian Renaissance

This style is closely related to the Beaux-Arts style and was popular between 1900–35. It is characterized by designs modeled on Italian Renaissance churches.

Neoclassical

The neoclassical style is also related to the Beaux-Arts style. Flourishing between about 1895 and 1950, this style was inspired by Roman and Italian Renaissance architecture; it was characterized by large entrance porticos with monumental columns.

Romanesque Revival

The Romanesque Revival continued well into the twentieth century; French and Italian Romanesque models were frequently copied.

Byzantine Revival

The term Byzantine is derived from the former name of the capital of the Eastern Orthodox church and the Holy Roman Empire, named Constantinople by its founder, Constantine, then called Byzantium and now known as Istanbul. The term refers both to architecture linked to the political identity of the eastern Roman Empire and to the buildings of the eastern Orthodox church, whether found in Greece, Turkey, or Russia. It is a medieval style, which originated in the fifth and sixth centuries and flourished until well after the fall of Constantinople in 1453. Later used for both synagogues and churches, this style was based on churches from the Byzantine empire in the Middle Ages in Venice and Constantinople. It is characterized by the use of domes and thick, planar walls encrusted with ornament, and frequently mosaics of Christ or other holy figures.

Russian Orthodox

The Russian Orthodox tradition is an offshoot of the Byzantine tradition. In America, Russian Orthodox churches, with their characteristic onion domes, were built

Above: Clarence Blackall, Clapp, and Whittemore: Temple Obahei Shalom (Lovers of Peace), 1187 Beacon Street, Brookline, MA, 1928. A Byzantine-influenced synagogue.

Left: Sts. Peter and Paul, Russian Orthodox church, Minnesota Highway 65, Bramble, MN, 1915–18. Distant view of this remote church, built by Russian immigrants.

Above: Jaroslaw A. Korsunsky: Sts. Volodymyr & Olha Church, 739 North Oakley Blvd., Chicago, IL, 1975. Detail of mosaic on front wall.

by Russian immigrants as early as 1844 in Alaska, and later in areas with concentrations of Russian immigrants, such as Chicago and New York. This included frontier settlements such as northern Minnesota and large urban centers such as Brooklyn, New York.

Spanish Eclectic

Revival styles based on the Spanish Colonial period were especially popular in the Southwest and California between about 1890–1930. These churches feature stucco walls and red tile roofs, with Spanish-inspired detailing. Spanish-influenced churches were built from Florida to New York City. The style was given a major boost from the 1915 Pan-American exhibition in San Francisco and the contemporary studies of Spanish architecture by Bertram Grosvenor Goodhue, designer of the exhibition.

Scandinavian Revival

The distinctive forms of southern Swedish medieval churches were occasionally copied in America as well. The Swedish-born architect Martin Gravely Hedmark created fine examples in Providence, Rhode Island (Gloria Dei Evangelical Lutheran Church, 1925–28), and New York City (Trinity Baptist Church, 1929–31).

Mormon, or Latter-day Saint, Temples

These continued to be built in traditional form, but were less constrained by tradition and were thus free to experiment with nontraditional styles. There were Prairie Style Mormon churches, as well as Art Deco and modernist designs.

Specialized forms of non-European origin were built for different faiths; these are found wherever large groups

Above: Jean-Baptiste Louis Bourgeois (1856–1930): Baha'i House of Worship, 100 Linden Avenue, Wilmette, IL, 1920–53. Overall view.

Above: Hindu Temple of Chicago, 10915 Lemont Avenue, Lemont, IL, 1985. Based on tenth-century temples in Southern India, but adapted to a harsher Midwestern climate.

of immigrants are located. These are primarily shaped by the national traditions of the immigrant group and their religious beliefs. Among the most distinctive are Hindu temples and Islamic mosques. Other examples include temples for the Baha'i and Zen faiths.

These eclectic styles represented the vast majority of churches and temples built in the early twentieth century, despite the critical enthusiasm for modernist building. Most people, in fact, preferred the traditional styles and their links to European or other national roots.

The question of a truly American style was more urgently raised in the early twentieth century. It coincided with the search for a style expressive of the new technological age, and the two were often seen as synonymous. The most important effort in this regard was the Prairie Style; an indigenous American style created by Frank Lloyd Wright and his Midwestern counterparts, which flourished from

about 1893–1920. The style includes aspects of the Shingle Style, fused with elements from Japanese architecture and a rejection of European historicism. Wright's later Organic Architecture builds on the principles of the Prairie School. Both Wright and Louis Sullivan strongly condemned American architects' continued borrowing of European forms. Wright felt that a new architecture based on modern living patterns, technologies, and concepts of space had to be created. Rather than seeing the church as a box containing various rooms, he wanted to create the interiors first, and then shape the building around them. By emphasizing the flow of space instead of mass, Wright helped shift American architecture from an architecture of solid mass to one of volume and transparency. With windows treated as banks of light screens, walls became more dynamic as well. Wright's Unity Temple (1906) in Oak Park, Illinois, inspired other architects to create modernist designs.

Right: Frank Lloyd Wright:
Unity Temple, 875 Lake
Street, Oak Park, IL, 1904–6.
Front view.

Below: Comparison: First
United Church of Oak Park,
Lake Street, Oak Park, IL,
1916. Directly across the
street from Wright's temple
is a Twentieth Century
Gothic church, highlighting
the innovative approach of
the Prairie School architect.
Rebuilt after a fire in 1916,
the congregation rejected
Wright's modernism.

After World War I, new modernist experiments emerged. Architects in Europe enthusiastically embraced modern materials such as metal and glass, and firmly rejected historical ornament. Many of them admired and were influenced by Frank Lloyd Wright, but they went even further in creating a new style for the new age. These modernist styles at first appealed only to a small elite seeking a new mode of life, but eventually were embraced by a broader segment of American society. The focus on the modern resonated with the longstanding American desire to create a new world, beyond Europe's borders, owing nothing to the past. These modernist styles include:

Art Deco, or Art Moderne

This was a style that embraced modernism, but was also rooted in past traditions. Churches built in this style, which flourished between about 1920–40, generally modify Gothic ornamental features with streamlined, simple geometry and planar walls.

International Style

The most important current of the new architecture was the International Style, which began about 1925 and continues to the present day. A modernistic style that rejects historical ornament, the International Style was named for a 1932 exhibition of the works of LeCorbusier, Mies van der Rohe, and Walter Gropius at the Museum of Modern Art in New York. Modern building technology is revealed by the frequent use of curtain walls, ribbon windows, and cantilevered floors. European-born architects such as Rudolph Schindler and Richard Neutra brought firsthand knowledge of these new directions to America. Significantly, both men came to the United States to work with Frank Lloyd Wright in the early 1920s. Two of the main sources of the International Style, Walter Gropius and Ludwig Mies van der Rohe, immigrated to America in the late 1930s to escape Nazi Germany. Both Gropius and Mies had a tremendous effect on American architecture through their teaching as well as their buildings; Gropius headed the Harvard School of Design and Mies directed the Illinois

Above: Ludwig Mies van der Rohe: St. Saviour Chapel, Illinois Institute of Technology, Chicago, IL, 1952. A deliberately understated chapel by one of the leading International Style architects.

Institute of Technology in Chicago. The reductionist quality of this style has made it unpopular for churches, although Mies created a model chapel at the Illinois Institute of Technology campus in Chicago in 1952.

Gropius and Mies van der Rohe are both associated with the most influential design school of the twentieth century, the Bauhaus in Germany. Although the Bauhaus was one of the main points of origin of the International Style, the emblem of their 1919 prospectus was a Gothic cathedral. The very name Bauhaus derives from *bauhutte,* the mason's huts, which were used during the construction of a Gothic cathedral. Just as Gothic cathedrals brought together the entire community and united the Arts and Crafts, the idealists of the Bauhaus hoped to create a new world order based on collective work and technology. The Gothic cathedral employed a skeleton of stone ribs to display great expanses of stained glass; the Bauhaus architects used steel skeletons to create volumes of space enclosed within transparent walls of plate glass. Medieval architecture was intended to support religious narratives in sculpture and stained glass; the modernist design refused to define or limit the meaning, offering a clear package that could be filled with a variety of interpretations.

In 1951, Reinhold Niebuhr castigated the rampant eclecticism of the previous era, calling for a more meaningful program of modern church design:

> In a sense the formless exuberance of American church architecture in most of the churches built between 1870 and 1930 is a perfect expression of the formlessness inside the church. Neither Gothic architecture nor the chaste New England meetinghouse is the only possible architecturally poetic frame to outwardly symbolize the spiritual of the church. A vital Christianity will express in new architectural forms or in novel adaptations of old forms to the new realities of a technical society. But American church architecture in the period mentioned revealed no discipline of any kind. It was merely the expression of free imagination and the fruit of some architects' conviction that a church should not look like a grain elevator. Therefore it was distinguished from the latter by as many turrets, arches, and other curious gingerbread elements as the architect could dream up.
>
> It is neither necessary nor possible for the "free churches" to return to the traditional forms of the liturgical churches. There can well be more freedom and spontaneity than these forms allow. [13]

Above: Eliel and Eero Saarinen: Christ Church Lutheran, 3244 Thirty-fourth Street South, Minneapolis, MN, 1949. Front view.

The post-WWII era brought the tensions between the traditionalists in church design and the inventiveness of modern architects to the fore. Following the shocks to traditional faith posed by the Holocaust and the revolutions of modern science and technology, some churches and temples tried to find a new symbolic language of form.

The Modern Age

The tensions between high culture and mass culture have never been more intense or led to more interesting results than in the last 100 years. The formal language of architecture was expanded, and the basis of its meaning reconsidered. Architectural symbolism had been the defining factor in almost all the styles associated with the eclectic revivals of the late nineteenth and early twentieth centuries. The modernist movement had suddenly discarded nearly all traditional symbolism. At the same time, increasing attention was being paid to the theoretical structure of

Above: Frank Lloyd Wright: Unitarian Meeting House, Shorewood Hills, Madison, WI, 1947.
Front view.

communication and architectural symbolism. Theoreticians such as Charles Jencks applied modern theories of semiotics (the study of signs and symbols) to architecture. Sign theory recognized the importance of the role of the viewer in the structure of meaning; it was not just the architect's intentions that mattered, nor could the building be said to simply "speak for itself." There is a dynamic relationship between the architect/author, the building (the signifier), and the interpretation, or the viewer.

The last decades of the twentieth century saw a proliferation of stylistic options, including:

Formalist

Precisely because the International Style was perceived as lacking in emotional and spiritual expression, many modernist architects experimented with more expressionist shapes in their designs for churches and temples. Frank Lloyd Wright and Le Corbusier were the leaders in this.

Wright's extraordinary range of designs was shown in his Unitarian Church (1947) in Shorewood Hills (near Madison), Wisconsin; the Beth Sholom Synagogue (1954–59) in Elkins Park, Pennsylvania; and the Annunciation Greek Orthodox Church (1956) in Wauwatosa, Wisconsin. This demonstrated how far he had come from the early Prairie Style and inspired the next generations of architects. Le Corbusier's Church of Notre Dame du Haut (1954) at Ronchamp, France, and the monastery and abbey church of La Tourette (1956–60) near Lyons, France, were equally influential. Other fine examples of modern churches include the Air Force Academy Chapel (1956–62) at Colorado Springs, designed by Walter Netsch; and Wallace Harrison's "Fish Church" (1958) at Stamford, Connecticut. One of the most striking was Marcel Breuer's designs for St. John's Abbey (1961) at Collegeville, Minnesota. The best of these match the power and depth of feeling of abstract expressionist painting of the same era.

Above: Frank Lloyd Wright: Beth Sholom Synagogue, Elkins Park, PA, 1954–59. Front view.

Above: Frank Lloyd Wright: Annunciation Greek Orthodox Church, 9400 West Congress Street, Wauwatosa, WI, 1956. Front view.

Left: Russell Gibson von Dohlen, Inc.: Blessed Sacrament Roman Catholic Church, 15 Millbrook Drive, East Hartford, CT, 1973. The spare abstraction of modernism is dressed up with traditional symbolic statuary.

Above right: Comparison: The Big Duck, Route 24, Flanders, Long Island, NY, 1931.

Right: Edward Slater: Trinity Church ("Fish Church"), 716 Route 25A, Rocky Point, NY, 1964. Front view.

Above: Eric Mendelsohn: Mount Zion Temple; 1300 Summit Avenue, St. Paul, MN, 1951, altered in 1967.

Recycled Structures—Adaptive Reuse

The same age that saw the abandonment of historic ornament in the new modernist styles also brought a renewed respect for the past and the development of the modern historic preservation movement. Compared to houses and commercial buildings, which were often casually destroyed, churches have fared better because of their historic and religious significance.

A by-product of the historical preservation movement, which gained strength in the 1970s, was the conversion of older building types into new uses. Examples of structures that have been successfully converted include storefronts, theaters, drive-in banks, and auto repair centers. The tradition of adaptive reuse fits well into the religious trend to find sacred meaning in all things; these humble vernacular buildings are literally reborn into a new life of worship.

Homeschooling has been a growing trend in the last three decades; there has also been a similar growth in people turning to worship in their homes. The Home Church move-

ment is still somewhat underground, but there is a network of websites and publications devoted to the trend. The parallels to the early Puritan meetings held in homes of congregation members are deliberate.

Vernacular Structures or Contemporary Folk Architecture

Ordinary domestic-style buildings have continued to be built or converted for smaller churches throughout the twentieth century. Larger congregations have frequently built meeting halls reminiscent of modern commercial architecture, also a kind of vernacular style. Although they might look more like convention centers or exhibition halls, they serve the purpose of creating a large, flexible space for the worshipers. Tent revivals, which were popular in the late nineteenth and early twentieth centuries, have also never disappeared and continue to thrive in both rural and urban areas.

Inexpensive churches in this era include mass-produced modular structures and even Quonset huts, which were utilized during and immediately after World War II. The noted

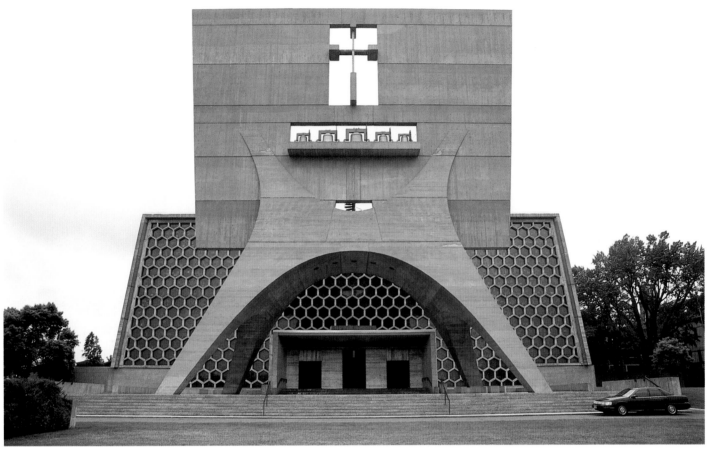

Above: Marcel Breuer: St. John's Abbey, Collegeville, MN, 1961. Front view, "banner" bell tower.

Above: Comparison: Le Corbusier: Notre Dame du Haut, Ronchamp, France, 1954.

Above: New Holyland M.B. Church, Chicago Avenue, Chicago, IL. A converted storefront.

Above: First Church of the Nazarene, 175 Mulberry Street, Claremont, NH. A small, vernacular church.

architect Bruce Goff, who served with the Seabees in the war, designed a chapel using a Quonset hut. It was later moved to a new congregation after the war. Other experimental, pre-fabricated religious structures of this period include very geometric geodesic domes and A-frames. Modular construction, which is also very popular in the housing industry, has made generic churches available. These can be built quickly and offer the economies of standardized production.

Late Modern

There is also a large group of High Style architect-designed churches and temples in this era of 1970 to the present that continue the research of modernist architects. Some of these work well and create an almost theatrical setting for worship. Others are merely bleak reminders of how the asceticism of modernism can work against its success. One of the most striking is the Garden Grove Church, also known as the Crystal Cathedral, in Los Angeles (1978–80), by Philip Johnson and John Burgee. This was built for the large congregation of one of the most successful televangelists.

Postmodernism

Rejecting the ascetic geometry of modernist architecture, Robert Venturi and other architects sought to reintroduce complexity and rich human experience into their architecture. Postmodernism began in the 1960s and continues to the present. Historical ornament and contextual allusions were no longer taboo, although they were frequently used with irony. Philip Johnson has designed several postmodern churches based on exotic historical precedents in Texas, including the Thanksgiving Chapel (1976) in Dallas, which emulates the spiral form of an early minaret in Iraq, and the Chapel of St. Basil (1996–97) at the University of St. Thomas in Houston, which derives from Eastern Orthodox traditional forms. Johnson's Cathedral of Hope in Dallas is a free exercise in abstract form. One of the most noted designs of recent years was Steven Holl's St. Ignatius Chapel (1998) in Seattle, Washington, which uses the structures of modernism to shape the church building into a series of "tubes of light" that create a powerful and contemplative mood.

Above: Revival Meeting, Middletown, CT, 2002. Rev. Douglas E. Lawrence, aka "Preacher on the Move."
The statue in the foreground is a Civil War memorial.

Above: Temple of Eck, 7450 Powers Blvd., Chanhassen, MN, 1990. A gathering place for a relatively recent religion.

Above: Chicago Illinois Temple, 4151 West Lake Avenue, Glenview, IL, 1985. A modernist house of worship for the Church of Latter-day Saints.

The most ancient forms of worship have been revived in recent years, by New Age seekers constructing primitive labyrinths for devotional purposes. Native American groups have also sought to find the roots of their cultural identity in the architectural forms of their ancestors and to adapt these to modern needs. As a result, there are fascinating examples of churches built on Indian reservations in the shape of traditional round hogans and tepees. Sacred architecture serves as a badge of identity, a shelter from contemporary pressures, and a vehicle to transport one out of this world and its chaos, into a spiritual realm. This transcendent and life-affirming role is one of the oldest for architecture; the act of construction reveals ideas about creativity and the creation of the world. The house of worship is both a sacred temple and a symbol.

Notes

1. A. J. Downing, "A Few Words on Our Progress in Buildings," in *Rural Essays*, quoted in Wayne Andrews, *American Gothic: Its Origins, Its Trials, Its Triumphs* (New York: Random House, 1975), 42.
2. James Jackson Jarves, *The Art-Idea: Sculpture, Painting and Architecture* (New York, 1864).
3. Ralph Adams Cram, "The Philosophy of the Gothic Restoration" (1913), quoted in Leland M. Roth, ed., *America Builds: Source Documents in American Architecture and Planning* (New York: Harper & Row, 1983), 462.
4. Leopold Eidlitz, *The Nature and Function of Art, More Especially of Architecture* (London, 1881), quoted in Roth, *America Builds*, 274–75.
5. See Alan Taylor, *American Colonies* (New York: Viking, 2001), for a recent survey of this period.

Above: Beth El Synagogue, 5224 West Twenty-sixth Street, St. Louis Park, MN, 1968.

Above: William Rawn Associates: Glavin Family Chapel, Babson College, Wellesley, MA, 1997–2000.

6. Kenneth Hafertepe and James O'Gorman, eds., *American Architects and Their Books to 1848* (Amherst, MA: University of Amherst Press, 2001), 22; for the size of Thomas Jefferson's second library, 61.

7. Daniel D. Reiff, *Houses from Books: Treatises, Pattern Books, and Catalogs in American Architecture, 1738–1950: A History and Guide* (University Park: Pennsylvania State University Press, 2000).

8. Johann Joachim Winckelmann, *On the Imitation of the Painting and Sculpture of the Greeks*, translated by Henry Fuseli (1755), quoted from Winckelmann's *Writings on Art*, David Irwin, ed., 61.

9. Leopold Eidlitz, "Christian Architecture," *The Crayon* 5, no. 2 (1858), quoted in James Early, *Romanticism and American Architecture* (New York: A. S. Barnes, 1965), 124.

10. Ralph Waldo Emerson, "Thoughts on Art" (1841), quoted in Roth, ed., *America Builds*, 97. The reference to Gothic architecture and frost is cited in James Early, *Romanticism and American Architecture*, 92.

11. David Handlin, *American Architecture* (London, 1985), 114–15.

12. Randolf Rock, "Our Church-Erection Interests," *United Brethren Review* 5:2 (April 1894), 179–80.

13. Reinhold Niebuhr, "The Weakness of Common Worship in American Protestantism," *Christianity and Crisis* 9:9 (May 28, 1951), 68–70.

Chapter 1

Early Religious Architecture in the U.S.—
the First Houses of Worship

The Heavenly Mansions—the Earth a Shadow:

*A King from heaven has sent for you: by faith he is showing you the New Jerusalem,
and is taking you along in the Spirit, and showing you all the rooms for rest and
dwelling in heaven. He says, "All these are yours, this palace is for you and Christ."
Indeed, if you alone were the only person chosen by God for salvation, Christ would have
built that one house for you and Himself: now it is for you and many others also.*

—Samuel Rutherford, letter 247, from Aberdeen, Sept. 9, 1637

This chapter focuses on structures built for worship by various groups inhabiting
America, including both Native American cultures and the first European
colonists. Although much has been lost from this early period, there are still
many impressive remains, and historical reconstructions and drawings help sup-
plement the visual record. The American continent is vast, and the varied climate

Right: Kiva, Pueblo Bonito
(Anasazi), Chaco Canyon, NM,
A.D. 900–1300.

Above: Photo of Southwestern kiva interior.

Above: Mandan earth lodge reconstruction, Like-a-Slant village, Mandan, ND.

zones and biological zones shaped the early cultures that inhabited them.

The seventeenth century in America was marked by strong regional differences. There was no unity among the colonies founded by rival nations. They were competing ventures, seeking to establish themselves and to gain primacy over the native inhabitants and each other. Nor did the multicultural settlements of the time lead to mutual cooperation. Each rival group sought a foothold: the Spanish in Florida and the Southwest, the British along the eastern seaboard in New England and Virginia, the Dutch in New Amsterdam (now New York) and the Hudson River valley, the French in Canada and Louisiana,

and Swedes and Germans in the Delaware valley.[1] Each colonial group had to adapt its national building traditions to the American environment, which frequently was much more extreme than the European climate. In the Northeast, winters were much colder and the summers much hotter than in England. In the South and Southwest, the range of temperatures was also much more extreme. The life of the colonists was hard; the importance of home as a source of security and shelter cannot be overestimated. There was little energy for, or interest in, stylistic innovation, and American building lagged considerably behind the fashions of European architecture.

Above: The Devil's Tower, known to Native American peoples as Mato Tipi—the Bear's Lodge, WY.

Left: Woodhenge and
Mounds, Cahokia, IL.

Native Americans

Although the details are lost in prehistory, the origins of
Native American religion can be traced back 30,000 to
50,000 years, with the arrival of the first groups of people
from northeast Asia over a land bridge from Siberia. Those
early ancestors brought with them their hunting taboos and
rituals, beliefs in spirits, and shamanism. These original
hunting beliefs eventually fused with or were replaced by
agricultural beliefs.

When the European colonists arrived, there were many
distinct Native American groups speaking over 300 different languages in North America, with a total population
almost as large as Europe's. These cultures were as varied as
the land they occupied. Tragically, the vast majority of
Native Americans perished within a few decades of the
European arrival from disease and conquest. Their lack of
immunity to common European diseases was fatal; when
Old World diseases spread to Native American populations,
as much as 90 percent of the local population died.

This short chapter cannot give a complete account of
the Native American religious architecture, but the extensive variety of traditions will be briefly surveyed, including
those of coastal groups, Plains Indians, and the American
Southwest. Building types include *kivas* (circular underground chambers for worship) at the ancient pueblos of
the Southwest, sacred sites marked in various ways, and
enormous mounds and earthworks from the great cultures
of the central United States, such as the Hopewell tribes.
Sophisticated wooden architecture and mythological traditions are reflected in the plank houses and totems of the
Northwest coast tribes of the Haida, Tlingit, and Kwakiutl.

For the most detailed account, the reader is referred to specialized studies, such as *Native American Architecture* by Peter
Nabokov and Robert Easton.

Native American buildings were strongly shaped by the
geographic and climactic region; nine broad cultural areas
have been defined. Building materials were taken from the
local area and consisted of wood, bark, plant materials such
as grass or reeds, earth (rammed or dried adobe bricks),
stone, as well as animal hides and bones. In the far north,
snow was used. The Native Americans lived much closer to
the natural environment than modern people and their
structures were well adapted to their lifestyle. Nature was
imbued with sacred forces and even their domestic architecture reflected those spiritual values. Some groups were
nomadic, such as the Plains Indians, while others lived in
larger groups in more permanent locations. The great cities
of the Mississippi River valley such as Cahokia, Illinois, comprised many structures, including temples built on large
earthen mounds. The great pueblos of the Southwest were
built by settled groups who depended on agriculture. In the
Pacific Northwest, villages based on fishing and hunting
developed a unique plank-style architecture.

Dwellings were not only related to patterns of social
order, but the spiritual understanding of the cosmos. The
creation of the world was sometimes compared to the building of a house, with the gods as the first builders. Building
or renewing a house could be a sacred ritual. Orientation
toward the compass points was nearly always meaningful,
and buildings with domed roofs were considered to reflect
the shape of the heavens. The vertical dimension was particularly meaningful in the Hopi and Navajo kivas, where the
underground chamber was connected to the sky by a

ladder. The underworld and the heavens were the realm of the gods; people occupied the middle zone. The origins of architecture were often ascribed to the gods, and it was a ritual duty to re-create the original methods and materials. Nearly any house could become a site for religious ritual; the tepees of the Great Plains could be sanctified by painting them with sacred symbols and dedicating them to vision quests. The ideal pueblo re-created the form of the sacred mountains and contained ritual plazas and kivas.

Sacred Sites

Religion and spirituality were very important to the Native Americans. Architecture in its widest sense includes the entire built environment, and Native Americans worshiped not just in buildings, but at sacred sites where the spiritual forces were directly linked to humans. Even domestic architecture incorporated spiritual principles in orientation and structural plans that reflected religious beliefs.

A recent archaeological document published by the Department of Defense attempts to explain the relationship between Native Americans and the land:

> Native Americans are attached to the land in some ways that others can easily understand, but also in other ways that are almost impossible to explain. The Christian-Islamic-Hebrew concept called holy land perhaps best describes where the Indian people perceive they were created. Here in their holy lands are origin mountains where the supernatural created them and gave them responsibilities for using and protecting the land. Here also…are places best described by the Christian-Islamic-Hebrew term sacred site. However, Native Americans have places that they consider powerful or religiously significant, such as where a mythic being spent one night or where lighting struck the earth. Such places lack cognates in European and Mid-Eastern religions making it more difficult to explain to non-Native Americans that such places are truly sacred and worthy of protection and reverence by everyone.[2]

Above: Serpent mound, Adams County, OH, between 800 B.C. and A.D. 400. This mysterious mound is over 600 feet long.

Native American

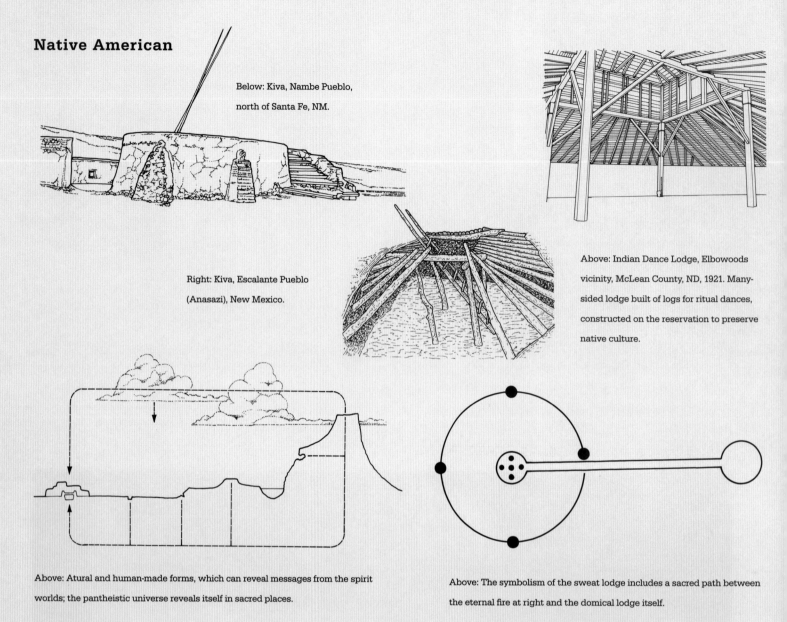

Below: Kiva, Nambe Pueblo, north of Santa Fe, NM.

Right: Kiva, Escalante Pueblo (Anasazi), New Mexico.

Above: Indian Dance Lodge, Elbowoods vicinity, McLean County, ND, 1921. Many-sided lodge built of logs for ritual dances, constructed on the reservation to preserve native culture.

Above: Atural and human-made forms, which can reveal messages from the spirit worlds; the pantheistic universe reveals itself in sacred places.

Above: The symbolism of the sweat lodge includes a sacred path between the eternal fire at right and the domical lodge itself.

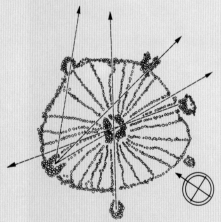

Above: Bighorn Medicine Wheel, Wyoming. A structure apparently used for early astronomical observations and rituals. Markers in the circle point to sunset and sunrise at the summer solstice, as well as to other planets.

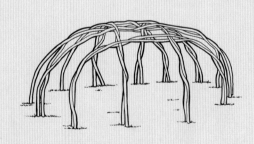

Above: Native American sweat lodge. A simple frame structure of lashed poles was covered with bark or other materials to create a space for the cleansing ritual.

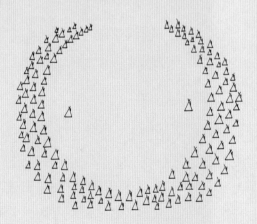

Above: Tepees were often arranged in a circle open toward the east.

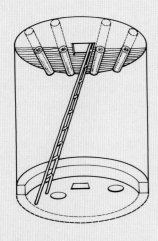

Above: Diagram of a Southwest kiva, showing the connection between the world beneath the surface fo the earth and the sky, symbolized by the ladder.

Above: The ladder emerging from the kiva points to the sky.

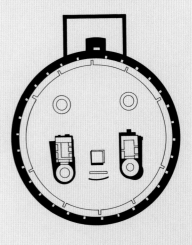

Above: Plan of the Great Kiva, Chaco.

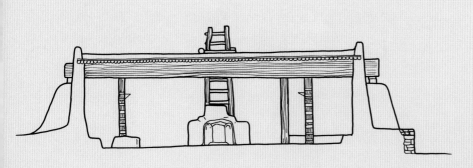

Above: Section of Kiva Nambé Pueblo, Santa Fe County, NM.

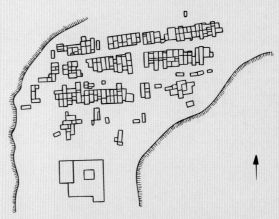

Above: Plan of Acoma Pueblo, NM, twelfth century. All the buildings face the south for optimum solar exposure, except for the Spanish mission, which faces east.

Above: Navaho Hogan; wooden frame is covered with earth. Exterior view. The hemispherical shape of the Hogan re-creates the sacred dome of heaven.

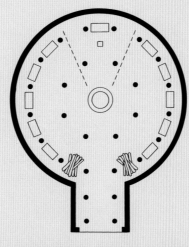

Above: Plan of a Pawnee earth lodge. The circular plan and axis toward the altar have spiritual significance. The entrance is oriented toward the east.

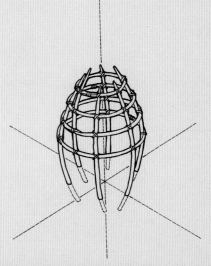

Above: Shaman symbolism; the "shaking lodge." This was a light structure used for mediumistic rituals by shamans in the north-central United States.

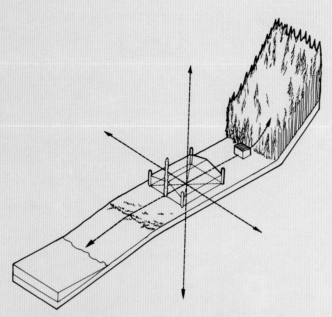

Above: Cosmic patterns in the Northwest coast Native American culture and landscape. Living beneath the sea and forest, and beneath the sky and above the earth; both horizontal and vertical directions held symbolic significance.

Above: Northwest coastal plank house and totem pole; from a photograph by Edward Curtis.

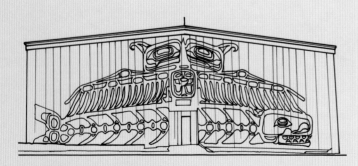

Above: A Northwest coast symbolic painting of a mythical thunderbird carrying a whale from the Kwakiutl tribe.

Another conceptual difference between Native American and modern American cultures is the use of the term "symbol." Especially in modern European and American culture, symbols are considered to be arbitrary signifiers, said to stand for a concept or belief or deity in a very limited sense. For the Native American, the understanding of reality is very different. A symbol does not just represent a spirit or a god, but actually is imbued with its presence. For example, when a religious practitioner in an American Indian ceremony states that a rock represents the earth or a sacred mountain, he means that the earth or the mountain is actually present in the ceremony. The ceremony is not just an empty ritual, but is directly connected to the cosmic forces.

Natural and human-made forms were understood to reveal messages from the spirit worlds; the pantheistic universe reveals itself in sacred places. These include burial sites and ruins, mourning sites, ceremonial sites, and creation story locations and boundaries. The so-called Devil's Tower in northeastern Wyoming, known to Native American peoples as Mato Tipila (the Bear's Lodge), was a place of particular power. The 867-foot-high plateau was often used for vision quests. According to a widely shared native myth, the rock formation was created when a group of seven young girls on a small hill was attacked by a large grizzly bear. Their prayer to the gods for deliverance was granted when the hill grew higher into the sky, until the seven girls were transformed into the seven stars of the constellation we call Pleiades. The giant bear's claws scratched the sides of the mountain, leaving the deep grooves that sculpt it. In modern American culture, it was featured in the film *Close Encounters of the Third Kind* as the most likely spot for extraterrestrials to contact us, updating the tribal mythology.

The movements of the stars were thought to be particularly important signs; the Bighorn Medicine Wheel in Wyoming is a structure apparently used for early astronomical observations and rituals. The eighty-foot-diameter wheel has been described as an American Stonehenge. It is made of stones set into the ground, the tallest standing about three feet tall. The shape is like that of a wagon wheel, with a large outer ring, a small central cairn, and twenty-eight spokes connecting them. The number twenty-eight may relate to the number of days in a lunar month. The wheel aligns with the four points of the compass, and additional piles of stone align with the rising and setting sun at the summer solstice. There may also be alignments with different stars in the night sky. The Bighorn Medicine Wheel is surrounded by evidence of many other ceremonial and religious sites; the area shows evidence of having been occupied for nearly 7,000 years. Evidence for dating the actual construction of the Medicine Wheel is inconclusive, but it certainly preceded the period of European contact by hundreds of years. The wheel should not be seen in isolation, but in the context of its relationship to the surrounding forests and mountain peaks. The national historic site is located on the edge of Medicine Mountain, near Lovell, Wyoming. In recent years, archaeologists have studied other Native American structures for evidence of astronomical use. Between seventy and 150 medicine wheels have been identified in the western states and Canada. The oldest is the 5,500-year-old Majorville Cairn in the Canadian province of Alberta.

Navajo Hogans were domelike, timber frame structures covered with earth. The hemispherical shape of the Hogan re-creates the sacred dome of heaven. The plan of Pawnee earth lodges also reflected cosmic symbolism. The circular plan and axis toward the altar have spiritual significance; the entrance is always oriented toward the east.

Correlation between the buildings and the human body was widely found. Sweat lodges were simple frame structures of lashed poles covered with bark or other materials to create a space for the cleansing ritual. These structures are designed to generate hot moist air, similar to a Finnish sauna. The sweat lodge is used for rituals of purification and spiritual renewal and healing. A special sort of religious architecture used for divinatory rites by the Chippewa in the Great Lakes area is the shaking tent, or "conjuring lodge." It is a small ovoid booth made of six or seven saplings bound into a domical shape by wooden hoops. Only a little larger than the shaman, it was covered with bark or cloth after he entered the structure. The flimsy structure would shake while the shaman was in his trance, an effect amplified by rattles attached to the frame.

The kivas of the southwestern pueblos are among the most distinctive of the Native American religious structures. *Kiva* is Hopi for "ceremonial room." Although the entire pueblo can be said to have sacred significance as a re-creation of the sacred mountain shape, the kiva is a special space. One of the largest pueblos, Chetro Ketl in Chaco Canyon, built between 1010 and 1109, had twenty-one kivas. Pueblo Bonito (*c.* 920–1300) was even larger and had forty

Above: Great Circle Earthworks, Hopewell culture, Newark Earthworks State Memorial, OH.

kivas. A kiva is a circular chamber, excavated deep in the ground. A low wall of stone or adobe adds to the depth of the kiva chamber. It is roofed over with four main poles, representing aspects of the creation myth. A small hole dug in the floor of the kiva allows even more direct contact to the spirit world below. Entrance to the kiva is gained by a ladder, which signifies the contact between earth and heaven. Light comes from the hole in the roof and also from fire. In the brightly lit southwestern desert, the strong sunlight provides a powerful beam of light, which moves around the kiva as the sun completes its course in the sky.

The pueblos and kivas were early models of architecture utilizing solar and geothermal heating. By placing the kiva partially below ground and using an earthen roof, the builders took advantage of the relatively constant soil temperature and reduced heat losses from wind. Additional warmth was provided in the winter by the body heat of the worshipers and a central hearth. A separate ventilation shaft provided fresh air. The slanting shaft of light that fell

Above: Haida house with totem pole, photographed at Haina, Queen Charlotte Island, AK, *c.* 1900.

through the ceiling door creates a mysterious effect. Although the traditional view is that these round sunken chambers were solely for religious purposes, archaeological evidence suggests that at least some kivas were used for living quarters.

Good examples of kivas are found at the Escalante Pueblo and the Pueblo Bonito in Chaco Canyon. These were both built A.D. 900–1300 by the enigmatic Anasazi culture, which preceded the Navajo and Hopi in New Mexico. The word *anasazi* is Navajo for "ancient ones." The Anasazi mysteriously vanished before the coming of the Europeans. Later Pueblo tribes also built kivas for religious ceremonies; one example is at the Nambe Pueblo, north of Santa Fe.

In the western plains, the Mandan tribe built earth lodges for religious ceremonies. A reconstruction can be found at Like-a-Slant village in Mandan, North Dakota. In Mandan cosmology, the universe was considered to be a giant earth lodge, with the sky held up by four pillars just as their houses were held up by four central posts.

The round shape was prevalent for sacred structures. The Drum Dance Lodge built at Mille Lac, Wisconsin, is documented in photographs taken early in the twentieth century. It is a many-sided lodge built of logs, constructed on the reservation to preserve native culture through ritual dances.

Mounds and Earthworks

The enormous animal-figure earthworks constructed in Ohio between 800 B.C. and A.D. 400 are equally impressive and mysterious. Some of these, such as the Serpent Mound, Adams County, Ohio, are over 600 feet long. They can best be appreciated from the air, and even though made of earth mounds, they are recognizable after 2,000 years. Early maps from the nineteenth century show that they were the center of ceremonial complexes. The Newark Bird Mound complex in Newark, Ohio, covered an area of over four square miles. They were not cities, however; the population seems to have been widely dispersed. The earthen mounds began as burial sites, although some evolved for defensive purposes, and for others the meaning is still unclear. Besides the animal-shaped mounds, there are also geometric designs, such as the Great Circle Earthworks and the Octagon Mound built by the Hopewell culture. These mounds are now part of the Newark Earthworks State Memorial in Ohio.

The cultures of the Mississippi and Ohio River valleys lived in relatively large urban centers and built astonishingly large monuments of earth and wood. Cahokia was one of the greatest urban centers of the pre-Columbian period, and the intriguing Woodhenge and Mounds can be found there. Cahokia thrived in the period of 1050 to 1250; at its height, nearly 30,000 people lived in the urban area. The Cahokia mounds rivaled the Aztec pyramids in size. Built entirely of earth, the base of the largest mound measured 790 feet by 1,050 feet, and it was almost one hundred feet high. French priests later built a mission church on top of it. Many smaller mounds surrounded it, and there was also an astronomical observatory made of wood, now known as Woodhenge.

On the Northwest coast, a complex culture developed in the fishing villages. A unique architecture of houses made of thick planks was common here. These plank houses were oriented according to cosmic symbolism, particularly reflecting the importance of the sea and forest. The threshold was elaborately decorated, indicating the importance of and dangers seen in transitions and points of entry. The extraordinary carved totem poles are a part of the culture here. Difficult for outsiders to read, the various animal forms recount historical and sacred narratives. The conjoined animals represent points of contact and also the concept of metamorphosis. These are now recognized as highly important forms of sculpture. Some are preserved, while others have been reconstructed at historic preservation sites. One of these is T'Shan, a reconstructed Girksan village in Hazelton, British Columbia. Haida houses with totem poles were also found at Haina on Queen Charlotte Island, Alaska.

Whales were an important part of the culture of the Nootka tribe in the Pacific Northwest; to ensure a good hunt, the Nootka Whale House hunting shrine includes ancestor figures and symbolic representations of the whales.

In recent years, certain aspects of Native American spirituality have been adopted by various New Age groups in search of a more authentic spirituality that recognizes the important role of nature and the environment. While this has led to increased understanding and respect for Native American beliefs, some American Indians view this as another phase of exploitation. Commercialized "dream-catchers" and imitation sweat-lodges have inadvertently led to cultural misunderstandings.

Above: Houses with totem poles at T'Shan, reconstructed Girksan village, Hazelton, British Columbia.

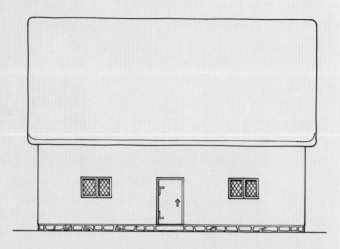

Above: First meetinghouse, Dedham, MA, early seventeenth century. The first New England meetinghouses were like houses of the period, built with heavy timber frames and roofed with thatch.

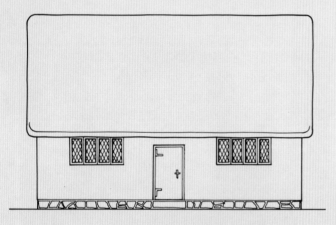

Above: First meetinghouse, Sudbury, MA, early seventeenth century. Notable for banks of casement windows and a thatched roof.

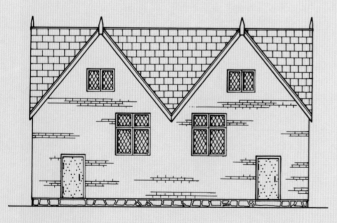

Above: Second meetinghouse, Sudbury, MA, mid-seventeenth century. The building was expanded with dual transverse gables intersecting the long roof.

Colonial Churches—the First Period

What can be a better or nobler work, and more worthy of a Christian, than to erect and support a reformed particular Church in its infancy, and unite our forces with such a company of faithful people, as by a timely assistance may grow stronger and prosper; but for want of it, may be put to great hazards, if not be wholly ruined.

—Cotton Mather, *Magnalia Christi Americana, or the Ecclesiastical History of New England, 1620–98*

When the English colonists first arrived in Massachusetts and Virginia, their immediate priority was for housing and defense. Their earliest worship services were held in very primitive shelters, the congregation seated on felled logs under a bit of canvas for a roof. A frequently quoted description from the seventeenth-century chronicle of Captain John Smith recounts the first services in Virginia:

> When I first went to Virginia, I well remember we did hang an awning, an old sail, to three or four trees to shadow us from the sun; our walls were rails of wood, our seats unhewed planks until we cut planks, our pulpit a bar of wood nailed to two neighboring trees. This was our church till we built a homely thing like a barn, set upon crotchets, covered with rafts, sedges, and earth, so were also the walls. Yet we had daily Common Prayer morning and evening, every Sunday two sermons, and every three months the Holy Communion, till our Minister died. But our Prayers daily, with an Homily on Sundays, we continued two or three years till more Preachers came.

The first settlements in New England made do with similar temporary structures or met in the houses of prominent citizens. In Boston, John Winthrop's parlor was used for services in 1630. Some early parsonages were also used for meetinghouses.

The first permanent meetinghouses were simple structures, essentially heavy timber frame houses dedicated to religious use. Dimensions were modest, perhaps twenty by thirty feet. This suited the Puritan values, which sought to find God in all things and rejected overt religious symbolism. Cotton Mather sneered at traditional symbolism used in English churches: "the setting of these places off with a theatrical gaudiness does not savor of the spirit of a true

Above: Old Ship Meeting House, 107 Main Street, Hingham, MA, 1681; with additions in 1731, 1755.

Above: Side view, Old Ship Meeting House, Hingham, MA.

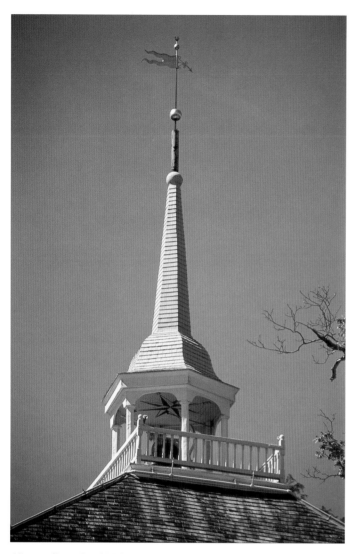

Above: Steeple, Old Ship Meeting House, Hingham, MA.

Christian society." Reconstruction drawings of the first meetinghouses in Dedham and Boston show small wooden structures with thatched roofs, basically rural English farmhouses built in America. Given the importance of religion to these separatist colonists, the simple structures were replaced with more elaborate buildings as soon as possible. These simple, barnlike structures were a new building type, however, an original architectural form. The building was known as a meetinghouse instead of a church, since it was used for all town meetings, and the colonists rejected the traditional term as well as the hierarchical associations of churches. The traditional church was oblong and oriented toward the altar, which was located at the far end of the church from the entrance, with all the seats facing it. The pulpit was set up on the middle of the long side. The Puritan meetinghouse did away with the altar and turned the seating benches toward the pulpit. The entrance was also moved to the long side, behind the benches. The plans typically became square, about forty to forty-five feet on a side.

In the first colonial period, only the Anglican houses of worship in Virginia were known as churches. Seating in the seventeenth century was on benches; men and women sat on separate sides with an aisle between. Box pews were introduced in the eighteenth century. These square enclosed pews held entire families and were sold or leased to the families by a committee, according to complex formulas weighing age, occupational status, wealth, and

Right: Interior of Old Ship Meeting House, Hingham, MA.

Above: Interior of Old Ship Meeting House, Hingham, MA.

number of generations that the family had been in the town. Additional seating in second floor balconies or galleries was used by young men and women between the ages of ten and twenty-one, seated separately, of course; servants, slaves and the town poor were also relegated to this area. Social hierarchies clearly did exist in Puritan culture and were inscribed in the use of the meetinghouse.

Early meetinghouses were not painted at first; later they might be painted in a much wider variety of colors than is commonly assumed. In the eighteenth century, stonelike colors were popular, including yellows as well as dark and light colors. Combinations of yellow and green were not unknown. The meetinghouse in Rowley, Massachusetts, was painted red, and in 1762 the meetinghouse in Pomfret, Connecticut, was painted orange, with chocolate and white trim. Other congregations followed their colorful lead. During the Greek Revival of the nineteenth century, the fashion for painting buildings white became dominant, and many meetinghouses were painted over at that time. If a steeple was built, it was not topped with a cross, which would have seemed too close to the Anglican or "Popish" tradition. Instead, a weather vane or "iron flag" might be used.

The oldest surviving meetinghouse in New England is the Old Ship Meeting House in Hingham, Massachusetts, built in 1681. It was built in the typical square plan of the Puritan meetinghouse, rejecting the implied hierarchy of a traditional English church with its longitudinal nave leading to the altar. For the Puritans, who insisted on the primacy of the Word of God, the pulpit was the center of the church. The Old Ship Meeting House was built entirely of wood with a massive oaken frame, which was raised in three days between July 26 and 28. The exposed timbers of the ceiling are curved, and these have given the church its name, since they are said to resemble the upside-down hull of a ship. This is a traditional framing format of late medieval building (a "cruck frame"), however, and not evi-

Right: Meetinghouse, Main Street, Deerfield, MA, 1696–1728 (reconstruction).

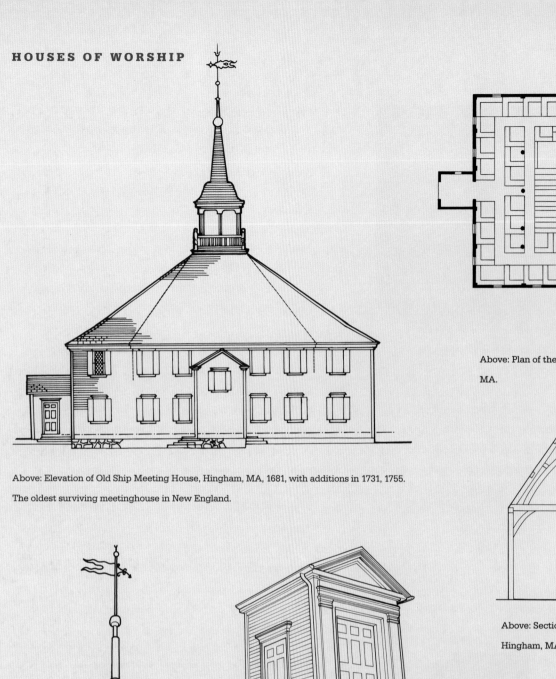

Above: Plan of the Old Ship Meeting House, Hingham, MA.

Above: Elevation of Old Ship Meeting House, Hingham, MA, 1681, with additions in 1731, 1755. The oldest surviving meetinghouse in New England.

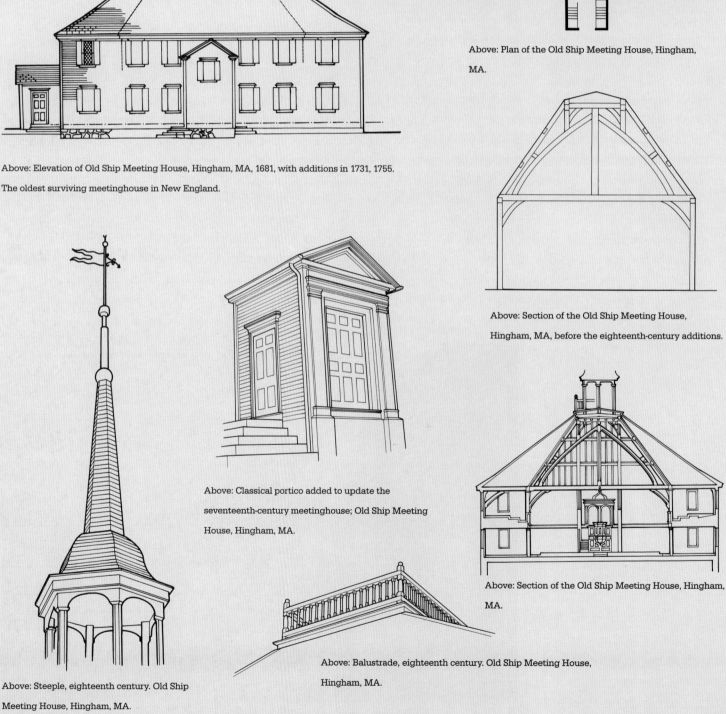

Above: Section of the Old Ship Meeting House, Hingham, MA, before the eighteenth-century additions.

Above: Classical portico added to update the seventeenth-century meetinghouse; Old Ship Meeting House, Hingham, MA.

Above: Section of the Old Ship Meeting House, Hingham, MA.

Above: Steeple, eighteenth century. Old Ship Meeting House, Hingham, MA.

Above: Balustrade, eighteenth century. Old Ship Meeting House, Hingham, MA.

dence that they copied a ship's hull or that ship's carpenters were the builders. The ship metaphor is appropriate for a church, since churches are often compared to vessels that protect one on the voyage of life. The image is rooted in the biblical stories of Noah's Ark and Christ on the Sea of Galilee, and the word "nave" derives from the Latin word for ship.

The Old Ship Meeting House, in its original form, had a tall hipped roof, surmounted by some form of balustrade and a simple cupola. It was covered with clapboards, and windows were casements with small diamond panes. The interior was very plain. The roof timbers were left exposed, and the only pews were simple benches. In 1731, the meetinghouse was expanded, with a fourteen-foot addition built to the northeast. At this time, the roof timbers were closed in with a plaster and lath ceiling, which made the unheated meetinghouse more comfortable, and the interior walls were plastered. In 1755, it was enlarged again, with a

fourteen-foot addition built to the south-southwest. This preserved the square footprint. A new hipped roof was added and was simply built over the earlier, more steeply pitched, roof. The first box pews were added at this time. By the mid-eighteenth century, the simple meetinghouse must have seemed too crude and archaic, for classical details were added to make it more elegant. The balustrade and cupola reveal eighteenth-century sophistication, and new classical pediments were incorporated into the entrance porticoes. Inside, the pulpit was set off by paneling with classical arches. Most dramatically, a false ceiling was added to disguise the medieval roof timbers and also to keep it warmer. The first stove was not added to the Old Ship Meeting House until 1822. Parishioners kept warm in their box pews with heavy clothes and charcoal foot warmers. The meetinghouse was modernized again in a renovation in 1869 and given Victorian decoration, with yellow print wallpaper and red carpeting. The box pews were

Above: Fort Church, Jamestown, VA, *c.* 1610. A reconstruction of the early timber frame and thatched roof church built by the first settlers.

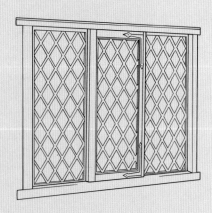

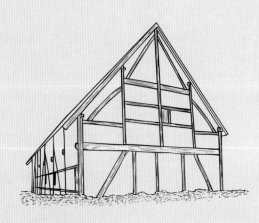

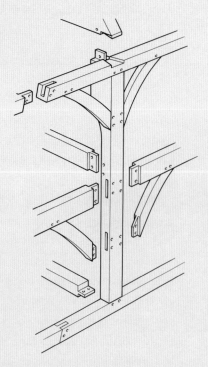

Above: Casement windows with small diamond-shaped panes of glass in leaded frames were typical in the seventeenth and early eighteenth centuries.

Above: Wall Construction: The pattern of the half-timber frame shows clearly against the white plastered infilling.

Above: Timber frame construction. The framing techniques are based on English traditional construction, with roots in the late Middle Ages.

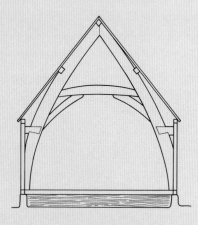

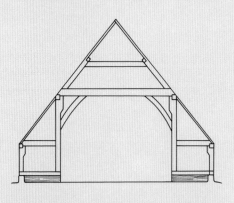

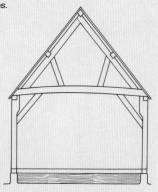

Above: Cruck frame.

Above: Aisled frame.

Above: Timber frame; post construction.

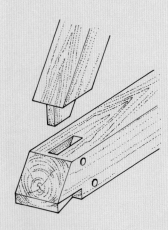

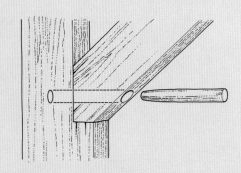

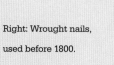

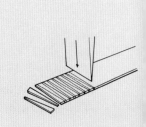

Above: Mortise and tenon joint. Before the introduction of standardized lumber and lightweight framing techniques in the nineteenth century, each joint was an individual construction.

Above: Treenails (trunnels), wooden pegs used for early timber frames. Typically made of oak, these anchored the heavy beams.

Right: Wrought nails, used before 1800.

Right: Cut nails, used after 1800. Cut from a sheet of iron, they are tapered only on one side. Later in the nineteenth century, inexpensive wire-cut nails replaced them.

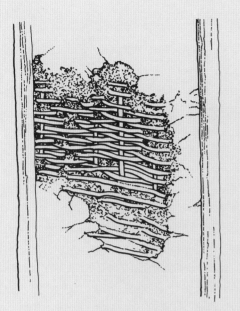

Above: With the outer surface damaged, the woven sticks of the wattle (sticks) and daub (clay or plaster) infilling show between the posts in this European example.

Above: Infilling between posts and beams in half-timber frame: brick fill, or nogging.

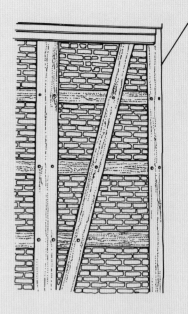

Above: Wall Construction: The brick infilling between the timbers shows clearly in this structure.

removed and replaced with Victorian bench pews. These cosmetic additions were not removed until the restoration of 1930, when the ceiling was removed and the box pews restored. The current state of the building now provides a window into the original seventeenth-century appearance and allows one to read the beginning stages of the evolution of eighteenth-century classicism.

The style of this first period of colonial architecture is often called Postmedieval English to indicate the essential conservative nature of this folk building style, rooted in late medieval building practices. This was true of both the New England and Virginia colonies. Reconstructions such as the Fort Church, Jamestown, VA, *c.* 1610, and other archaeological reconstructions show the character of the primitive buildings of this era. The Fort Church was built with a heavy timber frame and half-timbering effects with the plaster walls revealed. The harsher New England climate demanded clapboards ("clayboards") to protect the plaster against the elements, but this was less necessary in the South. William Strachey described the state of the church in 1610, when he and his shipmates arrived in Jamestown after a disastrous shipwreck in Bermuda. His description of this shipwreck was used by William

Shakespeare as a source for the shipwreck scene in *The Tempest*. Strachey's letter to an unknown woman in England provided these details about the Jamestown church:

> It is in length three-score foot, in breadth twenty-four, and shall have a chancel in it of cedar and a communion table of the black walnut, and all the pews of cedar, with fair broad windows to shut and open, as the weather shall occasion, of the same wood, a pulpit of the same, with a front hewn hollow, like a canoe, with two bells at the west end. It is so cast as it be very light within, and the lord governor and captain general doth cause it to be kept passing sweet and trimmed up with divers flowers, with a sexton belonging to it. And in it every Sunday we have sermons twice a day, and every Thursday a sermon, having true preachers, which take their weekly turns; and every morning, at the ringing of a bell about ten of the clock, each man addresseth himself to prayers, and so at four of the clock before supper.[3]

Although the Jamestown church was a primitive fort church, it was clearly made as attractive as possible.

Above left: St. Luke's Old Brick Church, Smithfield, Isle of Wight County, VA, 1632–75. Interior.

Above: St. Luke's Old Brick Church, Smithfield, Isle of Wight County, VA, 1632–75. Entrance.

Left: St. Luke's Old Brick Church, Smithfield, Isle of Wight County, VA, 1632–75. Exterior view of window.

Above: St. Luke's Old Brick Church, Smithfield, Isle of Wight County, VA, 1632–75. Front view. One of the oldest churches on the eastern seaboard.

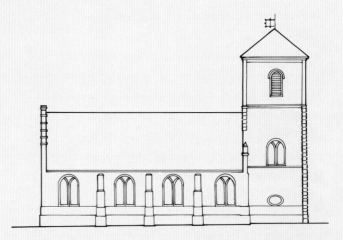

Above: Elevation of St. Luke's Old Brick Church, Smithfield, Isle of Wight County, VA, 1632–75.

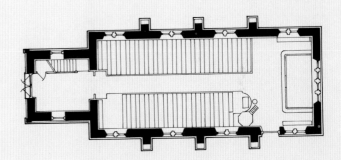

Above: Plan of St. Luke's Old Brick Church, Smithfield, VA.

Right: Window with tracery in rear wall of St. Luke's Old Brick Church, Smithfield, VA. Note also the stepped gables.

Virginia and Massachusetts were established under very different principles, with the Massachusetts Bay Colony founded by Puritans. Virginia, on the other hand, was a royal colony from the start, and the dominant church there was the Anglican church, the Church of England. The oldest surviving church in Virginia is the Newport parish church, now known as St. Luke's Old Brick Church (1632–75) in Smithfield, Isle of Wight County. St. Luke's is basically a very late English Gothic parish church. In fact, it is often referred to as a case of "Gothic Survival" to distinguish it from later Gothic Revival churches. The colonists who built it were simply continuing the traditional forms that they knew from their homeland. Style was less important to them than re-creating their familiar surroundings in their English parish.

The actual date of St. Luke's Old Brick Church is disputed; older sources assert that it was begun as early as

1632, which would make it the oldest surviving church in America, while other more recent sources propose a later date. It is certainly the oldest of seventeenth-century churches in Virginia, however. As with the Old Ship Meeting House, the church shows evidence of stylistic inconsistency. The nave is the oldest portion, and it is completely Gothic: It has the typical lancet (pointed arch) windows, attached buttresses to strengthen the wall, and a steeply pitched roof with a crow-step gable. The rear wall features a large window with intricate brick tracery. The stained glass was a later addition in all these windows. The brick walls are two feet thick. The twenty-foot-square entrance tower is somewhat later than the nave and shows a tentative classicism in the addition of brick quoins and rounded arches, which become more elegantly proportioned in the upper stages. The archway of the door is a flattened arch, derived from English Romanesque precedents. There is an awkward triangular pediment shape over the door, indicating a certain consciousness of style. The interior is distinguished by the exposed collar beams and roof timbers; like the Old Ship Meeting House, the medieval structure is revealed. The round-arched screen near the altar is clearly classical, however, and is a later addition. Virginia churches, although Anglican, were closer to the Low Church simplification of rituals and spaces. St. Luke's (which received its saint's name only in the nineteenth century) was originally built with no stained glass and no separation between the nave and the chancel.

Besides being unattainable in the seventeenth century, clear glass has been linked to the Enlightenment value of clarity.

Dutch Colonial

The New Netherlands Dutch colony in the New World was extensive, reaching from New Amsterdam (now New York) well up the Hudson River. Dutch was spoken in parts of the Hudson River valley area until the late eighteenth century. The dominant church was the Protestant Dutch Reformed Church. The earliest surviving example is that at Sleepy Hollow, New York, of about 1700. It is a small rectangular chapel built of stone, with a Flemish gambrel roof.

The Dutch Calvinists had split from the Catholic Church in the sixteenth century, and like the English Puritans, they rejected the religious symbolism of traditional churches. A plain style was prescribed by Calvin himself, and the emphasis was on preaching, so the pulpit was the focus of their churches. The octagon plan suited the rejection of hierarchy, and a number of small octagonal churches were built in New Netherlands in the seventeenth century, following Dutch precedents. None of these survive, but the appearance of one built at Bergen, New Jersey, in about 1680 is recorded in drawings.

The town of New Paltz in the Hudson River valley was established by French Huguenots who fled persecution in

Above: Dutch Reformed Church, Route 9, Sleepy Hollow, NY, c. 1700.

Above: Walloon Church, Huguenot Street, New Paltz, NY, 1717; replica built 1965.

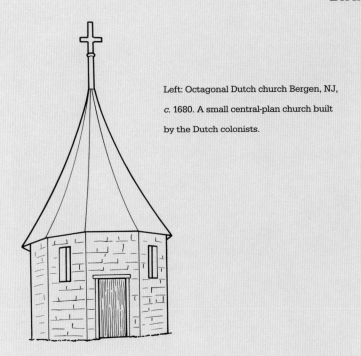

Left: Octagonal Dutch church Bergen, NJ, *c.* 1680. A small central-plan church built by the Dutch colonists.

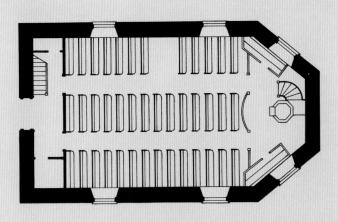

Above: Plan of Dutch Reformed Church, Sleepy Hollow, NY, *c.* 1700.

France and moved into a totally Dutch colony. Their architecture is very similar to the local Dutch building traditions. The Huguenots were Calvinists, like the Dutch, and were Walloons from northern France (and modern-day Belgium), near the Dutch linguistic border. The first church was the Walloon Church, built of logs in 1683. This was replaced by a stone building in 1717. The original has been destroyed; the current stone church in New Paltz is a reconstruction built in 1965. It is a small stone building with a steep, nearly pyramidal, hipped roof with a small cupola on top. It holds about sixty people. The interior is very plain, almost without decoration.

Mid-Atlantic

In the seventeenth century, various European powers competed for colonies in America. Swedish settlers established a short-lived colony in the Delaware valley in 1638. Perhaps the most enduring contribution of this group was the introduction of the log cabin into American building, built with horizontal logs laid in a square with notched corner joints. It is a kind of vernacular building known across Scandinavia, and although it took many decades to spread beyond this region, it has become a symbol of the American frontier culture. The Swedish colonists were Lutherans; two early churches built by the Scandinavian immigrants of New

Sweden still survive. One is the Holy Trinity Church (Old Swede's Church) in Wilmington, Delaware, which dates from 1699. This is the oldest Lutheran church in America. It is built with granite walls made of level courses of irregularly shaped stones and has a steep-pitched gable roof. A small belfry was added in 1802 at the center of the façade. The interior is white and plain; there is a wineglass pulpit at the left side with a flat sounding board above it.

The Swedish church of Gloria Dei, Philadelphia, Pennsylvania, was built between 1698 and 1700 by English builders. A small brick building with a steep pitched gable roof, it is the oldest church building in Pennsylvania; before it was built, the congregation worshiped in a simple log building of the Swedish tradition. Betsy Ross attended this church and was married here.

French Colonial

The French colonial style is the least well known of all the European styles in America. The French colonial territory in North America was vast and included most of the Mississippi River valley, from Canada to New Orleans. Towns and cities were few, however, and the major city of New Orleans lost most of its colonial architecture in disastrous fires in 1788 and 1794. French colonists arrived in 1718, and the first church was a temporary wooden struc-

Above: Holy Trinity Church (Old Swede's Church), 606 North Church Street, Wilmington, DE, 1699.

Above: Gloria Dei, 929 South Water Street, Philadelphia, PA, 1698–1700. A Swedish church, constructed by English builders. It is the oldest church building in Pennsylvania.

ture, which was soon replaced by a half-timbered building, which is also lost. Seventeenth-century settlements outside of Quebec were sparse and fortified. Catholic missionaries were among the first to explore and settle these frontier areas. In 1670, Jesuit Father Charles Dablon founded a birch-bark mission chapel on Mackinac Island in northern Michigan. This church was abandoned in 1706 and rebuilt as Sainte Anne de Michilimackinac at Fort Michilimackinac in Michigan, which was established in 1715. Reconstructions of the buildings of the fort show that the church was a simple log building with a small spire. The fort was surrounded with a palisade of logs, and many of the buildings were constructed with the vertical logs placed directly in the ground, using the French *poteaux-en-terre* (poles-in-ground) or *poteaux-en-sole* (poles-on-a-sill) technique.

The reconstruction of the Fort St. Jean Baptiste in Nachitoches, Louisiana, reproduces the likely appearance of the settlement in about 1730. The church here is a small wooden building, constructed using the poles-in-ground technique, which did not last long in the damp southern soil. The church had a small steeple to make it more familiar.

Spanish Colonial

Much of the southern and southwestern part of what would become the United States was initially part of New Spain. The Spanish colony included Florida, California, New Mexico, and Texas. Ponce de León was the first Spaniard to arrive in what would become the continental United States when he landed near St. Augustine in Florida in 1513.

Other Spanish explorers moved north from their bases in Mexico. In contrast to the predominant English influence in New England, characterized by simple meetinghouses, the Spanish colonies brought the lavish Catholic Baroque style to America.

The earliest Spanish colonial churches in Florida were simple, however, built of heavy timber frames and thatched roofs. None of these has survived. A reconstruction of the church at Mission San Luis, Tallahassee (Apalachee), Florida, originally built in 1656, shows the timber frame construction.

Spreading the word of God was important to the Spanish colonists, and they devoted considerable energy to trying to convert the Native Americans. Spanish Jesuits came to California and Arizona, and Franciscans to New Mexico and Texas. Both Jesuits and Franciscans were in Florida. Examples of important mission churches are found in Acoma and Taos, New Mexico; San Antonio, Texas; Tucson, Arizona; and Mission San Luis, Florida. By 1626, Spanish missionaries had built twenty-six churches in what is now New Mexico and converted thousands of Native Americans to Catholicism.

The mission churches were largely built by Native American laborers, working under the direction of the Spanish missionaries. In the Southwest, the favored building material had long been adobe, sun-dried earthen structures. The Indian technique was to take handfuls of mud and squeeze them into lumps which were placed in rows. Successive rows, or courses, would be placed on top of the first one, until the desired height was reached. This simple technique is called puddling. This was suitable for one- or, at most, two-story buildings. The Spanish colonists introduced a variation in the construction of adobe buildings, derived from the practice in Mexico and Spain. The bricks are molded into uniform shapes and reinforced with grass or straw, then dried. These improved bricks allowed them to build thicker walls and taller buildings, as in the mission churches. Nonetheless, the forms of these buildings are necessarily much more primitive than their Spanish models.

The builders of the mission churches of the Southwest found that adobe made an admirable material. First of all, it was cheap, readily available, and could be produced by unskilled labor. In the arid climate, the sun-dried brick was very durable and could easily be repaired. The thick walls required for adobe construction had additional benefits, as

Above: San Agustin de la Isleta, NM, begun *c.* 1613.

Above: San Estevan del Rey Mission Church, Acoma, NM, 1629–42.

Above: San José, Laguna, NM, *c.* 1700.

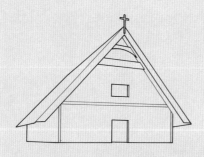

Above: Mission San Luis, Tallahassee, FL, 1656. Exterior (reconstruction). The earliest Spanish colonial churches were also built of heavy timber frames and thatched roofs. None of these has survived.

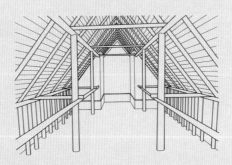

Above: Mission San Luis, Tallahassee, interior (reconstruction). An aisled, timber frame construction.

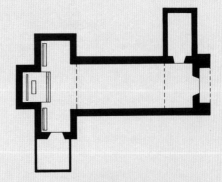

Above: Plan of a typical Spanish mission church.

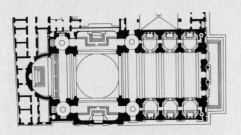

Above: Plan of Il Gesu, Rome, Italy, 1568–75. This Roman church inspired many Spanish churches in the Old World and in the colonies.

Above: Typical Spanish mission church—planar façade. Mission churches typically followed this pattern or had twin-towered façades.

Above: Typical Spanish mission church—twin-towered façade.

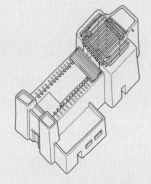

Above: Adobe church, roof construction.

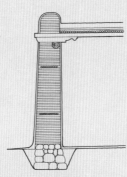

Above: Adobe wall construction.

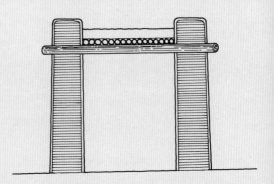

Above: Adobe construction with vigas, or stout logs.

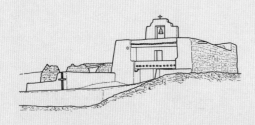

Above: Nuestra Señora de la Asunción at Zia Pueblo, NM, begun c. 1614.

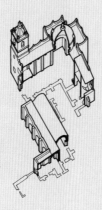

Left: Nuestra Señora de la Purísima Concepcion de Acuna, 807 Mission Road, San Antonio, TX, late 1730s–1755. Section view.

Right: Nuestra Señora de la Purísima Concepcion de Acuna, 807 Mission Road, San Antonio, TX, late 1730s–1755. Aerial view.

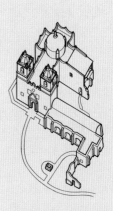

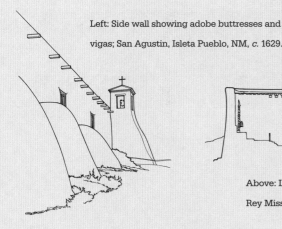

Left: Side wall showing adobe buttresses and vigas; San Agustin, Isleta Pueblo, NM, *c.* 1629.

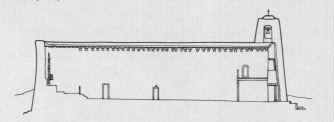

Above: Longitudinal section of San Estevan del Rey Mission Church, Acoma, NM, 1629–42.

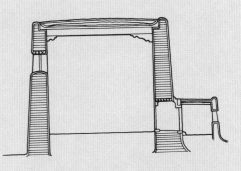

Above: End section of San Estevan del Rey Mission Church, Acoma, NM.

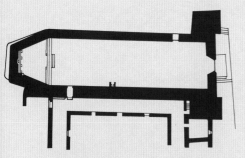

Above: Plan of San Estevan del Rey Mission Church, Acoma, NM.

Above: Belfry at San Estevan del Rey Mission Church, Acoma, NM.

Above: Nuestra Señora de la Asuncion, Zia Pueblo, NM, 1610–28; 1693.

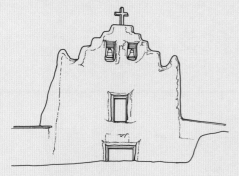

Above: Façade of San José, Laguna, NM, *c.* 1700.

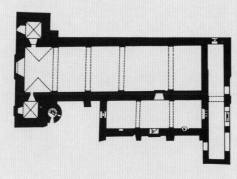

Above: Plan of San José y San Miguel de Aguayo, San Antonio, TX, *c.* 1720–31.

Above: Nambé Church, NM, 1725. Destroyed.

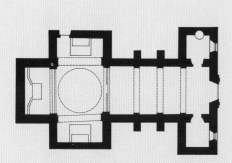

Above: Plan of Nuestra Señora de la Purisima Concepcion de Acuna, San Antonio, TX, 1743–45.

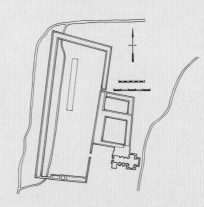

Above: Site plan of Mission San Antonio de Valero (the Alamo), San Antonio, TX, 1744–56. The extensive complex included many buildings.

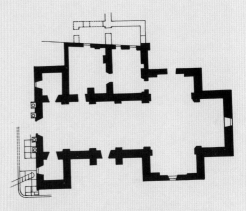

Above: Plan of Mission San Antonio de Valero (the Alamo), San Antonio, TX, 1744–56.

Above: San José y San Miguel de Aguayo, San Antonio, TX, *c.* 1720–31. Pedro Huizar, sculptor.

Above: Mission de Corpus Christi de la Ysleta, U.S. Highway 80, Ysleta, TX; rebuilt 1908.

Above: San Xavier del Bac, Tucson, Arizona, 1783–97.

Above: San Miguel Chapel, Santa Fe, NM, 1709.

Above: San Francisco de Asis, 3321 Sixteenth Street, San Francisco, CA, 1782–91.

the thick thermal mass of earth helped keep a relatively stable temperature in an area that was known for blazing heat in the summer and cold winters. The roofs of adobe structures are composed of thick logs known as vigas, which are covered with a layer of small branches and then layers of earth above that.

After preliminary explorations earlier in the century, mostly by those seeking legendary gold treasures, New Mexico was colonized in the 1580s. A royal decree in 1583 directed the viceroy of New Spain to organize the new settlements. Santa Fe was designated the colonial administrative center in 1609. The earliest surviving mission church is San Agustin de la Isleta, which was begun about 1613. The low and wide adobe façade is flanked by two low bell towers; a third bell is enframed in a center gable. A second church of Nuestra Señora de la Asunción at Zia Pueblo was begun c. 1614. It is very simple, with a low horizontal

façade broken only by a stepped gable encasing a church bell. One of the most important is the early church of San Estevan del Rey Mission, in Acoma, New Mexico, built between 1629 and 1642. It is a massive structure built of adobe. The walls are very thick and there is only one window and a doorway cut into the main façade. Two bell towers flank the entrance.

These early mission churches are built on a cruciform plan, with thick adobe walls. They re-create a simplified version of Spanish Baroque architecture. The cruciform plan is traditional, with the altar at the far end from the entrance. The entrance façades frequently incorporate simplified versions of the twin-towered façades of Baroque churches, or else they are planar, with scalloped gables. These two types dominate the façades of mission churches.

Although later in date, the adobe church of San José (c. 1700) at Old Laguna Pueblo, New Mexico, is simpler

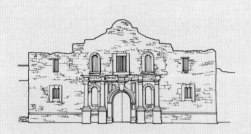

Above: Façade of Mission San Antonio de Valero (The Alamo), San Antonio, TX, 1744–56, as it is today.

Above: Façade of Mission San Antonio de Valero, reconstruction.

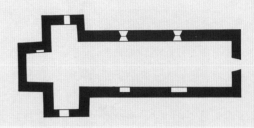

Above: Plan of old church of Santo Tomás, Abiquiu, NM, c. 1754–1770.

Above: New church of Santo Tomás, Abiquiu, NM, c. 1934–38.

Above: Santa Clara, Santa Clara Pueblo, NM, 1626–29; c. 1758. State of the church in 1899; it collapsed in 1905 and was rebuilt c. 1914 and in the late 1960s.

Above: Façade of the San José de Gracia de las Trampas, Las Trampas, NM, c. 1760.

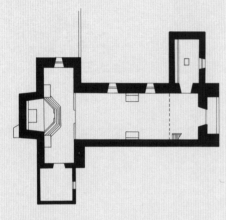

Above: San José de Gracia de las Trampas, Las Trampas, NM, c. 1760. Plan.

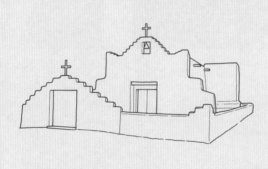

Above: San Lorenzo, Picuris Pueblo, NM, c. 1770. A planar façade.

Above: Façade of San Francisco de Asis, Ranchos de Taos, NM, 1805–15.

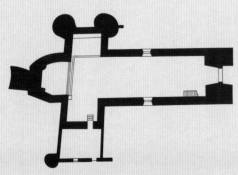

Above: Plan of San Francisco de Asis, Ranchos de Taos, NM.

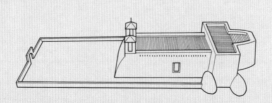

Above: San Francisco de Asis, Ranchos de Taos, NM; reconstruction.

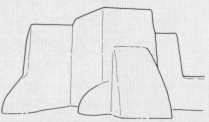

Above: Rear view of San Francisco de Asis, Ranchos de Taos, NM.

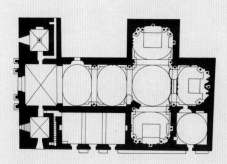

Above: Plan of San Xavier del Bac, Tucson, Arizona, 1783–97.

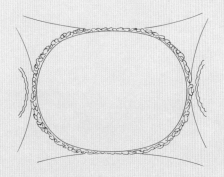

Above: Oval dome at San Xavier del Bac, supported by pendentives.

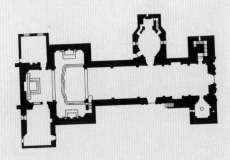

Above: Antonio Peyri: Plan of San Luis Rey de Francia, near Oceanside, CA, 1811–15.

Left: San Jeronimo, Taos Pueblo, NM, 1617; c. 1626; 1706; c. 1850.

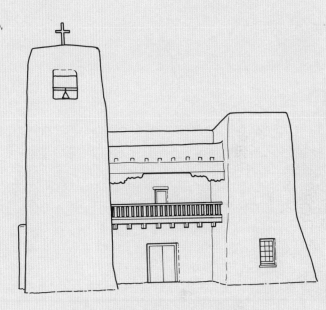

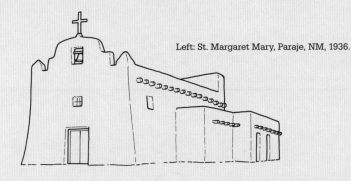

Left: St. Margaret Mary, Paraje, NM, 1936.

Above: Cristo Rey, Santa Fe, NM, 1939–40.

Above: St. Anne, Acomita, NM, 1939–40.

Above: McHugh and Hooker; Bradley P. Kidder: San Ildefonso, San Ildefonso Pueblo, NM, 1969; this new church replicates one first built in 1617 and rebuilt in 1711 and 1905.

Left: Mañuel Estevan Ruiz: San Carlos de Borromeo, 3080 Rio Road, Carmel, CA, 1793–97.

than San Estevan. The façade is totally flat and unornamented, and there are no flanking towers. The gable is stepped, with bells set into the upper portion. It is a long hall church, not cruciform. The interior has simple wall painting on the nave, and a primitive painted reredos (altar screen) at the rear. It features paintings of saints and twisted columns that look back to St. Peter's in Rome and other Baroque churches.

The tall central tower that marks the façade of the San Miguel Chapel in Santa Fe, New Mexico, 1709, seems almost Gothic with its verticality.

The richness of Spanish Baroque is evident at Mission San José y San Miguel de Aguayo near San Antonio, Texas.

Above: San Xavier del Bac, Tucson, Arizona, 1783–97. Interior.

It was built between 1720–31. The church was dedicated to the Marquis of San Miguel de Aguayo, who was the governor of Texas at that time. It is a very authentic example of Spanish Catholic Baroque. The cruciform church is built of stone and has a pair of flanking towers at the façade; one still has an ornate bell tower. The nave is narrow and vaulted with groin vaults. The crossing is topped by an actual dome on an octagonal drum. The drum is pierced with windows, which direct light over the altar. The carved entrance portal is unique in architecture at this time, for it is laden with three-dimensional carvings of saints and other figures. The sculptor was Pedro Huizar, a Spanish artist trained in Europe. William Pierson, Jr., has observed that such a sensuously theatrical portal was technically impossible in New Mexico at this time, due to the lack of sculptors, and conceptually unthinkable in New England, dominated as it was by the Puritan aesthetic. English Puritans in the time of Oliver Cromwell had smashed many sculptures in an iconoclastic fury.

The church of Nuestra Señora de la Purísima Concepcion de Acuna in San Antonio, Texas, was probably begun in the late 1730s and finished in 1755. It is a stone church, built on a cruciform plan with a dome over the central crossing. The restored interior is now white and plain, with a barrel-vaulted nave leading to the crossing dome, which is carried on pendentives. The church originally contained a number of ornate sculptures, paintings, and a decorated reredos, an ornamental screen behind the

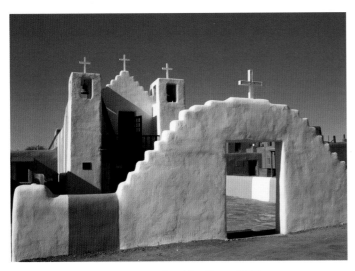

Above: San Geronimo, Taos Pueblo, Taos, NM.

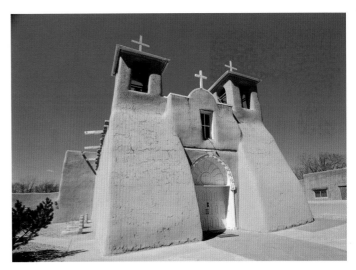

Above: San Francisco de Asis, Ranchos de Taos, Taos, NM, 1805–15.

altar. The exterior façade has two towers, and the central portal is covered by a tall pediment, which is almost shaped like an equilateral triangle. The pediment contains a niche that once held a sculpture of the Immaculate Conception.

The Mission Corpus Christi de la Ysleta (1744), Ysleta, Texas, is an example of modern restoration. The eighteenth-century church on this site was burned in a fire in 1907, and the church now largely dates from 1908. The façade and interiors were completely redone. The Baroque scalloped gable and bell tower continue the mission style, however.

An important group of mission churches in Texas were built in the area of San Antonio, of which the most well known is Mission San Antonio de Valero, more famous as the Alamo. It was built between 1744 and 1756, and unlike the New Mexico churches, was built of stone. Therefore the detailing is crisper, and the design closer to the Spanish precedents. The ornament around the doorway is particularly fine. The church has played an important role in Texas and American history and exists today in an incomplete state. The scalloped façade was originally intended to be much taller, with two tall flanking bell towers. The nave crossing was to be covered by a dome. The interior held richly carved altarpieces, which have long since vanished. The Alamo had been abandoned by the Franciscan monks by the early nineteenth century. It began to be used as a military compound and fortress in 1813. In 1836 it was the site of the legendary battle between the Mexican forces of Santa Anna and the Americans commanded by William

Travis, including Davy Crockett and Jim Bowie. At that point the Alamo attained its mythic status, a historic ruin as celebrated as any in Europe. The façade was restored in the 1850s, when the present gable was added. A restoration in 1915 gave the church its present form.

The small church of Mission San Francisco de Asis (Mission Doloros), in San Francisco, California, was built in 1782–91. The much restored façade features a double level of columns; at the upper level the columns rise in graduated heights under the shallow gable roof.

The mission church of San Xavier del Bac stands on the edges of the Sonoran Desert near Tucson, Arizona. When built in 1783–97, it was indeed remote. The mission was originally founded in 1700 by a Spanish Jesuit priest. When the Jesuits were banished from the area in 1767, it was taken over by the Franciscans, who built the current church. It is very European in conception, with a cruciform plan and stone vaulted domes over the nave, transepts, and crossing. The high crossing dome is circular on an octagonal drum, while the others are oval, carried on pendentives. The forms are simplified, however, and more primitive than the European precedents, undoubtedly the result of the frontier conditions and isolation. The church is made of brick, covered with stucco and whitewash. On the exterior, the church is all white and simple. The entrance portal is encased in paintings and sculpted columns and shallow figures. The painted sculptural decoration of the apse, however, is a riot of bold shapes and colors. Painted columns create a series of niches for sculptures and paintings.

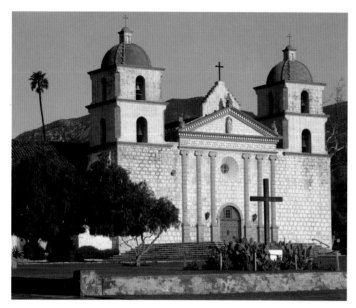

Above: Santa Barbara Mission, 2201 Laguna Street, Santa Barbara, CA, 1815–20.

Directly above the altar is a statue of the Virgin Mary dressed in blue, surrounded by a field of red, with crudely painted angels pulling back a curtain to reveal her. In the section above her, there is a representation of the cross inset into the wall, with two saints flanking it. Additional saints appear in the flanking niches on either side. Baroque church interiors in Spain, Italy, and Austria were noted for the almost delirious explosion of visionary forms and colors. This colonial church becomes a theatrical setting that provides a convincing vision of heaven. It has the most complete surviving ornament of any of the Spanish mission churches.

The mission church of San Geronimo at Taos Pueblo, in Taos, New Mexico, has a two-story portico supported by spiral wooden columns. Two symmetrical bell towers flank the façade, projecting slightly. The central portion of the façade is capped with a stepped gable. The adobe

Above: Cathedral of St. Augustine, 38 Cathedral Place, St. Augustine, FL, 1797. Restored 1887 by James Renwick after fire.

Above: Antonio Peyri: San Luis Rey de Francia, 4050 Mission Avenue, Oceanside, CA, 1811–15.

church is now painted with contrasting dark browns and white, giving it a strong visual presence.

The massive adobe walls of the church of San Francisco de Asis at Ranchos de Taos, Taos, New Mexico, were built in 1805–15. The crude primitiveness here makes a powerful set of forms that have inspired many modern artists. The monumental form of the rear of the church is especially powerful. The façade is characterized by two symmetrical flanking bell towers. The interior of the nave is dark, but with dramatic lighting near the altar from hidden windows. In European Baroque churches, the altar would be lit from a dome, but it was not possible to build domes in the colonial Southwest at this time. Similar dramatic effects were created with small windows on high, hidden from direct view. The mysterious lighting creates an effect appropriate to the mystery of the mass.

*

After developing the missions of New Mexico, Arizona, and Texas, the Spanish turned to coastal California. The missions there were even more remote from the centers of Spanish cultural influence, and the means were more limited, so the mission churches tend to be simpler. Nonetheless, they have a raw beauty and considerable historical interest. The administrative center for the California missions was the church of San Carlos de Borromeo in Carmel, built by the master stonemason Mañuel Estevan Ruiz in 1793–97. Like many of the other missions, it was built by Native Americans working under Spanish direction. The material in this case is a local sandstone. The façade is flanked with two towers, which are not symmetrical. The left tower has a tall oval dome, one of the most Baroque features of the church. A star-shaped window above the round-arched doorway in the middle of the façade is scalloped into a quatrefoil, or four-leaf, shape. The ground plan is that of a long hall church, with a narrow nave. On the inside, the nave is vaulted with a long barrel vault that is parabolic in shape, giving it an unusual profile.

The largest of the Spanish missions in California was the Santa Barbara Mission, built between 1815–20. The broad stone façade is flanked by two symmetrical bell towers capped with small domes. The center of the façade is emphasized with a large classical pediment supported by tall Ionic engaged columns. Thick bands of mortar join the courses of ashlar masonry. The influence of European tradition is very strong and clearly reflected here.

The most prosperous of the Californian missions was San Luis Rey de Francia in Oceanside, California. It was built by Father Antonio Peyri in 1811–15. The mission buildings cover over six acres. The church has a cruciform plan with a long nave. The whitewashed façade has a single tower on the right and a scalloped gable over the nave. The mission was closed in 1831, when the Mexican government secularized the missions. In 1893 it was reconsecrated as a church.

Mission San Francisco Solano in Sonoma, California, was founded in 1823. It was the last and northernmost of the twenty-one Franciscan missions in California. Three years later the wooden buildings burned down and were replaced with an adobe structure. In 1834, the Mexican government closed all the missions, and San Francisco Solano fell into disrepair, with roof tiles and adobe bricks taken for other buildings. In 1841, a smaller adobe church was built nearby. After passing into various commercial uses, the church was damaged in the 1906 earthquake and repaired in 1913. The low adobe church and *convento* (priest's quarters) were restored again in the 1940s and turned into a historic museum.

*

St. Augustine, Florida, is the oldest continuously occupied European settlement in the United States. It was founded in 1565. The Cathedral of St. Augustine has been rebuilt several times. The present building dates from 1797, when it was constructed out of the local coquina stone, composed of sedimentary layers of seashells. The stone is easily cut when soaked with water, but becomes hard when dried. The interior was destroyed by a fire in 1887. The architect James Renwick helped restore and enlarge the church, adding a transept and bell tower. On the interior, the ceiling is supported by massive decorated timbers.

Log Churches

Log buildings are popularly associated with the frontier experience in American culture. True log buildings were introduced by Swedish colonists in the Delaware valley in

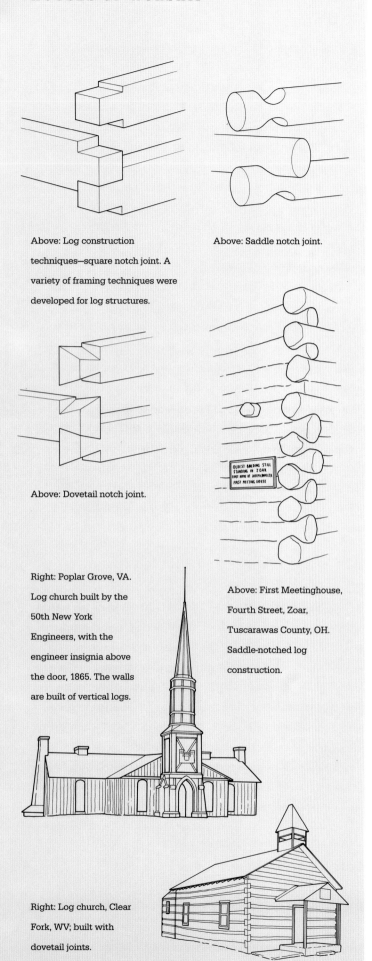

Above: Log construction techniques—square notch joint. A variety of framing techniques were developed for log structures.

Above: Saddle notch joint.

Above: Dovetail notch joint.

OLDEST BUILDING STILL STANDING IN ZOAR
FIRST HOME OF JOSEPH BIMELER
FIRST MEETING HOUSE

Above: First Meetinghouse, Fourth Street, Zoar, Tuscarawas County, OH. Saddle-notched log construction.

Right: Poplar Grove, VA. Log church built by the 50th New York Engineers, with the engineer insignia above the door, 1865. The walls are built of vertical logs.

Right: Log church, Clear Fork, WV; built with dovetail joints.

the seventeenth century. Eventually the form spread westward. In the preindustrial era, in areas with abundant timber, hand-hewn logs were the most convenient building material. Log buildings were constructed directly on the ground, or on fieldstone foundations. The logs were joined at the corners with a variety of joints: square notches, saddle notches, or dovetail joints. The spaces between the logs were filled with clay chinking to make them weather tight. The typical church was a single room structure, occasionally with a gallery on a second level. One surviving example of an early log church is the First Meetinghouse, in Zoar, Tuscarawas County, Ohio. It is made with saddle-notched log construction. Although the coming of the railroad spread sawed lumber and wire nails, which replaced the hand-hewn log technique, this technique did recur under certain circumstances. During the Civil War, the 50th New York Engineers built a church in Poplar Grove, Virginia, out of logs. An unusual technique was used in this 1865 building, for the walls are built of vertical logs.

Notes

1. See Alan Taylor, *American Colonies* (New York: Viking, 2001), for a recent survey of this period.
2. Report on Native American Sacred Sites and the Department of Defense, web page accessed on January 11, 2003: https://osiris.cso.uiuc.edu/ denix/Public/ES-Programs/Conservation/ Legacy/Sacred/ch1.html#onai.
3. William Strachey, letter, 1610; quoted in website: http://smith2.sewanee.edu/gsmith/courses/Religion 391/DocsEarlySouth/1610-WilliamStrachey.html.

Above: Mission San Francisco Solano, 16885 Sonoma Highway, Sonoma, CA, 1823.

Chapter 2

Colonial Churches—
the Eighteenth Century

Upon my arrival in the United States, the religious aspect of the country was the first thing that struck my attention; and the longer I stayed there the more did I perceive the great political consequences resulting from this state of things, to which I was unaccustomed. In France I had almost always seen the spirit of religion and the spirit of freedom pursuing courses diametrically opposed to each other; but in America, I found that they were intimately united, and that they reigned in common over the same country.

Religion in America takes no direct part in the government of society, but nevertheless it must be regarded as the foremost of the political institutions of that country; for if it does not impart a taste for freedom, it facilitates the use of free institutions. Indeed, it is in this same point of view that the inhabitants of the United States themselves look upon religious belief.

—Alexis de Toqueville, *Democracy in America* (1835)

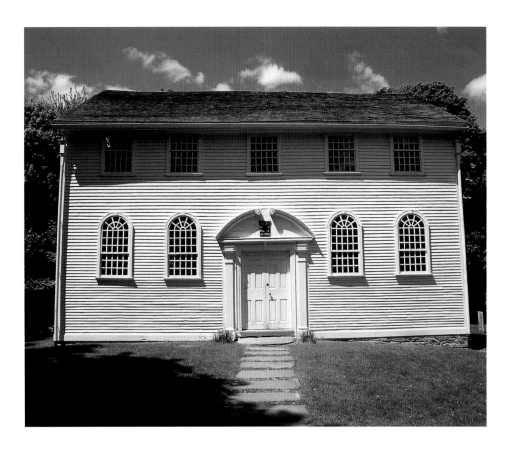

Right: St. Paul's Church (Old Narragansett Church), Wickford, RI, 1707. Front view.

The American Revolution of 1776 brought an end to the colonial era. Church architecture of the 1700s, however, was marked by increasing British influence on church design. The Revolution did not bring a corresponding transformation of style.

A greater homogeneity of style developed on the east coast in the eighteenth century, as the classically inspired Georgian style spread across the region. The Anglican church assumed new prominence in New England, although many Congregational meetinghouses continued to be built. The time lag between European styles and their introduction in America began to shorten, although it was still considerable. The two main developments were the spread of Wren-type churches in the first part of the eighteenth century, inspired by Christopher Wren's plans for fifty-one new churches for London. Later, the influence of James Gibbs's church of St. Martin-in-the-Fields (1722–26) became more prevalent.

Greater religious diversity appears among the colonists in the eighteenth century. The first Jewish synagogue in New England dates from this time: the Touro Synagogue (1760) in Newport, Rhode Island. It was designed by Peter Harrison, a classically oriented architect. In the last quarter of the century, Shakers came to America and built their distinctive settlements and meetinghouses.

New England had been colonized by dedicated Puritans. Over time, the religious zeal seemed to dissipate, but it was rekindled by a new wave of evangelism and church building in the 1740s known as the Great Awakening. Preachers such as Jonathan Edwards and George Whitehead reignited religious passion. There was a Second Awakening in the 1770s and 1780s, coinciding with the American Revolution. A considerable number of churches were built at this time.

Meetinghouses

Traditional foursquare meetinghouses of the sort developed in the seventeenth century continued to be built in the next period, especially in new frontier settlements, although these would be superseded by more elaborate classical buildings as a greater consciousness of style developed. The Old Brick Meetinghouse in Boston (1712) was

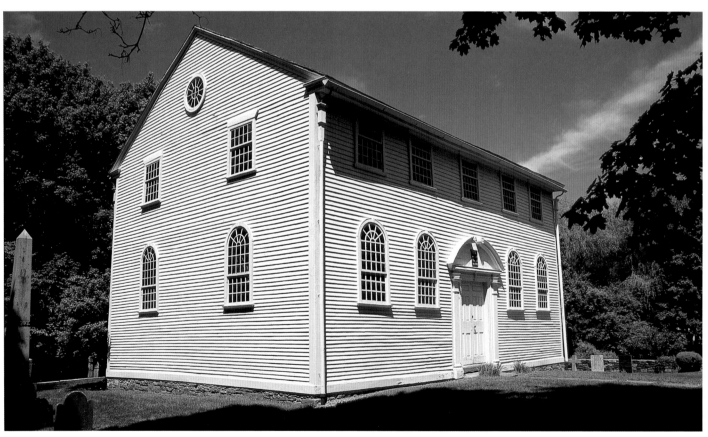

Above: St. Paul's Church (Old Narragansett Church), Wickford, RI, 1707. Side view.

an exceptionally large square meetinghouse. It was three stories high, with belt courses dividing the stories. The hipped roof was topped with a balustrade and cupola. A two-story pedimented entrance porch projected from the center of the building. This meetinghouse was the last of its kind to be built in Boston, and it was demolished in the nineteenth century. These early meetinghouses generally lacked steeples; if there was a bell tower, it was often a separate structure; old prints of the nearby Lexington meetinghouse and battle green show such a separate structure.

In new communities such as Narraganset, Rhode Island, even an Anglican church was built in the meetinghouse form in these early years, as seen in the Old Narraganset Church (St. Paul's) of 1707. This church was later moved to Wickford. An earlier bell tower fell in the mid-nineteenth century and has not been replaced. The only classical features of the essentially domestic structure are the round-arched windows on the first floor and the broken pediment over the door. The entrance is found at the long side of the church, in typical meetinghouse fashion.

Quakers

Quakers were in some ways even more radical than the Puritans. The Society of Friends, or Quakers, was a movement initially led by George Fox (1624–91) in England. He insisted on the primacy of a direct and personal relationship with God, rather than through the intermediary of a church hierarchy. Revelation could, and should, be experienced by the congregant, which led to physical and emotional states accompanied by movements which gave rise to the term "Quaker." The first Quakers to arrive in Massachusetts in 1656 were banished and found refuge in the more tolerant Rhode Island. At first they generally worshiped in houses; specialized meetinghouses were built later. Newport was an early Quaker center, and an early simple but large meetinghouse was built there in 1699. After the Revolution, the numbers of Quakers in Rhode Island began to decline.

Pennsylvania, under the tolerant policies of William Penn, himself a convert to Quakerism, became the home of the largest concentration of Quakers. William Penn received a royal charter for his colony in 1681, and by the 1690s attracted many Quakers from Britain. Quakers shared with the New England Puritans a distaste for outward show,

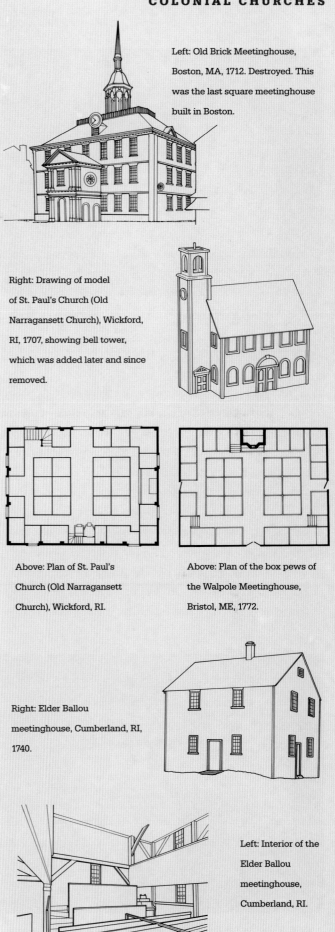

Left: Old Brick Meetinghouse, Boston, MA, 1712. Destroyed. This was the last square meetinghouse built in Boston.

Right: Drawing of model of St. Paul's Church (Old Narragansett Church), Wickford, RI, 1707, showing bell tower, which was added later and since removed.

Above: Plan of St. Paul's Church (Old Narragansett Church), Wickford, RI.

Above: Plan of the box pews of the Walpole Meetinghouse, Bristol, ME, 1772.

Right: Elder Ballou meetinghouse, Cumberland, RI, 1740.

Left: Interior of the Elder Ballou meetinghouse, Cumberland, RI.

Above: Friends Meetinghouse, North Pembroke, MA, 1706.

Above: Friends at Stony Brook, Princeton, Mercer County, NJ, 1760. Stone Quaker meetinghouse.

and, if anything, their meetinghouses were even more simple than those in New England. Quaker meetinghouses are deliberately plain and reflect the conviction that the meetinghouse is no more or less sacred than any other place. Meetinghouses were generally built in the manner of other simple houses or vernacular architecture. There are no steeples or bell towers. There are generally two separate entrance doors for men and women, taken to symbolize the equality of men and women. On the inside, men and women sat on separate sides of the house on plain benches, facing a group of elders and "weighty friends." They held separate meetings for business, with movable wooden

partitions between men and women used for privacy. During the worship service, the divider was removed, however, and women were able to preach as often as men.

The Friend's Meetinghouse in North Pembroke, Massachusetts (1706), is the oldest in the state. It was originally located in Scituate, on the property of Edward Wanton. Earlier, he had been an official who participated in the hangings of Quakers in Boston and was so moved by their calm grace that he became one himself. The meetinghouse was later moved to its present location. It is a small structure, strongly resembling contemporary domestic architecture. On the interior, benches line all four sides,

Above: Friends Meetinghouse, 141 Central Avenue, Dover, NH, 1768.

Above: Friends Meetinghouse, Amesbury, MA, 1851. The traditional design is essentially unchanged.

Above: Old Brooklyn Meetinghouse, Town Green, Brooklyn, CT, 1771. Front view.

Above: Old Brooklyn Meetinghouse, Town Green, Brooklyn, CT, 1771. Interior.

Above: Trinity Episcopal Church (Malbone Church), Brooklyn, CT, 1771.

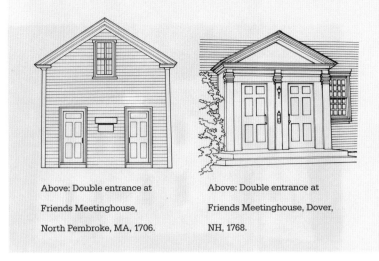

Above: Double entrance at Friends Meetinghouse, North Pembroke, MA, 1706.

Above: Double entrance at Friends Meetinghouse, Dover, NH, 1768.

facing the center. The later Friends Meetinghouse in Dover, New Hampshire (1768), is much larger, but similar in design. There is an early stone Quaker meetinghouse at Stony Brook in Princeton, New Jersey, from 1760, which is similarly plain.

Often political and religious disputes were marked by the establishment of a new church or meetinghouse. In the small town of Brooklyn in northern Connecticut, two meetinghouses bear evidence to both stubborn religious convictions and resistance to taxes, perennial themes in American culture. The Old Brooklyn Meetinghouse was built in 1771, replacing an earlier structure. The new Congregational meetinghouse was to be paid for with taxes on the town, which did not sit well with Captain Godfrey Malbone, who was an Episcopalian. Rather than contribute to the building of the new Congregational meetinghouse, Captain Malbone built his own church—reportedly drawing the plans himself—the Trinity Episcopal Church (now also known as the Malbone Church), a short distance away in Brooklyn, also in 1771. Malbone was originally from Newport, Rhode Island, and his design is a simplified form of the Touro Synagogue by Peter Harrison (built 1759–63). It is a square meetinghouse, with hipped roof.

The Old Brooklyn Meetinghouse had a side entrance, and a tall steeple at the end, which had to be rebuilt as early as 1774 and was badly damaged in a 1938 hurricane. It is currently in the process of restoration.

Several well-preserved pre-Revolutionary meeting-houses are preserved in close proximity on the coast of Maine. The Walpole Meetinghouse in Bristol was built in 1772 and is a two-story shingle-covered structure with a gable roof. Little distinguishes it from a residence of the period. The name of the church is derived from the origi-

Above: Meetinghouse, State Highway 111A (Main Street), Danville, NH, *c.* 1755.

Above: Meetinghouse, State Highway 121A at its junction with Fremont Road, Sandown, NH, 1773.

Above: Walpole Meetinghouse, South Bristol Road, Route 129, Bristol, ME, 1772.

Above: Union Episcopal Church, Old Church Road, West Claremont, NH, 1773. Steeple added later.

Above: German Lutheran Meetinghouse, one mile south of Waldoboro Village on ME 32, Waldoboro, ME, 1772.

Above: Timothy Palmer (attributed): Rocky Hill Meetinghouse, 4 Portsmouth Street, Amesbury, MA, *c.* 1785. Side view.

nal name of the township, which was renamed Bristol in 1767. When the church was built it retained the earlier name. It was originally a Presbyterian parish and became Congregational after 1800.

German Lutheran immigrants built the Waldoboro (or Old German) Meetinghouse in Waldoboro, Maine, in 1772. This is also a domestic-style meetinghouse, two stories high with a gabled roof. There is a porch entry on the narrow side, and this leads to an axial interior, which focuses on the prominent pulpit. The exterior is a traditional New England meetinghouse, but the interior recalls the hierarchical plan of European churches.

Other well-preserved meetinghouses from this era can be found in New Hampshire, including the Fremont Meetinghouse (1773) in Sandown. It is a wide meetinghouse with the entrance in the middle of the long side. The windows are symmetrically placed, and two stair towers and entrances flank the building as well. The meetinghouse has a gabled roof and is covered with clapboards.

The oldest Anglican church in New Hampshire is Union Episcopal Church in West Claremont. It was begun in 1773, but not completed until 1789 because of the Revolution. The church underwent later alterations; the tower and belfry were added in 1801. It was originally only four bays long, with two additional bays added in 1820. At first the color was gray, with the rear wall painted red, using the cheapest color. Now it is all painted white. The orientation of the church is longitudinal, with entrance through the entrance tower.

The Rockingham Meeting House (*c.* 1787–1800) in Rockingham, Vermont, was built at the end of the century. Its present site on the top of a steep hill was not the one chosen in the town meeting; despite losing the vote for its location, a cantankerous group simply moved all the building materials to their preferred site the night before construction was to begin, and the rest went along with the preemptive move. It is a large, two-story, wooden building with a gabled roof and two porch entries at the narrow ends. The interior is very light, with a second-story gallery on three sides. The carved decoration of the pulpit is simple but skillful. The church took many years to complete due to lack of organization, and it fell into disuse in the mid-nineteenth century. It was carefully restored in 1906.

An unusual example of sectarian cooperation and New England thriftiness is found in the Old Round Church in Richmond, Vermont (1812–13). It was constructed by the

Above: Rockingham Meeting House, Meetinghouse road, Rockingham, VT, *c.* 1787–1800. Fully restored, 1906.

Above: Rockingham Meeting House. Interior.

Above: Old Meetinghouse, NH 107, Fremont, NH, 1800.

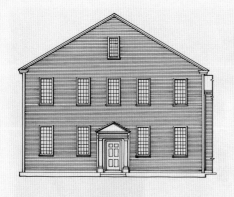

Above: Timothy Palmer (attributed): Rocky Hill

Meeting House, Amesbury, MA, 1785. West elevation.

Above: Rocky Hill Meeting House. South elevation.

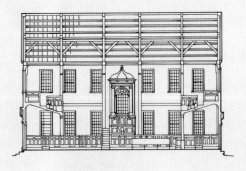

Above: Rocky Hill Meeting House. Section.

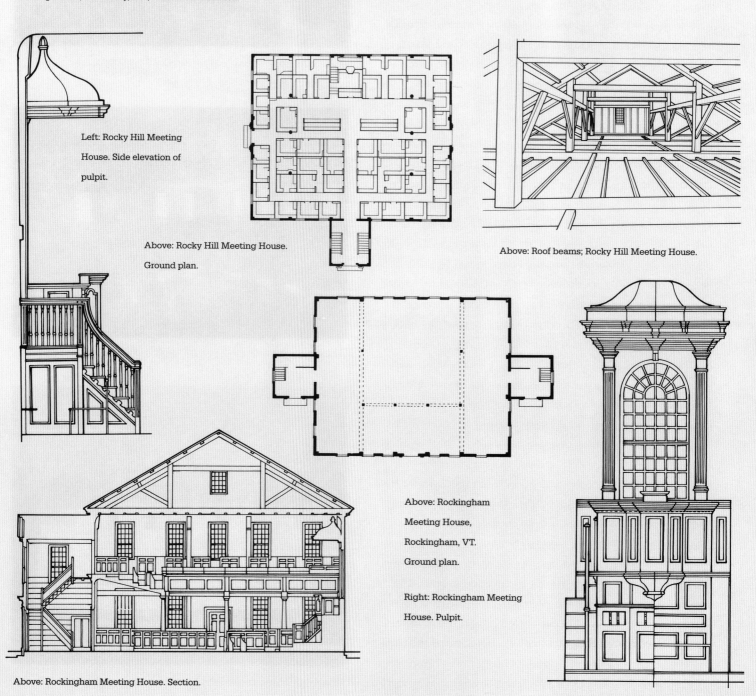

Left: Rocky Hill Meeting

House. Side elevation of

pulpit.

Above: Rocky Hill Meeting House.

Ground plan.

Above: Roof beams; Rocky Hill Meeting House.

Above: Rockingham

Meeting House,

Rockingham, VT.

Ground plan.

Right: Rockingham Meeting

House. Pulpit.

Above: Rockingham Meeting House. Section.

Above: Old Stone Presbyterian Church, Church and Foster Streets, Lewisburg, West VA, 1796; 1830.

Above: William Rhoades, master builder: Old Round Church, Bridge Street, Richmond, VT, 1812–13. Built to serve five denominations.

master builder William Rhoades to serve five denominations who shared the building. The land it sits on was donated. It is not actually round, but sixteen-sided. An open-arched cupola with eight sides sits atop an octagonal drum on the roof, and a crude weather vane, shaped like an arrow or a comet, caps the building. The interior includes a second-story gallery.

Communitarian Groups

Some of the most distinctive houses of worship were created by sects who practiced communal living and strict devotion, in some cases including celibacy for all church members.

The unique Ephrata Cloister was created for a group of devout separatists, followers of the Pietist mystic Georg Conrad Beissel (1691–1768), who was inspired by earlier German reformers. Built in the early 1740s in the manner of earlier German timber architecture, it is located in Lancaster County, Pennsylvania. The most striking building is the central Saal (1741), or meeting hall, with steep

pitched roofs and many small windows. Adjoining the Saal is the sisters' house where the women lived, known as the Saron (1743). It has three floors of dormitory cells. The members of this community committed themselves to celibacy and a strict regimen of work, simple diet, and prayer. Men and women alike wore long white robes. The group led a regimented life; bedtime was at nine. Beds were

Above: Ephrata Cloister, 632 West Main Street, Ephrata, PA, 1741/43.

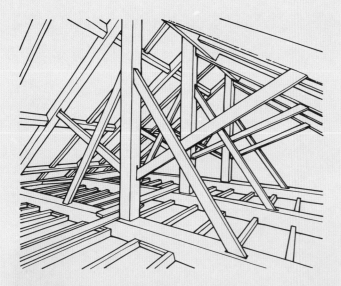

Above: Roof trusses, Chestnut Hill Meetinghouse, Chestnut St., Millville vicinity, Worcester County, MA.

Above: William Rhoades, master builder: interior of the Old Round Church, Richmond, VT, 1812–13.

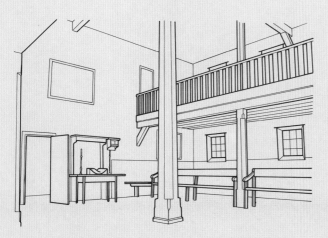

Above: Ephrata cloister, Ephrata, PA, 1743. Interior of meetinghouse.

narrow and made of wood; Beissel thought that feather beds were sinful. All rose at midnight for a two-hour prayer vigil to await the second coming, after which they went back to bed, but rose again at five for morning services and work. Music and printing provided creative outlets. The group was at its height in the mid-eighteenth century with over three hundred members, and the community owned over twenty buildings. Internal dissension in later years led to the dissolution of the group, although their doctrines had an important legacy in the Seventh Day Baptists.

Shakers

The late eighteenth century brought other new religious groups to America, including the Shakers. Led by the charismatic Mother Ann Lee (1736–84), who left England in 1774 to find greater freedom in the colonies, the Shakers were guided by personal visions and a dedication to strict celibacy and a simple lifestyle. Mother Ann had been part of a group of "Shaking Quakers" in England and found many new followers in New York and New England. Her followers came to consider her almost as a second coming of Christ, in female form. Rejecting the formal symbolism of the Anglican church, Shaker chapels were deliberately based on domestic architecture. Excellent examples survive at Canterbury, New Hampshire (1792); Sabbathday Lake,

Above: Moses Johnson, master builder: Shaker Meetinghouse, Canterbury Shaker Village, 288 Shaker Road, Canterbury, NH, 1792.

near New Gloucester, Maine (1794); and Hancock Village, Massachusetts (1786). These are basically gambrel roof houses, typical of Georgian house design, and built with exacting craftsmanship. The Canterbury and Sabbathday Lake Meetinghouses were designed by the master craftsman Moses Johnson, who built ten Shaker meetinghouses. There are large windows on the first floor and in the shed dormers. The brightly lit first-floor meeting room occupies the entire first floor, which is forty-four by thirty-two feet in size. There are separate entrances for men and women.

The Shakers were known for their devotion to excellence and efficiency in all things, since all actions could be considered a form of prayer. Their furniture designs are highly prized. They were an unusually inventive group and originated such, now commonplace, items as the peg clothespin, washing machine, circular saw, and the flat broom, which replaced the round broom. At their peak in the nineteenth century, there were over 5,000 Shakers in communities from Maine to Kentucky and Ohio. The order nearly disappeared in the 1990s, though a handful of reorganized Shakers now live at the Sabbathday Lake site in Maine.

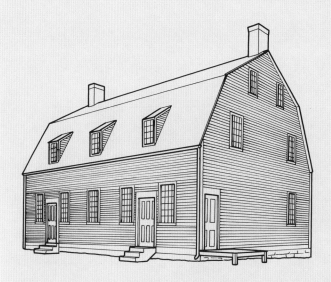

Above: Shaker Meetinghouse (first), Watervliet Shaker Road, Colonie Township, Watervliet, Albany County, NY, 1792. Gambrel roof type.

Above: Shed dormer; Shaker Meetinghouse, Canterbury, NH, 1792.

Above: Shaker Meetinghouse, Sabbathday Lake, 707 Shaker Road, New Gloucester, ME, 1794.

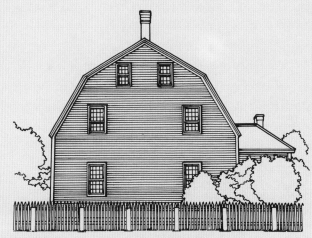

Above: Gambrel Roof; Shaker Meetinghouse, Canterbury, NH, 1792.

Above: Old Indian Church, 410 Meetinghouse Road, Mashpee, MA, 1717 (founded 1684), rededicated 1923. A simple vernacular meetinghouse.

Above: Mohegan Congregational Church, Church Lane, Montville (near Uncasville), CT, 1831. Front view.

Native American Christian Churches

Many Native Americans were converted to Christianity and organized into villages of "Praying Indians." The General Court of Massachusetts passed an act for the Propagation of the Gospel among the American Indians. Reverend John Eliot learned the Algonquin language of the Native Americans and preached his first sermon to Chief Waban in his own wigwam in Nonantum (now a part of Newton). Eventually Praying Indian towns were set up in a ring around Boston as an outer wall of defense during King Philip's war in 1675. Unfortunately, the English colonists did not trust their Native American allies, and other American Indians saw them as enemies. Caught between the warring factions, their numbers were reduced by over two thirds between 1674 and 1680.

A number of early churches built for and by these Native Americans survive in New England. On Cape Cod in Massachusetts, the Old Indian Church in Mashpee was founded in 1684; the current church was built in 1717 and rededicated in 1923. It is a nearly square wooden meeting-house structure covered with shingles. The simple vernacular structure lacks the formality of European reli-gious architecture, which might have seemed too alien to their experience. The considerably later Mohegan Congregational Church, in Montville (near Uncasville),

Connecticut, was built in the Wren-Gibbs church format in 1831. It completely adopts the current Christian style of construction.

Georgian Architecture

The colonies on the East Coast became more unified in the eighteenth century, with a more homogeneous style of architecture based on British classicism. The period is called Georgian, after the ruling English monarchs. After the reign of Queen Anne (1702–14), George I ascended the throne (ruled 1714–27), followed by George II (1727–60) and George III (1760–1820), who ruled during the American Revolution. Classical details, such as columns, pediments, and porticos, began to appear, and there was a greater emphasis on symmetry.

Wren-Style Churches

The most important development in the early eighteenth century was the introduction of the Wren-style church. The greatest British architect of the Baroque era, Christopher Wren (1632–1723) had been given the task of designing fifty-one new churches to replace the eighty-seven that had

Above: Bruton Parish Church, Williamsburg, VA, 1710–15. The first example of a Wren-style church in America.

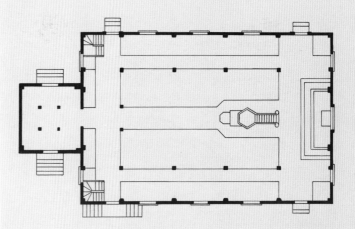

Above: Richard Munday: Trinity Church, Newport, RI. 1725. Plan.

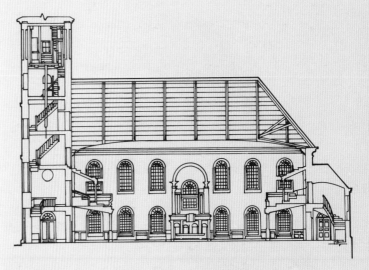

Above: Robert Twelves, designer; Joshua Blanchard, builder: Old South Meeting House, Boston, MA, 1729–30. Section.

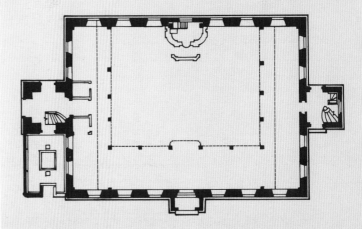

Above: Robert Twelves, designer; Joshua Blanchard, builder: Old South Meeting House, Boston, MA, 1729–30. Plan.

burned down in the Great Fire of London in 1666. The style for these was classical and strongly derived from the Italian Renaissance, except for the steeples. The Gothic steeple had been out of favor since the Renaissance; classical architecture tended toward a horizontal rather than vertical emphasis. Wren's revival of the steeple had a tremendous impact. He devised a basic formula that included an oblong nave combined with a smaller entrance tower and steeple at the short end. This gave a pronounced axial orientation to the churches, though not so exaggerated as the attenuated plans of medieval churches. Although the exterior walls were built of stone, the ceilings were wooden, covered with plaster and lath. This lighter structure saved expense and allowed a more open and delicate interior. Wren's simple design pattern allowed considerable variation, and this type became extremely popular in America. Indeed, the steeple associated with this design became one of the most familiar symbols of colonial America.

The first example of a Wren-style church in the colonies was the Bruton Parish Church in Williamsburg, Virginia (1710–15). Its simple classicism contrasts sharply with the Gothic St. Luke's Old Brick Church of a few decades earlier. The Bruton Parish church is also built of brick, but features tall, round, arched windows set in flat planar walls. The body of the nave has a steep pitched gable roof. It is preceded by a square three-story tower, which is topped by

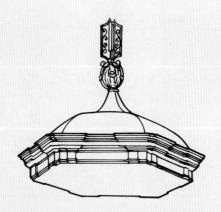

Right: Wineglass pulpit, with sounding board above. Peter Harrison: King's Chapel, Boston, 1750.

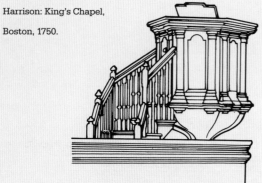

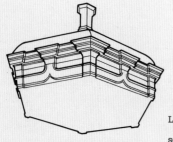

Left: Wineglass pulpit, with sounding board above. Richard Munday: Trinity Church, Newport, RI, 1729.

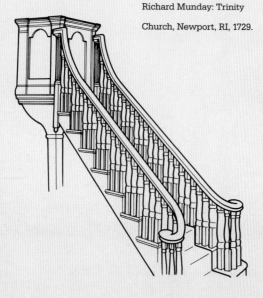

two octagonal sections and capped by a spire roof. The Bruton Parish Church has at least one major link to medieval tradition in its cruciform plan, however, which Wren had abandoned. This is the only Wren-style church built in the South in the first half of the eighteenth century, but the type would become very important in New England.

The first fully developed Wren-style church in Boston was Christ Church, also known as Old North Church. It was designed by William Price, a print dealer who presumably had knowledge of Wren's designs for the London churches. Old North Church was built for the second Anglican congregation in Boston. It is made of brick, with a large oblong main block and smaller entrance tower at the front of the church. The church measures seventy by fifty feet. The exterior walls are very planar, and there is a shallow apse at the rear of the church. The tall tower is closest in design to Wren's St. James Garlickhythe (*c.* 1680), which was built near St. Paul's Cathedral in London. The 175-foot steeple may be a composite of some of Wren's other projects. This church has a legendary place in American history, for it was

Above: William Price, print seller: Old North Church, 193 Salem Street, Boston, MA, 1723. Front view.

Above: William Price: Old North Church, 193 Salem Street, Boston, MA, 1723. Side view.

Above: Richard Munday: Trinity Church, Queen Anne Square, Newport, RI. 1725. Front view.

Above: Robert Twelves, designer; Joshua Blanchard, builder: Old South Meeting House, 310 Washington Street, Boston, MA, 1729–30.

from this steeple that two lanterns were lit to signal Paul Revere of the coming of the British troops in 1775, spurring his famous ride to warn the rebels at Lexington and Concord.

The interior of Old North Church is simple and very light, due to the large windows and bright white paint. The detailing is much plainer than in Wren's more ornate London churches. There is a second-story gallery on two

sides, and the wineglass pulpit is arched over with a sounding board, an ingenious device that amplified the voice of the preacher. The congregation sat in box pews.

The influence of Old North Church is seen almost immediately in the design of Trinity Church in Newport, Rhode Island. Built in 1725–26, the steeple was not finished until 1741. The builder here was a local craftsman, Richard Munday, who designed many buildings in Newport. William

Above: William Price: Old North Church, 193 Salem Street, Boston, MA, 1723. Interior.

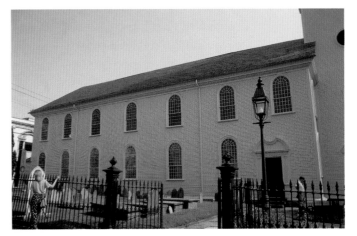

Above: Richard Munday: Trinity Church, Queen Anne Square, Newport, RI. 1725. Side view.

Above: Comparison: Christopher Wren: St. James Garlickhythe, London, 1676–83.

Above: Comparison: Christopher Wren: St. Mary-Le-Bow, London, 1670–77.

Price, designer of Old North Church in Boston, was also one of the founders of Trinity Church. Trinity Church closely copies the basic design of Old North Church, but it is made of wood, covered with clapboards. The Newport church was lengthened by the addition of two bays and a shallow apse in 1762, elongating its proportions and making it even more like the English Anglican churches.

Although it was perhaps natural that the Anglican churches should follow the lead of London churches, even the Congregational churches began to imitate the new design. The Old Brick Meetinghouse in Boston (1712; demolished) was a large square meetinghouse of the traditional type, but it was the last of its kind in that town. In 1729, the Old South Meetinghouse was built in Boston. It was apparently designed by Robert Twelves and built by Joshua Blanchard. Rejecting the traditional foursquare meetinghouse plan, this new brick structure copied the Wren format of the oblong box with entrance tower,

although there was still an entrance on the long side of the building. This church also played an important historic role in the American Revolution and is featured on the Boston Freedom Trail. The open colonnaded steeple stems from Wren's design for St. Mary-Le-Bow (1670–77) in London.

The most impressive Anglican church in Boston was the new King's Chapel (1750), designed by Peter Harrison. Harrison was a leading gentleman architect in Newport, Rhode Island, and this was one of his first major buildings. Although most of his designs are pastiches of images he found in books, he had the greatest knowledge of classicism in the colonies, and his designs are invariably skillful. The plan of this one is close to the designs of Wren's churches in London, as published in James Gibbs's *Book of Architecture* (1728). King's Chapel is built of stone, one of the first buildings of that material in Boston. Although Harrison planned a tower, it was never completed and has no steeple. The monumental columns were made of wood in the end,

Above: Peter Harrison: King's Chapel, 58 Tremont Street, Boston, MA, 1750. Front view.

Above: Peter Harrison: King's Chapel, Boston, MA, 1750. Side view.

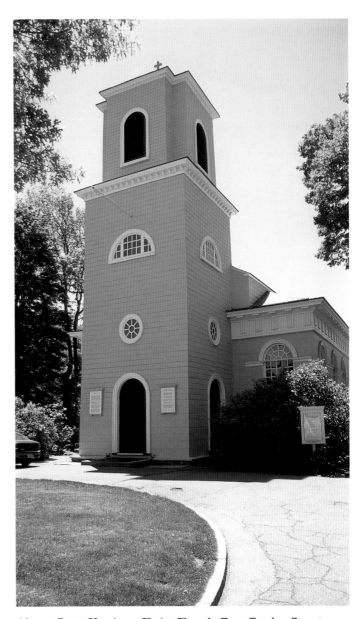

Above: Peter Harrison: Christ Church, Zero Garden Street, Cambridge, MA, 1760. Front view.

Above: Peter Harrison: King's Chapel, Boston, MA, 1750. Interior.

Above: Peter Harrison: Christ Church, Cambridge, MA, 1760. Interior.

Above: Peter Harrison: Touro Synagogue, 85 Touro Street, Newport, RI, 1759. The congregation dates back to 1658, when Sephardic Jews arrived from Barbados. The temple was named after the congregation's first rabbi, Isaac Touro.

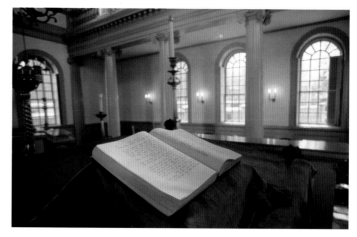

Above: Peter Harrison: Touro Synagogue, Newport, RI. Interior. Although the exterior is similar to an eighteenth-century meetinghouse, the plan of the interior follows the Sephardic ritual and resembles the Spanish and Portuguese Synagogue of Amsterdam.

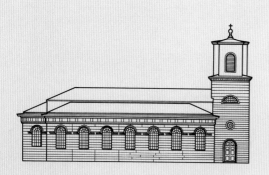

Above: Peter Harrison: elevation of Christ Church, Cambridge, MA, 1760.

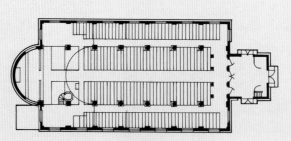

Above: Plan of Christ Church, Cambridge.

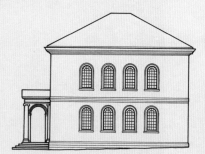

Above: Peter Harrison: Touro Synagogue, Newport, RI, 1759. Drawing of side elevation.

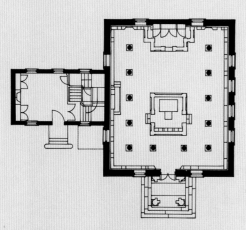

Above: Touro Synagogue, Newport, RI. Plan.

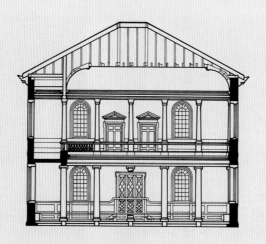

Above: Touro Synagogue, Newport, RI. Section.

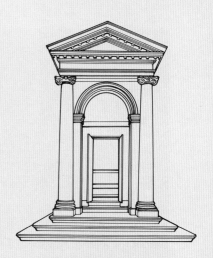

Above: Touro Synagogue, Newport, RI. Classical portico.

but they follow Harrison's design. The interior is more elegant than any earlier churches in Boston and features a second-story gallery supported by slender Corinthian columns. The apse is terminated with a Palladian window, and the ornate wineglass pulpit is surmounted by a suspended sounding board. King's Chapel replaced an earlier wooden structure from 1686, built just two years after Massachusetts was reclaimed as a royal colony.

Harrison also designed the Touro Synagogue in Newport in 1759–63. This was more of a challenge for him, since he had little knowledge of Jewish architecture and his books offered no direct models. Touro Synagogue is the oldest synagogue in America, since earlier examples in New York have not survived. The congregation was established in 1658, when Sephardic Jews arrived in Newport from Barbados. (The Sephardim derived from Jews expelled from Spain in 1492.) The temple was named after the congregation's first rabbi, Isaac Touro, who had recently arrived from the rabbinical academy in Amsterdam. For this house of worship, Harrison created an almost cubic building with a low hipped roof and an adjacent lower ell structure. The painted brick exterior is plain, with simple round-arched windows, but the entrance portico carries a graceful pediment on Ionic columns. The interior is simple, with light plastered walls and gray painted trim. There are second-story galleries where women sat during the services. The raised bimah for the rabbi is in the center, and the Torah shrine is against the eastern wall. In the second-story level is a pedimented alcove with paintings of the tablets of the law. The overall layout resembles the Spanish and Portuguese Synagogue in Amsterdam (1675), suggesting that Harrison drew on a wide range of sources. Members of the congregation may have provided him with engravings of the synagogue in Amsterdam.

The Gibbs-Type Church

James Gibbs was one of the most successful architects in London in the early eighteenth century. His *Book of Architecture* of 1728 was one of the most important sources for American building. His most influential church design was for St. Martin-in-the-Fields (1727) in London. It was the model for a large number of American churches in the second half of the century and replaced the Wren type with a more unified design.

Above: Dr. John Kearsley: Christ Church, Second and Market Streets, Philadelphia, PA, 1727–44. Spire by Robert Smith, 1750–54.

Above: Samuel Cardy: St. Michael's Church, 14 St. Michael's Way, Charleston, SC, 1752–53.

Above: Thomas McBean: St. Paul's Episcopal Chapel of Trinity Church, Broadway, between Fulton and Vesey Streets, New York, NY, 1764–66.

Above: Joseph Brown: First Baptist Church, Providence, RI, 1771–75. Front view.

Above: Joseph Brown: First Baptist Church, 75 North Main Street, Providence, RI, 1771–75. Side view.

Above: First Baptist Church, Providence, RI. Detail of entrance portico.

Right: Comparison: James Gibbs: St. Martin-in-the-Fields, London, England, 1727.

Above: Federated Church (1st Congregational and 2nd Baptist Churches), Townsend, VT, 1790. False Gothic tops added to the windows in the nineteenth century.

Above: Asher Benjamin: Meeting House, Route 103, Windsor, VT, 1798 (portico added 1922).

Above: First Religious Society (Unitarian), 26 Pleasant Street, Newburyport, MA, 1801.

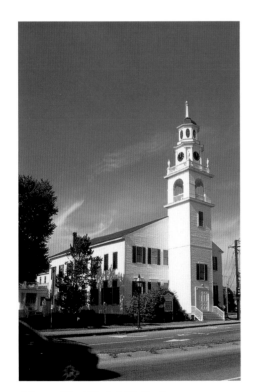

Above: First Parish Unitarian Universalist Church, 114 Main Street, Kennebunk, ME, 1804.

Above: Lavius Fillmore: Congregational Church, 27 North Pleasant Street, Middlebury, VT, 1806.

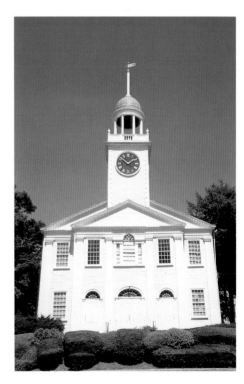

Above: New North Church, 1 Lincoln Street, Hingham, MA, 1807.

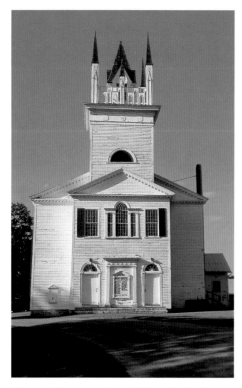

Above: Congregational Church, Sudbury, VT, 1807.

Above: Daniel Wadsworth, builder: Center Church (First Church of Christ), 675 Main Street, Hartford, CT, 1807.

Above: Peter Banner: Park Street Church, 1 Park Street, Boston, MA. 1809.

Above: First Parish Unitarian Universalist, Ashby Common, Ashby, MA, 1809.

Above: Meetinghouse, Beverly, MA, 1809.

Above: Elias Carter: Federated Church, Templeton, MA, 1811.

Left: Typical eighteenth-century Georgian-style door with triangular pediment.

Right: Typical eighteenth-century Georgian-style door with swan's neck pediment.

Dr. John Kearsley's design for Christ Church (1727–44) in Philadelphia was one of the first in America to be modeled after Gibbs' church. It is made of brick and has numerous classical touches, including a large Palladian window on the rear wall. The distinctive spire was added by Robert Smith in 1750–54; it was also modeled on the plates in Gibbs's *Book of Architecture*. The interior is a simplified version of St. Martin-in-the-Fields, with a flat plaster ceiling.

The stone tower of St. Michael's Church in Charleston, South Carolina, built by Samuel Cardy in 1752–53, is further evidence of the prestige of Gibbs's famous London church. Cardy was an Irish-born architect, who came to

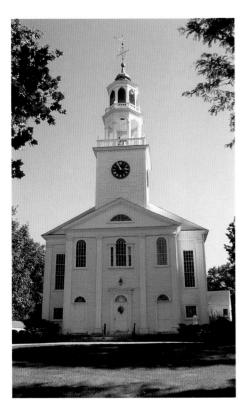

Above: Andrews Palmer: Unitarian Church, 50 Cochituate Road, Wayland, MA, 1814.

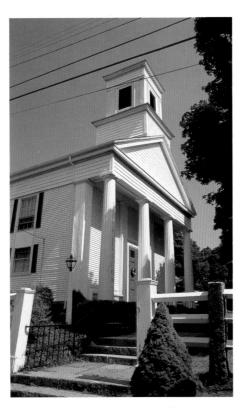

Above: First Congregational Church, Route 156, Lyme, CT, 1814.

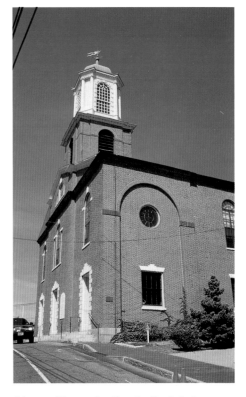

Above: Alexander Parris: St. John's Episcopal Church, 101 Chapel Street, Portsmouth, NH, 1807–18.

Above: United Church, Town Green,
New Haven, CT, 1815.

Above: John Holden Green:
First Unitarian Church (formerly
Congregational), 1 Benevolent Street,
Providence, RI, 1816.

Above: Samuel Belcher: First
Congregational Church, 1 Sterling City
Road, Old Lyme, CT, 1817.

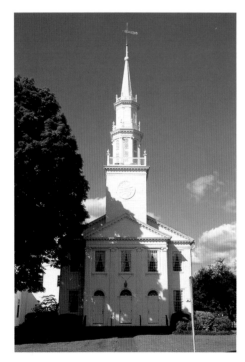

Above: David Hoadley, builder/architect:
Congregational Church, 6 West Main
Street, Avon, CT, 1818–19.

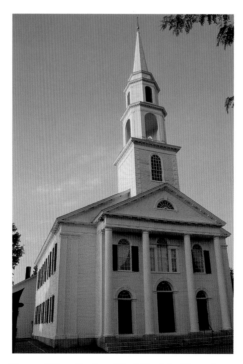

Above: Elias Carter: First Parish Church,
Unitarian, 13 Maple Street, Mendon, MA,
1820.

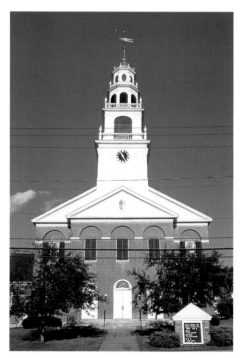

Above: John Leach, builder: South
Congregational Church, 320 Church
Street, Newport, NH, 1822. (Follows
design of Elias Carter, Templeton
Church.)

Above: South Congregational Church, Temple Street, Kennebunkport, ME, 1824.

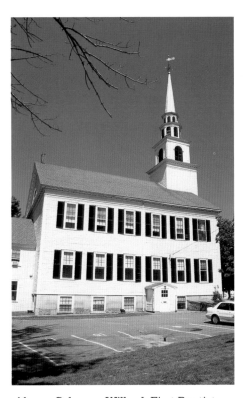

Above: Solomon Willard: First Baptist Church, Worcester Road and Pleasant Street, Framingham, MA, 1825.

Above: South Congregational Church, 277 Main Street, Hartford, CT, 1827.

Above: Center Congregational Church, 193 Main Street, Brattleboro, VT, 1843.

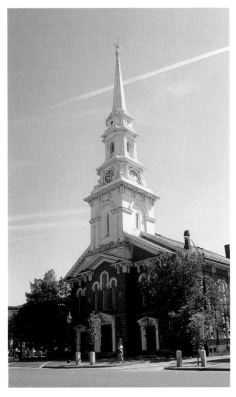

Above: John D. Towle and Foster: North Congregational Church, Market Square, Portsmouth, NH, 1855.

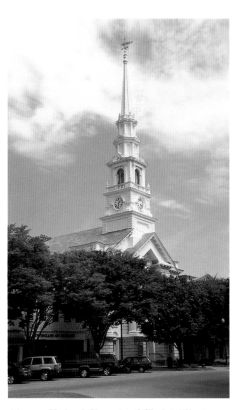

Above: United Church of Christ (First Congregational Church), Central Square, Keene, NH, 1786.

Above: Arthur Gilman: Arlington Street Church, 351 Boylston Street, Boston, MA, 1859–61. Unitarian.

Charleston in 1752. St. Michael's is Charleston's oldest church and features an imposing 185-foot-high steeple, with three octagonal upper tiers over a square tower. The classical entrance portico clearly echoes Gibbs's design as well. The church is made of brick and covered with stucco painted white.

Thomas McBean was a Scotsman who had actually studied with James Gibbs in London. His design for St. Paul's Episcopal Chapel of Trinity Church (1764–66) in New York City is one of the closest copies of St. Martin-in-the-Fields in America. The tall spire was added to the square tower in 1794. It is built of a local stone known as Manhattan schist and brownstone. It is the only pre-Revolutionary church surviving in New York City. The interior of the church was exceptionally elegant, with Corinthian columns and an elliptical ceiling vault. A sounding board hangs over the pulpit, and a large Palladian window fills the chancel wall. The colonial governor regularly worshiped here. The religious services after George Washington's inauguration were held in this church. After September 11, 2001, the church was touched by history again when it provided a sanctuary and relief for emergency workers.

The First Baptist Church (1775) in Providence, Rhode Island, was built just before the Revolution. It was designed by Joseph Brown (1733–85), who was not an architect, but a mathematician and astronomer. He had already designed the first college building at Rhode Island College (now Brown University) and several houses. The First Baptist Church has been described as transitional between the meetinghouse and church plan. It is nearly square, and although there is a prominent entrance tower with the high pulpit on an axis from it, there are also entrances on both long sides. With the original arrangement of the box pews, these were of equal importance to the tower entrance. The church can hold 1,400 people. The steeple is clearly based on one of the alternative designs for St. Martin-in-the-Fields, which was included in his copy of Gibbs's *Book of Architecture* (1728). The tower is fronted by a small Ionic

Above: Entrance portico at the Rocky Hill Meeting House, Amesbury, MA, 1785.

Above: Entrance portico of a particularly elaborate type; Joseph Brown: First Baptist Church, Providence, RI, 1771–75.

Right: Joseph Brown: First Baptist Church, Providence, RI, 1771–75.

Above: Joseph Brown: First Baptist Church, Providence, RI, 1771–75. Interior.

entrance portico, and includes many classical details—such as a Palladian window, quoins, other pediments, and a succession of urns and columns—as the tower rises and grows more slender.

Federalist, or Adam, Style

The second half of the eighteenth century saw increasing sophistication in terms of style and craftsmanship. The Georgian style was succeeded by a classical style influenced by Robert Adam, called the Adam Style, or the Federalist Style. It brings the Wren-Gibbs model of church up to date with classical detailing and a greater symmetry and simplicity. This period also saw the rise of more professional architects, such as Charles Bulfinch and Asher Benjamin.

Although he is more known for his public buildings and houses in the Federalist style, Charles Bulfinch also designed a number of churches in and around Boston. One of the finest is the brick church of St. Stephen (originally built as the New North Church) in 1802–4 in Boston.

Asher Benjamin wrote seven books on architecture, including the first ever published in the United States, *The Country Builder's Assistant*, printed in Greenfield, Massachusetts, in 1797. This was followed by *The American Builder's Companion; or, a New System of Architecture Particularly Adapted to the Present Style of Building in the United States of America* (Boston, 1806). His books appeared in many editions and had an enormous influence on American builders. His books were deliberately practical; in the preface to *The American Builder's Companion*, he wrote: "We do not conceive it essentially necessary to adhere exactly to any particular order, provided the proportion and harmony of the parts be carefully preserved…. Attempts which have sometimes been made to compose fancy orders have only spoiled the work, and

Above: Asher Benjamin: Charles Street Meeting House, Boston, MA, 1804.

Above: Charles Bulfinch: St. Stephen's Church (built as New North Church), 401 Hanover Street, Boston, MA, 1802–4.

Above: Asher Benjamin: Old West Church, 131 Cambridge Street, Boston, MA, 1806.

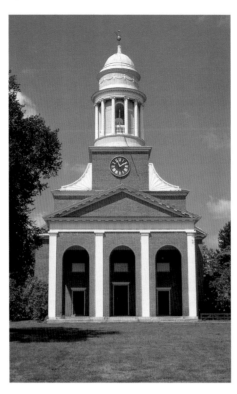

Above: Charles Bulfinch: Meeting House, Town Common, Lancaster, MA, 1815–17.

Above: Charles Bulfinch: Meeting House, Lancaster, MA, 1815–17. Detail of portico.

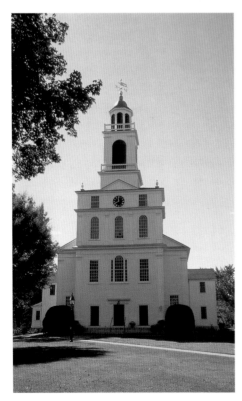

Above: Unitarian Church, 75 Great Road, Bedford, MA, 1817.

Above: Meetinghouse, Weathersfield Center Road, Weathersfield, VT, 1821.

Above: Elisha Scott: Baptist Church, Route 140, East Poultney, VT, 1805.

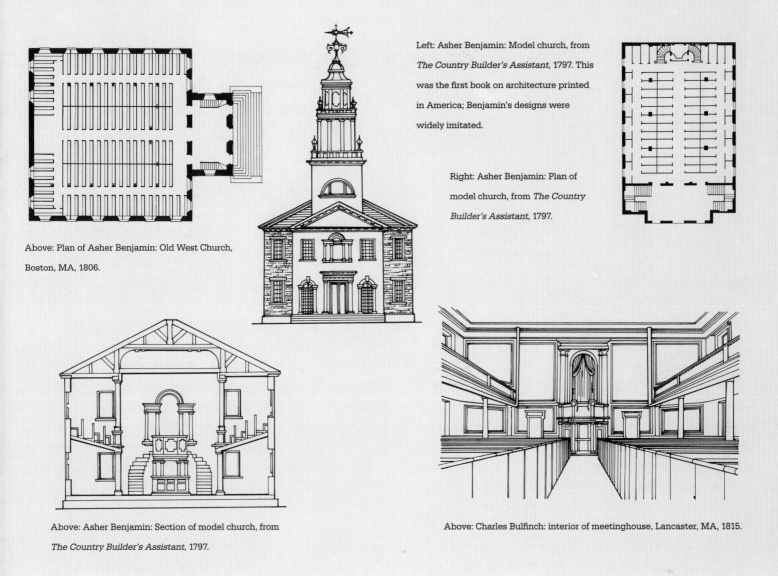

Above: Plan of Asher Benjamin: Old West Church, Boston, MA, 1806.

Left: Asher Benjamin: Model church, from *The Country Builder's Assistant*, 1797. This was the first book on architecture printed in America; Benjamin's designs were widely imitated.

Right: Asher Benjamin: Plan of model church, from *The Country Builder's Assistant*, 1797.

Above: Asher Benjamin: Section of model church, from *The Country Builder's Assistant*, 1797.

Above: Charles Bulfinch: interior of meetinghouse, Lancaster, MA, 1815.

no reduction of the expense has been effected." The model churches published in *The Country Builder's Assistant* of 1797 and the *American Builder's Companion* of 1806 were widely imitated.

One example by Benjamin himself is the large meeting-house in Windsor, Vermont, built in 1798. The elegant classical portico was added in 1922 to give a more formal air to the old meetinghouse. Benjamin also built the Charles Street Meeting House in Boston in 1804 and the Old West Church, also in Boston, in 1806.

Asher Benjamin's published designs inspired the Baptist Church in East Poultney, Vermont, built by Elisha Scott in 1805. Benjamin's designs also strongly influenced the meetinghouse in Weathersfield, Vermont (1821), which has a steeple that is particularly close to the plans in Benjamin's books. This meetinghouse continued the New England tradition of combining town and church functions in one building. The town hall was downstairs and the church above.

Built in 1817, the Unitarian Church in Bedford, Massachusetts, also closely follows the plans in Benjamin's *American Builder's Companion*. The rectangular central pavilion is wide, with three widely spaced entrance doors. Patterns of three are emphasized, with three stories of windows above the doors; the first two have three windows and the third has two windows flanking the clock. A square steeple topped by a lantern terminates the composition.

One of the finest Federalist meetinghouses is Charles Bulfinch's meetinghouse in Lancaster, Massachusetts, built in 1815–17. Many consider it to be Bulfinch's masterpiece. It is built of brick; even the pilasters are simply another thickness of brick, painted white to set them off from the red brick arches. The proportions are perfectly balanced, from the triple arched entry to the tall cupola.

Left: Large Federalist window. Asher Benjamin: Meeting House, Windsor, VT, 1798.

Right: Oval window. First Church of Templeton, Templeton, MA, 1811.

Above: Fan light window, First Parish Church, Mendon, MA, 1820.

The scalloped wooden fans between the tower and the body of the nave help smooth the transition.

The iconic New England meetinghouse, painted white and graced with a tall steeple, proliferates at this time, especially in the villages. The majority follow the Wren-Gibbs format, with elegant classical detailing. Palladian and fan light windows are often seen.

The meetinghouse for the First Religious Society (Unitarian) in Newburyport, Massachusetts, was built in 1801. The white frame church has crisp decorative details in the carvings on the façade. The tall steeple consists of two square sections topped by a two-stage octagonal lantern, with a spire on top. The pedimented doorway has a delicate sunburst pattern in the fan light window. Other classical details include pilasters and a Palladian window.

Further examples include the First Parish Unitarian Universalist Church (1804) in Kennebunk, Maine; the Congregational Church (1806) in Middlebury, Vermont, designed by Lavius Fillmore, a cousin of president Millard Fillmore; and the New North Church (1807) in Hingham, Massachusetts. The Congregational Church (1807) in Sudbury, Vermont, is something of a hybrid, with almost Gothic spires placed on top of the steeple of this meetinghouse.

One of the most elegant of early nineteenth century meetinghouses is the Center Church (First Church of Christ), Hartford, Connecticut, built by Daniel Wadsworth in 1807.

Asher Benjamin's influence can be seen in the First Parish Unitarian Universalist church (1809) in Ashby,

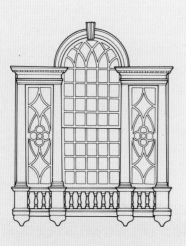

Above: Palladian window, Baptist Church, East Poultney, VT.

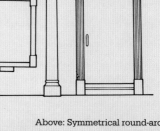

Left: Elaborate carvings ornament this meetinghouse door; First Religious Society (Unitarian), Newburyport, MA, 1801.

Above: Symmetrical round-arched doorways flanking a blank central portico; Congregational Church, Sudbury, VT, 1807.

Above: Fan light over door; New North Church, Hingham, MA, 1807. Such windows were a common Federalist decorative device.

Left: Quoins, from Samuel Belcher: First Congregational Church, Old Lyme, CT, 1817.

Right: Palladian window. A symmetrical design invented by the Italian Renaissance architect Andrea Palladio, and disseminated in this country by books.

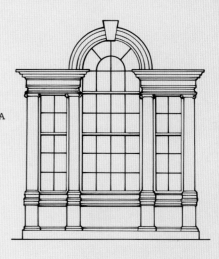

Massachusetts. The steeple is modeled after Benjamin's designs. The meetinghouse in Beverly, Massachusetts, of 1809 is also a fine example. An urban variation is found in Peter Banner's design for the urban Park Street Church in Boston of 1809.

Elias Carter (1781–1864) developed a church design that was copied many times across New England. Carter's first example was the Federated Church in Templeton, Massachusetts, built in 1811. The wide nave of this wood frame church is preceded by a projecting monumental pediment, supported by two pairs of columns. Behind this pediment is a tall steeple modeled on James Gibbs' designs, with two square stages and two octagonal stages. The South Congregational Church of 1822 in Newport, New Hampshire, generally follows the design of Carter's

Templeton Church, although it is made of brick and omits the pediment with paired columns. It was built by John Leach, a local builder. Solomon Willard's First Baptist Church (1825) in Framingham, Massachusetts, closely follows the design of Elias Carter's church at Templeton.

Elias Carter also built the First Parish Church, Unitarian, in Mendon, Massachusetts, in 1820. This church is simpler than his Templeton design, especially the steeple, but it was also much copied.

Throughout New England, one finds attractive examples of these quintessentially American churches. Excellent examples are found in Wayland, Massachusetts; Lyme and Old Lyme, Connecticut; Portsmouth, New Hampshire; and Kennebunkport, Maine. The Town Green of New Haven, Connecticut, has notable churches in several styles, includ-

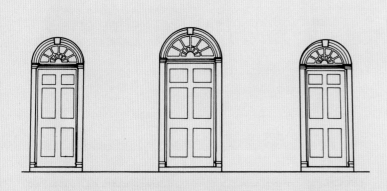

Above: Simple entrance to a Federalist meetinghouse, Weathersfield, VT, 1821.

Right: Round arched doorway; John Leach, builder: South Congregational Church, Newport, NH, 1822.

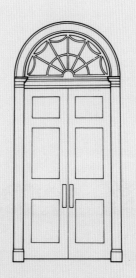

Above: Round arched doorway; Mohegan Congregational Church, Montville (near Uncasville), CT, 1831.

Right: Steeple; Union Episcopal Church, Old Church Road, West Claremont, NH, 1773. Steeple added later.

Right: Steeple; Asher Benjamin: Meeting House, Windsor, VT, 1798.

Above: Steeple; Richard Munday: Trinity Church, Newport, RI, 1725.

Above: Steeple; Lavius Fillmore: Congregational Church, Middlebury, VT, 1806.

Above: Steeple; Elisha Scott: Baptist Church, Route 140, East Poultney, VT, 1805.

Above: Steeple; New North Church, Hingham, MA, 1807.

Above: Steeple; Daniel Wadsworth, builder: Center Church (First Church of Christ), 675 Main Street, Hartford, CT, 1807.

ing the United Church of 1815. The First Unitarian Church (formerly Congregational) in Providence, Rhode Island, has a dramatic site on the side of a hill; one can't help but look up to it. The church was designed by John Holden Green and built in 1816.

In the small town of Avon, Connecticut, one finds a lovely example of a New England meetinghouse. The Congregational Church in Avon was built in 1818–19 by David Hoadley, a local builder and architect. The entrance pavilion has three identical round-arched doors, and four two-story pilasters support the pediment. The square tower of the steeple carries two octagonal stages and a spire. Nearby in Hartford, the South Congregational Church (1827) has an impressive steeple and portico.

These prototypical New England churches continued to be built well into the nineteenth century. Steeples especially became more elaborate. In Keene, New Hampshire, the United Church of Christ (First Congregational

Church) was originally built in 1786. In 1860–61 the steeple was constructed.

One of the most elaborate designs is found at the Arlington Street Church in Boston. It was designed by Arthur Gilman and built between 1859–61. This Unitarian church is built in stone, with a monumental steeple. It was the first major public building in the newly filled Back Bay district of Boston. The interior is notable for one of the largest collections of Tiffany stained glass windows in a single church. These were installed between 1898 and 1933.

The Seamen's Bethel in New Bedford, Massachusetts, was built for sailors in the city's whaling industry in 1832. It was immortalized in Herman Melville's *Moby Dick*: "In the same New Bedford there stands a Whaleman's Chapel, and few are the moody fishermen, shortly bound for the Indian Ocean or Pacific, who fail to make a Sunday visit to the spot." Melville describes at length a pulpit, which was shaped like the prow of a ship:

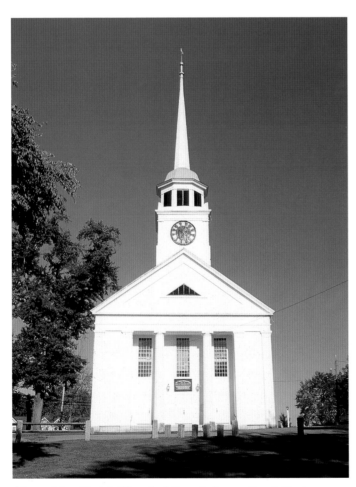

Above: First Parish Church, 1 Powderhouse Road, Groton, MA, 1755. Remodeled and partially turned in 1839 to make it more like a church; the Greek Doric columns were also added.

Above: First Parish Meeting House, Town Green, Shirley Center, MA, 1773. This church was moved to this place on the Town Green in 1851.

Left: Seamen's Bethel,
15 Johnny Cake Hill, New
Bedford, MA, 1832. Rebuilt
after 1866 fire.

Nor was the pulpit itself without a trace of the same sea-taste that had achieved the ladder and the picture. Its panelled front was in the likeness of a ship's bluff bows, and the Holy Bible rested on the projecting piece of scroll work, fashioned after a ship's fiddle-headed beak. What could be more full of meaning?—for the pulpit is ever this earth's foremost part; all the rest comes in its rear; the pulpit leads the world. From thence it is the storm of God's quick wrath is first descried, and the bow must bear the earliest brunt…. Yes, the world's a ship on its passage out, and not a voyage complete; and the pulpit is its prow.

This intriguing pulpit was only a product of the author's imagination. However, the popularity of the 1956 film version of *Moby Dick*, starring Gregory Peck, drew many tourists to New Bedford, who were disappointed not to find the ship prow pulpit. The current pulpit was built in 1961 to remedy that lack. This is one of the first cases where literature and film combined to shape the historical and liturgical re-creation of a church.

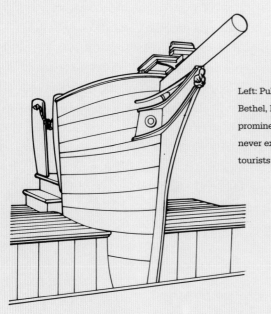

Left: Pulpit in the shape of a ship's prow; Seaman's Bethel, New Bedford, MA, 1832. This pulpit is prominent in Herman Melville's *Moby Dick*, but it never existed until 1961, when it was added to satisfy tourists who had seen the film version of the novel.

Right: Guilberto Guillemard: Cathedral of St. Louis, King of France, Jackson Square, New Orleans, LA, 1779. The central tower was built according to the design of Benjamin Latrobe in 1820.

French Colonial

The Great Fire of 1788 in New Orleans destroyed the first Cathedral of St. Louis, King of France. It was rebuilt to new classical designs by Gilberto Guillemard in 1789. Two side towers flank the three-story portico of the main façade. The cathedral has undergone many changes; the central tower was added in 1820; it was designed by Benjamin Latrobe. This tower burned down in 1850, but was rebuilt. The church was enlarged between 1849 and 1851 by J. N. B. de Pouilly with even more classical motifs. The nave interior is one large barrel vault, flanked with side aisles and second floor galleries. The ceiling is painted with Renaissance decoration.

Right: Seamen's Bethel, 15 Johnny Cake Hill, New Bedford, MA, 1832. Interior; the pulpit is shaped like the prow of a ship and features prominently in the novel *Moby Dick*.

Log Churches

One of the most enduring and mythic building types in American history is the log cabin, which is fixed as an almost iconic image of the settlement of the continent. This vernacular tradition comes from the middle colonies of Maryland, Pennsylvania, Delaware, and New Jersey. It is a timber tradition brought by Swedish, German, and other Central European colonists. The tradition of log buildings was spread by frontiersmen whose movements across the region of Appalachia and the Smoky Mountains transferred this architectural design deep into the culture of America for many generations to come.

In the frontier areas of West Virginia and Kentucky, a number of log churches still survive. These are clearly folk-style, or vernacular, designs, and are of great historic interest. One surviving example is the Rehoboth Methodist Episcopal Church (1786) in Monroe County, West Virginia. It is one of the earliest Methodist churches in America, constructed only two years after the founding of the Methodist Society in 1784 in Baltimore. At the time it was built, it was on the western frontier, and it has a fortified appearance, testifying to its use as a refuge from Indian conflict. There is only one door and two small windows. On the interior is a gallery around three sides. The benches are simple split logs.

Above: Rehoboth Methodist Episcopal Church, two miles east of Union off State Road 3, Monroe County, WV, 1786. A log church built in part as a shelter against American Indian attacks.

Other historic log churches include the Old McKendree Chapel, a United Methodist Historic Shrine, in Jackson, Missouri, 1819. The chapel was built just three years after Missouri became a U.S. territory and is the oldest surviving Protestant church west of the Mississippi. The huge poplar logs are sawn square—some of them were up to thirty inches in diameter—and white plaster serves as chinking. At one end is a massive stone fireplace.

The Andrews Methodist Chapel (also known as the McIntosh Log Church), was built in the vicinity of McIntosh in Washington County, Alabama, in 1860 and was in use until 1952. It is a single-room log structure, with a gabled roof covered with wooden shingles. A building that illustrates the intrinsic interest of vernacular architecture is the Mount Vernon African Methodist Episcopal Church in Monroe County, Kentucky. It is one of the earliest African American churches in Kentucky, built about 1848. It was constructed by three freed slaves, George Pipkin, Albert Howard, and Peter West, who lived in the settlement called Freetown. The church was named Mount Vernon in honor of George Washington. These early log structures are precious relics of past ages.

Weather Vanes

One of the most distinctive features of the New England meetinghouses is the wide variety of weather vanes that surmount many of the steeples. Congregationalists and other groups who rejected the traditional symbolism of the European churches, which were typically topped with crosses, substituted weather vanes. These were functional—they showed the direction of the wind—and also aesthetic. In fact, they were one of the few forms of sculpture found in the colonies and early republic. Considerable ingenuity was employed in the design of these weather vanes, and they use a variety of symbols, such as comets or shooting stars, arrows, and later, even three-masted ships.

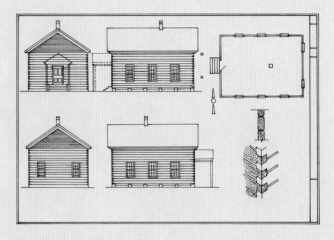

Above: Andrews Methodist Chapel (McIntosh Log Church), U.S. Highway 43, vicinity of McIntosh, Washington County, AL, 1860.

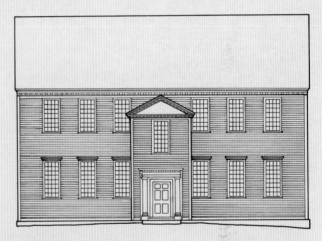

Above: The Old McKendree Chapel, United Methodist Historic Shrine, Country Road 306, Jackson, MO, 1819. The oldest surviving Protestant church west of the Mississippi.

Above: George Pipkin, Albert Howard, Peter West, builders: Mount Vernon African Methodist Episcopal Church, State Road 100 north of Gamaliel, Monroe County, KY, c. 1848.

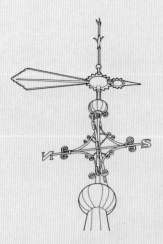

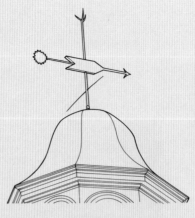

Above: Shooting star weather vane, Baptist Church, East Poultney, VT.

Above: Shooting star weather vane, Congregational Church, designed by Lavius Fillmore, Middlebury, VT, 1806.

Above: Shooting star weather vane, Old Round Church, designed by William Rhodes, Richmond, VT, 1812–13. This is a simple version of the shooting star motif.

Above: Ship weather vane; Seaman's Bethel, New Bedford, MA, 1832. Rebuilt after 1866 fire. The pulpit of this church is shaped like a ship's prow.

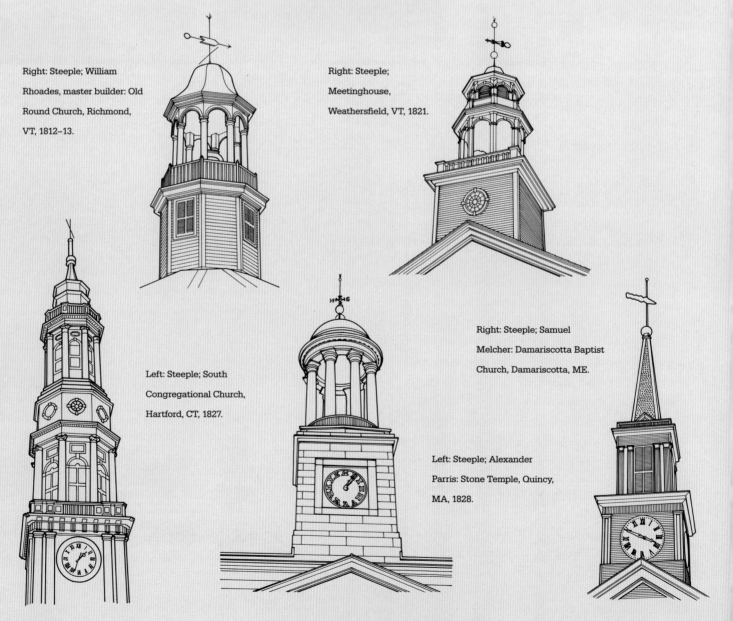

Right: Steeple; William Rhoades, master builder: Old Round Church, Richmond, VT, 1812–13.

Right: Steeple; Meetinghouse, Weathersfield, VT, 1821.

Left: Steeple; South Congregational Church, Hartford, CT, 1827.

Right: Steeple; Samuel Melcher: Damariscotta Baptist Church, Damariscotta, ME.

Left: Steeple; Alexander Parris: Stone Temple, Quincy, MA, 1828.

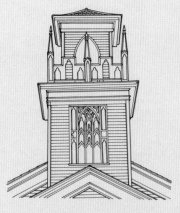

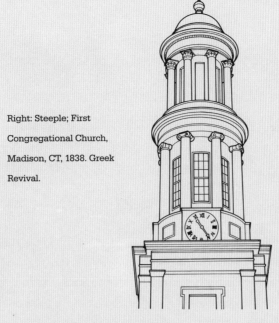

Right: Steeple; First Congregational Church, Madison, CT, 1838. Greek Revival.

Right: Minard Lafever: First Presbyterian Church (Old Whaler's Church), Sag Harbor, NY, 1842–43. Original steeple.

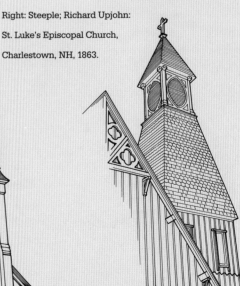

Above: Steeple; St. John's Episcopal Church, East Poultney, VT, 1831. The portico is a combination of a Greek Revival pediment and Gothic pointed arches; Gothic pointed arch forms predominate in the steeple.

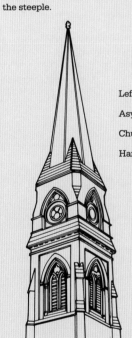

Left: Steeple; Patrick Keely: Asylum Hill Congregational Church, 814 Asylum Avenue, Hartford, CT, 1865.

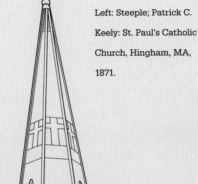

Left: Steeple; Patrick C. Keely: St. Paul's Catholic Church, Hingham, MA, 1871.

Right: Steeple; John Murphy: St. Peter's Church, Hartford, CT, 1865–68.

Right: Steeple; Richard Upjohn: St. Luke's Episcopal Church, Charlestown, NH, 1863.

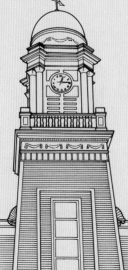

Right: Steeple; First Baptist Church, Essex, CT, c. 1845. Egyptian pylon, with Greek Revival lantern.

Right: Steeple; Patrick C. Keely: St. Bridget's Roman Catholic Church, West Rutland, VT, 1860–61.

Chapter 3

European Revivals of the Nineteenth Century

Architecture has frequently served as a vehicle for time travel or travel to far-off lands. The nineteenth century brought a great increase in historical knowledge and an increasingly sophisticated awareness of the relationship of style and religious and social values. For the first time, architects and church builders were faced with the need to consciously choose a style when they built a new church. The range of historical reference and stylistic expression expanded dramatically, with styles consciously chosen to reflect specific emotional or ideological associations. These linkages were particularly important for religious buildings. Some called for a new style for the new country, but the prevailing sentiment still favored revivalism. The sculptor Horatio Greenough explained in 1843 that the United States was itself something new made from old and various parts:

> We have heard the learned in matters relating to art express the opinion that these United States are destined to form a new style of architecture. Remembering that a vast population, rich in material and guided by the experience, the precepts, and the models of the Old World, was about to erect durable structures for every function of civilized life, we also cherished the hope that such a combination would speedily be formed.
>
> We forgot that though the country was young, yet the people were old, that as Americans we have no childhood, no half-fabulous, legendary wealth, no misty, cloud-enveloped background. We forgot that we had not unity of religious belief, nor unity of origin; that our territory, extending from the white bear to the alligator, made our occupations dissimilar, our character and tastes various.[1]

The new nation was not yet mature enough or unified enough for an authentic new style to emerge.

Meetinghouses

Traditional meetinghouses continued to be built throughout New England, reflecting the conservatism of the New England region and the continuing relevance of the meetinghouse form for modern worship.

Neoclassical

Early neoclassical churches frequently echo the forms of Roman churches, either as a sign of religious affiliation or as a symbol of enlightenment values. Neoclassicism is a more accurate revival of classical forms than the earlier Georgian classicism, and the architects draw directly from ancient examples, rather than through the intermediary of Palladio or James Gibbs. The neoclassical style tends to be more severe, with larger columns and arches than were found in the more delicate Georgian style. Examples include Benjamin Latrobe's Catholic Cathedral (Basilica of the Assumption), Baltimore, Maryland, of 1804–18; and the Monumental Church (1812) of Richmond, Virginia, designed by Robert Mills.

Benjamin Latrobe (1764–1820) was born in England, where he trained with the architect A. P. Cockerell and absorbed the influence of Sir John Soane. From these two, he learned a new, rational approach to classicism where columns and arches played structural and not merely decorative roles. The new style was less delicate than the earlier Adam Style. Latrobe emigrated to America in 1796 and brought a new level of technical and theoretical expertise to America. In 1806, he wrote to his fellow architect Robert Mills:

> The profession of architecture has been hitherto in the hands of two sorts of men. The first, of those who from traveling or from books have acquired some knowledge of the theory of the art but know nothing of the practice; the second, of those who know nothing but the practice and in the habits of a laborious life, have no opportunity of acquiring the theory.[2]

Latrobe combined both technical skill and a thorough knowledge of architectural history.

He was the architect of many public buildings and banks in Philadelphia and Washington, D.C., including the national Capitol. His most important church was the new Roman Catholic Cathedral for Baltimore (1804–18), the first monumental Catholic cathedral in America. It is a large classical building with Roman-style dome, which is vaulted in stone.

The church is now known as the Minor Basilica of the Assumption of the Blessed Virgin Mary in Baltimore. Bishop John Carroll chose Latrobe for his professionalism. Latrobe's virtuosity was shown by the fact that he offered

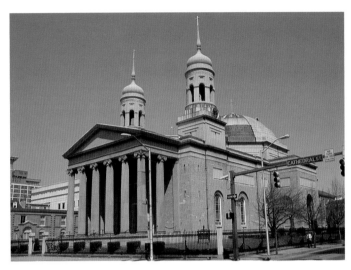

Above: Benjamin Latrobe: Minor Basilica of the Assumption of the Blessed Virgin Mary, Cathedral and Mulberry Streets, Baltimore, MD, 1804–18. Roman Revival.

Above: Minor Basilica of the Assumption of the Blessed Virgin Mary, Baltimore, MD. Side view.

Above: Minor Basilica of the Assumption of the Blessed Virgin Mary, Baltimore, MD. Detail.

Left: Benjamin Latrobe: Minor Basilica of the Assumption of the Blessed Virgin Mary, Baltimore, MD, 1804–18. Interior.

Bishop Carroll a choice of styles—a Roman-style cathedral that would make clear the connection to Rome as the center of Catholicism, or a Gothic design. This would have been one of the first Gothic Revival churches in America, and although Latrobe indicated that he favored the Roman design, the choice was left to the client. This is the beginning of the period of eclecticism in American architecture, where style choices were consciously made for emotional or historical associations.

The bishop chose the Roman style, and its design is a traditional cruciform plan with a twin-towered façade and a monumental Ionic portico. The overall scheme recalls

Above: Robert Mills: Monumental Church, Richmond, VA, 1812.

Above: Maximilian Godefroy: Unitarian Church, Chas and Franklin Streets, Baltimore, MD, 1817–18.

Wren's Baroque St. Paul's Cathedral in London. The complex interior volumes are created by a sequence of domed spaces, with a large central dome over the crossing. These domes were actually vaulted with stone in a thoroughly rationalist manner not merely implied through a false ceiling of wood and plaster. This would not have been possible for any earlier American architect. The sixty-five-foot central dome is carried on a cylindrical drum, which is reduced to a ring of eight substantial piers at the ground level, so that the interior is as open as possible. The nave and choir also have smaller domes, which repeat the design motif and help buttress the central dome. The complex series of interlocking spaces create a coherent and majestic interior. The cool gray colors are enhanced by the tracery of linear moldings similar to the work of Sir John Soane's Bank of England. The dome ceilings have sunken oval coffers. Construction was begun in 1806 and was essentially complete in 1818. The church was enlarged in 1863, with the choir stretched to accommodate a full dome, which was actually in keeping with Latrobe's original intentions.

The Baltimore cathedral represents a complete break with the Wren-Gibbs tradition, which would have been inappropriate for the Roman Catholic cathedral in any event. The new level of engineering proficiency and stylistic sophistication mark it as one of the most important buildings of the new era. It would not be out of place in any European capital.

Robert Mills (1781–1855) was born in Charleston, South Carolina. He worked briefly with James Hoban in Washington, D.C., and then with Thomas Jefferson at his home in Monticello in the early 1800s. Final training with Benjamin Latrobe gave him unequaled preparation as an American architect. He practiced a severe neoclassical style; one of his favorite design motifs was the central rotunda, which he incorporated into several early churches. The Circular Congregational Church (1804–6) in Charleston included a portico of stolid Doric columns and no steeple, reflecting the Rational Neoclassicist influence of his mentor, Latrobe. Mills's church burned and was replaced in 1892 with a Richardsonian Romanesque design. The circular design provided a central position for the pulpit or altar, focusing the attention of the congregation in a dramatic way. Thus it is equally suitable for different religious traditions, such as Protestants, who give priority to the spoken word of the sermon, and Catholics, who emphasize the ritual altar. The rotunda form has origins in both ancient

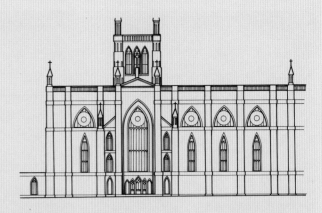

Above: Benjamin Latrobe: Minor Basilica of the Assumption of the Blessed Virgin Mary, Baltimore, MD, 1804–18. Drawing of alternate Gothic design. Maryland Historical Society, Baltimore.

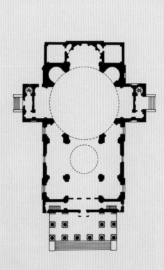 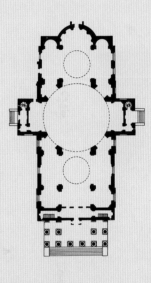

Above: Cathedral (Basilica of the Assumption), Baltimore, MD, 1804–18. Original plan.

Above: Cathedral (Basilica of the Assumption), Baltimore, MD. Final plan; the rear of the church was expanded, and the half-dome over the choir was replaced with a full dome.

Left: St. Patrick's Roman Catholic Church, Pond Road, Newcastle, ME, 1808.

Above: St. Patrick's Roman Catholic Church, Pond Road, Newcastle, ME, 1808. The oldest Catholic church in New England.

Above: Baptist Church, 34–44 Main Street, Wickford, RI, 1816.

Above: St. Patrick's Roman Catholic Church, Pond Road, Newcastle, ME, 1808. Detail.

classical architecture and in medieval and Renaissance baptisteries in Italy. One of the earliest surviving examples of this new type, which would become very common in American religious architecture, is the Monumental Church (1812) in Richmond, Virginia. Mills's neoclassical design has a simple stone portico with an austere Doric order. Massive piers flank the two columns of the front pediment. The main body of the church is a domed rotunda; the segmental dome is of wood with a plaster ceiling.

Neoclassical severity is evident on the exterior of Maximilian Godefroy's Unitarian Church in Baltimore, Maryland. Built in 1817–18, it was the last work in America by the French architect. The exterior is a plain cubic form, with a shallow pediment, which is entered through an arcade of three Renaissance arches. The interior is a square space under a hemispherical dome supported by four pendentives that bridge the span between four wide arches. An oculus at the top of the dome admits light. Decorative elements combine Renaissance and classical details.

St. Patrick's Roman Catholic Church in Newcastle, Maine, was built in 1808 and is the oldest Catholic church in New England. This small brick church speaks of the relative isolation of Catholics in New England. It was built by Irish architect Nicholas Codd. It is a Wren-Gibbs–type church, with rounded windows and slight classical detailing. Although small, the brick walls are one and a half feet thick.

A good example of a folk-style neoclassical church is the Baptist Church built in Wickford, Rhode Island, in 1816. The white gable-end frame building is only slightly adapted to assume the character for a pedimented temple.

Greek Revival

Latrobe and Thomas Jefferson were dedicated to the revival of Roman classicism, which is characterized by the use of arches and domes. Starting about 1818, however, a more severe style based on Greek precedents, especially the Parthenon (447–432 B.C.) appeared. The Greek Revival flourished between 1820 and 1850; it was the first national style in the U.S., spreading across the continent, and was used for all levels of building, from high style to folk architecture. Greek architecture was associated with the birth of democracy and the striving for perfection. As an older style, it appealed to the taste for primitivism in the early nineteenth century; there was a widely held conviction that earlier periods of history and earlier forms of art were purer and simpler. With greater historical understanding, Greece was now perceived as the source of much of Roman culture, and both its architectural language and vocabulary were quickly adopted. At the beginning of the nineteenth century there was an increased interest in the culture of ancient Greece both in Western Europe and in the United States. This was heightened by archaeological excavations and particularly by the transfer of Greek treasures to European museums, such as Lord Elgin's acquisition of the famous sculptures of the Parthenon for London's British Museum in 1801. This also coincided with the political ferment of the War of Independence in Greece between 1821 and 1829, which aroused much support in European countries such as France and England. These factors made Greek architecture more appealing for public monuments and for houses where the owners wanted to declare their taste. The Greek temple form was also used for both Christian and Jewish houses of worship.

The First Church of Quincy (also known as the Stone Temple) of 1828 in Quincy, Massachusetts, was designed by Alexander Parris. Parris had worked for Charles Bulfinch while the Lancaster Meetinghouse was under construction, and the overall plan of the Stone Temple resembles the earlier Federalist building. It is built of local Quincy granite, however, and has a more massive, simplified appearance. The monumental entrance portico is a stark Doric design, with unfluted columns. Although the integrated steeple links it to the Wren-Gibbs tradition, this hybrid is unmistakably part of the Greek Revival.

Two good examples of Greek Revival churches in New York City are the St. James Roman Catholic Church of

Above: Parthenon, Athens, Greece, 447–432 B.C. The Parthenon came to be regarded as the finest example of Greek architecture.

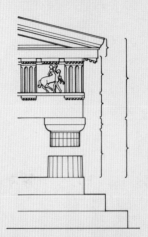

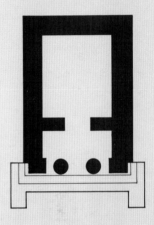

Above: Doric order: Classical architecture has characteristic sets of forms, called orders, which must be combined according to rules. The Doric is the oldest and most severe of these orders.

Above: Greek temple: With columns in antis, set back between the walls at the entrance. Greek temples used a wide variety of configurations of columns.

Above: Colonnade; a row of columns.

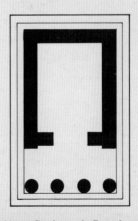

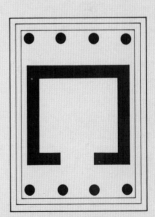

Above: Greek temple: Prostyle, with columns at the entrance.

Above: Greek temple: Amphiprostyle, with columns at each end.

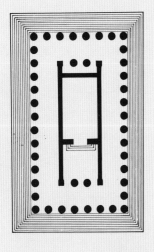

Above: Greek temple: Peripteral, with columns all around the temple.

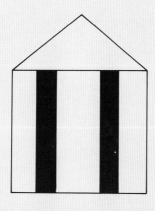

Above: Greek distyle temple, with two columns at the front.

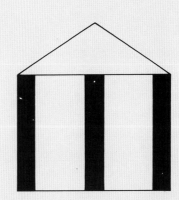

Above: Greek tristyle temple, with three columns across the front.

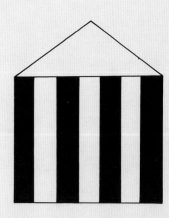

Above: Greek tetrastyle temple, with four columns across the front.

Above: Greek pentastyle temple, with five columns across the front.

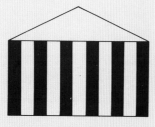

Above: Greek hexastyle temple, with six columns across the front.

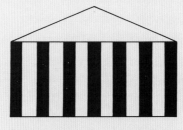

Above: Greek heptastyle temple, with seven columns across the front.

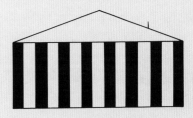

Above: Greek octastyle temple, with eight columns across the front.

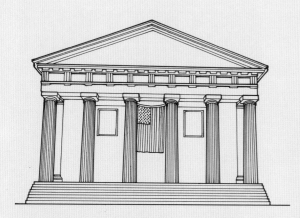

Above: First Congregational Church, Madison, CT, 1838. Detail of Doric portico.

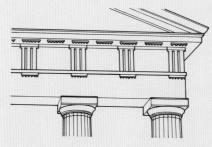

Above: Triglyphs and metopes; Doric frieze from the First Congregational Church, Madison, CT, 1838. The forms of Greek architecture are based on their origins in wooden building, the triglyphs represent the ends of wooden beams, and the metopes the blank spaces between them.

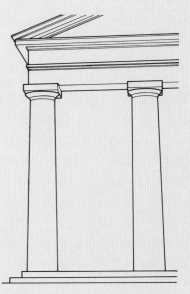

Above: Simplified Doric order; Alexander Parris: Stone Temple, Quincy, MA, 1828. Parris's columns have no flutes, but also have no bases. They are made of hard Quincy granite, which may have influenced the simplification.

Left: The Tuscan order. Tuscan Doric was a simplified form of the Doric order, introduced by the Romans. Columns have no flutes and are on bases.

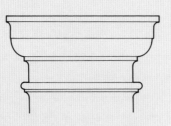

Above: Tuscan Doric capital.

Right: Ionic order. The Ionic order is similar to the Doric, but the columns are slimmer, are set on bases, and have scroll-like capitals.

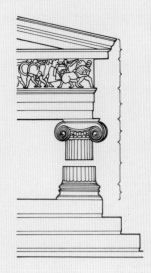

Above: Ionic capital, from Samuel Belcher: First Congregational Church, Old Lyme, CT, 1817.

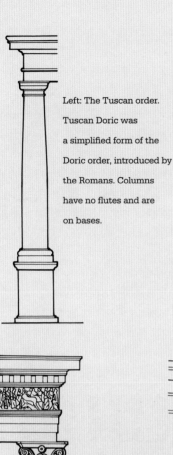

Left: Corinthian order. The Corinthian order is the most ornate; the capitals are based on acanthus leaves.

Above: Ionic capital, Damariscotta Baptist Church, ME,

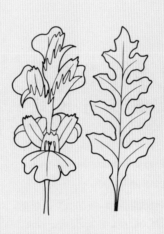

Above: Acanthus leaves, carved in Corinthian capitals.

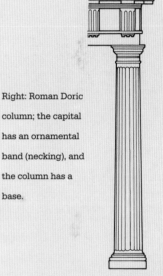

Right: Roman Doric column; the capital has an ornamental band (necking), and the column has a base.

Left: Composite column, combining aspects of the Corinthian and Ionic orders.

Above: Cross section from above of a classical column, showing channels (flutes) and dividing ridges (arrises).

Above: Caryatids, columns in the shape of young women, on the Erechtheion, Athens. Fifth century B.C.

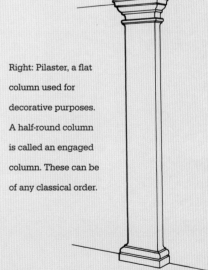

Right: Pilaster, a flat column used for decorative purposes. A half-round column is called an engaged column. These can be of any classical order.

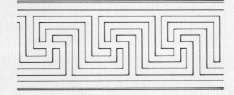

Above: Greek meander, or fret, pattern, used as a decorative motif.

Above: Twisted column, sometimes called Solomonic columns, associated with the temple of Solomon in Jerusalem.

Above: Greek Revival pillars in their simplest form; columns are suggested by boards nailed in a boxlike shape. Chestnut Hill Baptist Church, Exeter, RI, 1838.

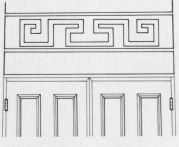

Left: Greek fret pattern, over door of Chestnut Hill Baptist Church, Exeter, RI, 1838.

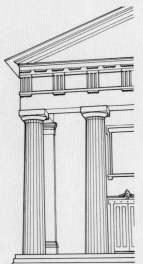

Above: Elegant Doric columns, First Congregational Church, Madison, CT, 1838.

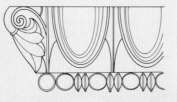

Above: Egg and dart decorative pattern, over bead and reel design, common classical motifs.

1835–37, possibly by Minard Lafever, and St. Peter's Roman Catholic Church of 1836. St. James is a brownstone church with two columns (distyle) *in antis* (the columns are set between two walls).

Comparison with a real classical temple, such as the Maison Carrée (19 B.C.) in Nimes, France, which was so admired by Thomas Jefferson that he copied it for the Virginia State Capitol, reveals significant differences with modern churches. Most essentially, pagan temples were built as shrines to the gods and were not intended to hold masses of worshipers. Lighting was thus not an issue, but the modern church requires many windows for illumination. The entire function is different and can only be adapted by treating the temple form as a box or shell.

A split between liberal and Calvinist members of the Congregational Church in Uxbridge, Massachusetts, led the one group to build a Gothic Unitarian church directly

Above: Alexander Parris: Stone Temple, 1306 Hancock Street, Quincy, MA, 1828.

Above: Minard Lafever: St. James Church (Roman Catholic), 32 James Street, New York, NY, 1835–37.

Above: Alexander Parris and Solomon Willard: Cathedral Church of St. Paul, 138 Tremont Street, Boston, MA, 1820.

Above: Alexander Parris: Stone Temple, Quincy, MA, 1828.

across the street from this Greek Revival church in 1834. The First Evangelical Congregational Church of 1833 has a six-column (hexastyle) Ionic portico, with a stepped gable rising in two stages toward the steeple.

The First Congregational Church (1838) in Madison, Connecticut, has one of the finest Greek porticoes in New England. It was designed by Volney Pierce and is built of wood. The detailing is crisp and perfectly copied from ancient sources, especially the Parthenon. The steeple is first square, then ascends to two cylindrical stages, similar to the Choragic Monument of Lysicrates, a favorite of Greek Revival architects.

The Congregational Church in Slatersville, Rhode Island, of 1838–40 is a simpler but still crisp example of the Greek Revival. The entrance portico has only four columns instead of six (tetrastyle instead of hexastyle, like the Parthenon). The columns are widely spaced, creating a more static symmetry. The rectangular block and tower shows its roots in the Wren-Gibbs tradition, but the overall intent of participating in the new Greek Revival style is clear.

Even less accurate is the Chestnut Hill Baptist Church (1838) in Exeter, Rhode Island. The pediment and portico are only hinted at here, as the end gable of the church is

Above left: First Evangelical Congregational Church, Main Street, Uxbridge, MA, 1833. A split between liberal and Calvinist members led the one group to build a Gothic Unitarian church directly across the street from this Greek Revival church in 1834.

Left: Comparison: Maison Carrée, Nimes, France, 19 B.C. A Roman temple much admired by Thomas Jefferson and other neoclassicists.

Right: Volney Pierce: First
Congregational Church,
Madison, CT, 1838. Side view.

Above: Volney Pierce: First Congregational Church,
26 Meetinghouse Lane, Madison, CT, 1838. Front view.

Above: Congregational Church, Slatersville, RI, 1838–40.

Above: John Bishop: Huntington Street Baptist Church, 29 Huntington Street, New London, CT, 1843.

Above: Chestnut Hill Baptist Church, 10 Rod Road, Exeter, RI, 1838.

closed off and four paneled piers take the place of columns. There is a fragment of Greek fretwork above the door to reinforce the symbolic linking to the Greek Revival. This is a folk-style building, created by local carpenters with a smattering of stylistic references.

Although it now has an elegant Doric portico with four columns and a pediment at the front, the First Parish Church Unitarian Universalist in Billerica, Massachusetts, was not originally built in the Greek Revival style. When first constructed in 1797, it was a traditional meetinghouse.

Above: William Miller: William Miller Chapel, County Route 1, Low Hampton, NY, 1848.

In 1844, it was altered to the Greek Revival style and actually rotated ninety degrees to emphasize the entrance at what had been the gable end of the building.

Charleston, South Carolina, was devastated by a great fire in 1838; after the fire, many of the new buildings were constructed in the Greek Revival style. One of the most impressive is the Kahal Kadosh Beth Elohim Synagogue of 1841–43. It was designed by Cyrus L. Warner and built by a congregation member, David Lopez. It is America's second oldest synagogue (after the Touro synagogue in Newport, Rhode Island) and the oldest in continuous use. The American Reform Judaism movement originated at this site in 1824. The Reform movement was an attempt to modernize synagogue worship and to update Jewish theology; it began in Germany early in the nineteenth century and quickly spread throughout central Europe and to the United States. The Greek Revival synagogue in Charleston has an excellent copy of the Doric portico of the Parthenon. The columns do not go all the way around the church, however, unlike the original peripteral Greek temple in Athens. The tall windows at the side are encased in elegant Greek moldings. As with many Greek Revival buildings, the pure Greek exterior is combined with an eclectic interior and a large central Roman-style dome.

Another Greek Revival synagogue is found in Baltimore, Maryland. The Lloyd Street Synagogue was

Above: Samuel Melcher: Damariscotta Baptist Church, King's Square, Damariscotta, ME.

Above right: First Parish Church Unitarian Universalist, 5 Concord Road, Billerica, MA, 1797. This church was altered to the Greek Revival style and rotated ninety degrees in 1844.

Right: Cyrus L. Warner, architect; David Lopez, builder: Kahal Kadosh Beth Elohim Synagogue, 90 Hasell Street, Charleston, SC, 1841–43.

Above: Cyrus L. Warner, architect; David Lopez, builder: Kahal Kadosh Beth Elohim Synagogue, Charleston, SC, 1843. An important Greek Revival synagogue.

Above: Kahal Kadosh Beth Elohim Synagogue. Side elevation.

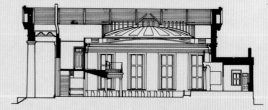

Above: Kahal Kadosh Beth Elohim Synagogue. Section.

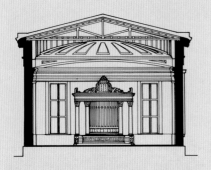

Above: Kahal Kadosh Beth Elohim Synagogue. Transverse section.

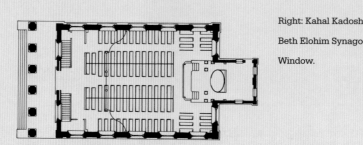

Above: Kahal Kadosh Beth Elohim Synagogue, Ground plan.

Right: Kahal Kadosh Beth Elohim Synagogue, Window.

designed by Robert Cary Long, Jr., in 1845. A four-column version of the Doric pediment of the Parthenon is attached to a brick synagogue, which now houses the Jewish Historical Society of Maryland.

The Greek Revival was the first national style in America; it permeated all levels of building, from the folk-style to the high-style, architect-designed buildings, and it spread from coast to coast. In Cincinnati, Ohio, the Cathedral of St. Peter in Chains was built between 1841 and 1845. This Greek Revival church was designed by Henry Walter; it follows the Wren-Gibbs model, with a large Corinthian entrance portico and a steeple above. The main body of the church is behind this first tower.

The Southern states have many excellent examples of the Greek Revival. Thomas S. Stewart designed St. Paul's church in Richmond, Virginia in 1845. The Government Street Presbyterian Church in Mobile, Alabama, was built almost a decade earlier, in 1836–37. It was designed by James Gallier, James Dakin, and Charles Dakin and is similar to the designs of Minard Lafever.

The South Park Presbyterian Church (1853) in Newark, New Jersey, had an impressive façade with an Ionic portico and two square towers, each of which terminated in an octagonal section and a round lantern modeled on the choragic monument of Lysicrates in Athens, one of the favorite motifs for Greek Revival designers. The church burned and only the façade survives.

One of the fascinating aspects of the Greek Revival is the way that it could be adapted to all levels of building, from the highest style to the folk level. The William Miller Chapel was built in the vicinity of Fairhaven, Low Hampton, New York, in 1848 by the visionary William Miller (1782–1849). A self-taught preacher who was fascinated by the Book of Revelations, Miller became famous for predicting the end of the world on a very specific date. Miller attracted a large number of followers who abandoned their worldly goods and anxiously awaited the second coming on October 22, 1844. When it did not occur, this became known as "the Great Disappointment." Miller returned to his early home near the Vermont border and built this

Right: Henry Walter: Cathedral of St. Peter in Chains, 325 West Eighth Street, Cincinnati, OH, 1841–45.

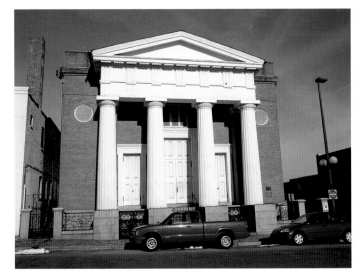

Above: Robert Cary Long, Jr.: Lloyd Street Synagogue, 11 Lloyd Street, Baltimore, MD, 1845.

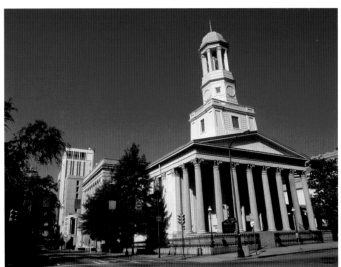

Above: Thomas S. Stewart: St. Paul's, 815 East Grace Street, Richmond, VA, 1845.

Above: James Gallier, James Dakin, Charles Dakin: Government Street Presbyterian Church, Government and Jackson Streets, Mobile, AL, 1836–37. The design of this church can be compared to those by Minard Lafever.

Above: Zoar Moravian Church, also known as the Zoar Church, County Highway 10, Chaska, MN, 1863. Greek Revival in a frontier setting.

small chapel in a rudimentary Greek style. His millenarian theology inspired later groups, notably the Advent Christian denomination and the Seventh Day Adventists.

In rural southern Minnesota, the tiny Zoar Moravian Church, also known as the Zoar Church, was built in 1863. The small wooden building brought the Greek Revival to a frontier setting.

Gothic Revival

The term "Gothic" is one of the great misnomers in history. The style of medieval architecture developed between 1100–1300 had nothing to do with the Goths who sacked Imperial Rome. Stylistic labels are frequently associated with value judgments, and this term originates with Giorgio Vasari's account of the "rebirth" of architecture in the fifteenth century. To distinguish the architecture of his own time from that of the preceding era, and to reinforce its superiority, Vasari labeled the earlier style, the style of the Goths, "barbaric." Vasari was incorrect; Goths were an early medieval tribe from the north that invaded Rome in A.D. 410, but they had nothing to do with the architecture created centuries later. The medieval architects' own term for their style was *opus modernum,* or "modern style." The term "Gothic" for architecture thus originated as a slur. The evo-

lution from Gothic to Renaissance reflected a conceptual shift in the purposes of architecture and the expressive means used to realize them.

It took several centuries and a new concept of architecture as a symbolic language to permit a revival of the medieval style. In realms other than literature, the Medieval Revival emerged first in the garden follies and romantic mansions of eccentric members of the English aristocracy in the second half of the eighteenth century. Strawberry Hill (1753), built for Sir Horace Walpole, and Fonthill Abbey (1795–1807) are the most conspicuous examples. Fonthill Abbey was a towering pleasure palace built for William Beckford at the outset of the nineteenth century. The architect was James Wyatt, who earned the nickname "Wyatt the Destroyer" for his scraping restorations of actual medieval cathedrals.

Gothic architecture originated in religious building in Europe, the churches and cathedrals of the later medieval period, 1190–1400. In contrast to the earlier Romanesque style, the Gothic is taller and uses pointed arches for windows and ribbed vaults to attain greater height with thinner walls. A major goal was to increase the amount of window space available for light and stained glass. As Otto von Simson points out in his classic study of *The Gothic Cathedral,* light was an important symbol for the immaterial but pervasive presence of God. A fully developed Gothic cathedral presented an image of heaven that was meant to transport the worshiper out of his everyday world into a transcendent vision. The Gothic style was a synthesis of engineering and profound symbolism. In 1858 the architect Leopold Eidlitz noted that the great height of Gothic churches, aided by the use of pointed arches, leads the eye "continually upwards, without a well defined, but rather a suggested conclusion, leading the mind to the infinite *above*, which conveys the idea of God, not only beyond the limits of the building but beyond the limits of space appreciable to the physical sense."[3] Gothic Revival architecture embodies the characteristics and tendencies that are opposed to classicism, that is: asymmetry, irregularity, and verticality.

The first Gothic Revival churches in America appear shortly after the turn of the century. One of the earliest is by Maximilian Godefroy in 1806–8, St. Mary's Seminary Chapel in Baltimore, Maryland. Even classically oriented architects designed Gothic churches, as seen in Christ Church, Washington, D.C., 1807; Charles Bulfinch's

Above: Maximilian Godefroy: St. Mary's Seminary Chapel, 600 North Paca Street, Baltimore, MD, 1806-8.

Above: Joseph Mangin: St. Patrick's Old Cathedral, 260–64 Mulberry Street, New York, NY, 1809–15. Restored after 1868 fire.

Above: John Holden Green: St. John's Church (now St. John's Cathedral), 271 North Main Street, Providence, RI, 1810. Episcopal.

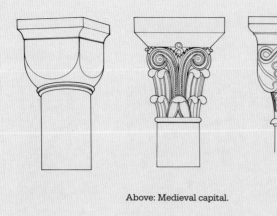

Above: Medieval capital.

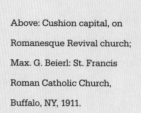

Above: Cushion capital, on
Romanesque Revival church;
Max. G. Beierl: St. Francis
Roman Catholic Church,
Buffalo, NY, 1911.

Above: Parts of a medieval church; the spandrels, flat
areas between arches.

Federal Street Church in Boston of 1809; and William
Strickland's St. Stephen's Episcopal Church, Philadelphia,
PA, 1822–23. Formerly attributed to Benjamin Latrobe,
Christ Church in Washington was designed by his friend
Robert Alexander. This early Gothic Revival church
replaced a log cabin church. The tower was added in 1848.

The major figure of the early Gothic Revival is Richard
Upjohn, whose Trinity Church in New York (1839–46) is
only the most prominent of his many commissions. Upjohn
adapted his Gothic style to simple wood frame structures,
which could be built for smaller rural congregations, in a

Carpenter's Gothic style. This style was based on medieval
precedents, encouraged by popular literary trends. The
first Gothic novels in the eighteenth century presented an
exotic and imaginative view of a romantic medieval past.

An early example of the Gothic Revival in America is St.
Mary's Seminary Chapel of 1806–8 in Baltimore, Maryland,
designed by Maximilian Godefroy (1765–1840?). This small
church has a prominent gallery and tiny rose window on
the second story, echoing the façade of the Gothic cathedral of Notre Dame in Paris. The design also recalls Roman
triumphal arches, especially with the Doric columns flank-

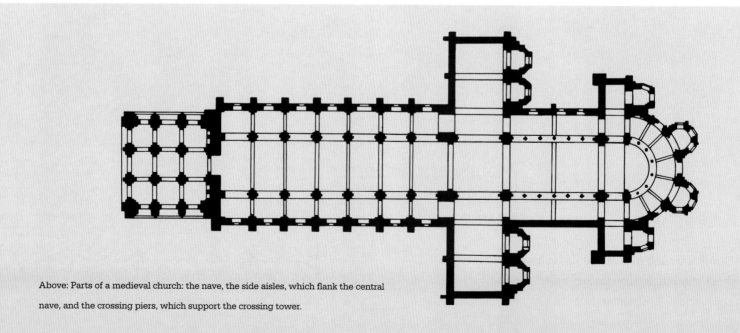

Above: Parts of a medieval church: the nave, the side aisles, which flank the central
nave, and the crossing piers, which support the crossing tower.

ing the building and doorway. Like Latrobe, Godefroy was generally committed to neoclassicism. Born in Paris in 1765, he moved to America from 1805 to 1819, while exiled by the Napoleonic regime in France. His original design called for St. Mary's Seminary Chapel to be built in stone, with a tall central tower. For cost reasons, it was made of brick and the tower was not built. A tower of different design was added in 1840 but this was removed in 1916. During construction, the height of the nave roof was reduced, leaving the upper gallery projecting above it like a false front.

Benjamin Latrobe had offered a Gothic design for the cathedral in Baltimore in 1804, but it was rejected by the client in favor of a Roman classical design. As an eclectic architect, Latrobe had already explored the Gothic style in smaller projects. In 1808, however, he designed Christ Church in Washington, D.C. This church has a crenellated central tower, with small rose windows in each wall, topped with four pinnacles. The walls are flat, an effect accentuated by the lack of moldings over the doors or windows. The wall is still the dominant structural element here, unlike the true medieval style.

The original Roman Catholic cathedral in New York City is St. Patrick's Old Cathedral (1809–15) in what is now Chinatown. It was designed by Joseph Mangin, a French immigrant and one of the architects of the New York City Hall. This is a very simple Gothic church, with flat walls built of stone, lancet windows, and a small rose window in the gable. Restored after a fire in 1868, the interior now features cast-iron columns supporting a timber truss roof.

Another of the earliest Gothic churches is St. John's Church (now St. John's Cathedral) in Providence, Rhode Island. It was designed by John Holden Green and built in 1810. This Episcopal church is basically a Wren-Gibbs type, with Gothic detailing. It is made of brownstones, which set it apart from the white-painted, wood frame churches of the preceding era. The entrance portico was inspired by the most influential pattern book for Gothic designers from the mid-eighteenth century, Batty Langley's *Gothic Architecture, Improved by Rules and Proportions* (1742). On the interior, the nave is almost square like a meetinghouse, and the slightly rounded plaster ceiling is ringed with a large wheel molding in the manner of Adamesque or Federalist architecture. The Gothic features of this church are more decorative than structural.

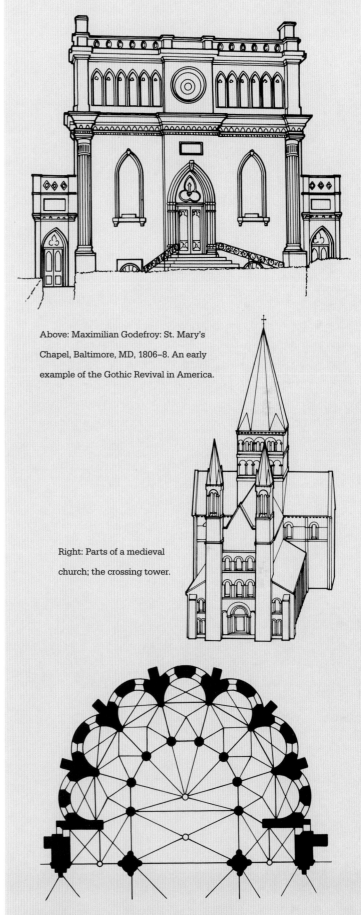

Above: Maximilian Godefroy: St. Mary's Chapel, Baltimore, MD, 1806–8. An early example of the Gothic Revival in America.

Right: Parts of a medieval church; the crossing tower.

Above: Parts of a medieval church; the ambulatory.

Above: Fanciful Gothic portico, inspired by Batty Langley's *Gothic Architecture Improved.* John Holden Green: St. John's Church (now St. John's Cathedral), Providence, RI, 1810.

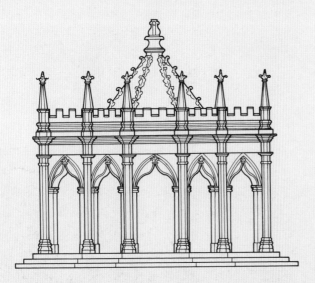

Above: Batty Langley: Gothic portico, from *Gothic Architecture Improved,* 1741–42.

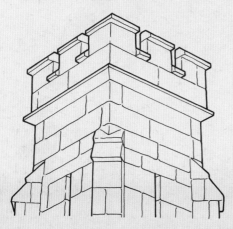

Left: Battlements. A. J. Davis: First Unitarian Church, New Bedford, MA, 1845.

Another architect mostly known for his classical designs was Ithiel Town, who created some of the finest Greek Revival public buildings in the 1820s and 1830s. In 1814–17, however, he designed Trinity Episcopal Church on the town green of New Haven, Connecticut, in a convincing Gothic style. The church has lost some of its original Gothic trim and the wooden tower was rebuilt in 1884–85 in stone in a heavier fashion. A chancel was added at this time to the rectangular block plan of the original building. Town's original tower design was borrowed from James Gibbs's *Book of Architecture* of 1728, which reproduced an early-sixteenth-century English Gothic church. While still copying from the book that was the chief source of Georgian classicism, Town took American architecture in the direction of Romantic and Picturesque medievalism. Town's Gothic church in New Haven was very influential; his own later and similar Christ Church Cathedral in Hartford, Connecticut, of 1827–29, extended this influence.

William Strickland's St. Stephen's Episcopal Church, Philadelphia, PA, 1822–23, is another Gothic design by a committed classicist; Strickland is credited with introducing the Greek Revival in America with his Second National Bank building in Philadelphia of 1818. His essay in Gothic is awkward, with a rectangular block of the church body flanked by two slender octagonal towers on the façade. The lancet windows are the chief sign of the Gothic style.

The Vermont architect Lavius Fillmore (1767–1805) is best known for his Federalist-style meetinghouses, but in 1827 he designed St. Stephen's Episcopal Church in Middlebury, Vermont, in a Gothic style. The Gothic elements are only skin-deep, however; it is basically a Wren-Gibbs type church, with lancet windows and some decorative trim. The interior of this church was redesigned in the 1860s in a Victorian mode. It is the first Gothic church in Vermont.

Gothic and Greek Revival styles were at times used as badges of identity in doctrinal conflict. A case in point is the First Congregational Society, Unitarian, in Uxbridge, Massachusetts. This church dates from 1834, when a split between liberal and Calvinist members of a congregation led one group to build this Gothic church directly across the street from the Greek Revival church of 1833.

A castellated form of Gothic, with thick walls and crenellations or battlements on top, was in vogue early on. The First Unitarian (North) Church, Salem, Massachusetts,

Above: Ithiel Town: Trinity Episcopal Church, New Haven, CT, 1815

Above: Ithiel Town: Christ Church Cathedral, 45 Church Street, Hartford, CT, 1827–29.

Above: Lavius Fillmore: St. Stephen's Episcopal Church, 3 Main Street, Middlebury, VT, 1827. Interior redesigned in the 1860s.

Above: Gothic door. South Parish Unitarian Church, Main Street, Charlestown, NH, 1843.

Above: Pointed arches mark this entrance at a Gothic Revival church; First Congregational Church, Claremont, NH.

Above: Sometimes Gothic arches and classical porticos are combined, as in this case. South Congregational Church, Temple Street, Kennebunkport, ME, 1824.

Right: First Unitarian (North) Church, 316 Essex Street, Salem, MA. 1836–37.

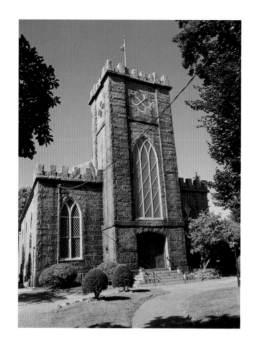

Below: First Congregational Society, Unitarian, 27 North Main Street, Uxbridge, MA, 1834.

Below: A. J. Davis: First Unitarian Church, 71 Eighth Street, New Bedford, MA, 1845.

1836–37, is one example. Built by an anonymous architect, this church is made of heavy brownstone and features a central tower with battlements on the top. Alexander Jackson Davis's First Unitarian Church in New Bedford, Massachusetts, of 1845 features similar construction and fortified aspects.

The early Gothic Revival also brought odd combinations of styles. St. John's Episcopal Church in East Poultney, Vermont, of 1831 includes a Greek Revival pediment combined with Gothic pointed arches.

The South Parish Unitarian Church in Charlestown, New Hampshire, of 1843 is a small brick church with a slightly projecting entrance section and a wooden steeple. The hood moldings over the windows are decorative, but the flamboyant molding around the door is the chief ornament.

The first book on Gothic architecture published in America was an *Essay on Gothic Architecture* in 1936, written by John Henry Hopkins. Hopkins was the bishop of Vermont at the time, where he had moved after serving in Boston. He urged the adoption of the Gothic style for symbolic and liturgical reasons; he felt that the verticality of the Gothic style evoked, "by a kind of physical association, an impression of sublimity more exalted than any other sort of architecture can produce."[4]

In England, two important ecclesiastical reform movements began in Oxford and Cambridge in the 1830s. The Oxford Movement was led by academics and theologians who wanted to reintroduce elements of the medieval liturgy back into the liturgy of the Anglican church. As with medieval Catholics, they emphasized the role of ritual and the sacrament of the Eucharist. They published a series of pamphlets entitled *Tracts for the Times*, which gave them the name Tractarians. These tracts included reviews of recent church architecture. Their "High Church" orientation toward the altar distinguished them from "Low Church"

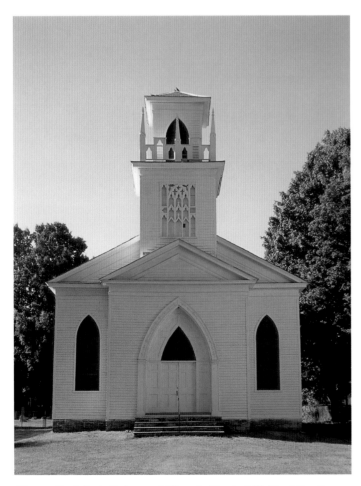

Above: St. John's Episcopal Church, Route 140, East Poultney, VT, 1831. Combination of Greek Revival pediment and Gothic pointed arches.

Above: South Parish Unitarian Church, Main Street, Charlestown, NH, 1843.

Above: Richard Upjohn: Trinity Church, New York, NY, 1839–46.

Above: Trinity Church, New York. Interior.

Above: Ithiel Town: Trinity Episcopal Church, New Haven, CT, 1815.

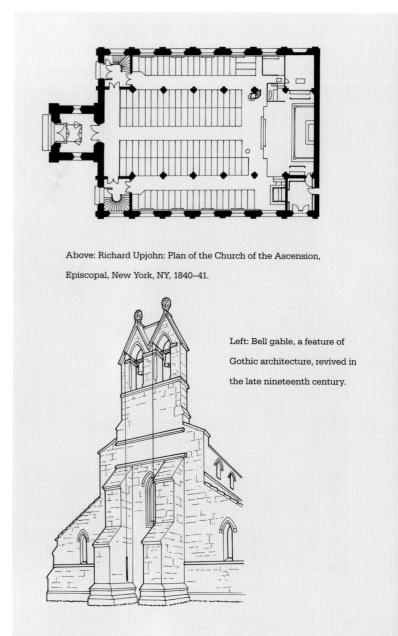

Above: Richard Upjohn: Plan of the Church of the Ascension, Episcopal, New York, NY, 1840–41.

Left: Bell gable, a feature of Gothic architecture, revived in the late nineteenth century.

Calvinists who emphasized the sermons and the pulpit. In Cambridge, a group of students with similar interests formed the Cambridge Camden Society in 1839, which published a journal called *The Ecclesiologist* beginning in 1841. The Camden society had strong antiquarian leanings, and promoted interest in English Gothic architecture as the best suited for modern England. These two groups had enormous influence on the development of Gothic architecture for churches in Britain and America.

Zealots such as A. W. N. Pugin began to identify the Gothic style with religious faith and moral reform. Pugin's book *Contrasts, or A Parallel Between the Noble Edifices of the Fourteenth and Fifteenth Centuries, and Similar Buildings of the Present Day; Shewing the Present Decay of Taste* (1836) left no room for doubt that the Gothic style was more than an option; it was a necessity. God himself weighed the Gothic against the classical, and in His scales, the classical was found wanting. The famous tailpiece illustration shows classical architecture weighed in the scales of God at the Last Judgment. Pugin, a convert to Catholicism, believed that a nation's architecture should give witness to its religious convictions, and as a Christian nation, England should choose a style untainted by pagan origins.

Pugin's idealism was highly persuasive in England and in the United States. Richard Upjohn built Trinity Church in New York (1839–46) following Puginian designs. Upjohn, a High Church Episcopalian, was conspicuously unwilling to design Gothic churches for other denominations. In 1846 he declined to build a church for the Unitarian Federal Street Church (later the Arlington Street Church) in Boston, citing the difference in beliefs and services. Upjohn's pious revival of the forms of Gothic architecture was motivated by associations of the style with an "age of faith" and was a ritual re-creation of the forms of an era that attempted to keep those values alive, just as faith is memorialized and reenacted through the liturgy.

With its 281-foot-tall spire, Trinity Church was the tallest building in New York City until 1890. The design closely follows some of Pugin's drawings of an ideal parish church, modeled on English churches of about 1300. Upjohn's

Above: Richard Upjohn: Church of the Ascension, Episcopal, New York, NY, 1840–41.

Above: Joseph C. Wells: First Presbyterian Church, 12 West Twelfth Street, New York, NY, 1846.

Left: The pointed arch results from the intersection of two circular arcs.

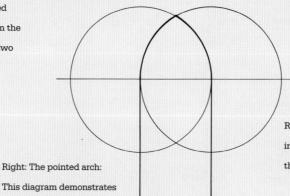

Right: The pointed arch: This diagram demonstrates the intersection.

Right: Gothic tracery, intersecting arches in the windows.

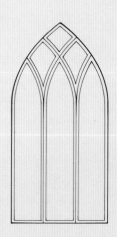

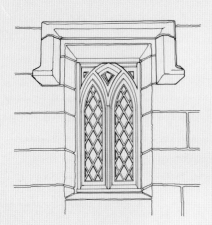

Left: Hood molding over lancet window. A. J. Davis: First Unitarian Church, New Bedford, MA, 1845.

Right: Rose window within lancet. Patrick Keely: Asylum Hill Congregational Church, 814 Asylum Avenue, Hartford, CT, 1865.

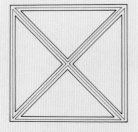

Above: Gothic ribbed vault; quadripartite (four-part) vault.

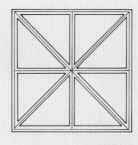

Above: Gothic ribbed vault; sexpartite (six-part) vault.

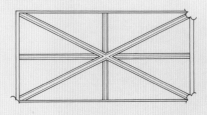

Above: Gothic ribbed vault; sexpartite vault with crossed ribs.

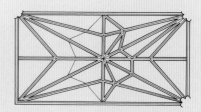

Above: Gothic ribbed vault; complex vault with tiercerons (secondary ribs) and liernes (tertiary ribs).

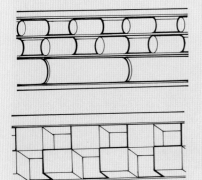

Above: Billet moldings; round and square, used in medieval architecture

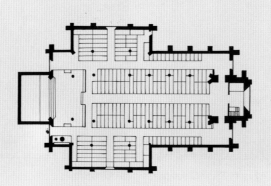

Above: James Renwick: plan of Grace Church, 800 Broadway, New York, NY, 1846.

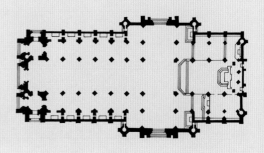

Above: James Renwick: plan of St. Patrick's Cathedral, New York, NY, 1857.

Above: Gothic windows: The foils are the lobes, or leaf shapes; the cusp is the point between them.

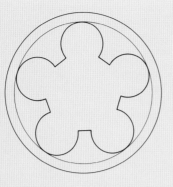

Above: Gothic windows: Multifoil, or window with multiple lobes.

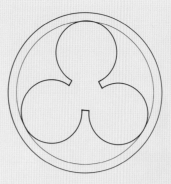

Above: Gothic windows: Trefoil, or window with three lobes.

Above: Gothic windows: Quatrefoil, or window with four lobes.

church is built of brown sandstone and features a rich variety of Gothic details: lancet windows, pinnacles, buttresses (not flying buttresses, however), tracery, and moldings. The interior of the nave has a high ceiling, traced with Gothic ribs, and enormous stained glass windows (forty-four feet high and twenty-eight feet wide). The ceiling was a compromise for Upjohn; to create truly authentic Gothic architecture, he wanted to vault the ceiling with stone, but it was deemed too

expensive. That being the case, he wanted to use large wooden trusses and leave them exposed. The building committee rejected the architect's plea for structural honesty, and in 1841 insisted on a ceiling of plaster and wood that imitates stone. The resulting ceiling is a perfect version of an English Perpendicular ribbed vault. Upjohn was always respected for his high standards; in 1857 he was named the first president of the American Institute of Architects.

Above: James Renwick: Grace Church, 800 Broadway, New York, NY, 1846.

Above: First Congregational Church, 34 Center and Williams Street, Fairhaven, MA, 1844.

Above: Saint Mary Star of the Sea, 10 Huntington Street, New London, CT.

Above: Second Congregational Church, River Road, Newcastle, ME, 1843.

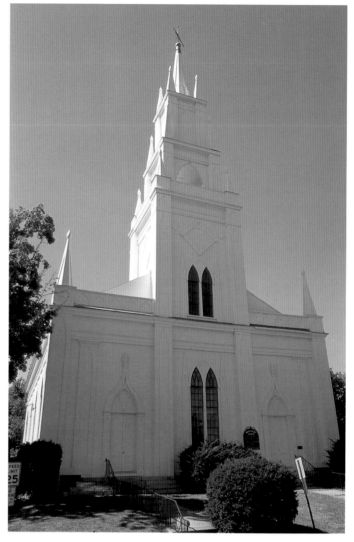

Above: Anthony C. Raymond: Winter Street Church (Congregational), Bath, ME, 1843.

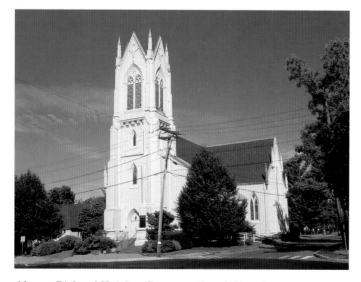

Above: Richard Upjohn: Congregational Church, 9 Cleaveland Street, Brunswick, ME, 1844–46. Front view.

Above: Congregational Church, Brunswick. Side view.

Very similar, but slightly more elaborate than Upjohn's nearby Church of the Ascension, the First Presbyterian Church, New York City, 1846, has a square pinnacled tower.

One of the finest churches of this period in New York was also built in 1846: James Renwick's Grace Church. It was constructed in the Middle Pointed, or Decorated, style of English Gothic, as recommended by the Ecclesiological Society. Renwick was also the architect of the Smithsonian Institution in Washington, D.C., and the later St. Patrick's Cathedral in New York City.

A number of churches with tall central towers were built in this phase of the Gothic Revival. One example is the Church of Saint Mary Star of the Sea in New London, Connecticut, which is elegantly constructed of stone. Although made of brick, the First Congregational Church (1844) in Fairhaven, Massachusetts, is equally powerful, with its massive central tower.

Gothic architecture was given significant support and direction by the church reform groups in England. The ecclesiologist declared that the Early Middle Pointed (or Early Decorated) style of English architecture was the most pure, and by 1843 was recommending specific models for High Church buildings. For smaller rural churches, St. Michael's, Long Stanton, Cambridgeshire (c. 1230), was singled out for its purity of design. A small gabled church, with a central bell-cote instead of a steeple, it was copied many times, sometimes in brick or wood instead of stone. The Church of St. James the Less in Philadelphia (1846–48) was actually built from measured drawings of St. Michael's executed by G. G. Place at the behest of the Ecclesiological Society, and sent to America. The American architect John E. Carver made very few changes to these plans, making this one of the purest of all revival buildings. The prevailing attitude was still that it was preferable to

Above: John E. Carver (from drawings by G. G. Place of St. Michael's, Long Stanton, Cambridgeshire, c. 1230): Church of St. James the Less, 3227 West Clearfield Street, Philadelphia, PA, 1846–48.

Above: A. W. N. Pugin noted that small, irregular stone masonry creates a richer texture than large blocks in his *True Principles of Pointed or Christian Architecture*.

Above: A. W. N. Pugin noted that large blocks provide a flatter surface and compete with the architectural forms.

Left: Board-and-batten siding at Little Brown Church, Rt. 32, Round Pond, ME, 1853.

Above: Diagram of board-and-batten siding.

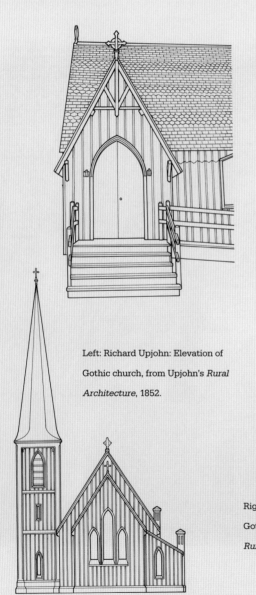

Left: Carpenter's Gothic; the simple sticklike ornaments of the bargeboards under the eaves were inexpensive and easy to build. Combined with the board-and-batten siding, the effect was a simple rural Gothic. This church was one of Upjohn's most popular designs. Richard Upjohn: St. Luke's Episcopal Church, Main Street, Charlestown, NH, 1863.

Left: Richard Upjohn: Elevation of Gothic church, from Upjohn's *Rural Architecture*, 1852.

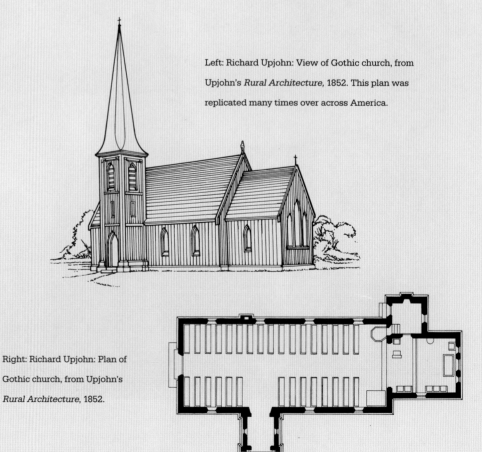

Left: Richard Upjohn: View of Gothic church, from Upjohn's *Rural Architecture*, 1852. This plan was replicated many times over across America.

Right: Richard Upjohn: Plan of Gothic church, from Upjohn's *Rural Architecture*, 1852.

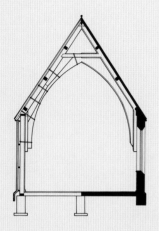

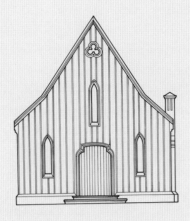

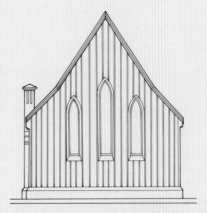

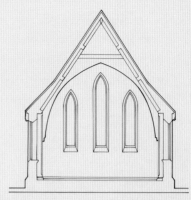

Above: Richard Upjohn: Section of Gothic church, from Upjohn's *Rural Architecture*, 1852.

Above: Richard Upjohn: Elevation of Gothic chapel, from Upjohn's *Rural Architecture*, 1852.

Above: Richard Upjohn: Rear elevation of Gothic chapel, from Upjohn's *Rural Architecture*, 1852.

Above: Richard Upjohn: Section of Gothic chapel, from Upjohn's *Rural Architecture*, 1852.

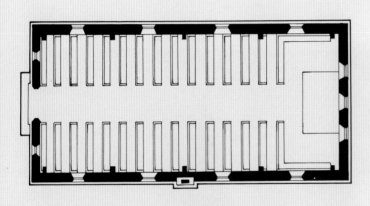

Above: Richard Upjohn: Plan of Gothic chapel from Upjohn's *Rural Architecture*, 1852.

Right: Balloon frame, from William Bell, *Carpentry Made Easy*, 1858. The balloon frame, consisting of light standardized two by fours and wire-cut nails, was invented in Chicago in 1833 by Augustine D. Taylor.

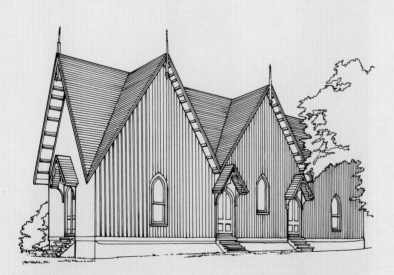

Above: Briery Church, Prince Edward County, VA, 1856. A board-and-batten Gothic church with multiple gables.

Above: St. Patrick's Roman Catholic Church, Austin, TX, *c.* 1854. A simple structure, with one pointed arch window and an inset cross pattern to indicate that it is a church.

171

copy the best models of the past than to invent new forms. This small parish church type was well suited for the American scene. The Covenant Congregational Church (1860) in Waltham, Massachusetts, is only one of many variants. Originally constructed for the Swedenborgian Church of the New Jerusalem, the church was rebuilt after a fire in 1870.

Upjohn also adapted his Gothic style to simple wood frame structures that could be built for smaller rural congregations, in the Carpenter's Gothic style. His 1852 book *Rural Architecture* provided plans and elevations for a simple wooden church, which could be, and was, duplicated inexpensively across America.

Board-and-batten siding is composed of vertical boards set close together, the joints between them covered with narrower wooden strips. The technique was developed for Gothic Revival residences by Andrew Jackson Downing and Alexander Jackson Davis. Richard Upjohn adapted this type of exterior wall covering for wooden Gothic churches, since it gave a vertical emphasis and was based on structure rather than mere decoration.

Upjohn's first church to use board-and-batten siding was the Congregational Church in Brunswick, Maine, built in 1845–46. It was exceptional for Upjohn in that it was not built for an Episcopal client. It is a cruciform church, which was originally built with a central square tower topped by a parapet. In 1848, however, the top of the tower was rebuilt and given a tall octagonal spire. This blew down in 1866 and was never replaced. The original color was also an earth-toned stone color, but it has since been painted white. The interior is remarkable for its intricate open-timber truss, which carries the double-pitched roof. This hammer-beam ceiling is derived from English precedents, but adapted to the special needs of this construction.

Above: Patrick C. Keely: St. Joseph's Roman Catholic Church, 92 Hope Street, Providence, RI, 1851–53.

Above: Patrick C. Keely: Asylum Hill Congregational Church, 814 Asylum Avenue, Hartford, CT, 1865.

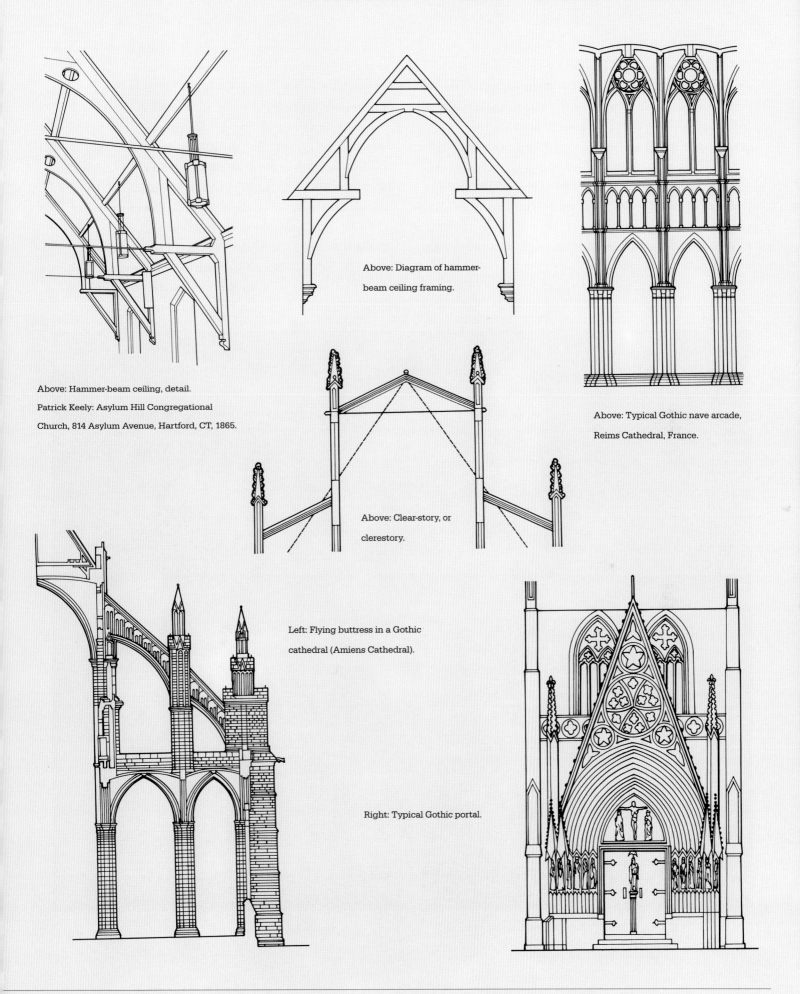

Above: Diagram of hammer-beam ceiling framing.

Above: Hammer-beam ceiling, detail.
Patrick Keely: Asylum Hill Congregational
Church, 814 Asylum Avenue, Hartford, CT, 1865.

Above: Typical Gothic nave arcade,
Reims Cathedral, France.

Above: Clear-story, or
clerestory.

Left: Flying buttress in a Gothic
cathedral (Amiens Cathedral).

Right: Typical Gothic portal.

The small rural Church of St. John Chrysostom in Delafield, Wisconsin, was built in 1851–53 using designs from Upjohn. This board-and-batten church retains its original red-stained color. An unusual feature is the separate bell tower, which recalls certain early American meetinghouses, such as the one at Lexington, Massachusetts. The pyramidal tower suggests that it may also be related to the separate bell towers constructed for Scandinavian medieval churches. The decorated verge boards, or bargeboards, are characteristic of the ornament of the "Carpenter's Gothic" found in houses as well as churches. Similar exquisite wood carving is found in the tiny country church of St. Luke's in Clermont, New York, built by Upjohn in 1857. This is also a board-and-batten wooden church, with carved bargeboards and a steeple made of open wooden trusses.

Upjohn received more job offers for rural churches than he could possibly handle, so he published his book *Rural Architecture* in 1852 to provide plans for smaller communities. St. Luke's Episcopal Church in Charlestown, New Hampshire, follows these designs very closely. There is also an addition to this church designed by Richard M. Upjohn, the architect's son, who continued his practice.

The Irish immigrant architect Patrick C. Keely (1816–1896) was one of the most prolific designers of churches in the nineteenth century. He came to the United States in 1842. Most of his churches follow Pugin's recom-

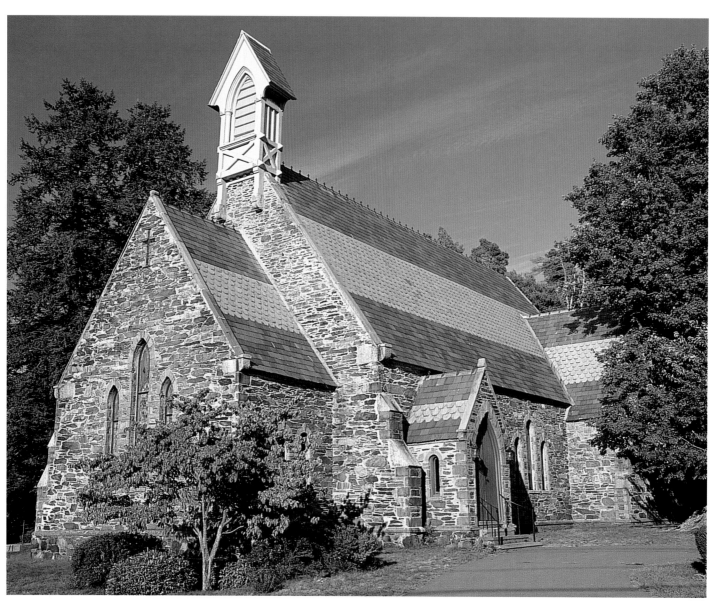

Above: Covenant Congregational Church, 375 Lexington Street, Waltham, MA, 1860. Built for the Swedenborgian Church of the New Jerusalem, the church was rebuilt after a fire in 1870.

mendation for English Gothic models, although some were executed in a Renaissance Revival style.

Gothic Revival churches follow several different typical patterns, including the single central tower façade, the single asymmetrical tower on the side, and the twin-tower façade.

Central Tower Churches

Central Vermont is known for its marble quarries and in the mid-nineteenth century, the town of West Rutland built a new Roman Catholic church in this beautiful stone.

Architect Patrick C. Keely designed St. Bridget's Church, which was built between 1860 and 1861 with a single central tower. The marble was donated for the church, and it was built by the local quarrymen. The interior is spacious and cool, with a central nave and small side aisles. The interior decoration includes traced Celtic motifs on the walls.

Mark Twain attended the Asylum Hill Congregational Church in Hartford, Connecticut. Built of brownstone and with a single central tower, it was designed by Patrick C. Keely and built in 1865. Also in Connecticut, Trinity Episcopal Church in Southport of 1862 was built of wood and is a lovely example of the central tower design.

Above: Church of St. Joseph, St. Joseph, MN. Minnesota's first consecrated Catholic church.

Above: Trinity Episcopal Church, 651 Pequot Avenue, Southport, CT, 1862.

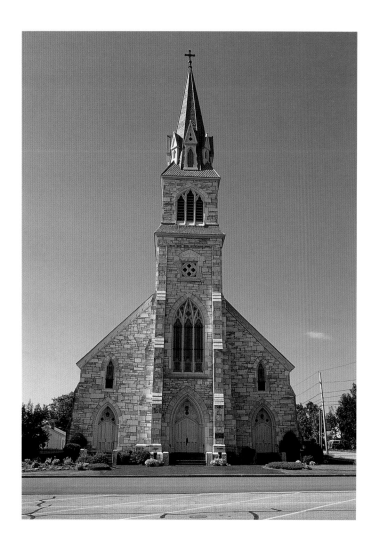

Above left: Patrick C. Keely:
St. Bridget's Roman Catholic
Church, Corner of Pleasant
and Church Streets,
Rutland, VT, 1860–61.

Above right: St. Bridget's
Roman Catholic Church,
Rutland, VT. Interior.

Left: Church of St. Joseph,
St. Joseph, MN. Side view.

Minnesota's first consecrated Catholic church was the Church of St. Joseph in the town of St. Joseph. It was built of stone with a single central tower in the front.

Single Asymmetrical Tower Churches

Churches with a single tower, set asymmetrically to the side, are based on English country models. A fine example is Richard Upjohn's St. Paul's Church in Brookline, Massachusetts, of 1848–51. It was built of Roxbury pudding-stone, one of the first buildings in the Boston area to use this stone. The rectory was added in 1886. The interior was destroyed by fire in 1976, but the exterior still retains the appearance of an English country church.

Richard Upjohn also designed the Church of the Covenant (the Central Congregational Church) in Boston in 1866 with an asymmetrical tower. A particularly fine example of the format is found in Grace Church, Newton, Massachusetts, designed by Alexander Esty and built in 1872–73. Esty was a noted local architect, who had earlier built some of the first Romanesque churches.

The asymmetrical tower plan adapted well for wooden churches also, as is evident at St. Catherine's Church, Charlestown, New Hampshire, 1879–80. This small church has fine stained glass windows by Louis Comfort Tiffany.

Above: Richard Upjohn: St. Paul's Church, 15 Saint Paul Street, Brookline, MA, 1848–51. Overall view.

Left: St. Paul's Church, Brookline, MA. Courtyard.

Above: Richard Upjohn: St. Luke's, Clermont, NY, 1857.

The prolific architect Patrick C. Keely provided the designs for St. Paul's Catholic Church, which was built of wood in Hingham, Massachusetts, in 1871. The popularity of this type is seen in numerous variants, such as the First Baptist Church in Lynn, Massachusetts, and rural churches such as St. James Episcopal Church in Keene, New Hampshire.

Thomas Ustick Walter was an architect most well known for his classical designs, but the Church of St. James in Wilmington, North Carolina, was designed by him in the Gothic mode in 1839.

The Church of St. Mark's in Philadelphia was built in 1847–49 by the architect John Notman. This church was founded on the principles of the Oxford Movement, and the architect based his design partly on plans furnished by the British Ecclesiological Society. It has a long nave, with transepts near the rear of the church; a massive buttressed tower rises at the right front of the church. The interior looks every bit like a British parish church of the Gothic

Above: Richard Upjohn: Church of St. John Chrysostom, 1111 Genessee Street, Delafield, WI, 1851–53.

Right: Richard Upjohn: St. Luke's Episcopal Church, Charlestown, NH, 1863. Interior.

Above: Richard Upjohn: St. Luke's Episcopal Church, 715 Main Street, Charlestown, NH, 1863. Addition by Richard M. Upjohn.

Above left: Richard Upjohn: Church of the Covenant (Central Congregational Church), Clarendon/ Newbury Streets, Boston, MA, 1866.

Above right: Alexander Esty: Grace Church, Church Street, Newton, MA, 1872–73.

Left: St. James Episcopal Church, 44 West Street, Keene, NH.

Above: St. Catherine's Church, Charlestown, NH, 1879–80.

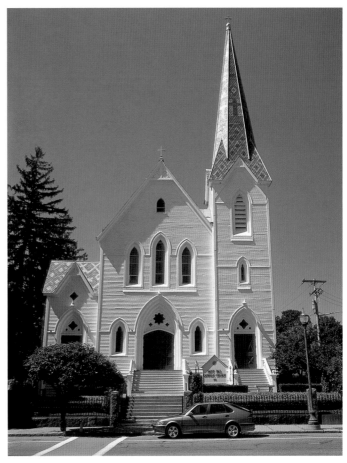

Above right: Patrick C. Keely: St. Paul's Catholic Church, 147 North Street, Hingham, MA, 1871.

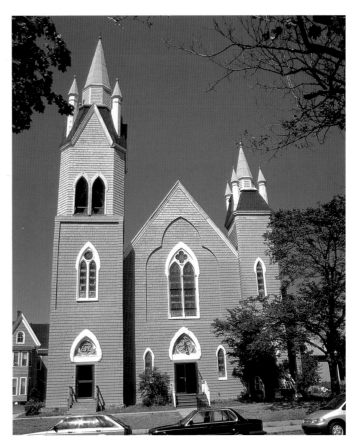

Right: First Baptist Church, 7 Park Street, Lynn, MA.

Above: John Notman: St. Mark's, 1625 Locust Street, Philadelphia, PA, 1847–49.

era, with high stone arches separating the nave and side aisles, and a deep chancel with a high altar and rich stained glass.

Twin Tower Churches

Twin-towered façades were typical of many French and English Gothic cathedrals. The Cathedral of Notre Dame at Chartres, France, built between 1145 and 1220, is only one of the most famous examples.

St. Patrick's Cathedral (1858–79) in New York City was designed by James Renwick, the architect who had previously created the Romanesque Smithsonian Institution (1846) in Washington, D.C. The twin-towered façade is

inspired by both French Gothic cathedrals and the Cologne Cathedral, which Renwick had seen on a tour in 1860. The 330-foot towers were finished after the church was opened in 1888. The plan is a large Latin cross; the church holds 5,000 people. It was intended to be a visible symbol on Fifth Avenue of the new prominence of the Irish Catholic immigrants. Renwick's original plan to vault the nave and build the towers of cast iron was vetoed by the clients. The use of iron in religious buildings was resisted by the clergy. Citing Christ's adjuration "Upon this Rock you shall build," it was argued that stone was the preferred material for churches. In England, the Archbishop of York refused to consecrate churches built of iron.

James Renwick also designed the Second Presbyterian Church (1874) in Chicago. It was rebuilt in 1900 by Howard Van Doren Shaw, and features Pre-Raphaelite interiors, a decorative counterpart to the Medieval Revival style of the architecture.

The Great Fire in Chicago of 1871 damaged the Episcopal Cathedral of St. James, which was designed by Edward J. Burling in 1857. The church was rebuilt in 1875 by the firm of Burling & Adler, which was formed when Dankmar Adler joined with Burling. This Gothic building is made of stone, but Adler would later make his name as one of the pioneers of early skyscraper design with his partner Louis Sullivan.

Burling and Adler also rebuilt the Scottish Rite Cathedral (Unity Church) in 1873 after the Chicago fire. The twin-towered stone Gothic church was originally designed by Theodore Vigo Wadskier in 1867. The south tower was constructed in 1882 by Frederick B. Townsend.

The Holy Cross Cathedral (1867–75) is the largest in Boston. It was designed by Patrick C. Keely (1816–96) in the early English Gothic style, with a cruciform plan. The length of the building is 364 feet and the width is 170 feet at the transepts. The nave is ninety feet wide, and the ceiling is 120 feet in height. Keely was also responsible for the Holy Name Cathedral in Chicago, built in 1874–75. One of the most prolific of all Gothic Revival architects, Keely is credited with designing over 600 churches and twenty-one cathedrals. The Cathedral of Saints Peter and Paul in Providence, Rhode Island, of 1878–89 is another Keely design.

Left: James Renwick: St. Patrick's Cathedral, Fifth Avenue between Fiftieth and Fifty-first Streets, New York, NY, 1858–79.

Right: James Renwick: St. Patrick's Cathedral, New York, NY, 1858–79.

Above: James Renwick: Second Presbyterian Church, 1936 South Michigan Avenue, Chicago, IL, 1874. Rebuilt 1900 by Howard Van Doren Shaw. Pre-Raphaelite interiors.

Above: Edward J. Burling: Episcopal Cathedral of St. James (Anglican), Huron & Wabash, Chicago, IL, 1857; rebuilt 1875 Burling & Adler.

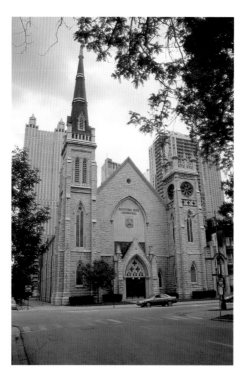

Above: Theodore Vigo Wadskier, with later alterations: Scottish Rite Cathedral (Unity Church), 935 Dearborn, Chicago, IL, 1867; rebuilt after fire in 1873 by Burling & Adler. South tower, 1882, by Frederick B. Townsend.

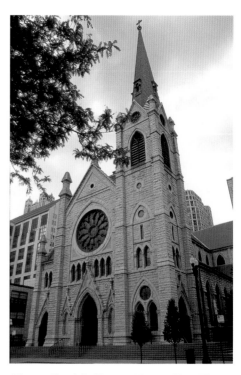

Above: Patrick Charles Keely: Holy Name Cathedral, State Street at Superior Street, Chicago, IL, 1874–75.

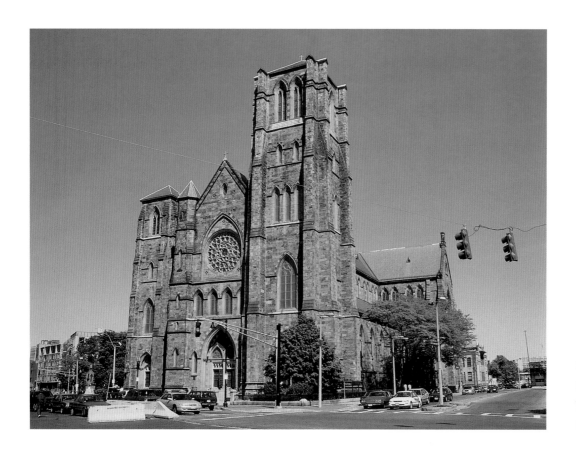

Left: Patrick C. Keely (1816–96): Holy Cross Cathedral, Washington Street at Union Park Street, Boston, MA, 1867–75.

Above left: John Murphy:
St. Peter's Church, 160 Main
Street, Hartford, CT,
1865–68.

Above: Comparison:
Chartres Cathedral, France,
1145–1220.

Left: Patrick C. Keely:
Cathedral of Saints Peter
and Paul, Cathedral Square,
Providence, RI, 1878–89.

Left: William W. Boyington, Sheire, Monroe & Romaine: First Baptist Church of St. Paul, 499 Wacouta Street, St. Paul, MN, Gothic Revival. Front view.

Folk-Style Gothic

Numerous small, folk-style churches were built with simple Gothic elements in the mid- and late nineteenth century across America. One early and unusual example is the Bremo Slave Chapel, Bremo Bluff, Fluvanna County, Virginia of 1835. This was a small board-and-batten Gothic chapel built on the plantation of General John Hartwell Cocke for his slaves, even though it was illegal to offer religious or other instruction to slaves at the time. After Cocke's death in 1866, the chapel was donated to the community of Bremo Bluff for use as a church. It is Virginia's only surviving slave chapel.

The Little Brown Church at Round Pond, Maine, dates from 1853 and is a small board-and-batten Gothic church. A more elaborate board-and-batten Gothic church with multiple gables is the Briery Church in Prince Edward County, Virginia, which dates from 1856. It is a longitudinal church, but intersected by three transverse gables on each side of the nave.

In southern Minnesota, one finds the simple Gothic Revival Svenska Mission Kyrka I Sodre Maple Ridge (also known as the Swedish Mission Church of South Maple Ridge) in Braham, a township in Isanti County, dating from the late nineteenth century. In 1869, the Reverend George Stewart designed the Good Samaritan Episcopal Church in Sauk Centre, Minnesota, and served as its minister. The stucco-covered church recalls the rural Gothic churches of the East Coast.

At the folk-style level, Gothic Revival churches could be very simple indeed. St. Patrick's Roman Catholic Church (*c.* 1854) in Austin, Texas, is a simple structure, with one pointed arch window and an inset cross pattern to indicate that it is a church.

Clearly, the Gothic Revival was also a national style. Frank Wills designed a model Gothic-style church, which was published in the *New York Ecclesiologist*, October 1849. Wills's design was derived from St. Michael's, Longstanton, England, a favorite model for High Church designs. Many churches were based on Wills's design, including the Chapel of the Cross in Mannsdale, Mississippi. It was built in 1852, but omits the tower and transepts.

Left: Little Brown Church, Route 32, Round Pond, ME, 1853.

Below: Svenska Mission Kyrka I Sodre Maple Ridge, also known as the Swedish Mission Church of South Maple Ridge, County Highway 1, Braham, MN, late nineteenth century.

Left: Reverend George Stewart: Good Samaritan Episcopal Church, Main Street, Sauk Centre, MN, 1869.

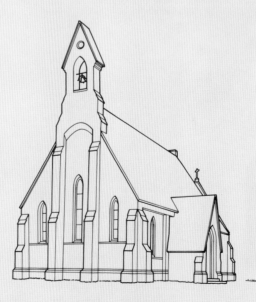

Above: Frank Wills: Gothic church published in the *New York Ecclesiologist*, October 1849. Derived from St. Michael's, Longstanton, England, a favorite model for High Church designs.

Above: Chapel of the Cross, Mannsdale, Mississippi, 1852. Based on Frank Will's design, but without the tower and transepts.

Above: Congregation Beth Israel, Stevens Point, WI, mid-nineteenth century.

Gothic Synagogues

Although the Gothic style is historically linked to Christian churches of the Middle Ages, its status as a style for houses of worship led to its adaptation for a number of interesting synagogues. Some were in rural areas, but others were in cities, including some lost examples in New York. The temple for Congregation Beth Israel in Stevens Point, Wisconsin, was built in the mid-nineteenth century in a simplified Gothic style. The small wood frame temple has no steeple, as those were too specifically tied to Christian churches, and features a clipped gable, or jerkinhead, roof.

The Temple Mickve Israel Synagogue in Savannah, Georgia, of 1878 is larger and has many more Gothic features, including the lancet windows, steeple, and cross-shaped plan. The top of the steeple ends with an unusual cupola, however. It was designed by Henry G. Harrison, an English Gothic Revival architect.

There is a precedent in European architecture for Gothic synagogues. The Old New Synagogue in Prague in the Czech Republic was built in the late thirteenth century, in the prevailing Gothic style of the period. It may have been built by Christian workmen—Jews were excluded from

Above: Henry G. Harrison: Temple Mickve Israel Synagogue, 20 East Gordon Street, Savannah, GA, 1878. A synagogue built in the Gothic style.

Above: Old New Synagogue, Prague, Czech Republic, thirteenth century. In medieval Europe, Jews were not allowed to join the building guilds, so many synagogues were built by gentiles.

the building trades—and the design is adapted for the Jewish service, with a central raised bimah and a separate section for women.

Italian Renaissance

Churches designed in imitation of Italian Renaissance examples were built for urban congregations in Philadelphia, Boston, and New York, then spread across the U.S. between the 1840s and 1900. These were frequently built for Roman Catholic congregations. As early as 1850,

Above: Father Anthony Ravalli: Coeur d'Alene Mission of the Sacred Heart, Caldwell, ID, 1850.

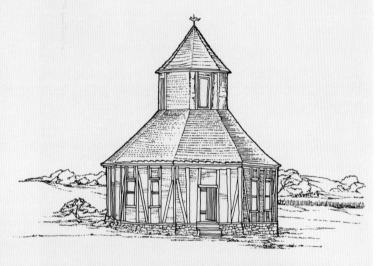

Above: Drawing of the Vereins Kirche, German immigrant church near San Antonio, TX, c. 1847. An octagonal church, on a half-timber base.

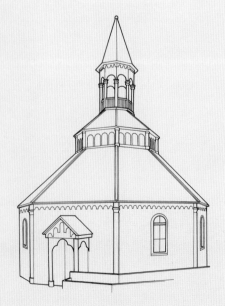

Left: Holy Ghost Roman Catholic Church, Kula, HI, 1894. An octagonal plan church.

one finds an example in the Coeur d'Alene Mission of the Sacred Heart, Caldwell, Idaho, designed by Father Anthony Ravalli in 1850.

Octagon Churches

The octagonal form had been important for medieval baptisteries, and the rotunda form had been revived by Robert Mills for larger churches. In the mid-nineteenth century there was also a brief craze for octagon houses, inspired by the writings of the phrenologist and reformer Orson Squire Fowler. A number of smaller churches drew upon these various currents and were constructed in octagonal form. The Vereins Kirche, a German immigrant church near San Antonio, Texas, was an octagonal church on a half-timber base. The precedent of German medieval churches, perhaps even the chapel of Charlemagne at Aachen, may have been the most important factor here. The church is known only through drawings, unfortunately. Another intriguing example is the Holy Ghost Roman Catholic Church, Kula, Hawaii, of 1894, also built on an octagonal plan.

Egyptian Revival

The Egyptian Revival was one of the most exotic revival movements in the nineteenth century. The culture of ancient Egypt was mysterious and highly compelling in the nineteenth century. Europeans viewed it as a site for colonization and plunder; Napoleon conquered Egypt and brought back artifacts, which made the first translations of the hieroglyphs possible. Accurate information about Egypt's ancient religious practices and beliefs thus slowly became available, but literary and mythic sources continued to be just as important. Americans knew Egypt through the texts of the Old Testament. The imagery of Moses winning freedom from Pharaoh struck a chord as a parallel to the American Revolution, and the association with funerary monuments made Egyptian forms doubly appropriate for cemeteries. The cemetery, enclosed with an Egyptian-style gate, could be read as a metaphor for the soul attaining freedom from earthly bondage, in a similar manner to the Jews escaping slavery in Egypt. Important Egyptian cemetery gates were built in Cambridge, Boston, and New Haven. Egyptian Pylon shapes, derived from ancient temple

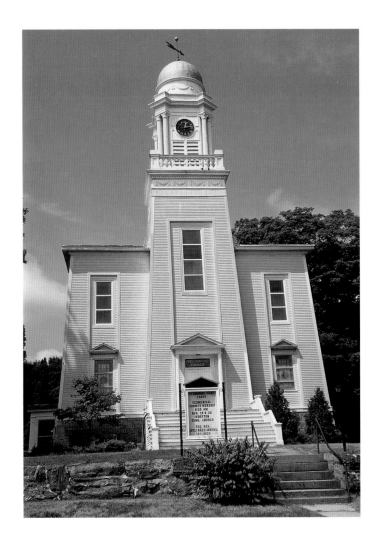

Above: Jeremiah Gladiven: First Baptist Church, 10 Prospect Street, Essex, CT, 1845–46. The central spire was originally conical and taller, but it fell in 1927 and was replaced by the current domed lantern in 1931.

Above right: Minard Lafever: First Presbyterian Church (Old Whaler's Church), Sag Harbor, NY, 1842–43. Side view.

Right: First Presbyterian Church, Sag Harbor, NY. Front view.

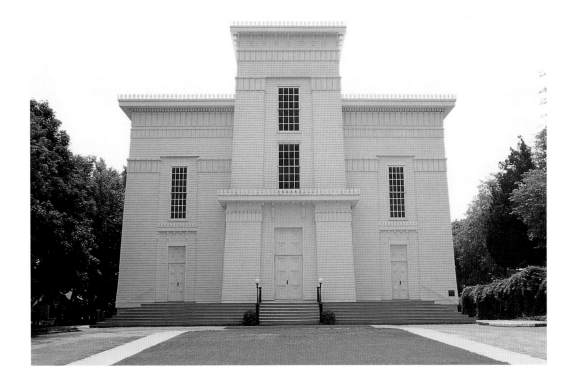

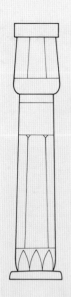

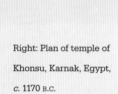

Left: Egyptian lotus bud column. Many of the forms in Egyptian art are derived from natural shapes.

Right: Egyptian lotus flower column.

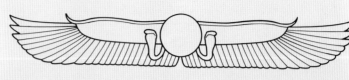

Above: Religious symbolism—the Egyptian winged sun disk; the sun flanked by serpents, carried on vulture wings.

Right: Religious symbolism—the Egyptian Eye of Horus.

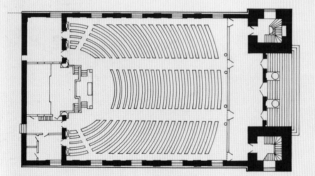

Left: Plan of William Strickland: First (Downtown) Presbyterian Church, Nashville, TN, 1849–51. An auditorium interior.

Right: Plan of temple of Khonsu, Karnak, Egypt, c. 1170 B.C.

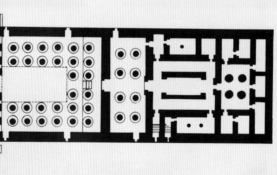

Above: Plan of temple of Horus at Edfu, Egypt.

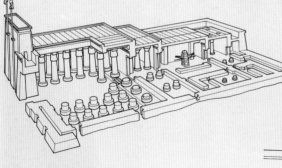

Above: Section of temple of Khonsu, Karnak, Egypt, c. 1170 B.C.

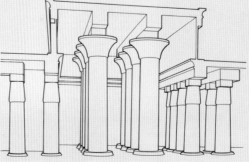

Left: Hypostyle hall, Karnak, Egypt. The hypostyle hall is named for its many columns; the effect created is like that of a massive forest.

Above: William Strickland: First (Downtown) Presbyterian Church, 4815 Franklin Pike, Nashville, TN, 1849–51.

Above: First (Downtown) Presbyterian Church, Nashville, TN. Interior.

Above: Pylon Temple of Horus, Edfu, c. 237 B.C. The pylon is one of the most distinctive Egyptian shapes and was frequently adapted for Egyptian Revival structures.

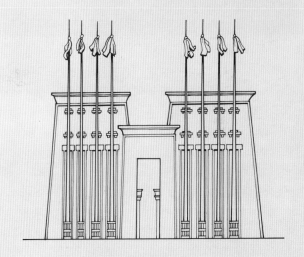

Above: Egyptian pylon temple.

Above: Thomas Ustick Walter: Beth Israel, the Crown Street Synagogue, Philadelphia, PA, 1849. Demolished.

Left: Martin Milmore: Sphinx, Mt. Auburn Cemetery, Cambridge, MA, *c.* 1870.

entrances, were the preferred form for these gates. The Mount Auburn Cemetery Gate in Cambridge was first built in wood painted to look like stone in 1832 and rebuilt in permanent stone in 1842. The designer was Dr. Jacob Bigelow, a founder of the garden cemetery. The Grove Street Cemetery Gate in New Haven (1844–48) was designed by the noted architect Henry Austin, who also designed many Greek- and Italianate-style houses. The winged sun disk is an appropriate symbol of resurrection

borrowed from the ancient Egyptians, clarified with Christian texts such as *The Dead Shall Be Raised*. The faith of Christians and ancient Egyptians overlapped in the hope for a blessed afterlife.

The extraordinary longevity and timeless quality of Egyptian art made it appealing for memorials, especially since it seemed to have a hidden meaning. Freemasons in Europe and America adopted imagery of Egyptian art and architecture, including pyramids and obelisks. The choice

Left: Jacob Bigelow: Mt. Auburn Cemetery Gate, Mt. Auburn Street, Cambridge, MA, 1832/42. Permanent stone version, 1842.

of obelisk shapes for the Washington Monument (1845–85) in Washington, D.C., designed by Robert Mills, and the Bunker Hill Monument (1827–43) by Solomon Willard in Charlestown, Massachusetts, was partly due to the influence of the Freemasons. The pyramid and all-seeing eye on the back of the American dollar is additional evidence of their influence. In the aftermath of the Civil War, the mysterious and devouring sphinx seemed an appropriate symbol for the incomprehensibility of the enormous sacrifices of the troops. The sculptor Martin Milmore carved an impressive sphinx of local granite in 1871 that broods over the graves in Mount Auburn Cemetery, Cambridge, Massachusetts.

A few churches and temples were built in this style. Perhaps the first was designed by William Strickland for the congregation Mikvah Israel in 1825 in Philadelphia. Although this was destroyed, old engravings show that the Egyptian aspects were confined to details such as sloping pylonlike shapes for moldings around the windows and door. The most important Egyptian Revival house of worship still standing is the First Presbyterian Church (Old Whaler's Church), in Sag Harbor, New York (1843–44), designed by Minard Lafever. Lafever was mostly known for his Greek Revival architecture, and this white, wood framed church has affinities with the most stark Greek Revival monuments. The battered (sloping) walls of the entrance, however, are an unmistakable pylon shape. The Sag Harbor

Above: Henry Austin: Grove Street Cemetery entrance, New Haven, CT. 1844–48. Detail.

Right: Henry Austin: Grove Street Cemetery entrance, New Haven, CT. 1844–48.

church seems to have directly inspired Jeremiah Gladiven to build the First Baptist Church in Essex, Connecticut (1845–46), in a similar shape. It, too, is quite eclectic and was originally even more of a hybrid of styles. The central spire was originally conical and taller, but it fell in 1927 and was replaced by the current domed lantern in 1931. The interior shows few overt references to the Egyptian style. A few years later, the noted classical architect William Strickland designed the First (Downtown) Presbyterian Church in Nashville, Tennessee (1849–51), in the Egyptian Revival style. The interior of this church is replete with Egyptian style décor. These churches fortunately still survive, however the early synagogue designed by Thomas Ustick Walter in Philadelphia has been demolished. This was the Beth Israel, or Crown Street, Synagogue built in 1849. The Egyptian Revival was at its height between 1840 and 1860 and then faded. Egyptomania was resurrected in the 1920s, however, and exerted a strong influence on the style of Art Deco.

Above: Isaiah Rogers: Old Granary Burying Ground entrance gate, Tremont Street, Boston, MA, 1840.

Notes

1. Horatio Greenough, *The United States Magazine and Democratic Review* 13 (August 1843): 206–210, quoted in Leland M. Roth, ed., *America Builds: Source Documents in American Architecture and Planning* (New York: Harper & Row, 1983), 78.

2. Benjamin Henry Latrobe, letter to Robert Mills, July 12, 1806; quoted in Roth, *America Builds*, 44.

3. Leopold Eidlitz, "Christian Architecture," *The Crayon*, 5, no. 2 (1858), quoted in James Early, *Romanticism and American Architecture* (New York: A. S. Barnes, 1965), 124.

4. Quoted in Early, *Romanticism and American Architecture*, 119.

Chapter 4

Victorian

Americans have long been torn between the pursuit of materialism on earth and the devotion to spiritual rewards in the afterlife. In 1835, in *Democracy in America*, the French author Alexis de Tocqueville observed that the American passion for the good life had pervaded religious discourse:

> Not only do the Americans follow their religion from interest, but they often place in this world the interest that makes them follow it. In the Middle Ages the clergy spoke of nothing but a future state; they hardly cared to prove that a sincere Christian may be a happy man here below. But the American preachers are constantly referring to the earth, and it is only with great difficulty that they can divert their attention from it. To touch their congregations, they always show them how favorable religious opinions are to freedom and public tranquillity; and it is often difficult to ascertain from their discourses whether the principal object of religion is to procure eternal felicity in the other world or prosperity in this.

Although materialism may have seemed dominant, de Tocqueville also noted the influence of evangelical preachers, who gave over their lives to religion and even created new sects:

> Here and there in the midst of American society you meet with men full of a fanatical and almost wild spiritualism, which hardly exists in Europe. From time to time strange sects arise which endeavor to strike out extraordinary paths to eternal happiness. Religious insanity is very common in the United States.

This chapter will focus on religious architecture just before and after the Civil War, when a rich variety of highly decorated styles flourished. This was an age of both economic and geographic expansion in the U.S. Although styles are still derived from European precedents, increasing signs of innovation appear. A new professionalism emerged in architecture at this time, with the first school of architecture founded at MIT in 1868. Illustrated journals of architecture also appear in the 1880s.

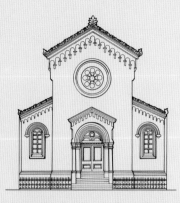

Above: Otto Blesch and Leopold Eidlitz: Shaaray Tefila, Wooster Street Synagogue, New York, NY, 1847.

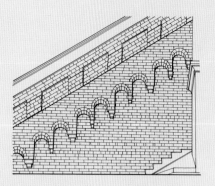

Above: Blind arcades, from Alexander R. Esty: Christ the King Presbyterian Church (Prospect Congregational Church), 99 Prospect St., Cambridge, MA, 1851.

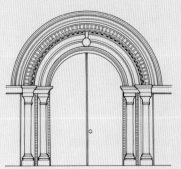

Above: An Early Romanesque portal: Christ the King Presbyterian Church (Prospect Congregational Church), Cambridge, MA.

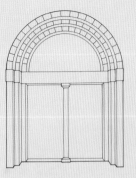

Above: Diagram of a Romanesque portal.

Above: Steeple: Henry Hobson Richardson: Grace Episcopal Church, Medford, MA, 1867-69.

Above left: Steeple: Baptist Church, Ludlow, VT, late nineteenth century.

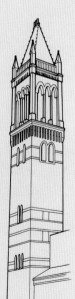

Left: Steeple: Charles A. Cummings and Willard T. Sears: New Old South Church, Copley Square, Boston, MA. 1874–75.

Early Romanesque Revival

Romanesque architecture originally appeared in Europe around the year 1,000. As the name implies, it was itself a revival of aspects of the Roman style of building, particularly featuring round arches. These were frequently gathered together in arcades, or running series of arches, and were often quite narrow. The buildings of this period tended to emphasize the thickness of the wall; windows were narrow. Interiors were somewhat darker than the later Gothic style, although the effect of the light coming through the thick walls was intensified for that very reason. The Romanesque Revival was most active in the United States between about 1844 and 1880. It appeared a bit earlier in Germany, where it was known as the *Rundbogenstil* (round arch style). This early appearance of the medieval style was largely replaced by the Richardsonian Romanesque in the 1870s.

One of the earliest examples of this precocious Romanesque style was Shaaray Tefila, the Wooster Street Synagogue (1847) in New York City, designed by Otto Blesch and Leopold Eidlitz. This synagogue looked very much like a Romanesque church, with a high central nave and lower side aisles. The medieval detailing of the blind arcades and corbels in the gables, superimposed arches at the entrances, and the rose window all reinforce the Romanesque style.

Alexander R. Esty's design for Christ the King Presbyterian Church (the Prospect Congregational Church) in Cambridge, Massachusetts, of 1851 is very

Left: Alexander R. Esty: Christ the King Presbyterian Church (Prospect Congregational Church), 99 Prospect Street, Cambridge, MA, 1851. Front view.

Right: Charles Heard: Old Stone Church, 1380 Ontario Street, Cleveland, OH, c. 1855.

Above: Richard Upjohn: Old St. Paul's Episcopal Church, 233 North Charles Street, Baltimore, MD, 1854–56.

Above: Joseph Reidl: Church of the Assumption, St. Paul, MN, 1870–74. Side view.

Above: Alexander R. Esty: Christ the King Presbyterian Church (Prospect Congregational Church), Cambridge, MA, 1851. Detail.

Above: George Keller: Temple Beth Israel, 21 Charter Oak Avenue, Hartford, CT, 1876. High Victorian eclectic/ Romanesque.

Above: John Notman: Holy Trinity, 1904 Walnut Street, Philadelphia, PA, 1856–59.

Above: Joseph Reidl: Church of the Assumption, 51 West Seventh Street, St. Paul, MN, 1870–74. Front view.

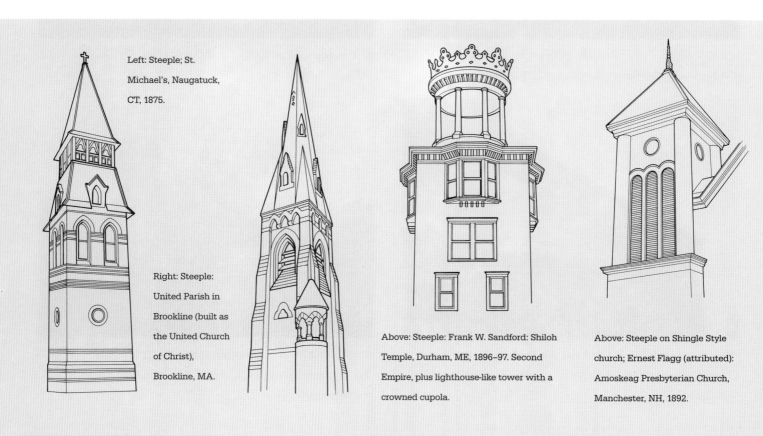

Left: Steeple; St. Michael's, Naugatuck, CT, 1875.

Right: Steeple: United Parish in Brookline (built as the United Church of Christ), Brookline, MA.

Above: Steeple: Frank W. Sandford: Shiloh Temple, Durham, ME, 1896–97. Second Empire, plus lighthouse-like tower with a crowned cupola.

Above: Steeple on Shingle Style church; Ernest Flagg (attributed): Amoskeag Presbyterian Church, Manchester, NH, 1892.

similar to the Wooster Street synagogue. This brick church also features a tall central section and similar blind arcades, corbels, and rounded arches.

Richard Upjohn explored the simpler forms of Romanesque architecture in Old St. Paul's Episcopal Church in Baltimore, Maryland, built between 1854 and 1856. The high gabled roof of this brick church is preceded by a triple-arched entrance porch and flanked by asymmetrical square towers. The taller one on the left is no higher than the roof gable and the shorter one is just slightly higher than the porch. The blind arcades and recesses, round arches, and rose window are all Romanesque.

An even more accurate rendition of the Romanesque style is found at the Church of the Holy Trinity (1856–59) in Philadelphia, designed by John Notman (1810–65). Notman was born in Edinburgh, Scotland, and emigrated to Philadelphia in 1831. Set in elegant Rittenhouse Square, the church displays picturesque asymmetry with a tall tower inspired by the eleventh-century Abbaye-aux-Hommes in Caen, France. The rector of this church was the Reverend Phillips Brooks, who later led the congregation of Trinity Church in Boston, when it erected a landmark Romanesque church by Henry Hobson Richardson in the 1870s.

The records of Hartford, Connecticut, show that Jews were living there as early as 1659. Hartford's first synagogue did not appear until the mid-nineteenth century, however. The 1876 Temple Beth Israel was built by George Keller in Romanesque Revival style, with round arches and twin towers on the façade. Keller was an Irish-born architect. Romanesque was also being used for Jewish temples in Europe as well as America at this time, perhaps because the Gothic Revival was so closely associated with Christianity.

Renaissance Revival

The Renaissance Revival flourished from about 1845 to 1890; the basilica plans of Early Italian Renaissance and Early Christian churches were revived by architects seeking a simple yet not overly austere style rooted in the past.

One of the grandest High Renaissance–style churches in America is the Cathedral of Sts. Peter & Paul in Philadelphia. It is reminiscent of Palladio's S. Giorgio Maggiore in Venice, with its tall temple front covering the nave, while the lower section for the side aisles slides right

Above: LeBrun & Notman: Cathedral of Sts. Peter & Paul, Eighteenth and Race Streets, Philadelphia, PA, 1846–64.

Above: Patrick C. Keely: Immaculate Conception Church, Harrison Avenue, Boston, MA, 1858–61.

Above: Church of the Sacred Heart, 1321 Centre Street, Newton, MA, 1891–99.

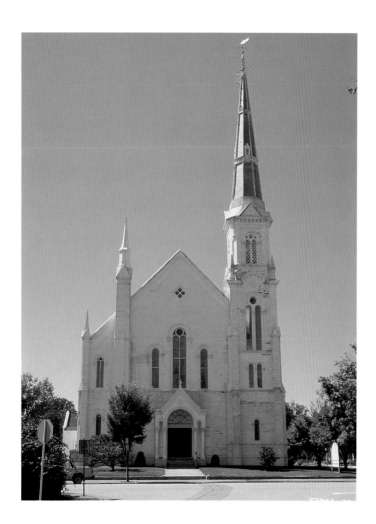

Left: First Baptist Church, 8 Lafayette Street, Wakefield, MA, 1872. Renaissance details combine with Gothic forms in this eclectic church.

Below left: McKim, Mead & White: Judson Memorial Church, Washington Square South, New York, NY, 1888–93.

Below: Judson Memorial Church, Washington Square South, New York, NY. Detail of classical doorway.

Above: Schickel & Ditmars: Church of St. Ignatius of Loyola, (Roman Catholic), 980 Park Avenue, New York, NY, 1895–1900.

behind the monumental columns. There is a tall dome over the central crossing. The church was designed by Napoleon LeBrun & John Notman, and built between 1846 and 1864 by the Irish Catholic community.

In Boston, Patrick C. Keely designed the Immaculate Conception Church; it was built between 1858 and 1861 by the Jesuit order in a Renaissance Revival style. The church replaced a short-lived Gothic Revival style building by Gridley J. F. Bryant, which was built in 1843–45, but burned down in 1848. The new church is 208 feet long by seventy feet wide; it is a long rectangular box. The entrance has a small projecting center pavilion with a large Palladian window in the center. On the inside, the nave is covered by a long barrel vault, ornamented by rich plasterwork. The side aisles are separated by Ionic arcades. The arch forms are echoed in tall round-arched windows on the exterior walls.

At times Renaissance ornament is applied to what is basically a typical Gothic church. The First Baptist Church (1872) in Wakefield, Massachusetts, looks at first glance just like many other Gothic churches with one tower to the right side, until one notices the round arches of the windows and the Renaissance columns flanking the entrance, and the classical pediments included in the tower itself. American eclecticism frequently combined styles in this manner.

Other churches strove for greater unity of style. The Church of the Sacred Heart in Newton, Massachusetts, was built in 1891–99 with no medieval holdovers. The twin-towered façade and the triple-arched entryway make a simple, yet pleasing composition.

Renaissance-style synagogues were also built; one example is Kenesseth Israel in Philadelphia, designed by Louis C. Hickman and Oscar Frotches in 1892.

Early Italian Renaissance features abound at McKim, Mead & White's Judson Memorial Church in Washington Square South, New York City, built 1888–93. The church was built by Dr. Edward Judson to commemorate his father, Adoniram Judson. Located in a wealthy neighborhood, it was intended to serve lower Manhattan's burgeoning immigrant classes as well as the wealthy. It is a rectangular auditorium church, with a separate 165-foot-tall campanile. The designers may have used Italian churches as models in an attempt to lure immigrant worshipers. As an example of the American Renaissance, the church contains seventeen large stained glass windows by John Lafarge and sculpture by Augustus Saint-Gaudens. The visual arts are thus united with the architecture.

The Church of St. Ignatius of Loyola (Roman Catholic) in New York City was built by Schickel & Ditmars in

Above: Saint Francis de Sales (Roman Catholic), 135 East Ninety-sixth Street, between Park and Lexington Avenues, New York, NY, 1890s.

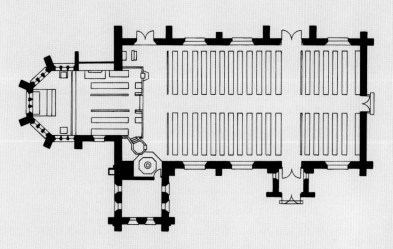

Above: Henry Hobson Richardson: Plan of Grace Episcopal Church, Medford, MA, 1867–69.

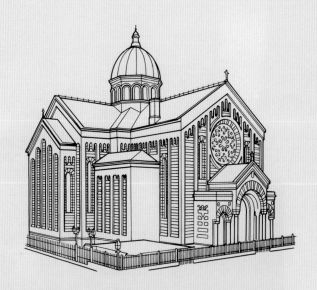

Above: Jacob Wrey Mould: All Soul's Unitarian Church, NY, 1853–55. An eclectic combination of Byzantine, Venetian, and Romanesque features. The first Ruskinian building in the U.S.

1895–1900 in the style of Italian Renaissance churches by Vignola. The façade is rather flat, but with a central pediment supported by two stories of paired pilasters.

Paired columns support the pediment of Saint Francis de Sales (Roman Catholic) in New York City. The church, built in the 1890s, is named for a late-sixteenth-century priest, and the Renaissance style seems fitting.

High Victorian Gothic

High Victorian Gothic was an ornate and vibrant style that flourished between about 1855 and 1880. The style originated in England and was strongly influenced by British architectural examples and the writings of John Ruskin.

Ruskin had become the chief advocate of Gothic architecture after Pugin; his books *The Seven Lamps of Architecture* (1849) and *The Stones of Venice* (1852–53) were highly influential in their arguments for the moral and aesthetic superiority of Gothic. Although the Oxford Museum is the only major architectural project he was directly involved with, the High Victorian Gothic style is often called Ruskinian Gothic. *The Seven Lamps of Architecture* included adjurations to the Lamp of Obedience, which prescribed revival of earlier styles, and the Lamp of Memory, which highlighted the role of architecture as the chief repository of cultural memory. In *The Stones of Venice*, Ruskin defined the nature of the Gothic as:

1. Savageness, 2. Changefulness, 3. Naturalism, 4. Grotesqueness, 5. Rigidity, 6. Redundance.

The High Victorian Gothic differed from the earlier Gothic Revival in being less bound to archaeological accuracy; the Gothic forms were adapted to new uses and new compositions. Ruskin called for freedom in applying the Gothic style:

> Do not be afraid of incongruities—do not think of unities of effect. Introduce your Gothic line by line and stone by stone; never mind mixing it with our present architecture; your existing houses will be none the worse for having little bits of better work fitted to them; build a porch or point a window, if you can do nothing else; and remember that it is the glory of Gothic architecture that it can do *anything*.[1]

After the strict discipline of the ecclesiological Gothic Revival, this modern Gothic was liberating.

One of the first High Victorian Gothic churches was William Butterfield's All Saints Margaret Street (1849–59) in London. Although clearly Gothic, it is eclectic and does not copy a single period of medieval design. It was known as modern Gothic in its time. This urban church featured bold patterns of red brick and black tar-dipped brick. The interior was richly colored as well, with much stained glass and bold patterns of

Above: Charles A. Cummings and Willard T. Sears: New Old South Church, Copley Square, Boston, MA, 1874–75.

Above: Charles A. Cummings and Willard T. Sears: New Old South Church, Boston, MA, 1874–75. Aerial view.

gold tracery and paintings set against the red walls.

One of the first architects to bring this new style to America was Jacob Wrey Mould (1825–86). His All Souls Unitarian Church (1853–55) in New York City was an eclectic combination of Byzantine, Venetian, and Romanesque features. Mould was an English-born architect and former pupil of Owen Jones, whose *Grammar of Ornament* of 1856 was a major source for all architects of

the second half of the nineteenth century. This was the first Ruskinian building in the U.S. It was a cruciform plan building with a small dome over the crossing; the most distinctive feature was the bold striped pattern of alternating courses of dark and light stone, which continue up even under the narrow, blind arcades at the gables.

Leopold Eidlitz (1823–1908) was born in Prague and emigrated in 1843 to the United States where he first

Left: Charles A. Cummings and Willard T. Sears: New Old South Church, Boston, MA, 1874–75. Detail of tower.

Above: William Ware and Henry Van Brunt: First Church, Boston, MA, 1868.

Above: William Ware and Henry Van Brunt: First Church, Boston, MA, 1868. Restored by Paul Rudolph, 1971.

Left: St. Michael's, 210 Church Street, Naugatuck, CT, 1875.

Right: Comparison: William Butterfield: All Saints Margaret Street, London, England, 1849.

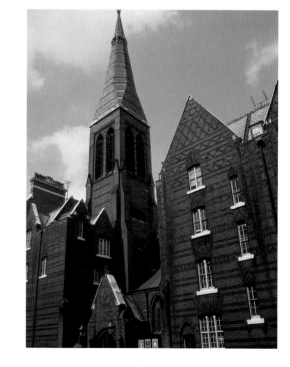

Above: William Ware & Henry Van Brunt: St. Stephen's Episcopal Church, 74 South Common Street, Lynn, MA, 1881.

Above: William Ware & Henry Van Brunt: St. Stephen's Episcopal Church, Lynn, MA, 1881.

worked for Richard Upjohn as a draftsman. He struggled to find a resolution between the conflicting demands of tradition and authentic expression of religious and cultural ideals. In 1881, he wrote:

> The confessional, the mass, the saints, and all the methods of Catholic worship pertaining to these, are examples of material expressions of ideas as created in the past. They must continue to command our respect, and will continue to live in Christian poetry. We have discarded them. We should now prove to the world that we are capable of replacing them with other and better expressions of religious ideas. [2]

Eidlitz's ecclesiastical designs include the Church of the Holy Trinity in New York City of 1873 and his Temple Emanu-El (1866–68, designed with Henry Fernbach) was a key example of Victorian synagogue architecture.

One of the most vibrant of High Victorian Gothic church designs is the New Old South Church in Copley Square, Boston, built in 1874–75 by the architects Charles A. Cummings and Willard T. Sears. The New Old South Church was built when the congregation of the Old South Church migrated to the new and fashionable Back Bay district of Boston. It was built on the new landfill at Copley Square, helping define this square as the finest ensemble of Victorian design in America, along with the High Victorian Gothic Museum of Fine Arts and H. H. Richardson's Romanesque Trinity Church. The church measures 200 by ninety feet, and holds up to 900 people. The plan of the church is a short-armed cross, with a tall tower asymmetrically placed near the entrance. This is an eclectic design, with polychromy in the stonework and a crossing tower reminiscent of Venetian architecture. The Lamp of Life is observed with naturalistic carvings of foliage and animals near the street level. The interior is colored with deep red walls, and the open ceiling trusses are stained dark. Stained glass adds to the colorism. Because the filled soil was unstable, the tower had to be taken down and rebuilt around 1930, as it had started to lean to an alarming degree.

The First Church in Boston was built by William Ware and Henry Van Brunt in 1868. It was a fine example of High Victorian Gothic, which was devastated by fire in 1968. The shell of the façade and steeple were preserved, braced by visible steel beams when the church was rebuilt by Paul Rudolph in 1971. Ware and Van Brunt were among the most accomplished architects in Boston and founded

Above: Rose window from Hartwell & Richardson: First Baptist Church, Cambridge, MA, 1881.

Above: Rose window from United Parish in Brookline (built as the United Church of Christ), Brookline, MA.

Above: Rose Window; Henry Fernbach: Central Synagogue, New York, NY, 1872. Moorish-Islamic Revival.

Above: Rose Window; Schneider & Herter: Park East Synagogue, 163 East Sixty-seventh Street, New York, NY, 1890.

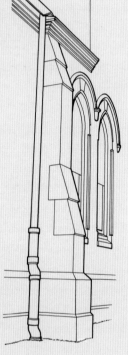

Left: Buttress from Hartwell & Richardson: First Baptist Church, Cambridge, MA, 1881.

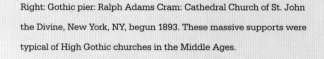

Right: Gothic pier: Ralph Adams Cram: Cathedral Church of St. John the Divine, New York, NY, begun 1893. These massive supports were typical of High Gothic churches in the Middle Ages.

Above: Simple pier footprint.

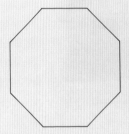

Above: Simple pier footprint; an octagonal shape.

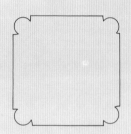

Above: Compound pier footprint; slender colonnettes engaged at the corners.

Above: Compound pier footprint: colonnettes engaged at the corner.

Above: Compound pier footprint; large and small colonnettes alternate.

Above: Compound pier footprint: Large colonnettes alternate with doubled small ones.

Above: Gothic capital from United Parish in Brookline (built as the United Church of Christ), Brookline, MA. Built in High Victorian Gothic style in 1873, destroyed by fire 1931, and rebuilt 1933.

Below: Cross section of a Gothic rib.

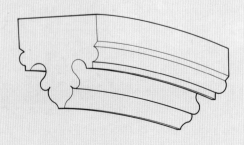

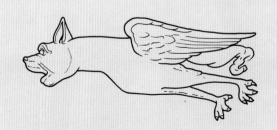

Left: Gargoyle, a colorful medieval feature revived in late nineteenth- and early twentieth-century American Gothic churches.

Above: United Parish in Brookline (built as the United Church of Christ), 210 Harvard Street, Brookline, MA. Built in High Victorian Gothic style in 1873; destroyed by fire 1931, and rebuilt 1933. Side view.

Above: Frank Furness: First Unitarian Church, 2125 Chestnut Street, Philadelphia, PA, 1883–86.

Above: United Parish in Brookline (built as the United Church of Christ), Brookline, MA. Detail of tower.

the MIT School of Architecture in 1868. Their design for St. Stephen's Episcopal Church (1881) in Lynn, Massachusetts, is an impressive composition with an irregular silhouette. It is constructed of red granite, with facings of red brick and trimmed with Nova Scotia freestone on the plan of a Latin cross. The nave and transepts are forty feet wide, with open timber trusses supporting the roof. The tower is 130 feet high, with a gable roof instead of a spire at the top.

The church of St. Michael's in Naugatuck, Connecticut,

Above: United Parish in Brookline (built as the United Church of Christ), Brookline, MA. Detail.

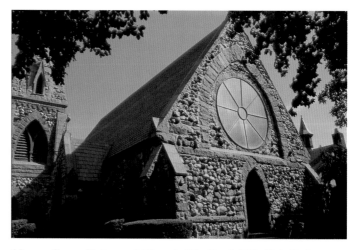

Above: Grace Episcopal Church, Medford, MA. Detail of glacial boulders.

Above: Henry Hobson Richardson: Grace Episcopal Church, 160 High Street, Medford, MA, 1867–69.

in 1933. This stone church embodies all of John Ruskin's *Seven Lamps of Architecture*, with its historic style, rough surface texture, and irregular and powerful forms.

Although Henry Hobson Richardson is more well known for his later Romanesque works, his first churches in the 1860s were in a Victorian Gothic mode. Grace Episcopal Church (1867–69) in Medford, Massachusetts, is a powerful composition. The exterior is largely monochromatic. His use of the large glacial boulders is unusual, however, and gives a rugged feeling to the church. He would use these boulders again in later houses.

*

was built in 1875 in a High Victorian Gothic style that owes much to Ruskin and William Butterfield. The church uses red and black bricks for permanent polychromy and has a powerful irregular silhouette, dominated by an asymmetrical corner tower and a steeply pitched gable.

The highly original architect Frank Furness designed the First Unitarian Church in Philadelphia. It was built between 1883 and 1886. His father, the Reverend William H. Furness was the minister here. Although altered, the exterior has strong forms. It is built on a cruciform plan, with a gabled nave and wide entrance porch with low, flattened arches. The interior has an elaborate hammerbeam ceiling.

The United Parish church in Brookline, Massachusetts (built as the United Church of Christ), has a dramatic High Victorian Gothic style, despite later remodeling. Originally built in 1873, it was destroyed by fire in 1931 and rebuilt

High Victorian Gothic was adapted for synagogue architecture as well. One of the earliest was Henry Fernbach's design for Shaaray Tefila in New York City of 1869. This was an eclectic temple, with pointed arch windows and polychromy. The center pavilion featured two arcades of three rampant arches on the first and second floors. The roof of this center section was a high-profile dome, ornamented with stars. A Star of David topped the lantern.

The Rodef Shalom Synagogue (1869–71) in Philadelphia was a new building for America's oldest Ashkenazic congregation, which was organized in 1795. (*Ashkenazic* is a term used to refer to Jews from France, Germany, and Eastern Europe, as opposed to the Sephardim, who came from Spain, Portugal, and the Middle East.) This was also a very eclectic building, with a Romanesque plan and elevation, Gothic buttresses, and

Moorish/Islamic horseshoe arches and multifoil banding around the upper windows. The bulbous dome of the asymmetrical corner tower is also derived from Moorish precedent. The interior featured both Islamic decoration and an English hammer-beam roof. It was designed by the firm of Fraser, Furness and Hewitt. Frank Furness (1839–1912) was a leading figure in the High Victorian Gothic style, and one of the most original architects of the era. This distinctive synagogue was demolished in 1927.

Richardsonian Romanesque

The Richardsonian Romanesque style, which flourished between about 1870 and 1900 is a paradox. Clearly derived from European precedents, it is generally regarded as one of the most original American styles and was viewed in its own day as a new contribution to world architecture. The style is named for the most original architect of the period, Henry Hobson Richardson (1838–86), who adapted the heavy stone construction of French and Spanish Romanesque architecture to new purposes and modernized forms. He was born in Priestley Plantation, Louisiana, and educated at Harvard. As there were still no architecture schools in America, he went to Paris to study at the Ecole des Beaux-Arts after graduating from Harvard. The Civil War broke out while he was in Europe, so he extended his stay abroad and worked with Henri Labrouste. The leading contemporary styles in France were the Second Empire

Above: Henry Hobson Richardson: Brattle Square Church, Commonwealth Avenue at Clarendon Street, Boston, MA, 1869–73. Side view.

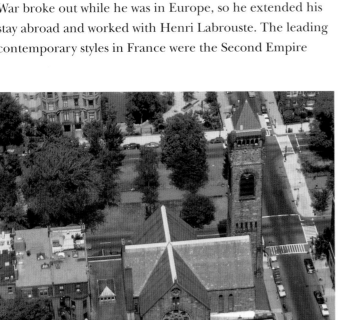

Above: H. H. Richardson: Brattle Square Church, Boston, MA, 1869–73. Aerial view.

Above: H. H. Richardson: Brattle Square Church, Boston, MA, 1869–73. Detail of tower, with sculptures by Frédéric Bartholdi, who also created the Statue of Liberty.

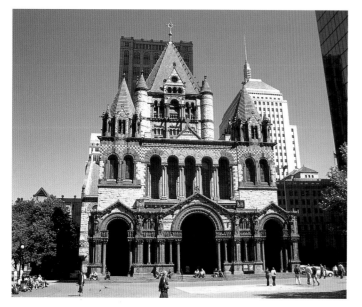

Above: H. H. Richardson: Trinity Church, Copley Square, Boston, MA, 1872–77.

Above: Photo of Richardson's Trinity Church, *c.* 1880. Porch has not yet been added.

Above: H. H. Richardson: Trinity Church, Boston, MA, 1872–77. Detail of tower.

Baroque and an academic classicism, but he was drawn into other modes of expression. His first major churches upon resuming his career in America were done in a High Victorian Gothic style, as seen at Grace Church in Medford, Massachusetts (1869). The influence of John Ruskin's *Seven Lamps of Architecture* and the earlier Gothic Revival were still strong.

In 1870, Richardson won the commission for the Brattle Square Church (now First Baptist Church) in Boston (1870–72). This was his first essay in a new blend of French Romanesque forms, updated for the new century. The church was built in the newly filled Back Bay section of Boston and featured a tall bell tower beside a cross-shaped

Above: Trinity Church, Boston, MA. Interior.

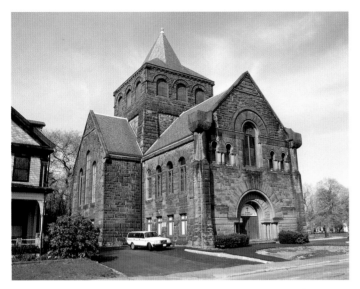

Above: H. H. Richardson: Immanuel Baptist Church, 187 Church Street, Newton Center, MA, 1885.

church with rather short transepts. He used the warm brownstone and Roxbury puddingstone for his materials, and handled the Romanesque details with great skill. The rose window with its thick tracery rings with authenticity. A highlight of the tower is the four large sculptures of the sacraments, executed by the French sculptor Frédéric Bartholdi, who was also the sculptor of the Statue of Liberty. These panels are flanked by four trumpet-playing angels at the four corners of the tower. Irreverent Bostonians quickly nicknamed this the "Church of the Holy Bean Blowers" because it looked as if the angels were hold-

ing pea-shooters and attempting to pick off pedestrians walking on the Commonwealth Avenue mall below.

The success of the Brattle Square Church helped Richardson win his next commission, which was to become his major work: Trinity Church in nearby Copley Square. A competition was held for a new building for this church, and Richardson won out over many competitors. He proposed a massive Romanesque church for this new square. As with the earlier project, he used the warm brown local stones, as well as Quincy granite. Although his works are one of the reasons the 1870s and 1880s are called the "Brown Decades," there is actually quite a bit of color in his architecture. The zigzag patterns and alternating checkerboards of different color stone remind one that Richardson is still heeding Ruskin's call for a vibrant, polychromatic architecture. In fact, Trinity Church is an excellent illustration of all of Ruskin's Seven Lamps: Life, Power, Beauty, Sacrifice, Truth, Memory, Obedience.

Since the church is built upon spongy landfill in the former Back Bay of the Charles River, the building committee was nervous about the weight of his original tower design and encouraged him to reduce the height forty feet. The new tower design was based upon the central tower of the Old Cathedral in Salamanca, a leading example of Spanish Romanesque. White and Charles McKim were working as assistants in Richardson's office at this point. They would later form one of the most successful firms in American architecture.

Trinity Church was also in some sense the beginning of

Left: H. H. Richardson: Trinity Church, Boston, MA, 1872–77. Detail of sculpture.

Right: John Lyman Faxon: First Baptist Church, 848 Beacon Street, Newton, MA, 1888. This church is frequently mistaken for one of Richardson's own works.

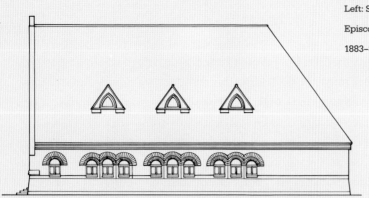

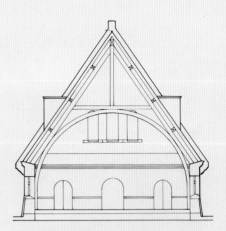

Left: Side elevation of Emmanuel Episcopal Church, Pittsburgh, PA, 1883–86.

Right: Section drawing of Emmanuel Episcopal Church, Pittsburgh, PA.

Right: Plan of Emmanuel Episcopal Church, Pittsburgh, PA.

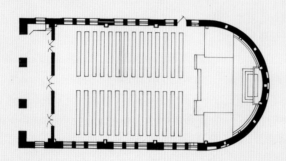

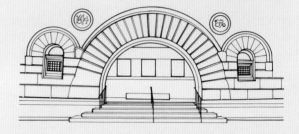

Above: Richardsonian arch: This massive arch form, perhaps inspired by Syrian early Christian designs, was a hallmark of the Richardsonian Romanesque. This example is from a follower of Richardson. H. H. Hartwell & W. C. Richardson: First Parish Congregational Church, One Church Street, Wakefield, MA, 1890.

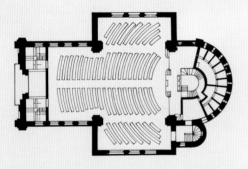

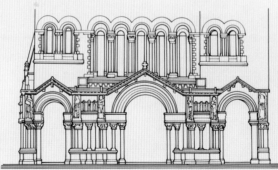

Above: Plan of Henry Hobson Richardson: Immanuel Baptist Church, 187 Church Street, Newton Center, MA, 1885.

Left: Romanesque arcades: The Romanesque style is characterized by heavier, narrower arches than the succeeding Renaissance period. H. H. Richardson: Trinity Church, Boston, MA, 1872–77.

Left: Dwarf columns, found in Richardsonian Romanesque buildings.

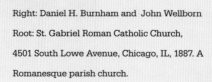

Right: Daniel H. Burnham and John Wellborn Root: St. Gabriel Roman Catholic Church, 4501 South Lowe Avenue, Chicago, IL, 1887. A Romanesque parish church.

the American Renaissance, for the project brought together architects, sculptors, painters, and stained glass artists to create a unified project for the first time in American architecture. Richardson's friend John Lafarge was given the task of directing the interior decoration, and he designed a richly coloristic interior, with warm red murals painted in the encaustic technique of the ancient Romans, which used hot wax to seal the color on the wall, making the paintings virtually permanent. He also designed stained glass windows, which enriched the interior and boosted that art in this country. A masterful window of King Solomon by the British firm of William Morris and Company, designed by Sir Edward Burne-Jones, also added to the stature of the decorations at Trinity.

Part of the innovation of Trinity Church stemmed from the overall impression of unity created by the architect. Whereas the previous High Victorian Gothic sometimes dissipated its effect in too much variety, Richardson continually tied the design together with common forms and colors and harmonious rhythms. His interior volumes are also very unified; the space flows and is as uninterrupted as possible.

The plan of Trinity Church is a Greek cross, with a separate chapel (now the parish house) and small cloister garden on the left side. The width of the church is 121 feet and the length is 160 feet. The tower is forty-six feet square on the inside. The entrance façade was originally flat and modeled after the Romanesque church of St. Trophime in Arles, France. After Richardson's death, his successor firm of Shepley, Rutan and Coolidge added a projecting porch in 1894–97.

Trinity Church was voted the best building in America by a poll of the readers of *The American Architect and Building News* in 1885 and is still regarded as one of the finest works of American architecture. Richardson's other church designs are less famous, but his Emmanuel Episcopal Church in Pittsburgh (1883–86) shows a striking unity in the horizontal composition. Another late work, the Immanuel Baptist Church in Newton Center, Massachusetts (1885), was only completed after his death and is not fully worked out. Richardson died in 1886 at age forty-eight of Bright's Disease, a kidney disorder.

Richardson's Romanesque style was repeatedly copied; adaptable to any building type, it quickly replaced the fussier Second Empire Baroque and High Victorian Gothic styles. One unusual example is the large urban Spiritualist

Above: Henry M. Congdon: St. James Church, 1991 Massachusetts Avenue, Cambridge, MA, 1888. Front view.

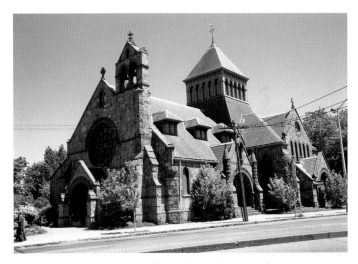

Above: St. James Church, 1991 Massachusetts Avenue, Cambridge, MA. Side view.

Above: H. H. Hartwell & W. C. Richardson: First Parish Congregational Church, One Church Street, Wakefield, MA, 1890; rebuilt after fire 1912.

Above: Franklin Welch, Chapel, Christian Science Center, Boston, MA, 1894. At left is the Mother Church by Charles Brigham & S. Beman; with Brigham, Coveney & Bisbee, 1906.

Above: Warren H. Hayes: Central Presbyterian Church, 500 Cedar Street, St. Paul, MN, 1889. Side view.

Temple in Boston (1884–85), designed by H. H. Hartwell & W. C. Richardson. Boston was a center of Spiritualist organizations in the late nineteenth century. This temple was built for Marcelleus J. Ayer, founder of the Temple of the Working Union of Progressive Spiritualists. The square, blocky building looks much like a commercial office building, although it had an auditorium inside it. The stonework is a mix of brownstone and granite, resembling the colors and textures used by Richardson. The broad arch over the

Above: H. H. Hartwell & W. C. Richardson: Spiritualist Temple, Exeter Street, Boston, MA, 1884–85. Built for Marcelleus J. Ayer, founder of the Temple of the Working Union of Progressive Spiritualists. Converted to a theater in 1913 by Clarence H. Blackall and later converted to commercial space.

entrance also recalls Richardson's designs. The temple was converted to a theater in 1913 by Clarence H. Blackall and ultimately transformed into commercial space.

Some of the imitators of Richardson are so good that their works are often mistaken for his own. The First Baptist Church in Newton, Massachusetts (1888), by local architect John Lyman Faxon is frequently mistaken for a true Richardson building. There are many other examples in his style.

After Richardson's death in 1886, monochromatic Romanesque churches become more common. The First Parish Congregational Church (1890) in Wakefield, Massachusetts, is an example. It was designed by H. H. Hartwell & W. C. Richardson, the same architects who built the Spiritualist Temple just six years earlier. The thick masonry walls use only two shades of gray, creating an image of solidity and repose. The deep Richardsonian arch over the entrance reveals its affiliation with the style of the earlier architect. The church was rebuilt after a serious fire in 1912.

The original chapel for the First Church of Christ, Scientist, was built in Boston in a monochromatic Romanesque style by Franklin Welch (1852–1930) in 1894. The triangular plan church is now just part of a much larger complex. The adjoining classical Mother Church (1906) is by Charles Brigham & S. Beman, with the firm Brigham, Coveney & Bisbee. The Christian Science church was founded by Mary Baker Eddy (1821–1910), who discovered that the healing power of prayer allowed her to escape

ROMANESQUE ORNAMENTAL PATTERNS USED IN ARCHES

Above: Romanesque ornamental patterns.

Left: Stanford White: Lovely Lane United Methodist Church, 2700 St. Paul Street, Baltimore, MD, 1882–87. A very archaic church, modeled on several early Italian churches in Ravenna.

Right: Episcopal Cathedral, 3723 Chestnut Street, Philadelphia, PA, 1906.

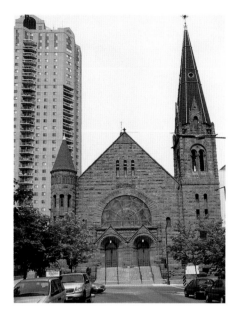

Above: Warren H. Hayes: Central Presbyterian Church, 500 Cedar Street, St. Paul, MN, 1889.

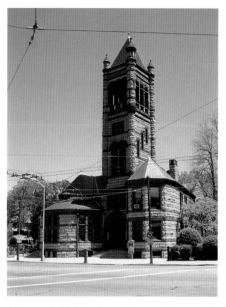

Above: A. P. Cutting: Harvard Epworth Methodist Church, 1551 Massachusetts Avenue, Cambridge, MA, 1891.

Above: Frederick G. Corser: Church of St. Stephen (Catholic), 2201 Clinton Avenue S., Minneapolis, MN, 1889.

her life as an invalid. Her book *Science and Health with Key to the Scriptures* was published in 1879. The new group attracted many followers and built this first, almost fortresslike chapel in 1894 on a triangular plot of land. Although it held 1,000 worshipers, a new church was built a decade later; this classical church will be discussed in the next chapter.

A massive square corner tower with thin Romanesque windows and a conical top dominates the Lovely Lane United Methodist Church in Baltimore, Maryland. Even the stone looks old. It was designed by Stanford White and built between 1882 and 1887. Exterior and interior elements are derived from several Italian churches, including several in Ravenna, Italy. The main body of the church is a square auditorium surmounted by a large dome. A tall, square tower with a broad brick wall pierced only by tiny slit windows stands on the corner; it is capped with a conical roof. The square tower is similar to that of a twelfth-century church near Ravenna. The dome of this very eclectic church is modeled on that of Hagia Sophia in Istanbul.

Daniel H. Burnham & John Wellborn Root were pioneers of the Chicago School and creators of some of the first skyscrapers. For the small Roman Catholic parish church of St. Gabriel in Chicago, however, they used the Romanesque style. The façade is covered by a large

sweeping gable, flanked on the right side by a 160-foot-tall tower with slender round turrets on each corner. A simple rose window fills the center of the façade. Originally built in 1887, the church has been greatly altered. A portico was added in 1914, and the tower was shortened in 1944; the interior has also been much changed.

Although now demolished, the Temple Israel in St. Louis, Missouri, of 1888 was a fine example of the Romanesque style. The exterior walls of rusticated granite and brownstone had a rich texture and warm color. A tall central hall was flanked by side aisles and preceded by an entrance porch. Small turrets swelled out from the corners of the façade and at the edges of an intersecting gable at the rear of the temple. The interior featured an ornate hammer-beam ceiling. Illumination was provided by lunette windows in the clerestory.

Another example of the later Romanesque style still stands in St. Paul, Minnesota: the Central Presbyterian Church (1889), designed by Warren H. Hayes. It is built of brownstone and has a rather flat façade with a tall, asymmetrical tower on the right side of the façade and a smaller tower at the left. The nearly square nave is laid out in the diagonal Akron Plan, with an elevated platform for preaching placed in the corner of the audience room and seating in a circular pattern. This plan, developed in Akron, Ohio, in 1868, provides good acoustics and sight lines. It became very popular for Protestant churches in the Midwest and West.

*

Certain styles more commonly associated with residential architecture were also used for churches, such as the Second Empire Baroque and Stick Style.

The Second Empire Baroque flourished between 1860 and 1880 in America. This richly ornate style, derived from French models, was the main competitor for stylistic dominance in public buildings and housing in the third quarter of the century. It is called the Second Empire Baroque because it was a Baroque Revival style that appeared during the reign of Napoleon III in France, which was known as the Second Empire (1851–70). The expansion of the

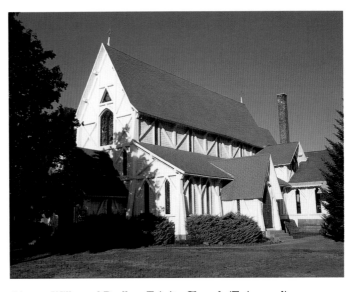

Above: Wills and Dudley: Trinity Church (Episcopal), 120 Broad Street at Chapel, Claremont, NH, 1852–53. An outstanding example of the Stick Style, which reveals its origins in the Gothic Revival.

Above: Frank W. Sandford: Shiloh Temple, Durham, ME, 1896–97. A Second Empire chapel, with mansard roofs and a lighthouse-like tower. Built for an evangelistic Protestant denomination called the Kingdom.

Louvre in Paris at this time contributed enormously to the prestige of this style. One of its hallmark features is the use of Mansard roofs, with their distinctive profile. The Second Empire, or Mansard, style was flexible and could be built on a very large and ornate scale in stone or on a much smaller cottagelike scale using wood, making it possible for different classes to utilize it. It was, however, seldom used for churches. A rare example is the Shiloh Temple (1896–97) in Durham, Maine, built by Frank Weston Sandford (1862–1948). It was constructed for a small Protestant sect known as the Kingdom. The charismatic Sandford, an ordained Baptist minister, founded this group after being convinced that he was receiving divine revelations. The main body of the temple is a basically a very large Second Empire-style house or inn, four stories high, with a seven-story-tall central tower. The cupola was known as the Jerusalem Turret, and members of the group prayed twenty-fours hours a day in a small room at the top, foreshadowing the Prayer Tower of Oral Roberts later in Tulsa. The tower has an ornate crown of metal and an inscription over the door proclaiming "The Truth." Although a complex of larger buildings, including over 500 rooms, was later attached to the original church, the group collapsed in the twentieth century after some failed missionary expeditions to Africa and Greenland. The other buildings have all been demolished and only the first chapel remains.

Left: Stick Style framing: Wills and Dudley: Trinity Church (Episcopal), Claremont, NH, 1852–53. The timber frame is on the exterior of the church.

Right: Stick Style framing: Trinity Church (Episcopal), Claremont, NH. The timber buttress almost resembles a flying buttress.

Stick Style

The Stick Style is a highly decorated style of wooden architecture, which features angular and rectilinear patterns of boards used as ornament. The passion for ornament and individualism combined with the thriving lumber industry led to the creation of a less common but highly decorated style of wooden architecture known as the Stick Style. Named only when Vincent Scully called attention to it in the 1960s, the Stick Style flourished from about the 1850s to 1890 and featured angular and rectilinear patterns of boards used as ornament on the exterior of the house. It was rarely used for church architecture, but a few examples can be found, such as Trinity Church (Episcopal), Claremont, New Hampshire, 1852–53, by Wills and Dudley. This robustly framed church demonstrates the connection between the Gothic Revival and the Stick Style. The heavy timbers of the wooden frame are exposed on the exterior and serve also as decorative elements. The ornament derives from structure, as it did in the original Gothic style.

All Saints Episcopal Church, Chicago, 1883, is another example of the Stick Style. It was designed by John C. Cochrane. The steep gable roof is joined by a bell tower on the right side. Framing timbers are connected by decorative wooden members. The exterior is covered with a mix of wooden shingles and clapboards. The interior is notable for its large exposed wooden trusses.

Shingle Style

The Shingle Style flourished between about 1875 and 1900. Partly inspired by seventeenth-century colonial architecture, this style features a greater simplicity and unity than other styles of this period. The chief distinguishing feature is a continuous skin of wooden shingles for roof (now generally replaced by composition roofing) and wall surfaces. The Unity Chapel in Spring Green, Wisconsin, by J. Lyman Silsbee and Frank Lloyd Wright in 1886 is one example. This is perhaps the earliest architectural work of the young Frank Lloyd Wright, who assisted Silsbee on the chapel.

Another early example of the style is St. Paul's Episcopal Church, Newton Highlands, Massachusetts, built in 1883. The side view shows the broad surface of the roof gable barely broken by the small triangular dormer and the swelling of the emerging cupola. The front view shows a series of triangular shapes harmonizing with the overall roof gable, including small pyramidal roofs over the entrances. A skin of gray shingles covers all the walls and roofs.

Although more well known for creating some of the earliest skyscrapers and for planning the architecture of the 1893 World's Columbian Exposition with his partner Daniel Burnham, the Chicago architect John Wellborn Root demonstrated the great unity of the Shingle Style in the Lake View Presbyterian Church, Chicago, 1887–88. The main body of the church is dominated by the steeply pitched gable roof; the roof and walls are covered with similar shingles. An octagonal tower with a conical roof is integrated into the front corner of the church, along with two smaller gables. All are subsumed in the same integrative shingle covering. The church has been altered with later additions; the current two-tone white paint diminishes the original unity, but it still stands as a fine example of the style.

Similarly, Ernest Flagg is best known for his early-twentieth-century skyscrapers in New York City, most notably the Singer Building of 1906. The Amoskeag Presbyterian Church in Manchester, New Hampshire, of 1892, which is attributed to him, shows a skillful unity in the way the continuous skin of shingles adds to the integration of the corner entrance tower, broad cross gable, and the wide rounded apse. The tower is capped with a pyramidal roof, and rounded projections on the corners avoid sharp angles and increase the sense of unity. The one plane of the small gable over the side entrance is

Above: First United Methodist Church, Church and Riser Streets, Columbia, LA, 1911. An interesting Shingle Style church with broad overhanging eaves on the towers.

Above: Unitarian Universalist Church, 147 High Street, Medford, MA, 1894. An amalgam of the Shingle Style and Tudor Gothic.

subsumed within the larger roof gable, further tying the forms together.

The long, low, shingle-covered church of Our Lady of Mercy in Belmont, Massachusetts, is an unusual example of a Shingle Style church designed by Maginnis, Walsh & Sullivan, who are much more well known for their Gothic and Byzantine structures. The triple-arched entry evokes Romanesque designs, the bell-cote is based on the British Gothic of the Ecclesiological Movement, while the continuous skin of shingles recalls the New England tradition of shingle buildings.

Frequently churches combine aspects of the Shingle Style with related styles, such as the half-timbered Tudor style. One example of such an amalgam is the Unitarian Universalist Church of Medford, Massachusetts, built in 1894. The church is built on a foundation of random ashlar masonry; the broad gable that encompasses the main body of the church is covered with warm brown shingles and the crenellated stone tower evokes early English churches. A small transverse gable covers the porte-cochere, a covered entrance for carriages.

Queen Anne

Queen Anne was a highly elaborate style, primarily used for houses. It has only the loosest connection to the historical Queen Anne, who reigned just before George I. This style may have seemed too domestic for use in religious buildings, although a few have been found. The late-nineteenth-century Baptist Church in Ludlow, Vermont, is an exceptional example. Were it not for the scale and the rose window, one might easily mistake it for a large Queen Anne house or inn. It is completely made of wood and has an irregular silhouette and colorful trim.

George H. Edbrooke designed the interesting New Testament Missionary Baptist Church (South Congregational Church) in Chicago, built in 1886. This eclectic church has medieval elements, but the combination resembles the Queen Anne style with its many gables and turrets. The church has an irregular silhouette, dominated by a large, round, corner tower that juts out from the otherwise square plan.

The Swedish Congregational Church (1892) in Deep River, Connecticut, is smaller and simpler. The large multi-paned windows are similar to Arts and Crafts designs.

Above: Ernest Flagg (attributed): Amoskeag Presbyterian Church, 95 Brook Street, Manchester, NH, 1892.

Above: Maginnis, Walsh & Sullivan: Our Lady of Mercy, 401 Belmont Street, Belmont, MA. Shingle covered.

Above: St. Paul's Episcopal Church, 1135 Walnut Street, Newton Highlands, MA, 1883.

Above: Baptist Church, 99 Main Street, Ludlow, VT, late nineteenth century.

Above: Baptist Church, Ludlow, VT.

Above: Swedish Congregational Church, 132 Union Street, Deep River, CT, 1892. The large, multipaned windows are close to Arts and Crafts designs.

Above: Moravian Church, 114 East Fourth Street, Chaska, MN, 1889; remodeled 1968.

Louis Sullivan

The great Chicago architects Louis Sullivan and Dankmar Adler sought to create a new path for American architecture. They designed what is now the Pilgrim Baptist Church on the South Side of Chicago, originally built as the Kehilath Anshe Ma'ariv Synagogue in 1891. Adler's father had been the first rabbi at this synagogue. It is a massive square building, rising three stories before stepping back to another smaller square section, which is topped with a pyramidal roof. The entire building was to be made of stone, but the budget would only allow the lower section to be built in stone. A great semicircular arch frames the doorway, and other large arches span three window bays; these unifying arches were derived from H. H. Richardson's buildings, especially his Marshall Field Warehouse in Chicago (1885), which also influenced Adler and Sullivan's Auditorium Theater and Hotel (1887–89). Frank Lloyd Wright was employed by Sullivan at the time this building was under construction. The interior is a vast auditorium space, surmounted by a barrel vault. Sullivan noted that religious architecture must transcend the physical, and represent "the out-working of the Great Spirit which makes nature so intelligible to us that it ceases to be a phantasm

Above: Louis Sullivan and Dankmar Adler: Pilgrim Baptist Church, originally built as Kehilath Anshe Ma'ariv Synagogue, 3235 East Ninety-first Street, Chicago, IL, 1891. Front view.

and becomes a sweet, a superb, a convincing Reality."[3] The synagogue is now the Pilgrim Baptist Church, which required some changes to the interior to accommodate a baptistery and choir.

At the turn of the century, Sullivan again was asked to design a house of worship, this time for a Russian Orthodox congregation: the Holy Trinity Russian Orthodox Cathedral and Rectory (1899–1903) in Chicago. His distinctive ornamental flourishes surface even in a project with such strict requirements as this. The interior is a square central plan, covered with an octagonal dome. The traditional *iconostasis*, a screen in Byzantine churches separating the sanctuary from the nave and pierced by three doors and covered with icons, separates the sacred space of the apse from the congregation. Construction of this church was partially paid for by Russian Czar Nicholas II.

Latter-day Saints, or Mormon, Temples

America has been the birthplace of several major religions. With the establishment of the Church of Jesus Christ of Latter-day Saints, distinctive temples were built, first in Illinois and then Utah. The denomination originated in Vermont with the prophetic visions of Joseph Smith

Above: Louis Sullivan: Holy Trinity Russian Orthodox Cathedral and Rectory, Chicago, IL, 1899–1903. Detail.

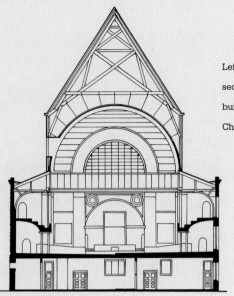

Left: Louis Sullivan and Dankmar Adler: section of Pilgrim Baptist Church, originally built as Kehilath Anshe Ma'ariv Synagogue, Chicago, IL, 1891.

Right: Plan of Pilgrim Baptist Church, Chicago, IL.

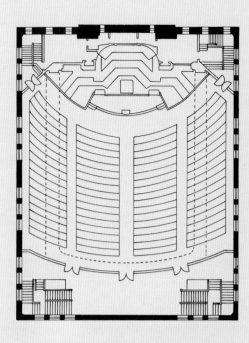

Above: Louis Sullivan and Dankmar Adler: Pilgrim Baptist Church, originally built as Kehilath Anshe Ma'ariv Synagogue, Chicago, IL, 1891. Postcard, 1908.

(1805–44). He and his followers moved west to Illinois, but after he was lynched in 1844, the group followed the leadership of Brigham Young (1801–77). The first Mormon temple (1846) at Nauvoo, Illinois, was dedicated shortly before the group migrated to Utah. This fell into ruins early in its existence, but has recently been reconstructed (1999–2002). The original architect was William Weeks.

The fortuitously named Truman O. Angell (1810–87) designed the main Mormon Temple in Salt Lake City, Utah. It was built in 1853–93 in a creative Gothicizing style with six towers and many pinnacles, which all point upward to heaven like a visual chorus. The very un-Gothic round windows underscore its eclectic nature, however. The site for the temple was chosen by Brigham Young, leader of the Mormons, and the town was laid out around it. Built to hold large numbers, the Salt Lake City Temple is 186 feet long and 118 feet wide, and the tallest tower is 210 feet high. The walls are nine feet thick at the bottom, tapering to six feet thick at the top. By 1883, the temple was only half finished; the architect Joseph Don Carlos was appointed to complete the project. The temple was open to non-Mormons for one day just before its dedication, but since then is open only to the faithful. The seldom-photographed interior consists of a number of rooms for special ceremonies, corresponding to the stages of the soul's progress.

The Logan Utah Temple (1877–84) in Logan, Utah, was built in a castellated style based on the Gothic Revival. Built on a rectangular plan, it has symmetrical towers at

Above: Manti Utah Temple, Temple Hill, Manti, UT, 1877–88.

each end. The square towers are flanked by smaller octagonal towers, with crenellations at the top.

The Manti Temple (1877–88) in Manti, Utah, is very similar—a tall, rectangular structure, with a strong vertical emphasis created by rows of external buttresses and tall towers at each end of the building. In this case, the towers are capped with curving roofs derived from the Second Empire style. The dedication prayer by Lorenzo Snow (1888) explains some of the temple's significance:

> We dedicate the ground and the hill on which it stands, that the same may be holy unto the Lord our God; that its steps, its terraces, its trees and shrubbery, with all its adornments and its approaches may be the

pathways of the just to the house of the Lord, the temple of our God. Let the foundation of this house be made permanent and never be moved from its place. May the stones and the cement of which the building is composed become compact and strong as if it were one solid rock.

> We consecrate the basement of the lower story, which is in likeness of the home of the dead, with its baptismal font, for the service of the living and the dead, with its steps, the oxen on which the font rests, its seats, its rooms for changes, with all its doors and windows, their hangings and fastenings, the furniture, and all that appertains to it.…

> We dedicate and consecrate unto Thee and the serv-

Above: Truman O. Angell: Mormon Temple, 50 West North Temple Street, Salt Lake City, UT, 1853–93.

Above: Logan Utah Temple, 175 North 300 East, Logan, UT, 1877–84. A castellated-style Mormon temple.

Above: William Weeks: Nauvoo Mormon Temple, 50 Wells Street, Nauvoo, IL, 1846; reconstructed 1999–2002.

ice of Thy Saints, the lower and upper main courts, with all other apartments in this building which are sheltered by its roof, according to the various uses for which they have been designed, with their stands, their altars, their desks, the stairs by which they are reached, their doors and windows, their hangings and fastenings, together with floors, partitions, ceilings, finishings, furnishings and ornamentations, also all apparatus and fixtures for ventilating, warming, lighting and seating the same, whether they are for public worship, administering in the holy sacraments and ordinances of this holy temple or for private prayer and secret devotion; also all rooms that are used for study and learning words of wisdom from the best books, or by lectures and the experience of righteous and learned men able to teach the will and ways of the Lord, all these we dedicate unto Thee that all may be most holy and acceptable unto the Lord our God.[4]

The entire structure was thus consecrated.

Moorish/Islamic Revival

The Moorish, or Islamic, Revival appeared in the second half of the nineteenth century; this style was especially used for synagogues because of its association with the golden age of Jewish life in Spain during the period of Muslim rule. Although none survive in Spain from this era, there had been Islamic-style synagogues in the Spanish city of Toledo. For at least fifty years, the style was very popular for synagogues in America and Central Europe. Perhaps the first Moorish-style synagogue in the United States was the eclectic Isaac Mayer Wise Temple (1863–65) in Cincinnati, Ohio. It was designed by James Keyes Wilson and features two tall minaret-like spires on the façade, Gothic arches, thirteen small domes, and vibrant polychromy. The tracery in the rose window in the middle of the façade is based on Islamic precedents, as are the horseshoe arches below it and the panels of arabesque decoration. The Islamic elements are primarily decorative; the plan of the temple is that of a basilica. The temple is named for Rabbi Wise, the leader of the Jewish Reform movement in America.

Henry Fernbach was the first Jewish architect in America. The Central Synagogue he designed in New York City in 1872 was built for a congregation organized by Bohemian Jews. The synagogue is built in the Moorish/Islamic Revival style, and imitates one in Budapest, Hungary. The colorful ornament has been described as "a carnival of delight." The distinctive rose window is actually a geometric design based on Islamic patterns, starting with intersecting pentagons at the center, which generate a ten-pointed star. The outer band is a series of five-pointed stars. The interior was severely damaged by a fire in 1998, but was skillfully restored by Hardy, Holzman, Pfeiffer Associates, who re-created much of the original lavish decoration that had been removed in previous alterations. The full panoply of Victorian lavishness is here, with sixty-nine different shades of color based on the original tones but adapted for modern electric light.

A rich blend of eclectic influences is found in the Chizuk Amuno (Strengthening the Faith) Synagogue in Baltimore, Maryland. It was built in 1876 by the architect Henry Burge. The exterior has a mix of Romanesque corbeled arches at the gables, Gothic lancet windows, and Islamic horseshoe arches at the entrance. The interior features an ornate Torah shrine with a large Moorish arch flanked by bulbous columns. The raised reading platform, or bimah, is in the center of the temple. The Temple of Israel Synagogue in Wilmington, North Carolina, is much simpler, but similarly includes horseshoe arches in the façade. It was built in 1876 by the architect Alex Strausz.

The first major synagogue established on the Lower East Side of New York City by the Orthodox Eastern European Ashkenazic Jews was Congregation K'hal Adath Jershurun, or the Eldridge Street Synagogue. It was built by the Herter Brothers in 1887. It is an eclectic mix of Moorish architecture—the prominent horseshoe arches are the key—and a Gothic rose window. The horseshoe arches over the doors are crisply notched with toothlike shapes, and an outer ring of ornate molding surrounds them. This molding is punctuated with Star of David designs. Bands of curling leafy carved moldings and rosette patterns add further ornament to the surface.

The Park East Synagogue in New York City was designed by Schneider & Herter and built in 1890. The temple was originally founded as Congregation Zichron Ephraim, a conservative temple to counteract the growing Reform movement. The building is quite eclectic, with horseshoe arches from the Islamic tradition, a rose window from the Romanesque period, and two towers. The rose window and towers echo certain European

Above: Henry Fernbach: Central Synagogue, 652 Lexington Avenue, New York, NY, 1872. Moorish/Islamic Revival.

Above: James Keyes Wilson: Isaac M. Wise Temple, 8329 Ridge Road, Cincinnati, OH, 1863–65. One of the first Moorish-style synagogues in the United States.

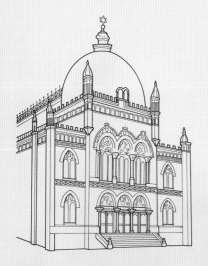

Above: Henry Fernbach: Shaaray Tefila, West Forty-fourth Street, New York, NY, 1869.

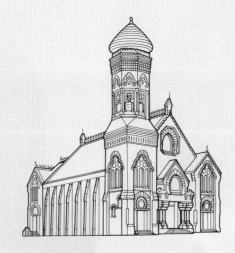

Above: Fraser, Furness & Hewitt: Rodef Shalom Synagogue, Philadelphia, PA, 1869–71. Demolished 1927.

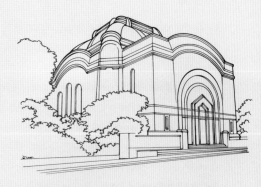

Above: Henry Hornbostel: Rodef Shalom Temple, 4905 Fifth Avenue, Pittsburgh, PA, 1906.

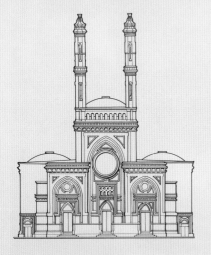

Above: James Keyes Wilson: Isaac M. Wise Temple, Cincinnati, OH, 1863–65. Elevation.

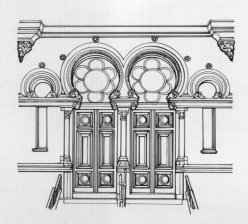

Above: Horseshoe arches, derived from Islamic precedents. Herter Brothers: Congregation K'hal Adath Jershurun, the Eldredge Street Synagogue, New York, NY, 1887.

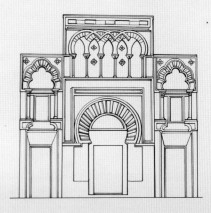

Above: Horseshoe and interlaced arches from the Great Mosque at Cordoba, Spain, 785–961. This mosque provided inspiration to a number of American Synagogues in the nineteenth century.

Above: Multifoil arch on window. Schneider & Herter: Park East Synagogue, New York, NY, 1890.

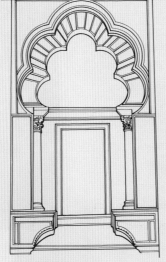

Above: Multifoil arch from the Great Mosque at Cordoba, Spain, 785–961.

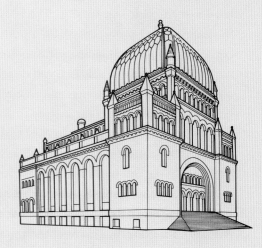

Above: Arnold Brunner: Temple Beth El, Fifth Avenue and Seventy-sixth Street, New York, NY, 1891. Demolished 1947.

synagogues of the nineteenth century, such as the Dohány Synagogue (1854–59) in Budapest, designed by Ludwig Förster. The center of the rose window is a star of David. Multifoil windows on the façade are derived from similar windows at the Great Mosque in Cordoba, Spain, of 765–961. Seven lobes surround the window, which contains stained glass in an Islamic floral pattern above a Star of David.

In the same year, the imposing Temple Beth El (1891) was built in New York City. The large stone building featured many Romanesque arches, but was dominated by a four-sided curving roof that rose like a dome over the façade. The interior was one large auditorium, with the torah shrine and raised platform at the end. The temple was demolished in 1947.

Several smaller wooden synagogues are of considerable

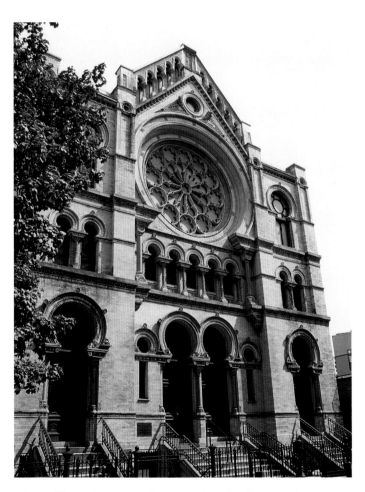

Above: Herter Brothers: Congregation K'hal Adath Jershurun, the Eldridge Street Synagogue, 14 Eldridge Street, New York, NY, 1887. Eclectic mix. This was the first major synagogue established on the Lower East Side by the Orthodox Eastern European Ashkenazi Jews.

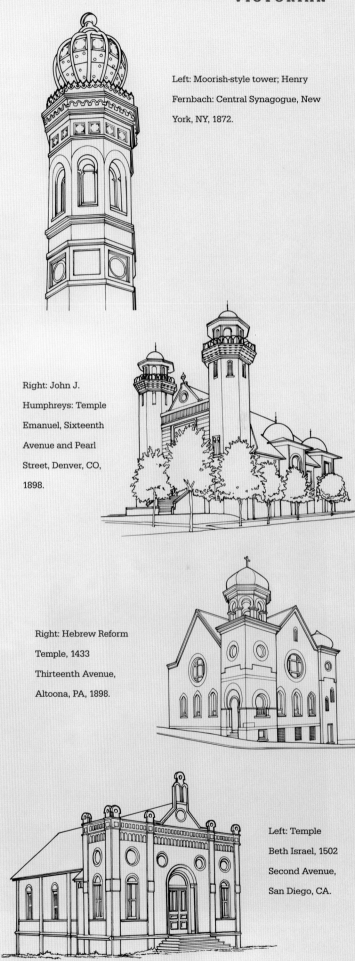

Left: Moorish-style tower; Henry Fernbach: Central Synagogue, New York, NY, 1872.

Right: John J. Humphreys: Temple Emanuel, Sixteenth Avenue and Pearl Street, Denver, CO, 1898.

Right: Hebrew Reform Temple, 1433 Thirteenth Avenue, Altoona, PA, 1898.

Left: Temple Beth Israel, 1502 Second Avenue, San Diego, CA.

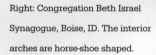

Left: Congregation Beth Israel Synagogue, 1102 State Street, Boise, ID. A shingle covered synagogue in Idaho.

Right: Congregation Beth Israel Synagogue, Boise, ID. The interior arches are horse-shoe shaped.

Above: Henry Fernbach: Central Synagogue, New York, NY, 1872. Detail.

Above: Alex Strausz: Temple of Israel Synagogue, 1 South Fourth Street, Wilmington, NC, 1876.

Above: Beth Israel Synagogue, 31 Concord Street, Norwalk, CT, 1906. Now the Canaan Institutional Baptist Church.

interest. Beth Israel Synagogue in Norwalk, Connecticut, was built in 1906. (It is now the Canaan Institutional Baptist Church). This is the only synagogue in Connecticut with onion domes. The shingle covered Congregation Beth Israel Synagogue, Ada County, Idaho, is an unusual rural synagogue. The interior arches are horseshoe shaped.

The Moorish style is also found in Denver, Colorado, which is the home of the Temple Emanuel (1898), designed by John J. Humphreys. This temple has two symmetrical towers at the front that resemble minarets. The gabled roof is intersected by two transverse sections covered with small domes.

Distinctive Islamic horseshoe arches are found over the entrance and in the tower of the Hebrew Reform Temple built in 1898 in Altoona, Pennsylvania. The building has a square plan with intersecting gables. The flattened, bulbous domes of the two corners also evoke the traditions of the Near East.

The Temple Beth Israel in San Diego, California, is a wood frame building, which is basically a typical gabled structure with a slablike rectangular entrance section in front of it. Originally, the gable and porch were topped with shapes symbolizing the tablets of Mosaic law.

Above left: Schneider & Herter: Park East Synagogue, 163 East Sixty-seventh Street, New York, NY, 1890.

Above: Henry Burge: Chizuk Amuno Synagogue (Strengthening the Faith), 27–35 Lloyd Street, Baltimore, MD, 1876.

Left: Schneider & Herter: Park East Synagogue, New York, NY, 1890. Detail.

Flemish Revival

The characteristic stepped gables of Flemish architecture were revived in a number of churches in New York and elsewhere. The West End Collegiate Church and School in New York City was built in 1891–93 by Robert W. Gibson. This is a Reformed Church and the use of Dutch Baroque motifs seems appropriate. The foundation of this congregation dates back to 1628, when the city was a Dutch colony. The stepped gable includes small pinnacles on every fourth step and the façade is pierced by a large, round window with square tracery. Raised stone quoins give a bumpy texture to the masonry. Dormers with miniature stepped gables are found on the side of the gable roof. A lantern with a small cupola echoes the spiky theme. The overall look is similar to a Flemish guild hall, such as those in Antwerp or Ghent. A similar stepped gable and round window are found at Mahanaim, Eglise Adventiste (formerly Ancient Divine Theological Baptist Church) in Brooklyn, c. 1890.

Baroque Revival

Northern Baroque forms were revived for Polish churches in Chicago and New York. Ethnic groups who emigrated from the Austro-Hungarian Empire also favored this style.

Above: Stepped gable, typical of the Flemish or Dutch Revival. Robert W. Gibson: West End Collegiate Church and School, New York, NY, 1891–93.

Left: Mahanaim, Eglise Adventiste (formerly Ancient Divine Theological Baptist Church), 814 Park Place, Brooklyn, NY, c. 1890.

Right: Robert W. Gibson: West End Collegiate Church and School, West End Avenue and West Seventy-seventh Street, New York, NY, 1891–93.

Although Patrick C. Keely is more well known for his Gothic churches, he created a northern Baroque design for St. Stanislaus Kostka Roman Catholic Church in Chicago, 1876–81. The façade features a stepped gable with small Baroque pinnacles on each step. Paired towers were added in 1892 by Adolphus Druiding; the one on the right side was destroyed by lightning in 1964 and hasn't been replaced.

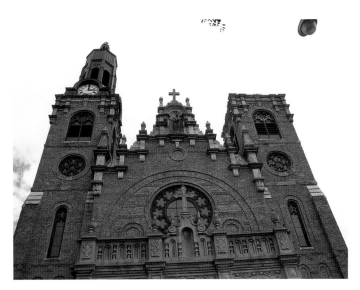

Above: St. Stanislaus Kostka Roman Catholic Church, Chicago, IL, 1876–81.

Above: Patrick C. Keely: St. Stanislaus Kostka Roman Catholic Church, 1327 North Noble Street, Chicago, IL, 1876–81; towers 1892 by Adolphus Druiding. Northern Baroque.

Russian Orthodox

Russian traders began to settle on the west coast of Alaska in the eighteenth century. The first Russian Orthodox monks arrived in 1794. The earliest surviving Russian Orthodox church is St. Michael's Cathedral in Sitka, Alaska. It was designed and built by Father John Veniaminov in 1844. Veniaminov, who had traveled between settlements in a kayak and learned the Tlingit language, was canonized as St Innocent, Enlightener of the Aleuts, Apostle to America and Siberia by the Russian Orthodox Church in 1977. Alaska was transferred to the United States in 1867 and most of the native Russians returned to their homeland. New waves of immigrants after 1890 led to many new churches being founded in areas with concentrations of Russian immigrants, such as Chicago and New York, but also in the northern states. One good example is Holy Resurrection Orthodox Church (1915) in Berlin, New Hampshire, designed by John Bergesen.

Left: St. Michael's Cathedral, Sitka, AK, 1844.

Left: John Bergesen: Holy Resurrection Orthodox Church, 20 Petrograd Street, Berlin, NH, 1915.

Right: George B. Rogers: Government Street United Methodist Church, 901 Government Street, Mobile, AL, 1889–90; 1907.

Spanish Colonial Revival

The Spanish Colonial style was revived not only in the Southwest, but also in New England and the South by academically trained architects, who saw it as another alternative.

Spiritualists

The Spiritualist movement was strong in the late nineteenth century, and while the most established groups adopted traditional historical styles, such as the Richardsonian Romanesque Spiritualist Temple in Boston (1884), there

Right: Ralph Adams Cram, Charles Francis Wentworth & Bertram Grosvenor Goodhue: Newton Corner Methodist Church, 515 Centre Street, Newton, MA, 1895. This Spanish/Mexican Baroque church has recently been converted to condominiums.

were also variant styles. One of the earliest spiritualists was Timothy Brown, who built his own house in 1855 in Georgetown, NY, according to directives from spirit guides, incorporating esoteric detail and features in this highly ornate Victorian house. Many spiritualist mediums claimed they relied upon the ghosts of dead Indians for their "spirit guides." In 1894 the Boston medium Mary Weston had the On-I-Set Wigwam Spiritualist Camp built in Onset, MA, in the form of a large tepee in honor of Native American spirituality.

Revival Meetings and Tent Crusades

Revival meetings held in outdoor tents were extremely popular in the frontier states in the early nineteenth century,

Above: Timothy Brown House, South Main Street and State Route 26, Georgetown, NY, 1850s.

Above: On-I-Set Wigwam Spiritualist Camp, 9 Crescent Place and Thirteenth Street, Onset, MA, 1894.

imbued as they were with a dual sense of contact with nature and a return to the primitive simplicity of the early church. After the Civil War, permanent meeting camps were established in resortlike settings. The New Jersey seacoast town of Oak Grove was the first of these. The Great Auditorium building was constructed for the Methodists by Fred T. Camp in 1893–94. The building resembles a large exhibition hall at one of the World's Fairs, such as the 1876 Centennial in Philadelphia. The large meeting hall holds thousands, and the interior deliberately echoes the simplicity of the earlier revival tents. The front façade is symmetrical, with two pedimented entrances flanking a larger central pediment. The number three is repeated again with two smaller towers flanking the tall central tower. All are topped with crosses. the exterior is shingled, and the roof is of sheet metal. Another permanent revival shelter is the Methodist Tabernacle, Barhamsville, Virginia, which was built in 1922.

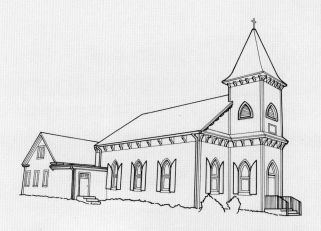

Above: Methodist Tabernacle at Mathews, VA, 1922. A traditional style church associated with a revival camp.

Chinese

Chinese immigrants brought the Taoist religion with them to California in the nineteenth century. The Won Lim Temple (Chinese Joss House) in Weaverville is the oldest continuously used Chinese Temple in California. It was built in 1874, replacing an earlier one destroyed by fire. It is a small wood frame building, painted red, with a gable roof. The Taoist religion does not hold services in the Western sense; the temple is a place for individual worshipers to pray and consult the gods. The Temple of Kwan Tai in Mendocino may date back to 1854. It is a simple vernacular building, made of redwood. It has a balloon frame, gable roof, and simple porch. The interior is very plain, with an unadorned altar and prayer table. Wooden benches line the walls.

Above: Fred T. Camp: The Great Auditorium, Methodist, 54 Pitman Avenue, Ocean Grove, NJ, 1893-94.

Above: Won Lim Temple (Chinese Joss House), Oregon and Main Streets, Weaverville, CA, 1874.

Above: Antioch Baptist Church, Highway 90, near Edgerly, LA, *c.* 1869. A simple vernacular meetinghouse.

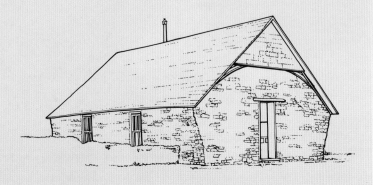

Above: Sod Friends Church, Haviland, KS, 1885. Churches and houses were made of sod in the prairie settlements, which lacked wood for construction.

Vernacular

Vernacular architecture is the style of ordinary building, the everyday language of structure. Many rural churches have been built in this plain-spoken style. The humble Antioch Baptist Church from about 1869, which stood near Edgerly, Louisiana, was a good example. A simple vernacular meetinghouse, this church recently burned. It was a rectangular frame building, with a gabled roof covered with corrugated sheet metal. The original congregation had been formed in 1827.

Sod Churches

On the western plains states, timber was scarce, so in the first wave of settlements, many houses and even churches and public buildings were made of sod—thick blocks of turf cut from the prairie and stacked up to make the walls of the buildings. This "Nebraska marble" was not an ideal building material—keeping the buildings clean, dry, and free from insects was difficult—but it was abundant, and shows the ingenuity of the "sodbusters." Although these early churches were replaced as soon as better materials became

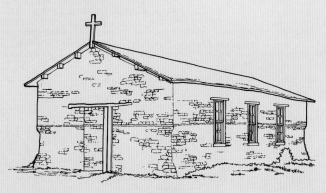

Above: An early sod church in Nebraska, *c.* 1880s.

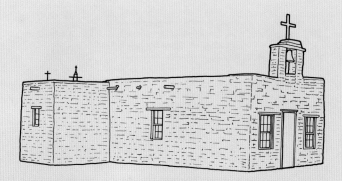

Above: Sod church: Mexican Catholic Church, Deming, NM, 1910–19. This church re-creates the form of earlier adobe churches.

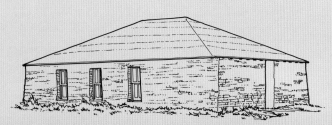

Above: Sod church: Lake View Methodist Episcopal Church, Tripp County, SD, *c.* 1911.

Left: Pilgrim Holiness straw bale church, Arthur County, NE, 1928. Buildings made of straw bales were also found in the prairie and western states.

available, early photographs document their history. Quakers built the Sod Friends Church in Haviland, Kansas, in 1885. Other sod churches were built in Nebraska in the 1880s. In Tripp county, South Dakota, the Lake View Methodist Episcopal Church was built about 1911. Around the same time, the Mexican Catholic Church was built of sod in Deming, New Mexico, 1910–19. This mimicked the earlier Spanish colonial adobe architecture.

Straw bale architecture has recently been revived for building houses, but this material was also used for frontier churches. As late as 1928, the Pilgrim Holiness Church in Arthur County, Nebraska, was made of straw bales. In this technique, tightly compacted bales of straw are stacked up on vertical reinforcing rods and finally plastered over. This makes a well insulated, durable structure. Several of these still survive, including the Pilgrim Holiness Church.

Late Gothic Revival

At the end of the century, a new wave of Gothic Revival churches was built, influenced by the Arts and Crafts movement and also liturgical considerations. Ralph Adams Cram was one of the leading architects of this movement.

As the industrial revolution progressed, urban populations began to explode, with many cities experiencing enormous growth. Boston went from a population of about 15,000 at the time of the revolution to over a half million by 1900; Chicago grew from a population of less than 30,000

in 1850 to over one million by the end of the century. Suburbs also grew at a tremendous pace, made possible by the development of streetcars and later, subways. In response to this sudden industrialization and urban growth, there was a reconsideration of preindustrial society and its values. In particular, the religious and social values of the Middle Ages received new appreciation. The centrality of religion during that era, and the direct connection between the people's lives and the arts and crafts, seemed very attractive. William Morris and John Ruskin in England promoted the idea that a return to medieval practice could provide an antidote to the alienation of modern industrial society. The Arts and Crafts movement that they inspired was enthusiastically received in the United States.

On the rocky coast of Maine, St. Ann's Church (1887) in Kennebunkport was built in the style of early English medieval churches from shore rocks gathered at the site. A

Above: H. H. Hartwell & W. C. Richardson: First Baptist Church, 5 Magazine Street, Cambridge, MA, 1881. Front view.

Above: H. H. Hartwell & W. C. Richardson: First Baptist Church, Cambridge, MA, 1881. Side view, showing clerestory.

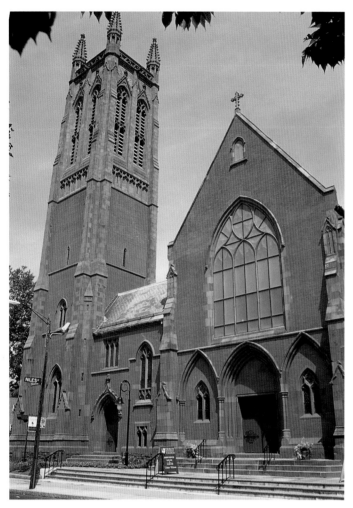

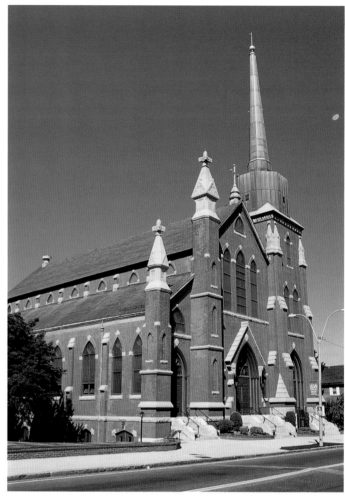

Above: Trinity Episcopal Church, 120 Sigourney Street, Hartford, CT, 1892–98.

Above: St. Patrick's Church, 44 East Central Street, Natick, MA, 1892–1902. Red brick, urban church.

square tower of rubble masonry stands before the gabled chapel. The interior is notable for the semicircular trusses carried on hammer-beams. The architect was H. P. Clark.

An even more massive tower dominates the early masterpiece of Ralph Adams Cram, the Church of All Saints in Dorchester (Boston), Massachusetts. It was built between 1892–95. The tower and block of the church are made of polygonal masonry of Quincy granite, and although the church is based on English perpendicular precedents, it nonetheless creates a feeling of originality. Cram was so profoundly steeped in the knowledge and feeling for Gothic that he made his own original creations within the style, and did not merely copy earlier buildings.

The late nineteenth century saw many urban churches built in the Gothic style. The First Baptist Church in Cambridge, Massachusetts was built by H. H. Hartwell & W. C. Richardson in 1881. The Gothic style is skillfully

handled here; the long nave and side aisles are unified by long sloping gable roofs. The asymmetrical façade, with one tall tower at the left, is well proportioned and ornamented with a variety of hood moldings, patterns, and gables in the brickwork. A rose window composed of wheels and circles completes the theme. Another typical redbrick urban church is that of St. Patrick's, Natick, Massachusetts, 1892–1902; the tower is a modern replacement.

Trinity Episcopal Church in Hartford, Connecticut, was built in the same decade, between 1892–98. It is a more elaborate structure, made of brick and brownstone. A square tower capped with pinnacles is set asymmetrically to the left of the façade. Westminster Presbyterian Church in Minneapolis, Minnesota, is a similarly impressive urban church, built of light-colored stone in 1897. The square tower lacks pinnacles, but the overall effect is as successful as the Hartford example.

RALPH ADAMS CRAM: CATHEDRAL CHURCH OF ST. JOHN THE DIVINE

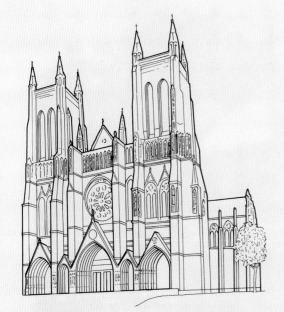

Above: Cathedral Church of St. John the Divine, New York, NY, begun 1893. Drawing showing projected façade with completed towers.

Above: Construction of the nave arch.

Above: Diagram of rose window.

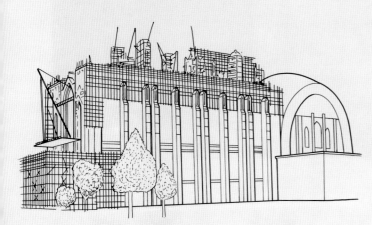

Above: Shown with the nave nearly complete.

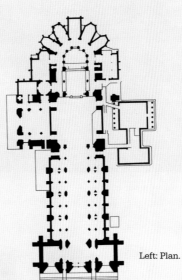

Left: Plan.

Above: Plan of the narthex.

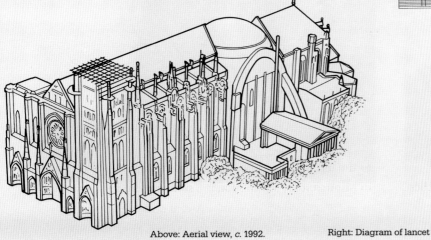

Above: Aerial view, c. 1992.

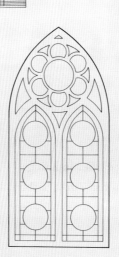

Right: Diagram of lancet window with stained glass.

Above: Capital with image of Nelson Mandela.

Above: H. P. Clark: St. Ann's Church, Ocean Avenue, Kennebunkport, ME, 1887.

Above: Westminster Presbyterian Church, 83 South Twelfth Street, Minneapolis, MN, 1897. Gothic.

Above: Ralph Adams Cram: Cathedral Church of St. John the Divine, 1047 Amsterdam Avenue, New York, NY, begun 1893.

Above: Ralph Adams Cram: All Saints, 209 Ashmont Street, Dorchester, Boston, MA, 1892–95.

Above: Westminster Presbyterian Church, 83 South 12th Street, Minneapolis, MN, 1897. Gothic.

Many of the great cathedrals of Europe took generations to build. This is also the case with the Cathedral Church of St. John the Divine in New York City. Intended to be the largest cathedral in the world, it can hold 8,000 people. The church was begun in a Romanesque style by the relatively inexperienced firm of George Heins and Christopher Lafarge in 1891. Progress was slow in the first two decades of construction. After the death of Heins in 1907, the great Gothic Revivalist Ralph Adams Cram was hired to revise the design, and he made it more like the French High Gothic cathedrals of Amiens or Reims. The nave and choir were complete by 1916 and work on the nave began in 1925. Construction was halted by the out

break of World War II and not resumed until 1980. In an unusual program to benefit the neighborhood, unemployed youth were taught the art of stonecutting. The church is still under construction.

The Church of St. James the Less (1846–48) in Philadelphia (and its English medieval model, St. Michael's, Long Stanton) continued to exert a strong influence on church design in the Late Gothic Revival. The Church of the New Jerusalem (Swedenborg Chapel) in Cambridge, Massachusetts, of 1901 is a small church with integrated bell-cote. Despite being constructed for a relatively new sect, it looks much like a traditional English parish church of the thirteenth century.

Gargoyles and Other Delights

As the Gothic Revival became more and more archeologi-
cally accurate, many more traditional aspects of the style
were revived. The carved gargoyle was used in many late
nineteenth and early twentieth century churches. Gargoyles
were carved decorations around the downspouts in
medieval architecture; the water typically runs out of their
mouths. These marginal figures provided an opportunity
for creative sculpting. Some depicted demons or monsters,
which symbolized the threats faced by the sinner outside
the church. Others were more whimsical, based on animal
or human forms.

Above: Christ Church, 750 Main Street, Waltham, MA, 1902.
A revival of H. H. Richardson's use of glacial boulders for the
walls and tower.

Above: H. Langford Warren (1857–1917): Church of the New
Jerusalem (Swedenborg Chapel), 50 Quincy Street,
Cambridge, MA, 1901.

Notes

1. John Ruskin, "Lectures on Architecture and Painting"
   (*Works*, 12), quoted in Kristine Ottesen Garrigan,
   Ruskin on Architecture: His Thought and Influence
   (Madison: University of Wisconsin Press, 1973) 111.
2. Leopold Eidlitz, *The Nature and Function of Art, More
   Especially of Architecture* (London, 1881), quoted in
   Don Gifford, ed., *The Literature of Architecture, The
   Evolution of Architectural Theory and Practice in Nineteenth
   Century America* (New York: E. P. Dutton, 1966), 413.
3. Louis Sullivan, quoted in Roger G. Kennedy, *American
   Churches*, (New York: Stewart, Tabori & Chang, 1982),
   26.
4. Manti Utah Temple dedicatory prayer, by Lorenzo
   Snow, 1888; reprinted in website:
   http://www.ldschurchtemples.com/cgi-
   bin/prayers.cgi?manti&geographical.

Chapter 5

Pre-WWII—Eclectic Revivals

The period 1880–1940 saw a wide variety of historical styles utilized for religious architecture. Many architects had extensive academic training, and the revivals were frequently more historically accurate than in the preceding decades. These historical revivals provided a counterpoint to the modernism that was also to develop in this period.

Many of these churches are built by specific ethnic groups who sought to maintain their cultural identity through the symbolism of their traditional religious architecture. The design of their houses of worship provides a link to their ancestral home, just as it did for the first European colonists in America. Religious architectures provides continuity in exile.

Right: Ralph Adams Cram:
Ruggles Street Church, Audubon
Circle at 874 Beacon Street,
Boston, MA, 1913–17.

Above: McKim, Mead & White: Congregational Church, 9 Division Street, Naugatuck, CT, 1901–03.

Above: First Church of Christ, Scientist, 391 Walnut Street, Newtonville, MA, 1924.

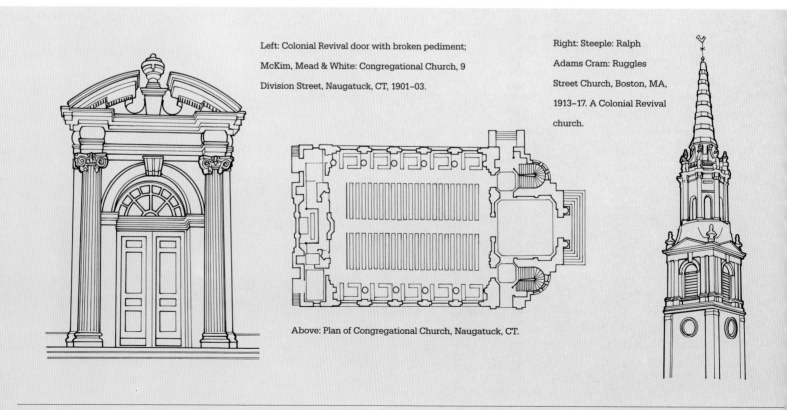

Left: Colonial Revival door with broken pediment; McKim, Mead & White: Congregational Church, 9 Division Street, Naugatuck, CT, 1901–03.

Right: Steeple: Ralph Adams Cram: Ruggles Street Church, Boston, MA, 1913–17. A Colonial Revival church.

Above: Plan of Congregational Church, Naugatuck, CT.

Above: Gargoyle in the shape of an angel, sculpted by John Angel between 1925–47; St. John the Divine, New York, NY.

Above: Gargoyle in the shape of a griffin; National Cathedral, Washington, D.C., 1964. The playfulness of medieval grotesques has been well captured in many of these modern gargoyles.

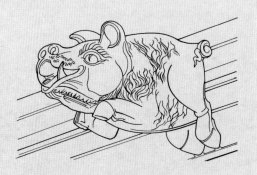

Above: Gargoyle in the shape of a boar: National Cathedral, Washington, D.C., 1964.

Above: Gargoyle in the shape of an African dog: National Cathedral, Washington, D.C., 1964.

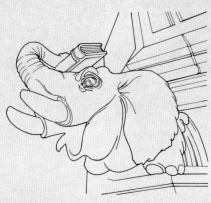

Above: Gargoyle in the shape of an elephant with a book: National Cathedral, Washington, D.C., 1975.

Above: Walter S. Arnold: Pacifist gargoyle, National Cathedral, Washington, D.C., early 1980s.

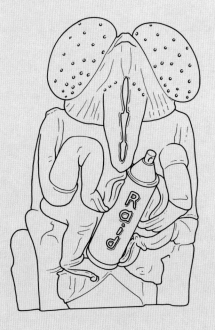

Left: Walter S. Arnold: Fly with can of Raid insecticide, gargoyle, Washington National Cathedral, Washington, D.C., early 1980s.

Right: Walter S. Arnold: Modern gargoyle, robot with computer, National Cathedral, Washington, D.C., early 1980s.

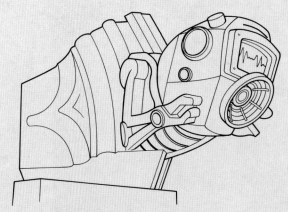

Colonial or Georgian Revival

This was a revival of American eighteenth-century forms that flourished between about 1880 and 1955, the first revival of American buildings in American architecture. It is a sign of the growing maturity of the United States and the increased status of American design. The Centennial exhibition in 1876 in Philadelphia provided some impetus for this revival. There are many examples across the U.S. Some of the most impressive include McKim, Mead & White's Congregational Church in Naugatuck, Connecticut, 1901–3; the Ruggles Street Church of 1913–17 in Boston by Ralph Adams Cram; and Memorial Church at Harvard University in Cambridge, Massachusetts of 1931, designed by Coolidge, Shepley, Bulfinch and Abbott. This style was popular not only on the East Coast where it had originated, but across the country.

*

European revivals in this era included the Twentieth Century Gothic, the Byzantine, Classical, and Renaissance Revivals, plus a wide variety of national traditions, from the Spanish colonial styles to the Scandinavian, Russian Orthodox, and various Oriental styles.

Above: Coolidge, Shepley, Bulfinch and Abbott: Memorial Church, Harvard Yard, Cambridge, MA, 1931.

Left: Coolidge and Shattuck: All Souls Unitarian Church, Eighteenth Street and Harvard Square, NW, Washington, D.C., 1924.

Right: National Baptist Memorial Church, Eighteenth Street and Harvard Square, NW, Washington, D.C.

Twentieth Century Gothic

This was an era of ambitious cathedral building, reflecting the new prosperity and confidence. American capitalists reveled in the comparison of their towering skyscrapers to medieval cathedrals. Gothic skyscrapers were called "cathedrals of commerce." The Woolworth Building in New York (1913) and the Chicago Tribune Building (1922) were two of the most conspicuous examples.

As the skyscrapers increasingly overshadowed the churches, many critics condemned the triumph of commercial over spiritual values and the reversed status of sacred and profane architecture in modern times. Attempts were made to reconcile the conflicting values; the Chicago architectural firm of Holabird and Roche built the tallest church in the world by combining a skyscraper with a Methodist church in the Chicago Temple (1924). The peak of the church spire is more than 500 feet from the ground. The body of the skyscraper is commercial office space; the church is above. At the entrance level is a plaque showing Christ overlooking Jerusalem; in the chapel is a plaque showing Christ overlooking Chicago. All the landmarks of the new Jerusalem are shown, including the latest Chicago skyscrapers.

The link between Gothic architecture and spiritual values was still taken for granted, and optimistic Gothic Revivalists such as Ralph Adams Cram believed that the widespread Gothic church architecture portended a spiritual revival:

> We are at the end of an epoch of materialism, rationalism, and intellectualism, and at the beginning of a wonderful new epoch, when once more we achieve a just estimate of comparative values, when material achievement becomes the slave again and no longer the slave-driver; when spiritual intuition drives mere intellect back into its proper and very circumscribed sphere; and when religion… assumes again its rightful place as the supreme element in life and thought.[1]

The revival of Gothic architecture meant a spiritual revival of the society: "And that is what the Gothic restoration means, a returning to other days—not for the retrieving of pleasant but forgotten forms, but for the recovery of those impulses, which made these forms inevitable."

Above: Charles Brigham: Unitarian Memorial Church, 102 Green Street, Fairhaven, MA, 1901–2.

Above: Ralph Adams Cram: First Unitarian Society, 1326 Washington Street, West Newton, MA, 1906.

Ralph Adams Cram was the leading architect of the Twentieth Century Gothic style. He consistently advocated the Gothic style in his writings. Among his early churches, Calvary Episcopal Church (1907) in Pittsburgh is a particularly successful evocation of the English High Church Gothic, with a detailed plan of symbolic stained glass and sculpture designed by the architect. It is a cruciform plan, 208 feet long. The central crossing is topped with a 220-foot-high steeple.

Around the same time, Cram designed the First Unitarian Society (1906) in West Newton, Massachusetts, in an accurate English Gothic style.

The firm of Cram, Goodhue & Ferguson won the commission for the Cadet Chapel at West Point, New York. The granite chapel was dedicated in 1910. It is also a cruciform plan, with a more stocky crossing tower. The Gothic style here is designed to resemble a medieval fortress; the academy refers to the style of the campus as "military Gothic."

The noted Boston architect Charles Brigham designed a particularly fine Gothic church in Fairhaven, Massachusetts, in 1901–2. The Unitarian Memorial Church was one of many commissions he completed for this town.

The Gothic church with a massive square tower, as created by Ralph Adams Cram at All Saints Ashmont (1895) was frequently emulated. One example is the Greek

Evangelical Church (originally the First Congregational Church) of Newton, Massachusetts, of 1903. This is a cruciform church dominated by a massive square tower with buttresses and crenellations at the front. The light-colored stone used for quoins contrasts strongly with the brownstone of the masonry.

One of the most prominent examples of twentieth-century Gothic Revival architecture is the Cathedral Church of St. Peter and St. Paul (also known as the Washington Cathedral) in Washington, D.C., which was begun in 1907 by the English architects George F. Bodley and Henry Vaughan. Vaughan was born in England and came to the United States in 1881, where he became a leading church architect. The cathedral is based on English Perpendicular Gothic and has two symmetrical towers on the façade and another over the crossing. The central portal of the triple-arched entryway is surmounted with a taller pointed arch, which contains the large rose window. The Washington Cathedral was finished in 1990 and features many modern carvings of modern themes, including robots and computers as well as fanciful medieval animals. One chapel incorporates a portion of a rock brought back from the moon. The Gothic style was popular across the nation. The Boston architectural firm of Shepley, Rutan & Coolidge, which had begun as H. H. Richardson's successor

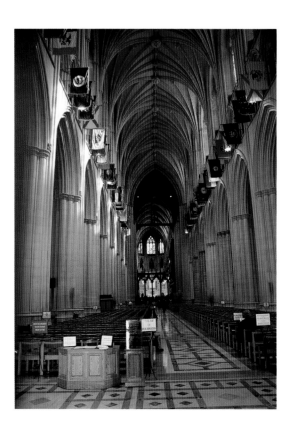

Left: George F. Bodley and Henry Vaughan: Cathedral Church of St. Peter and St. Paul (Washington Cathedral), Massachusetts and Wisconsin Avenues, Washington, D.C., 1907–1990. Interior of the Gothic nave.

Right: Cathedral Church of St. Peter and St. Paul (Washington Cathedral), Washington, D.C. Detail of entrance portal.

Left: George F. Bodley and Henry Vaughan: Cathedral Church of St. Peter and St. Paul (Washington Cathedral), Washington, D.C., begun 1907. Front view.

Above: Cathedral Church of St. Peter and St. Paul, Washington, D.C. Gargoyle.

Right: Cathedral Church of St. Peter and St. Paul, Massachusetts and Wisconsin Avenues, Washington, D.C., 1907-1990. Side view.

Above: Shepley, Rutan & Coolidge: Plymouth Congregational Church, 1900 Nicollette Avenue at Franklin, Minneapolis, MN, 1907.

Above: Edwin Hewitt and Edwin Brown: Cathedral Church of St. Mark, 519 Oak Grove, Minneapolis, MN, 1911.

Right: Edwin Hewitt & Edwin Brown: Hennepin Avenue United Methodist Church, 511 Groveland, Minneapolis, MN, 1914.

Below: Thomas H. Poole & Co.: St. Thomas the Apostle Church (Roman Catholic), 260 West 118th Street, SW corner St. Nicholas Avenue, New York, NY, 1907. Venetian Gothic.

firm working in the Romanesque style and then adopting a classical idiom, moved easily into the Gothic style in the twentieth century. They built the Plymouth Congregational Church, Minneapolis, in 1907 in a medieval style.

One of New York's more colorful eclectic churches is St. Thomas the Apostle Church (Roman Catholic) by Thomas H. Poole & Co., 1907. This profusely ornamented façade recalls Venetian Gothic with its colorful mosaics, trefoil arches, and delicate tracery. The many pinnacles also evoke memories of Milan Cathedral. Although it needs restoration, this is a gem waiting to be rediscovered.

Bernard Maybeck's First Church of Christ, Scientist (1910), in Berkeley, California, is eclectic and highly individualistic, a hybrid of Romanesque and Gothic motifs with modern construction materials. It is an early example of a church built of concrete; the roofs were originally covered with sheet metal. The exterior façade is predominantly horizontal, with a succession of low-pitched gable roofs that recall Japanese and Prairie Style architecture. The broad, overhanging eaves have pronounced rafter tails in the manner of California bungalows. Large panels of glass, made possible by the modern construction, dissolve the wall into a diaphanous curtain, which was also a goal of Gothic architecture. The interior is dominated by a square central auditorium spanned by two massive diagonal timber beams that arch slightly over the center. These beams are carried on concrete piers and are actually modern trusses, with infilled panels of Gothic ornament.

The Minneapolis firm of Edwin Hewitt & Edwin Brown was more concerned about being faithful to the architectural precedents of the Middle Ages. The Cathedral Church of St. Mark (1911) and the Hennepin Avenue United Methodist Church (1914), both in Minneapolis, represent accurate English Gothic adaptations.

English influence is particularly strong in the Trinity Episcopal Church in Newton, Massachusetts, begun 1913. It is closely based on King's Chapel, Cambridge, England. This kind of archaeological accuracy is not uncommon in this academic period.

Ralph Adams Cram and Howard Van Doren Shaw built a very authentic Gothic Revival design for the Fourth Presbyterian Church (1914) in a prominent location on Michigan Avenue in Chicago. The church is adjoined by

Above: Trinity Episcopal Church, 11 Homer Street, Newton, MA, begun 1913.

Above: Bernard Maybeck: First Church of Christ, Scientist, Berkeley, CA, 1910.

Above: Ralph Adams Cram: St. Elizabeth's Chapel, 1 Morse Road, Sudbury, MA, 1914. This was Cram's personal chapel, built on the grounds of his summer estate.

Left: Bertram Grosvenor Goodhue: Church of St. Vincent Ferrer, Sixty-sixth and Lexington, New York, NY, 1916–18.

Above: Church of St. Vincent Ferrer, New York, NY. Detail of sculpture on tower.

Left: J. William Beal: Bethany Congregational Church, 8 Spear Street, Quincy, MA, 1926.

Above: Charles Collens & Henry C. Pelton: Riverside Church, New York, NY, 1927–30. Detail. The portal closely follows the sculptural programs of French Gothic cathedrals.

Above: Riverside Church, New York, NY, 1927–30.

low informal buildings creating a quiet courtyard in the midst of the city.

Cram built a private chapel on the grounds of his summer home in Sudbury, Massachusetts, in 1914. St. Elizabeth's Chapel is a small fieldstone chapel with a rounded apse. The round-topped door is covered with medievalizing iron strapwork of the highest quality; a round window filled with stained glass is centered above the door. Cram and his wife are buried near the church.

French Gothic models inspired Bertram Grosvenor Goodhue's Church of St. Vincent Ferrer, New York City, 1916–18. Along with his Church of St. Thomas in New York City, this church has been named one of the fifty most beautiful in the United States. It was originally intended to

have a fifteen-story steeple, but this was never completed.

French models also inspired the design by Charles Collens & Henry C. Pelton for Riverside Church in New York City. Built between 1927 and 1930, the portal closely follows the sculptural programs of French Gothic cathedrals, especially Chartres. The steel-framed tower is 392 feet high and contains the largest carillon in the world. The nave is one hundred feet high and 215 feet long; the church can hold 2,500 people.

Plans were laid in the 1920s to build one of the largest cathedrals in the world in Philadelphia. Construction began in 1932, but was halted by the Great Depression. Only the Lady Chapel was completed of the grand Episcopal Cathedral. Walled off and made usable, it resem-

Above: Ralph Adams Cram, Howard Van Doren Shaw: Fourth Presbyterian Church, 866 North Michigan Avenue, Chicago, IL, 1914.

Above: Holabird and Roche: Chicago Temple, Chicago, 1924. This Methodist church is 512 feet high, perched on top of a skyscraper, with a chapel on the first floor.

bles the fragmentary remains of Beauvais Cathedral, a French Gothic cathedral. The site was finally developed as retirement housing in 1977–80.

More fortunate in its building history was the Chapel at Duke University in Durham, North Carolina, which was built between 1930 and 1935. James B. Duke declared his intention for the chapel: "I want the central building to be a church, a great towering church, which will dominate all of the surrounding buildings, because such an edifice would be bound to have a profound influence on the spiritual life of the young men and women who come here." The architects were Horace Trumbauer and Julian Abele, America's first well-known African American architect.

Tudor Revival

The Tudor style was inspired by British Tudor and late medieval architecture; it is characterized by steep pitched sloping roofs, and generally has half-timbered facades. The style was reinforced by the British exhibition buildings in world's fairs held in Philadelphia in 1876 and Chicago in 1893. Examples of this style are widely distributed. There are many fine ones in New England, such as Henry Vaughan's Church of the Holy Name in Swampscott, Massachusetts, of 1891–93 and St. Lawrence Roman Catholic Church in Brookline. A simpler version is found in the Unitarian Universalist Church in Franklin, New Hampshire.

Right: Horace
Trumbauer and
Julian Abele: Chapel,
Duke University,
Durham, NC, 1930–35.

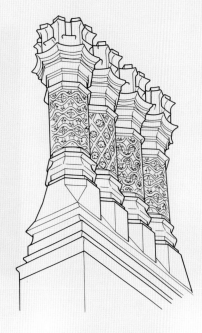

Left: Twentieth Century Gothic
Revival chimneys; Charles Brigham:
Unitarian Memorial Church,
Fairhaven, MA, 1901–2.

Left: Twentieth
Century Gothic
Revival finial; Charles
Brigham: Unitarian
Memorial Church,
Fairhaven, MA,
1901–2.

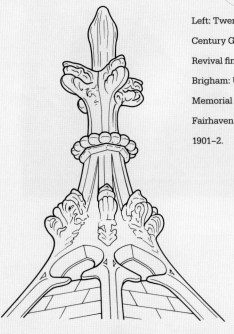

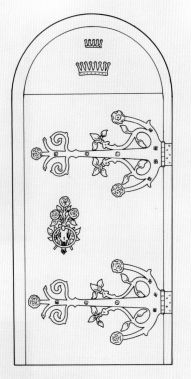

Above: Elaborate medieval ironwork on
door; Ralph Adams Cram: St. Elizabeth's
Chapel, Sudbury, MA, 1914.

Above: Twentieth Century Gothic
Revival pinnacle encrusted with
crockets; Charles Brigham: Unitarian
Memorial Church, Fairhaven, MA,
1901–2.

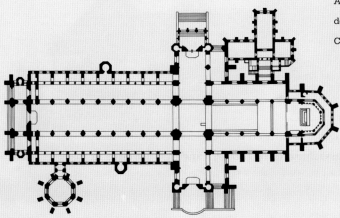

Left: George F. Bodley & Henry Vaughan: Plan of Cathedral Church of St.
Peter and St. Paul (Washington Cathedral), Massachusetts and
Wisconsin Avenues, Washington, D.C., begun 1907.

Beaux-Arts

The Beaux-Arts style flourished between 1885 and 1930. It was a Renaissance-inspired style popularized by the training of the French Ecole des Beaux-Arts. The Ecole des Beaux-Arts was formed in 1819 with a reorganization of the Académie Royale de Peinture et Sculpture and the Académie Royale d'Architecture. Richard Morris Hunt was the first American architect to be admitted to the Ecole, the second was Henry Hobson Richardson, and the third was Charles Follen McKim. The 1893 World's Columbian Exposition also helped promulgate the style. It is characterized by formality, symmetry, and lavish ornament. Because of the expense associated with the style, it is typically found only in churches and temples for large urban

Above; Henry Vaughan: Church of the Holy Name, 60 Monument Avenue, Swampscott, MA, 1891–93.

Above: Henry Vaughan: Church of the Holy Name, 60 Monument Avenue, Swampscott, MA, 1891–93. A small Tudor Revival church.

Above: St. Lawrence Roman Catholic Church, 774 Boylston Street (Rt. 9), Brookline, MA.

Above: Modern Tudor doorway; Unitarian church, Franklin, NH.

Above: Unitarian Universalist Church, 206 Central Street, Franklin, NH.

congregations. A prominent example is the synagogue for Congregation Shearith Israel in New York City, designed by Arnold Brunner and Thomas Tryon in 1896–97. This tall temple facing Central Park shows the influence of the World's Columbian Exposition as well as excavations of Near Eastern synagogues from Roman times.

A pared-down Beaux-Arts style is found at the Church of St. Paul and St. Andrew in New York City, designed by R. H. Robertson and built between 1895 and 1897.

One of the most striking monuments of the Beaux-Arts style is the First Church of Christ, Scientist (1899–1903), in New York City by Carrère and Hastings. It combines English Baroque massing and mannerist details with French Renaissance style. The façade has a tall entrance tower with a four-sided lantern and truncated polygonal spire. The effect is powerful and almost unsettling. The large auditorium seats

Above: R. H. Robertson: Church of St. Paul and St. Andrew, 540 West End Avenue, New York, NY, 1895–97.

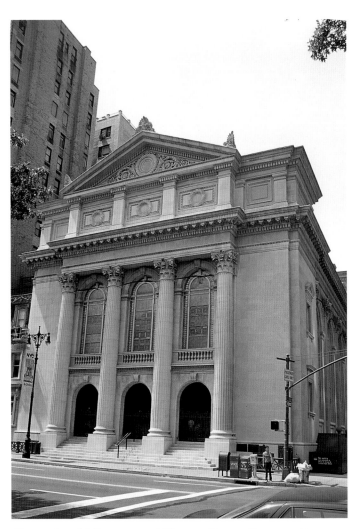

Above: Arnold Brunner and Thomas Tryon: Congregation Shearith Israel (synagogue), 99 Central Park West, New York, NY, 1896–97.

Above: John M. Carrère and Thomas Hastings: First Church of Christ, Scientist, Central Park West and Ninety-sixth Street, New York, NY, 1899–1903.

Above: Charles Brigham & S. Beman, with Brigham, Coveney & Bisbee: Mother Church, Christian Science Center, Boston, MA (chapel by Franklin Welch 1894, 1906). Front view.

Above: Mother Church, Christian Science Center, Boston, MA. Aerial view.

Above: Howard Hoppin and Frederick E. Field, First Church of Christ, Scientist, 71 Prospect Street, Providence, RI, 1906–13.

Above: S. J. Bowler: First Church of Christ, Scientist, 614–620 East Fifteenth Street, Minneapolis, MN.

Above: First Church of Christ, Scientist, 190 Court Street, Middletown, CT.

Above: First Church of Christ, Scientist, Massachusetts Avenue, Cambridge, MA, 1923.

2,000. The enormous vault of the ceiling is made possible by the use of steel girders, but is disguised with rich plaster ornament.

Although the Mother Church of the Christian Scientists was built in a Romanesque style in Boston, the Beaux-Arts came to be a hallmark of churches for that denomination. An unusually tall version is the First Church of Christ, Scientist, in New York City, 1899–1903, designed by John M. Carrère and Thomas Hastings. These classical architects were also responsible for the New York Public Library. As the Christian Science movement grew, the original Mother Church had to be expanded, and the architects Charles Brigham and S. Beman, with the firm of Brigham, Coveney & Bisbee, built a much larger church beside the old one in 1906. This Beaux-Arts church featured a large eighty-two-foot-diameter dome on a drum, resembling St. Peter's in Rome and St. Paul's Cathedral in London. The Boston dome is built with a steel frame and covered with white limestone. The new church could hold 3,000 people. Three

Above: Emmanuel Masqueray: Cathedral of Saint Paul, 226 Summit Avenue, Saint Paul, MN, 1906–15. Beaux-Arts.

Above: Emmanuel Masqueray: Basilica of St. Mary, Hennepin Avenue between Sixteenth and Seventeenth Streets, Minneapolis, MN, 1914.

Above: Emmanuel Masqueray: Church of King Louis (the Little French Church), Cedar Street, St. Paul, MN, 1909

Left: Beaux-Arts style doorway; Charles Brigham & S. Beman, with Brigham, Coveney & Bisbee: Mother Church, Christian Science Center, Boston, MA, 1906.

Right: McKim, Mead & White: Madison Square Presbyterian Church, New York, NY, 1906. A classic Beaux-Arts design.

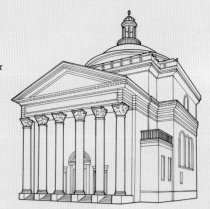

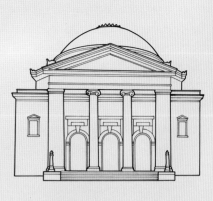

Above: Albert Kahn: Beth El, Woodward Avenue, Detroit, MI, 1903.

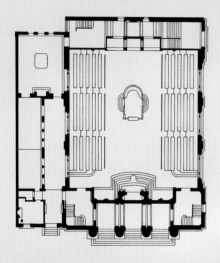

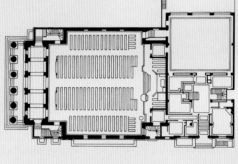

Above; McKim, Mead & White: plan of the Madison Square Presbyterian Church, New York, NY, 1906.

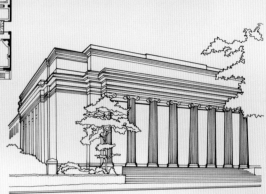

Above: Arnold Brunner and Thomas Tryon: Congregation Shearith Israel, New York, NY, 1896–97. This Beaux-Arts design was partly inspired by the classicism of the World's Columbian Exposition in Chicago of 1893.

Above; Albert Kahn: Beth El, Gladstone Avenue, Detroit, MI, 1922.

eras of building are represented in this structure, which includes the 1894 Romanesque church, the 1906 Beaux-Arts domed addition, and a semicircular entrance portico, which was added in 1975. The adjacent plaza is flanked by a series of modern concrete buildings, 1968–75.

The domed Beaux-Arts style is echoed in the smaller First Church of Christ, Scientist, in Providence, Rhode Island, of 1906–13, designed by Howard Hoppin and Frederick E. Field. Smaller, but still in the Beaux-Arts style is S. J. Bowler's First Church of Christ, Scientist, Minneapolis, built around the turn of the twentieth century. Similar examples are found in the First Church of Christ, Scientist, Middletown, Connecticut, and the 1923 First Church of Christ, Scientist, in Cambridge, Massachusetts, of 1923.

In the Midwest, Emmanuel Masqueray took a leading role in the Beaux-Arts style. He was born in Dieppe, France, and trained at the Ecole des Beaux-Arts in Paris. He emigrated to the United States in 1887. He worked for Richard Morris Hunt, the first American graduate of the Ecole des Beaux-Arts, and assisted in the design of the Breakers mansion in Newport in 1895. In 1904, he served as the chief architect for the world's fair in St. Louis. This led to the commission for the Cathedral of St. Paul in St. Paul, Minnesota, built between 1907 and 1915. Masqueray built over two dozen churches and cathedrals in the Midwest. His Basilica of St. Mary in Minneapolis of 1914 is equally impressive. One of his earliest works in Minnesota is the Church of King Louis (the Little French Church) in St. Paul, built in 1909.

Early Christian Revival

The simplicity of Early Christian basilicas was very appealing to many who appreciated either the links to primitive Christianity or the less fussy design compared to more elaborate (and costly) Gothic or classical styles. The design of St. John the Evangelist Catholic Church in Plaquemine, Louisiana, is heavily influenced by Early Christian churches, with some Romanesque details. The church is modeled on early basilicas, with a small rose window added; the freestanding tower to the left of the façade is a Romanesque campanile with narrow arches. The architect was Albert Bendernagal; it was built in 1927.

Italian Renaissance

The Italian Renaissance Revival style flourished between the 1890s and 1935. It is closely related to the Beaux-Arts style, differing in that it generally has less monumentality. Buildings in the Renaissance Revival style typically include distinct horizontal divisions, frequently separated by a belt or string course, and ornamental features copied from Italian examples, including window trim and/or surrounds, balustrades, and projecting cornices. The style was used for both churches and temples.

An early example is the synagogue of Kenesseth Israel in Philadelphia, designed by Louis C. Hickman and Oscar Frotches in 1892.

In Chicago, St. John of God Roman Catholic Church (1920) has a beautiful Renaissance façade, with two symmetrical bell towers. The nave features a barrel-vaulted ceiling. The church, designed by Henry J. Schlacks, is set in a landscaped park, which enhances the overall effect.

As in earlier eclectic revivals, specific European churches are sometimes copied. St. Sebastian's Roman Catholic Church in Middletown, Connecticut, of 1930–31 was inspired by the fourteenth-century Church of St. Sebastian in Melilli, Sicily.

Baroque Revival

The Baroque style in architecture developed out of the Late Renaissance in Rome in the late sixteenth century and lasted until the early eighteenth century with the rise of the Rococo style. It is basically a classical style, with greater spatial complexity on the interiors and more sculptural depth to the composition of façades. Twin bell towers and domes are frequently found. Baroque took on different characteristics in various European countries. The Roman Baroque was exceptionally classical, but also very sculptural. The French Baroque was more formal and less sculptural. German and Austrian Baroque architects emphasized soaring space and rich interior ornament, and onion domes are often found on the bell towers of these churches.

Northern Baroque styles appear at Holy Trinity Roman Catholic Church in Chicago, 1906. The church was

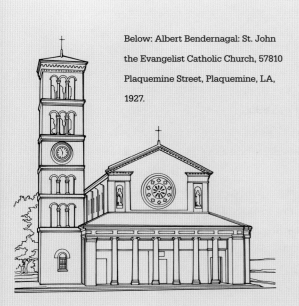

Below: Albert Bendernagal: St. John the Evangelist Catholic Church, 57810 Plaquemine Street, Plaquemine, LA, 1927.

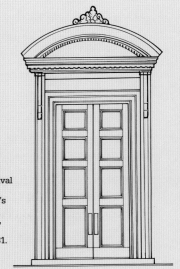

Left: An elaborate arch marks the doorway; Maginnis, Walsh & Sullivan: St. Catherine of Genoa, Catholic Church, Somerville, MA, c. 1915.

Right: Renaissance Revival style door; St. Sebastian's Roman Catholic Church, Middletown, CT, 1930–31.

Above: St. Sebastian's Roman Catholic Church, 147 Washington Street, Middletown, CT, 1930–31. The building is very similar to the fourteenth-century Church of St. Sebastian in Melilli, Sicily.

Above: St. Anne's Church and Shrine, 818 Middle Street, Fall River, MA, 1894–95/1902–6.

designed by Herman Olszewski and William G. Kriegl.

Austrian Baroque influences can be seen in St. Agnes Church in St. Paul, Minnesota, designed by George Ries and built between 1909 and 1912. Comparison to Austrian examples such as the Hofkirche in Innsbruck show similarities in the bell tower with onion dome and rich ornament.

French Baroque designs influenced Theo Daust's Church of Notre Dame de Mount Carmel in Grand Isle, Maine. The simplified Baroque church was built in 1909. The three-dimensional aspect of the composition, with twin bell towers flanking the façade and projecting forward, a domed cupola on each, and a lower entrance portico set back at a different level, connects the church to European Baroque sculptural architecture. The blocklike shape of the towers and the flatness of the walls, however, reveal the provincial aspects of the design.

American Revivalism was even appreciated in Europe.

The architect Nicholas Serracino designed a church in a late Roman Baroque style for a French-Canadian congregation in New York City, which won first prize in the International Exhibit at Turin, Italy, in 1911. This church, St. Jean Baptiste, was built between 1910 and 1913. It has a powerful freestanding Corinthian portico, twin bell towers, and a magnificent dome on a drum over the crossing of the nave and transepts. The towers are 150 feet high and the dome is 175 feet above the church floor.

J. F. Sheblessy designed the Church of the Holy Family (1915) in Cincinnati, Ohio. It is the only Cincinnati church executed in a simplified Baroque Revival style. The church has a massive Ionic freestanding portico, two bell towers, and a saucer dome at the crossing of the nave and shallow transepts of the church. This dome is barely visible on the exterior but it dominates the interior, which is decorated with ornate painting, including trompe-l'oeil illusionism.

Neoclassical

The neoclassical style flourished from about 1895 to 1950; it was inspired by Roman and Greek architecture, and is characterized by large entrance porticoes with monumental columns. It is also closely related to the Beaux-Arts style and was used for both churches and temples.

A massive neoclassic freestanding Corinthian portico dominates the façade of the Eglise de Notre Dame, New York City. The apse and sanctuary were built in 1909–10 by the architects Dans and Otto; the nave and façade date from 1915 and were designed by Cross and Cross. The church is unfinished; a large crossing dome on a drum was never built.

Neoclassicism is also seen in the monumental colon-

Left: Nicholas Serracino: St. Jean Baptiste Church (Roman Catholic), 1067–71 Lexington Avenue, New York, NY, 1910–14.

Above: Herman Olszewski & William G. Kriegl: Holy Trinity Roman Catholic Church, 1120 North Noble, Chicago, IL, 1906.

Above: George Ries: St. Agnes Church, 548 Lafond Avenue, St. Paul, MN, 1909–12. Austrian Baroque.

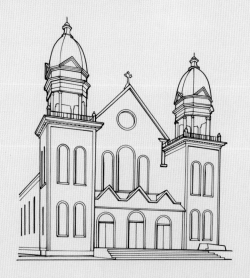

Above: Notre Dame de Mount Carmel, Grand Isle, Aroostook County, ME, 1909.

Above: Maginnis, Walsh & Sullivan: St. Catherine of Genoa, Catholic Church, Somerville, MA, *c.* 1915. Interior.

nade of the Temple Israel, Minneapolis, Minnesota. It was designed by Jack Liebenberg in 1928.

A small classical temple is the Temple Shalom (originally Congregation Sons of Joseph Temple), in Salem, Massachusetts. It is a late example of Classical Revival, built in 1952.

Romanesque Revival

Building on the earlier popularity of the Richardsonian Romanesque, Italian Romanesque models were frequently copied in the first decades of the twentieth century. Maginnis, Walsh & Sullivan was the most prominent

Catholic architectural firm; some of their best buildings are in the Romanesque style. St. John's Roman Catholic Church (1905) in Cambridge, Massachusetts, is an early example. One of their finest Romanesque buildings is the similar Church of St. Catherine of Genoa in Somerville, Massachusetts, built in 1915.

The city of Chelsea, Massachusetts, was devastated by a major urban fire in 1908. The following year, Henry Dustin Joll built a new temple for the Congregation Agudath Sholom (the Walnut Street Synagogue). This Romanesque building features two large, crenellated towers with bulbous roofs at the sides of the façade and a large central window surmounted with a Star of David. The church is built of brick. The interior follows the Orthodox layout, with the

Above: Jack Liebenberg: Temple Israel, 2324 Emerson Avenue South, Minneapolis, MN, 1928. Greek Revival.

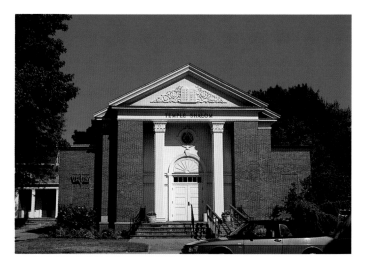

Above: Temple Shalom, originally Congregation Sons of Joseph Temple, 287 Lafayette Street, Salem, MA, 1952.

Torah shrine against the east wall and the raised bimah in the center of the temple.

The red brick of St. Paul's Church, Cambridge, Massachusetts, fits well into its urban environment. A basilica-type church, it was designed by Edward T. P. Graham in 1915. Blind arcades and a simple rose window identify it as Romanesque. A tall bell tower stands to one side at the rear of the church. A very similar design is found at Our Lady of Pity (Notre Dame de Pitié) Catholic Church, also in Cambridge. This church was built in 1920–21 for a French-speaking congregation; it is now Haitian.

Henry J. Schlacks was a leading architect of churches in Chicago, who drew on his extensive travels in Europe for his designs. Elements of various Early Christian churches are combined in the Roman Catholic Church of St. Mary of the Lake, built in Chicago between 1913 and 1917. The main body of the church is a basilica design modeled on St. Paul's Outside the Walls in Rome, with a separate bell tower (campanile) to the left side. The entrance is screened by a low arcade with a small arched gallery above it; the form recalls the forecourt, or narthex, of fourth- and fifth-century church designs.

An excellent example of the Romanesque style is found in St. Luke's Church (1924) in St. Paul, Minnesota, designed by John T. Comes (1876–1922). The massive central section is ornamented with a deeply recessed entrance with superimposed arches, a rose window of intricate tracery, and a blind arcade at the top.

Above: Henry Dustin Joll: Congregation Agudath Sholom (Walnut Street Synagogue), 145 Walnut Street, Chelsea, MA, 1909.

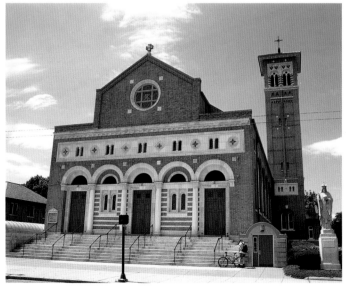

Above: Maginnis, Walsh & Sullivan: St. John's Roman Catholic Church, 2270 Massachusetts Avenue Cambridge, MA, 1905.

Above: St. Catherine of Genoa, Catholic Church, Somerville, MA, c. 1915. Front view.

Byzantine Revival

The Byzantine Revival was inspired by medieval churches built in the Eastern orthodox tradition in Venice and Istanbul (formerly Constantinople). After Constantine moved the capital of the Roman Empire to Byzantium in 323 and renamed it Constantinople, a new tradition grew up there and in Italy in the fifth and sixth centuries. The Eastern Orthodox Church developed under the influence of Middle Eastern, Hellenic, and Slavic history and culture, and in isolation from the Christian Churches of Western Europe and America, namely the Roman Catholic and the Reformed Protestant Churches. The formal break between the Christian East and West occurred in the medieval period, and from as early as the fourth century the Christians of the East were already living with very little contact with the Christians of the West.

The Byzantine Empire lasted until the fifteenth century. The most widespread Byzantine church design is a rotunda enclosed in a square and covered by a dome. This "cross-in-square" plan was adopted in Constantinople in the late

Above: Our Lady of Pity (Notre Dame de Pitié) Catholic Church, 35 Middlesex Street, Cambridge, MA, 1920–21.

Above: Henry J. Schlacks: St. Mary of the Lake, Roman Catholic Church, 4200 North Sheridan Road, Chicago, IL, 1913–17.

Above: John T. Comes: St. Luke's Church, Summit Avenue, 1079 Summit Avenue, St. Paul, MN, 1924.

Above: Edward T. P. Graham: St. Paul's Church, Bow and Arrow Streets, Cambridge, MA, 1915.

ninth century. It offers a square plan on the ground level, a cruciform shape above it, and finally the dome resting on a cylinder at the intersection of the arms of the cross and smaller domes or vaults over the four corners of the cube, between the arms of the cross. Byzantine churches typically face east. Other significant features include planar walls with rich ornament. The interior of the church is often richly decorated with mosaics or icons and much gold leaf, for the church is meant to provide a vision of heaven. In Orthodox belief, the icons are not simply images, but direct manifestations of the saints and holy figures, channels by which they may be known. After severe iconoclastic controversies in the ninth century, the Orthodox church concluded that icons were acceptable and necessary sacred images. The justification for images was found in the doctrine of the incarnation: Just as man was created in the image of God, Christ assumed the image of man in a perfected form. Icons that follow their original prototype are held to be equivalent to scripture. Therefore, style is rigid and conventional, governed by strict rules. An icon must be formally blessed to be complete.

In a sense, the entire Byzantine church is an icon, an image of heaven or a microcosm of the world, representing the setting of Christ's life on earth, the decorative sequence re-creating the imagery of the liturgical year, beginning with the Annunciation. The church is thus a symbolic counterpart to the reenactment of the sacred mystery in the liturgy.

The iconostasis is a distinctive feature of Orthodox

Above: Maginnis & Walsh; Frederick Vernon Murphy: National Shrine of the Immaculate Conception, Fourth Street and Michigan Avenue, NE, Washington, D.C., 1920.

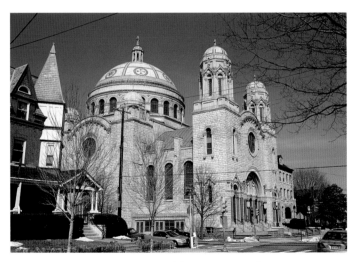

Above: Henry Dagit: Church of St. Francis de Sales, 4625 Springfield Avenue, Philadelphia, PA, 1906. Side view, showing dome.

Above: Bertram Grosvenor Goodhue: St. Bartholomew's, Park Avenue and East Fifty-first Street, New York, NY, 1919.

Above: Maginnis & Walsh; Frederick Vernon Murphy: National Shrine of the Immaculate Conception, Fourth Street and Michigan Avenue, NE, Washington, D.C., 1920. Side view.

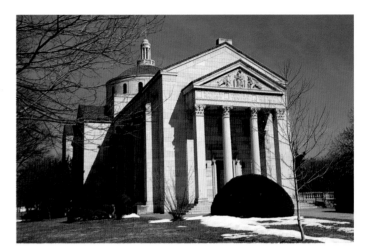

Above: Maginnis & Walsh: Chapel, Trinity College, 125 Michigan Avenue, NE, Washington, D.C., 1920–24. A simplified Byzantine-style church.

churches; it is a screen used in Byzantine churches to separate the sanctuary from the nave. It is pierced by three doors, originally a lattice of columns joined by a decorative parapet and coping. Since the fourteenth and fifteenth centuries it has become a wooden or stone wall covered with icons.

Above: Henry B. Herts & Walter Schneider: Congregation B'nai Jeshurun, 257 West Eighty-eighth Street, New York, NY, 1918. Byzantine/Romanesque.

The Byzantine style spread from Constantinople and Italy to Greece, the Balkans, and Russia. In America, it has been used for both synagogues and churches. Sometimes the Byzantine examples are closely copied, but often there is a strong sense of eclectic invention.

St. Bartholomew's church in New York City is one of the most impressive early Byzantine churches. It was designed by Bertram Grosvenor Goodhue and completed in 1919. The entrance portal, modeled on the Romanesque portal of St. Gilles-du-Gard in France, was created earlier by Stanford White for the old St. Bartholomew's Church in 1902 to commemorate Cornelius Vanderbilt II. In 1917, the portal was moved to the new church on Park Avenue.

The National Shrine of the Immaculate Conception, Washington, D.C., was built in the Byzantine style by Charles D. Maginnis and Timothy Walsh with Frederick Vernon Murphy in 1920. This is not a church for a neighborhood or parish, but a shrine intended for pilgrims. It is an eclectic combination of Byzantine and Romanesque forms. The tall center arch of the entry points to modernist styles as well. The mosaic-covered dome is Byzantine, while the tall bell tower, with its narrow arcades at the upper stories, recalls Italian Romanesque. The architects cited three reasons for their choice of style; one was that the Gothic was too expensive to build at that scale; also, the Episcopalian National Cathedral had just been completed in a Gothic style, and they did not want to seem to imitate it; finally, they felt the Byzantine domed style would blend better with the architecture of Washington, D.C.

Above: Charles R. Greco: Temple Beth Israel, 701 Farmington Avenue, West Hartford, CT, 1936.

Above: Rodeph Shalom Synagogue, 615 North Broad Street, Philadelphia, PA, 1927.

Above: Blackall, Clapp and Whittemore: Temple Obahei Shalom (Lovers of Peace), 1187 Beacon Street, Brookline, MA, 1928. Inspired by the Great Synagogue in Florence, Italy.

HOUSES OF WORSHIP

Left: Robert Kohn, Charles Butler, Clarence Stein: Temple Emanu-El, Fifth Avenue and Sixty-fifth Street, New York, NY, 1929. Byzantine/Romanesque.

Right: Emil Weil: Touro Synagogue, St. Charles Avenue at General Pershing, New Orleans, LA, 1908.

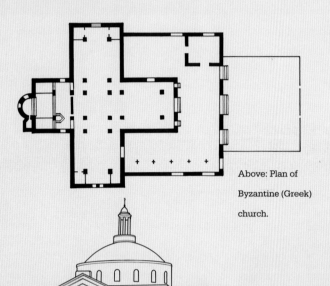

Above: Plan of Byzantine (Greek) church.

Above: Pendentives beneath dome.

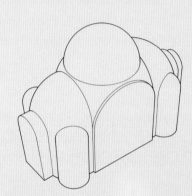

Above: Plaster model showing the interior volumes of the Hagia Sophia, Istanbul (formerly Constantinople), as solids.

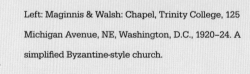

Left: Maginnis & Walsh: Chapel, Trinity College, 125 Michigan Avenue, NE, Washington, D.C., 1920–24. A simplified Byzantine-style church.

Left: Byzantine church; St. Taxiarchos at Cythnus.

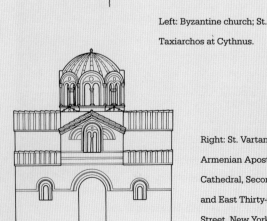

Right: St. Vartan, Armenian Apostolic Cathedral, Second Avenue and East Thirty-fourth Street, New York, NY, 1968.

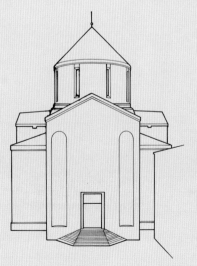

Above: Byzantine capitals; St. John the Baptist Carpatho-Russian Orthodox and Greek Catholic Church, Mill Hill Avenue, Bridgeport, CT, 1945.

Above: Classically inspired capitals, with the Star of David; Temple Shalom, originally Congregation Sons of Joseph Temple, Salem, MA, 1952.

Above: Ribbed dome: Bertram Grosvenor Goodhue: St. Bartholomew's, New York, NY, 1919.

Right: Domes: The ribbed dome of the Christian Science Mother Church in Boston is carried on an arcaded drum.

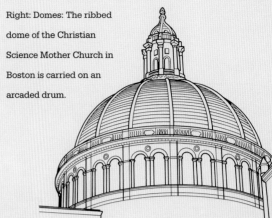

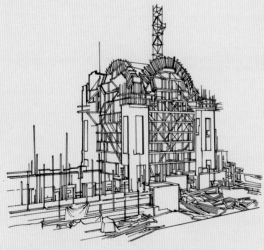

Above: Domes: a shallower dome, based on Byzantine precedents. Blackall, Clapp & Whittemore: Temple Obahei Shalom (Lovers of Peace), Brookline, MA, 1928.

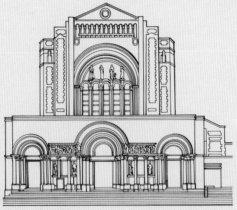

Above: Bertram Grosvenor Goodhue: St. Bartholomew's, New York, NY, 1919. Façade.

Above: St. Bartholomew's, New York, NY, 1919. Rose window on the transept.

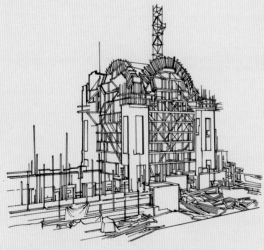

Above: St. Bartholomew's, New York, NY, 1919. Construction of the large crossing arches. This was an impressive building project.

Right: St. Bartholomew's, New York, NY, 1919. The pattern of ribs in the octagonal dome of the crossing is dramatic.

Left: St. Bartholomew's, New York, NY, 1919. The transition between the circular dome and square plan of the crossing is bridged by squinches.

Right: St. Bartholomew's, New York, NY, 1919. Detail of a squinch.

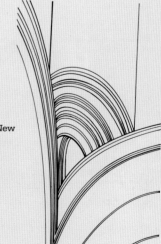

Above: Alfred S. Alschuler: Isaiah Temple, Chicago, IL, 1924. Interior.

Above: Isaiah Temple, Chicago, IL, 1924. A Byzantine-style temple.

Below: Walter S. Schneider and Henry Beaumont Hertz: B'nai Jeshurun, West Eighty-eighth Street, New York, NY, 1918.

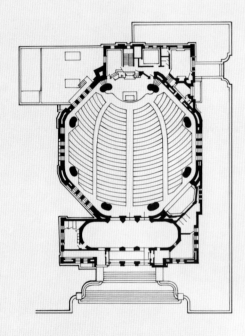

Left: Alfred S. Alschuler: Isaiah Temple, Chicago, IL, 1924. A Byzantine-style temple; the octagonal design is based on the Church of San Vitale, Ravenna, Italy.

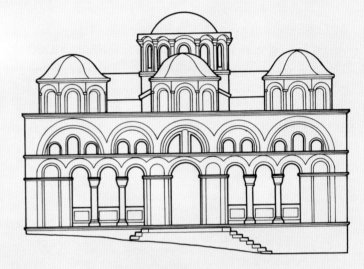

Above: A Byzantine church, Kiise Camii/St. Theodore, Istanbul (formerly Constantinople), eleventh century, with addition of outer narthex with three domes, c. 1320.

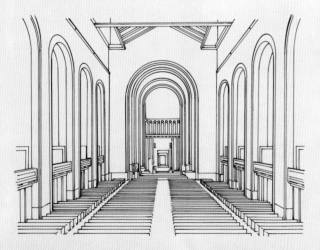

Above: Kohn, Butler and Stein: Temple Emanu-El, Fifth Avenue at Sixty-fifth Street, New York, NY, 1930.

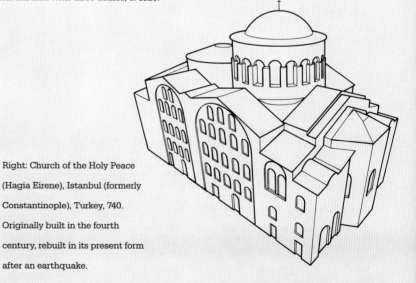

Right: Church of the Holy Peace (Hagia Eirene), Istanbul (formerly Constantinople), Turkey, 740. Originally built in the fourth century, rebuilt in its present form after an earthquake.

Above: Edward B. Stratton: Sts. Constantine and Helen Greek Orthodox Church, 14 Magazine Street, Cambridge, MA, 1935.

The church is a double-level church, like the church of St. Francis at Assisi. The cornerstone was laid in 1920 and the lower church was completed in 1931. The upper church was not finished until 1959, however. The shrine is 459 feet long and the bell tower is 359 feet high.

Ralph Adams Cram designed the deliberately ancient looking Byzantine/Romanesque Christ Church

(Methodist) on Park Avenue in New York City. It was built in 1932, using irregular limestone masonry and brick, with a tall central arch entry with a rose window and a narrow arcade at the top of the façade.

Many synagogues were built with large central domes inspired by the Byzantine tradition. The domed Byzantine-style Touro Synagogue in New Orleans, Louisiana, was named for Judah Touro, the son of a rabbi from Newport, Rhode Island. It was designed in 1908 by Emil Weil. In Chicago, Alfred S. Alschuler designed the Isaiah Temple (1924), which houses the oldest Jewish congregation in Chicago. San Francisco's Temple Emanu-El (1926) was modeled on the Hagia Sophia, Istanbul. It was designed by Arthur Brown, Jr. (of Bakewell, Brown & Schnaittacher), and features a large central dome, 150 feet high.

The Temple Obahei Shalom (Lovers of Peace) was built in Brookline, Massachusetts, in 1928 by Blackall, Clapp & Whittemore. The design with its monumental dome was inspired by the Great Synagogue at Florence, Italy. The hemispherical dome is supported by a sixteen-sided drum, which rises above a square section that rests upon the outer square of the building. A somewhat similar design is found in the Temple Beth Israel in West Hartford, Connecticut, designed by Charles R. Greco in 1936. The West Hartford

Right: Temple Beth-El Synagogue, 385 High Street, Fall River, MA, 1928.

temple has a ribbed dome that sits on a twelve-sided base, rather than the complex geometry of the Brookline synagogue. The flattened geometric design here is closer to Art Deco.

An even more simplified version is found in the Temple Beth-El Synagogue (1928) in Fall River, Massachusetts. The overall building is very cubic, with the exception of the central dome and the two towers with domed roofs on the façade.

The domed Byzantine church or temple was the most common form of the Byzantine Revival, but there was also a variation of this type that emphasized a single giant façade portal, found in urban churches such as Congregation B'nai Jeshurun (1918) in New York City, by Henry B. Herts and Walter Schneider. Another example is Temple Emanuel in New York City, 1929. This Byzantine/Romanesque

temple is the largest reform synagogue in the United States. It can hold 2,500 people; the main ceiling is 103 feet high.

Greek Orthodox congregations were naturally eager to build Byzantine-style churches. Although it is a small brick church, the Greek Orthodox church built in Brockton, Massachusetts, in 1933 has characteristic Byzantine features, including the narrow windows with stone light screens and the two domed lanterns on the façade. The stone building of Sts. Constantine & Helen Greek Orthodox Church in Cambridge, Massachusetts, designed by Edward B. Stratton in 1935 is very similar.

St. Gerasimos Greek Orthodox Church in New York City was designed by Kokkins and Lyons and completed in 1951. This very stylized Byzantine church has a two-tone façade, with white stone columns and arches topped with a flat wall of brick.

Above: Greek Orthodox church, Brockton, MA, 1933.

Russian Orthodox

The Russian Orthodox tradition is an offshoot of the Byzantine tradition. In America, Russian Orthodox churches with their characteristic onion domes were built by Russian immigrants as early as 1844 in Alaska and later in areas with concentrations of Russian immigrants, such as Chicago and New York. These included frontier settlements such as northern Minnesota and large urban centers such as Brooklyn, New York. With the Russian Revolution in 1917, the Russian Orthodox churches in America were left independent from their mother church.

The Ukrainian Catholic Church of Sts. Peter and Paul in Ansonia, Connecticut, was built in 1915. It is an impressive, if somewhat awkward, composition with a tall central dome resting on an octagonal drum. The plan is a Greek

Above: Sts. Peter and Paul, Ukrainian Catholic Church, 105 Clifton Avenue, Ansonia, CT, 1915.

Above: St. John the Baptist Carpatho-Russian Orthodox and Greek Catholic Church, 364 Mill Hill Avenue, Bridgeport, CT, 1945.

Above: Sts. Peter and Paul, Russian Orthodox church, Minn. Hwy. 65, Bramble, Koochiching County, MN, 1915–18.

cross, and there are four domed towers nested in the interior corners of the cross. The multiple domes recall old Slavic architecture.

In the far northern reaches of Minnesota, near the Canadian border, stands an isolated wooden church with an onion dome, a testament of the early Russian immigrants to this area. The Russian Orthodox church of Sts. Peter and Paul is located near the tiny town of Bramble, in Koochiching County. It was built during the years of the Russian Revolution, 1915–18, and the wood frame building is a product of a society that soon would exist only in exile. The exterior of the wood frame building is very plain, covered with clapboards. The interior is also made of simple wooden carpentry, but there is an elaborate iconostasis with many icons of the traditional saints.

Rising like a vision of Czarist Russia in western Chicago, the St. Nicholas Ukrainian Catholic Cathedral is a tall church with multiple domes and shimmering mosaics on the façade. It was designed by Worthmann, Steinbach & Piontek and built in 1915.

In a rural area of New Jersey, Russian immigrants began to build the monumental St. Vladimir's Memorial Russian Orthodox Church in 1934. Modeled on the historic Santa Sophia in Kiev (1037), the central-plan church features a

Left: St. Peter and St. Paul, Russian Orthodox church, Bramble, MN, 1915–18. Interior.

single large, gold onion dome on a drum. Located in Rova Farms in Cassville, New Jersey, the church was designed by Roman Verkovsky and Sergei Padukow. Portions of the church are still under construction.

The small Russian Orthodox Church of St. Nicholas in Stratford, Connecticut, was built in 1941 and is a gem of Slavic design, with multiple gilded domes. The interior features all the traditional decoration, including mosaics and an impressive iconostasis.

Eclecticism shaped the design of St. John the Baptist Carpatho-Russian Orthodox and Greek Catholic Church (1945) in Bridgeport, Connecticut. The light-colored stone building has seven domes, counting the large crossing dome. It recalls the design of the modern Romanesque church of Sacre Coeur in Paris by Paul Abadie, although the walls are flatter and less ornamented. The dome is supported by a circular drum, which is closer to Renaissance prototypes. The detailing is medieval Byzantine, however, including the mosaics at the entrance and in the interior, and the ornate carved columns.

Above: Worthmann, Steinbach & Piontek: St. Nicholas Ukrainian Catholic Cathedral, 2238 West Rice Street, Chicago, IL, 1915.

Above: Church of St. Nicholas, 1 Honeyspot Road, Stratford, CT, 1941.

Above: Roman Verkovsky, Sergei Padukow: St. Vladimir's Memorial Russian Orthodox Church, Rte. 57, North of Rte. 528, Rova Farms, Cassville, Jackson Township, New Jersey, begun in 1934.

Above: Onion domes: Church of St. Nicholas, Stratford Avenue, Stratford, CT, 1941.

Above: Doorway of a modern Russian Orthodox church: Church of St. Nicholas, Stratford, CT, 1941.

Above: Simplified diagram of an iconostasis: A partition covered with icons that separates the main space of the church from the sanctuary area behind it.

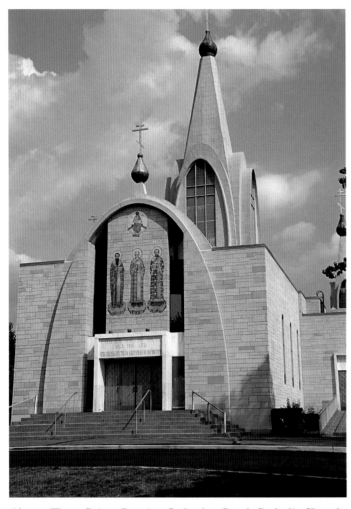

Above: Three Saints Russian Orthodox Greek Catholic Church, 26 Howard Avenue, Ansonia, CT, 1955. Parabolic arches form the nave.

Above: Three Saints Russian Orthodox Greek Catholic Church, Ansonia, CT, 1955. Detail of mosaic on façade.

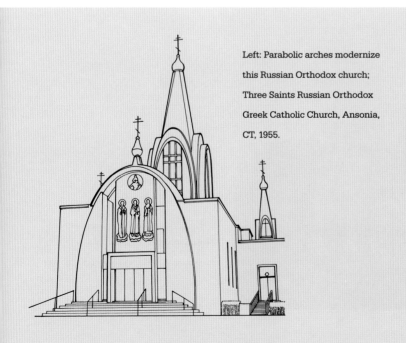

Left: Parabolic arches modernize this Russian Orthodox church; Three Saints Russian Orthodox Greek Catholic Church, Ansonia, CT, 1955.

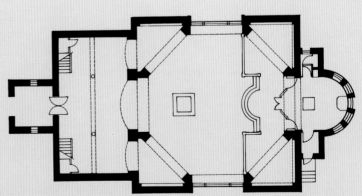

Above: Louis Sullivan: Plan of Holy Trinity Russian Orthodox Cathedral, Chicago, IL, 1899–1903.

Left: Sergi Padukow: St. Nicholas Russian Orthodox Church of Whitestone, 14-65 Clintonville St., Queens, New York City, 1969.

A modernistic variant of the Russian Orthodox church, with parabolic arches forming the nave, is found at the Three Saints Russian Orthodox Greek Catholic Church in Ansonia, Connecticut, of 1955.

Such modernism is rare in this normally conservative tradition. Much more traditional is the design by Sergi Padukow for the Russian Orthodox Church in New Kuban, New Jersey, of 1964. The church is a badge of identity for the community of exiled White Russians who resisted the Communist Revolution in 1917 and during World War II.

Built of brick and wood, the central dome is actually an octagonal spire; there are also five small turrets with onion domes. The interior is resplendent with icons and gold leaf. The iconostasis is particularly impressive.

A single broad, golden dome on a circular drum dominates the church of Sts. Volodymyr & Olha (1975) in Chicago, designed by Jaroslaw A. Korsunsky. There are smaller domes on four towers, but overall this church is closer to Byzantine designs than it is to the more vertical churches from Russia.

Left: Jaroslaw A. Korsunsky: Sts. Volodymyr & Olha Church, 739 North Oakley Boulevard, Chicago, IL, 1975.

Spanish Eclectic

Especially popular in California, the Mission Style (*c.* 1890–1920) re-created the look of earlier Spanish colonial architecture. Churches feature stucco walls and red tile roofs, with Spanish inspired detailing. Other Spanish-influenced churches were built from Florida to New York City. The style was given a major boost from the 1915 Pan-American Exhibition in San Francisco and the contemporary studies of Spanish architecture by Bertram Grosvenor Goodhue, designer of the exhibition.

Well before it became a national trend, the Spanish Revival was seen in Omaha, Nebraska, in the works of Thomas Rogers Kimball (1862–1934), who had studied at MIT and the Ecole des Beaux-Arts. St. Cecilia's Cathedral in Omaha is one of the ten largest cathedrals in the U.S. This church was designed in 1901 and construction began in 1905. It was used for services from 1916, although it was not actually completed until 1959. The two baroque towers flank a richly ornamented entrance.

Right: Albert C. Martin: St. Vincent de Paul Roman Catholic Church, 621 West Adams Blvd., Los Angeles, CA, 1925.

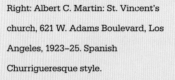

Left: Thomas Rogers Kimball: St. Philomena's Catholic Church (St. Frances Cabrini Catholic Church and Rectory), 1335 South Tenth Street, Omaha, NE, 1908–10.

Right: Albert C. Martin: St. Vincent's church, 621 W. Adams Boulevard, Los Angeles, 1923–25. Spanish Churrigueresque style.

Above: Thomas Rogers Kimball: St. Cecilia's Cathedral, 701 North Fortieth Street, Omaha, NE, 1901/1959. One of the ten largest cathedrals in the U.S., this church was designed in 1901; construction began in 1905, with services being held from 1916. Final completion took place in 1959.

Above: Madisonville Presbyterian Church, Pine and St. Joseph Streets, Madisonville, LA, 1905. A wood frame building, covered with clapboards, which mixes classical round-arched and Gothic pointed windows, and incorporates a Spanish Baroque style profile at the roofline.

Above: Church of Our Lady, San Mateo, CA. A simple Mission Revival style church.

Above: Church of Our Lady, San Mateo, CA. The interior is notable for the exposed scissor-trusses.

Also in Omaha, Kimball's St. Philomena's Catholic Church (now St. Frances Cabrini Catholic Church and Rectory), was built in the Spanish Revival style, 1908–10. The façade has a single tower at the right, a baroque parapet, and considerable ornament. The interior of the hall church has powerful exposed wooden ceiling trusses.

In Los Angeles, St. Vincent de Paul Roman Catholic Church was built in 1923–25. The architect was Albert C. Martin, who also designed the Los Angeles City Hall. This church has even more profuse ornament on the façade and has a single baroque tower at the left side. The crossing is crowned with a tall hemispherical dome. The decoration of this church is in the Spanish Churrigueresque style. The term is used from the late eighteenth century to denote the most exuberantly ornamental phase of Spanish architectural decoration, which lasted from about 1675 to 1750. The term derives from the Churriguera family in Salamanca, who were the principal exponents of the style.

Not all Spanish Revival churches are so elaborate. The Madisonville Presbyterian Church in Madisonville, Louisiana, built in 1905, is a simple wood frame building covered with clapboards. The exterior mixes classical round-arched and Gothic pointed windows, and incorporates a Spanish Baroque style profile at the roofline. Another example is the Church of Our Lady in San Mateo, California, a simple Mission Revival style church.

More recently, the distinctive Spanish colonial adobe style has been revived at Santa Maria De La Paz Catholic Community in Santa Fe, New Mexico. Constructed in 1994, this postmodern church re-creates the atmosphere of the earliest Spanish colonial churches of New Mexico.

Above: Faith Lutheran Church (Sv. Evang. Lutheran Augustana), 311 Broadway, Cambridge, MA, 1908–9.

Scandinavian Revival

The distinctive forms of southern Swedish medieval churches were occasionally copied in the U.S. The Swedish-born architect Martin Gravely Hedmark created fine examples in Providence, Rhode Island (Gloria Dei Evangelical Lutheran Church, 1925–28), and New York City (Trinity Baptist Church, 1929–31). The Gloria Dei Evangelical Lutheran Church is a large urban church built of brick upon a large limestone basement story. It is notable for the mix of medieval and modern Swedish motifs, including the Viking-style iron strapwork on the entrance doors and the remarkable tall bell tower, which has a

stepped gable top. This tower recalls aspects of the parish churches built in southern Sweden in the Middle Ages and even Baroque eras. Hedmark's Trinity Baptist Church in New York City is even more theatrical, with a tall false front with a stepped gable of brick. This church is close to Art Deco influences with its geometric patterning.

Many southern Swedish churches have stocky central towers, and this feature inspired the Faith Lutheran Church (Sv. Evang. Lutheran Augustana) in Cambridge, Massachusetts, which was built in 1908–9 for Swedish immigrants. A similar squat tower is found in the Church of the Epiphany (Episcopal) in New York City, designed by Wyeth & King, with Eugene W. Mason, associate architect, in 1939.

Left: Viking-style ironwork on door; Martin Gravely Hedmark: Gloria Dei Evangelical Lutheran Church, Providence, RI, 1925–28.

Right: Serpentine columns in window: Gloria Dei Evangelical Lutheran Church, Providence, RI, 1925–28.

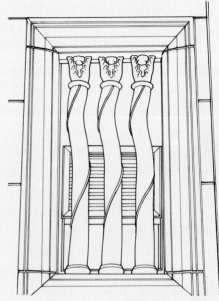

Above: Martin Gravely Hedmark: Gloria Dei Evangelical Lutheran Church, 15 Hayes Street, Providence, RI, 1925–28. Stepped gable bell tower.

Above: Comparison: Church, Asphult, southern Sweden.

Above: Martin Gravely Hedmark: Trinity Baptist Church (originally First Church), 250 East Sixty-first Street, New York, NY, 1929–31. Swedish Hansa gables, with Art Deco flair.

Above: Wyeth & King, Eugene W. Mason: Church of the Epiphany (Episcopal), 1393 York Avenue, East Seventy-fourth Street, New York, NY, 1939.

Mormon, or Latter-day Saint, Temples

Houses of worship for the Church of Latter-day Saints continued to be built in traditional form, but were occasionally influenced by modernist design. The Prairie School proved popular for Mormon temples in the early decades of the century. Later churches borrow aspects of Art Moderne or Art Deco.

*

Specialized forms of non-European origin were built for different faiths; these are found wherever large groups of immigrants are located. These are primarily shaped by the national traditions of the immigrant group and their religious beliefs. Among the most distinctive are Hindu temples and Islamic mosques. Other examples include temples for the Baha'i and Zen faiths.

Japanese Christians in Hawaii built churches which combined national traditions. The Makiki Japanese Christian Church in Honolulu is an example of transplanted Japanese-style architecture. It was built in 1904, with additions in 1915 and 1932. It is modeled on a Japanese castle of the sixteenth century, when Christianity was first brought to Japan.

Above: Makiki Japanese Christian Church, 829 Pensacola Street, Honolulu, HI, 1904 (additions 1915, 1932). Japanese style architecture, modeled on a sixteenth-century fortress.

Wrightian, or Prairie, Style

The Prairie Style, or Prairie School, was an indigenous American style, created by Frank Lloyd Wright and his Midwestern counterparts. It flourished from the 1890s to about 1920. The style includes elements from Japanese architecture and a rejection of European historicism. Wright's later Organic Architecture designs build on the principles of the Prairie School. The key example is Wright's Unity Temple in Oak Park, Illinois, 1906.

The question of a truly American style was more urgently raised in the early twentieth century. Both Wright and Louis Sullivan strongly condemned the continued borrowing of European forms by American architects. Wright felt that a new architecture based on modern living patterns, technologies, and concepts of space had to be created. Rather than seeing the house as a box containing various rooms, he wanted to create the interiors first and then shape the house around them. By emphasizing the flow of space in his houses, Wright helped shift American architecture from an architecture of solid mass to one of volume and transparency. With windows treated as banks of light screens, walls became more dynamic as well. In his *Autobiography* of 1932, Wright declared:

> I believe religious experience is outgrowing the church—not outgrowing religion, but outgrowing the church as an institution, just as architecture has outgrown the Renaissance and for reasons human, scientific and similar. I cannot see the ancient institutional form of any church building as anything but sentimental survival for burial.[2]

Unity Temple returns to the primitive simplicity of the first New England meetinghouses, avoiding the traditional symbolism of the steeple that points to heaven. Wright later explained that the church steeple, although traditional, was a misleading symbol and that humanity should focus on the earthly plane: "Was not the time come to be more simple, to have more faith in man on his earth and less anxiety concerning his Heaven about which he could know nothing?"[3] Wright rejected the traditional steeple—"Why point to

Above: F. L. Wright: Unity Temple, 875 Lake Street, Oak Park, IL, 1904–6. One of the earliest churches built using concrete.

Above: F. L. Wright: Unity Temple, Oak Park, IL, 1904–6. Detail; the cubic forms and abstract ornament break with historic tradition.

heaven?" he asked. Conventional symbols left him cold. His church was designed to celebrate people and their life and struggle here on earth. It was to be a "noble Room in the service of man for the worship of God."[4] Wright was descended from a long line of Unitarian ministers on his mother's side, the "God-Almighty Joneses" as they were known, and his father was an occasional preacher.

The budget for this church was extremely limited, and Wright managed to stay within the $45,000 allotted by using a relatively new material, poured concrete. The cubic form is starkly simple, alleviated with cast abstract patterns that Wright derived from plant shapes. Wright's term for this kind of abstraction was "conventionalization," and it played a large role in his thinking; it meant to him the discipline of intellect over disorder. In 1939, he wrote: "To me abstraction—to make anything in the abstract—is to make clear in some pattern the spirit of the thing."[5] The organization of Unity Temple is simple and clearly thought out. Form does follow function here. The church plan has a square form for the meetinghouse, joined to another square for the Sunday school by a passageway.

Wright's abstract use of poured concrete is in sharp distinction to the first concrete church in the world, which was cast in a Gothic style. That church is St. Jean the Evangelist in the Montmartre district of Paris, built by Anatole de Baudot between 1894 and 1902. The rediscovery of concrete was to have a profound effect on modern architecture. Concrete had been a staple of ancient Roman architecture, but the secret of its composition was lost with the fall of the Roman empire. Only in the nineteenth century was it rediscovered, and for decades it was used only for foundations and for landscaping purposes. Wright's Unity Temple is among the first concrete buildings in America.

The Unitarian service emphasizes the sermon and the contact between worshipers. The central meeting room facilitates this wonderfully. One cannot enter the central space directly; one has to turn ninety degrees, pass through a corridor, and then ascend a few stairs to the room, which is on a raised platform. The ceiling is set with square coffers between the concrete beams and translucent amber skylights. A ribbon window around the outer walls admits more light, like a clerestory. The alcoves were flooded with light from this window, and artificial light was used to create the same effect at night. The diffuse lighting emphasized the unity of the space. The colors are cool and highlighted

Above: F. L. Wright: Unity Temple, Oak Park, IL, 1904–6. Entrance.

Above: Comparison: Anatole de Baudot: Church of St. Jean the Evangelist, Montmartre, Paris, France, 1894–1902. First concrete church in the world, cast in a Gothic style.

by rectilinear patterns of wooden ornament and stencils. The motif of the right angle is carried throughout the design. Architect Philip Johnson has called this "the most beautiful room in America," and it is indeed an extraordinary space.

The room holds four hundred people. It was built with four interior piers that carry the overhead structure. These concrete posts were hollow and served as freestanding ducts to evenly distribute heat.

Wright's modernist style signified more than just freedom from outmoded European precedents—it meant for him the true architecture of democracy: "As a man is, so must he build. Just as a nation builds—so that nation is. We have the buildings we deserve to have.... There are many ways in life to conceal a man's true nature, but when he builds he cannot hide. You have him as he is."[6]

The flat roof and horizontal planes of Unity Temple blended with the Midwestern prairie landscape. Other

Above: William Drummond: First Congregational Church of Austin, 5701 West Midway Park, Chicago, IL, 1908. A Prairie Style church by a former assistant of Wright's.

Above: William Gray Purcell and George Feick, Jr.: Stewart Memorial Presbyterian Church, now the Redeemer Missionary Baptist Church, 116 East Thirty-second Street, Minneapolis, MN, 1909–10. Detail.

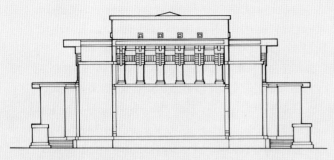

Above: Frank Lloyd Wright: Unity Temple, Oak Park, IL, 1904–6. Elevation.
Wright's design broke with traditional churches with steeples and tall naves.

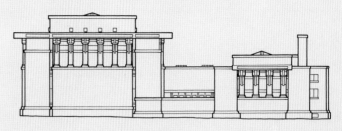

Above: Frank Lloyd Wright: Unity Temple, Oak Park, IL, 1904–6. Side elevation.

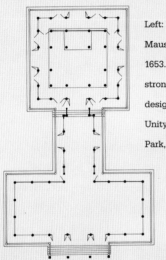

Left: Plan of Taiyu-in Mausoleum, Japan, 1653. This plan has strong parallels to the design of Wright's Unity Temple, Oak Park, IL.

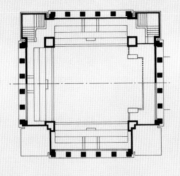

Above: Frank Lloyd Wright: Unity Temple, Oak Park, IL, 1904–6. Plan of auditorium at balcony level.

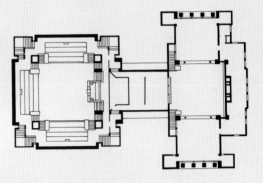

Above: Frank Lloyd Wright: Unity Temple, Oak Park, IL, 1904–6. Plan. The main meeting room was the focal point of the architecture.

Below: Frank Lloyd Wright: Unity Temple, Oak Park, IL, 1904–6. Longitudinal section.

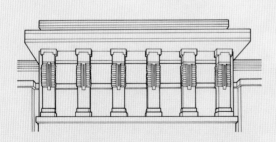

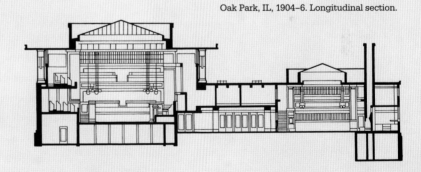

Above: Frank Lloyd Wright: Unity Temple, Oak Park, IL, 1904–6. Detail of upper windows.

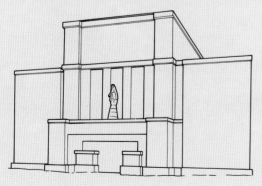

Left: William Drummond: First Congregational Church of Austin, 5701 West Midway Park, Chicago, IL, 1908. The Prairie Style is characterized by horizontal lines and geometric shapes. Drummond had been one of Wright's assistants.

Right: William Drummond: Plan of First Congregational Church of Austin, 5701 West Midway Park, Chicago, IL, 1908.

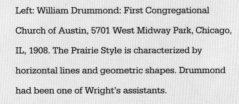

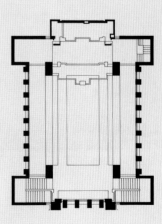

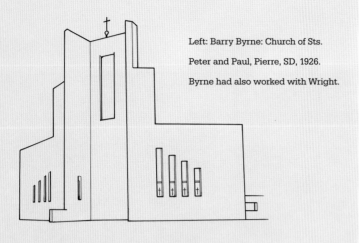

Left: Barry Byrne: Church of Sts. Peter and Paul, Pierre, SD, 1926. Byrne had also worked with Wright.

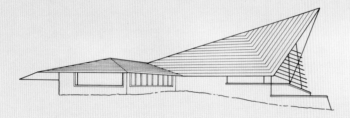

Above: Elevation of Frank Lloyd Wright: Unitarian Meeting House, Shorewood Hills (near Madison), WI, 1947. The configuration of the roof reminds many of praying hands.

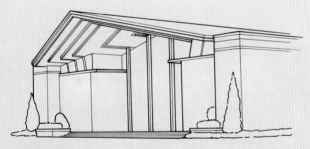

Above: Leonard Gabert and Mackie & Kamrath: Temple Emanu El, Houston, TX, c. 1948. A late Prairie School temple.

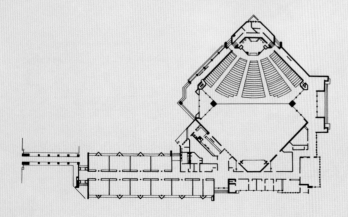

Above: Leonard Gabert and Mackie & Kamrath: Temple Emanu El, Houston, TX, c. 1948. Plan.

Prairie School churches were built in the Midwest. William Drummond (1876–1946) had been associated with Wright between 1899 and 1909, and his First Congregational Church of Austin (1908) in Chicago is clearly derived from Wright's Larkin Building in Buffalo, New York, and Unity Temple in Oak Park, Illinois. This church is built of bearing walls made of brick and heavy timber framing. The interior has a tall flat-roofed nave lit by glass skylights and flanked by side aisles. Interior wall treatments use earth colors, in the manner of Wright—sand-colored plaster and stained wood trim. Unlike Wright's Unity Temple, the social hall and kitchen are in the basement and not placed in an adjoining structure.

In Minneapolis, William Gray Purcell and George Feick, Jr., built the Stewart Memorial Presbyterian Church along similar lines in 1909–10. This is now the Redeemer Missionary Baptist Church. Further west, the Prairie Style was adopted for almost two dozen Mormon temples. The style persisted even after Wright abandoned it.

Barry Byrne (1883–1967), who had also worked with Wright, built the Church of Sts. Peter and Paul in Pierre, South Dakota, in a version of the Prairie Style in 1926. Born in Chicago, Byrne had no architectural training when he wrote to Frank Lloyd Wright in 1902 asking for an interview. Wright was impressed with his desire to become an architect and hired him as an apprentice. Byrne worked for Wright until 1908 and assisted with houses and the Unity Temple in Oak Park. In 1922, Byrne built his first church, and for the next forty years, he tended to specialize in religious buildings. His designs moved away from the Prairie Style toward a more expressionistic modern version of Gothic design. His Church of Christ the King in Tulsa, Oklahoma, was a major success, and in 1928 he was asked to design a church in Cork, Ireland, which has been described as the first European Catholic church built by an American architect. His work after 1945 will be discussed in the next chapter.

Wrightian, or Organic, Style

The later works of Frank Lloyd Wright go beyond his earlier Prairie Style, as he explored new formal vocabularies of circular, spiral, hexagonal, and triangular forms. Always original, he continued striving to create a new style for the national identity of America. He wanted to devise an "architecture for democracy" and felt that the outmoded styles of Europe were only a handicap. His architecture symbolized his view of human freedom and dignity with its originality and natural forms.

In 1946, Frank Lloyd Wright lamented the state of current church design:

> Cannot religion be brought into a human scale? Can it not be humanized and natural? Must "church architecture" be starched stiff as a hard collar and the symbols of worship be no more inspiring than a black bow tie or a pair of suspenders? What is a church? Isn't it a gratifying home for the spirit of human love and kindness?…Why must a church, even on a small scale, crucify the congregation just because Jesus was himself crucified?[7]

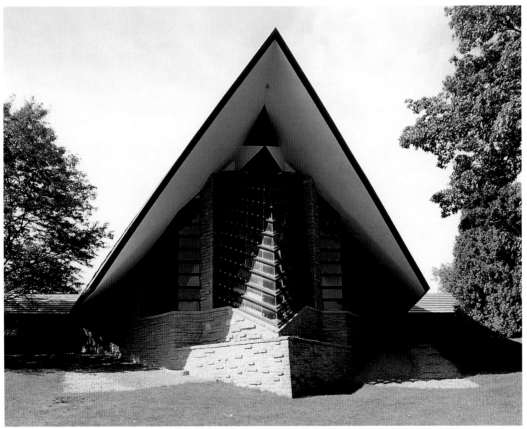

Above: Frank Lloyd Wright: Unitarian Meeting House, Shorewood Hills (Madison), WI, 1947. Side view. The congregation members hauled the stone from a nearby quarry.

Left: Unitarian Meeting House, Shorewood Hills (Madison), WI, 1947. Front view; the folded shape of the roof reminds many of praying hands, or the prow of a ship.

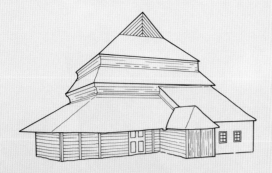

Above: Timber Synagogue, Gwozdziec, Galicia, seventeenth century. The pyramidal shape anticipates Wright's synagogue in Elkins Park, PA.

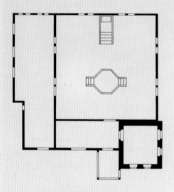

Left: Plan of Timber Synagogue, Gwozdziec, Galicia, seventeenth century.

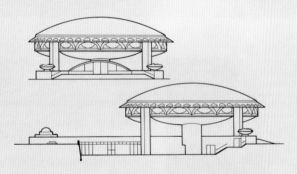

Above: Frank Lloyd Wright: Front and side elevation of Annunciation Greek Orthodox Church, Wauwatosa, WI, 1956.

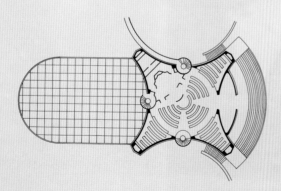

Above: Frank Lloyd Wright: Plan of Annunciation Greek Orthodox Church, Wauwatosa, WI, 1956.

Above: Frank Lloyd Wright: Beth Sholom Synagogue, Old York and Foxcroft Roads, Elkins Park, PA, 1954–59. Front view.

Wright congratulated the Unitarian church in Shorewood Hills near Madison, Wisconsin, for their forward thinking in theology and for hiring him to build a meetinghouse to lead in "taking the first courageous step over the threshold of the Atomic Era."[8] Wright believed that mankind was on the doorstep of a new age of cheap power and absolute freedom and that architecture needed to provide new models of community and integration. Wright's father had been a founding member of this Unitarian Society in 1879, and he renewed his membership in the congregation in 1938. This 1947 church is distinguished by a tall peaked roof with a projecting curtain wall of glass. The shape of the roof has been likened by the architect himself to a pair of praying

Above: Frank Lloyd Wright: Beth Sholom Synagogue, Elkins Park, PA, 1954–59. Detail.

hands, although many also see it as resembling the prow of a ship. Either association is appropriate to a church. The entrance is on the long side and sheltered under a wide overhanging eave, reminiscent of Wright's Prairie Style. The church members contributed their labor, as well as money, for this church, hauling tons of stone from a nearby quarry.

Wright designed the Beth Sholom Synagogue in Elkins Park, Pennsylvania, to give the effect of a mountain of light, recalling Mount Sinai where Moses received the tablets of the law from God. The pyramidal shape may also have roots in seventeenth- and eighteenth-century wooden synagogues in central Europe, which developed a distinctive tiered roof plan, sometimes nearly resembling pagodas. Wright designed this synagogue in consultation with the Rabbi; it was built between 1954 and 1959. In a letter to Rabbi Mortimer J. Cohen, Wright explained the simplicity of his plans for construction:

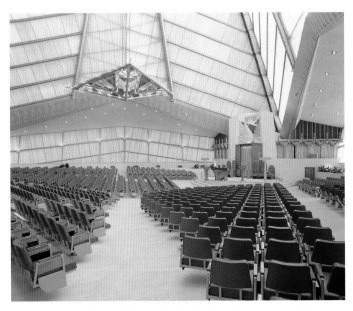

Above: Frank Lloyd Wright: Beth Sholom Synagogue, Elkins Park, PA, 1954–59. Interior.

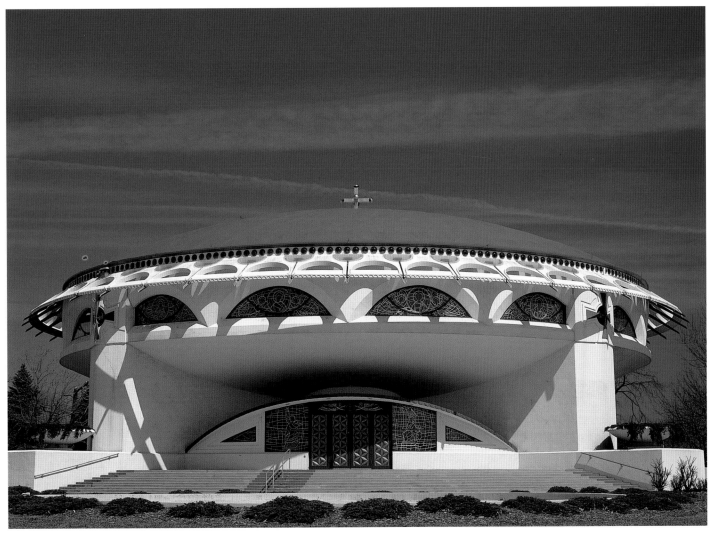

Above: Frank Lloyd Wright: Annunciation Greek Orthodox Church, Wauwatosa, WI, 1956. Exterior.

Left: Frank Lloyd Wright: Annunciation Greek Orthodox Church, Wauwatosa, WI, 1956. Side view.

The scheme is truly simple. Construction is modern as can be. Stamped copper shells erected for structural members are filled with concrete in which the necessary steel rods are embedded for stresses: The tops of the shells are removable for this purpose—thus no forming is necessary. The building is set up on an interior temporary scaffold. The outer walls are double wired glass outside—a blue tinted plastic inside—about an inch of airspace between. Heat rises at the walls from the floor.[9]

Left: Frank Lloyd Wright: Annie Pfeiffer Memorial Chapel, Florida Southern College, Lakeland, FL, 1941.

The tall pyramid of glass becomes a glowing pyramid of light at night, as the interior lights shine through the glass curtain walls.

*

One of Wright's most futuristic designs, the Annunciation Greek Orthodox Church (1956) in Wauwatosa, Wisconsin, features a broad concrete dome covering the entire church. The saucer dome is reminiscent of the domes of Byzantine architecture, but also evokes contemporary science fiction. Although the form broke with established precedents, Wright insisted he was guided by nature.

> Through nature we can sense anew the universal
> pulse, the inner rhythm of all being. We must do that
> if we are to recapture the reverence that gave life to
> the Gothic spirit.[10]

The dome and arch form repeat throughout the composition of the church. Inset cross-shaped windows link the church to earlier Byzantine designs.

Frank Lloyd Wright designed the entire campus of Florida Southern College, Lakeland, Florida, in 1938. Although some aspects of his designs were not carried out, the campus is a coherent ensemble of his later style. It is constructed of steel-reinforced concrete and makes frequent use of hexagonal modules for design. The Annie Pfeiffer Memorial Chapel was built in 1941. It is an irregular modernistic building, with a tall tower with patterns of hexagons and triangles. The interior space is lit by skylights and ribbon windows. A balcony circles the entire room.

Nature and geometry come together in a Swedenborgian chapel designed by Lloyd Wright, Frank Lloyd Wright's son. The Wayfarer's Chapel was built in 1949–51 in Rancho Palos Verdes, California. Lloyd Wright stated that he wanted this church to emphasize life, not death: "I wanted to get away from the concept of the sepulcher. The churches that we built in Europe are based mainly on the concept of the sepulcher; that is, the grave. I wanted the living thing, not the burial crypt." The overall concept was of a shrine in the redwood forest, overlooking the Pacific Ocean. As the plantings have grown over the last fifty years, the church fulfills this vision more than ever.

Above: Lloyd Wright: Wayfarer's Chapel, 5755 Palos Verdes Drive South, Rancho Palos Verdes, CA, 1949–51. A Swedenborgian chapel by the sea.

Craftsman Style Churches

A related American style was that of the Craftsman Style bungalows between 1905 and 1930. The style originated in California and was based on the Arts and Crafts inspired designs of Charles Sumner Greene and Henry Mather Greene. It was rarely used for churches, but one example is the Morgan Park Church of God in Christ (Morgan Park Congregational Church), by Patton, Holmes & Flynn in Chicago of 1916. This church is made of brick, with a long low profile, like a bungalow. The façade is opened with a large central window, divided by brick piers and recessed spandrels.

The simple bungalow form was used for St. Rita's Church, Marion, Massachusetts. This church is low and horizontal, with an open interior.

Although now extensively altered, the B'nai Israel Synagogue in Bridgeport, Connecticut, was built in the Craftsman Style by Leonard Asheim in 1911. It is now the

Left: St. Rita's Church, 113 Front Street, Marion, MA. This church is basically a large bungalow with an open interior.

Below: Leonard Asheim: B'nai Israel Synagogue, 1100 Park Avenue, Bridgeport, CT, 1911. Now the New Hope Missionary Baptist Church. Extensively remodeled; the diamond-paned windows are the most obvious link to the Craftsman Style.

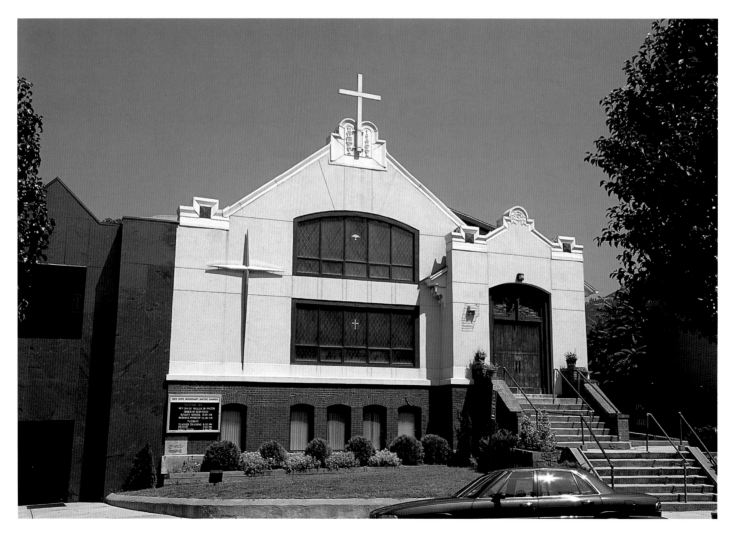

Above: St. Rita's Church, Marion, MA. Interior.

Left: Leonard Asheim: B'nai Israel Synagogue, Bridgeport, CT, 1911. Now the New Hope Missionary Baptist Church. Note the new Christian cross joined to the original tablets of the Mosaic commandments.

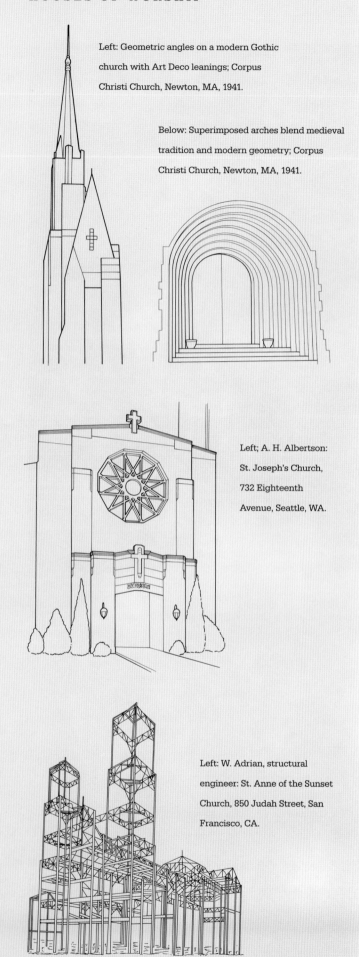

Left: Geometric angles on a modern Gothic church with Art Deco leanings; Corpus Christi Church, Newton, MA, 1941.

Below: Superimposed arches blend medieval tradition and modern geometry; Corpus Christi Church, Newton, MA, 1941.

Left; A. H. Albertson: St. Joseph's Church, 732 Eighteenth Avenue, Seattle, WA.

Left: W. Adrian, structural engineer: St. Anne of the Sunset Church, 850 Judah Street, San Francisco, CA.

home of the New Hope Missionary Baptist Church. The diamond-paned windows are the most obvious link to the Craftsman Style. The new Christian cross, joined to the original tablets of the Mosaic commandments, marks the transition in how this structure has been used.

Modernistic

A variety of modernistic idioms developed in the first few decades of the twentieth century, using new building technologies and adapting traditional forms to a greater or lesser degree. Modern structural techniques were found in St. Joseph's Church in Seattle, Washington, designed by A. H. Albertson. The desire for safety shaped the construction of the church of St. Anne of the Sunset Church in San Francisco, California. It was the first Catholic church in America with a complete steel frame and poured concrete for resistance to earthquakes. The structural engineer was W. Adrian.

Art Deco/Art Moderne

In the 1920s and 1930s, a group of churches approached the style of Art Deco, or Art Moderne. Churches built in this style blend Gothic ornamental features with streamlined simple geometry and planar walls. Traditional construction methods are generally used. Examples include the First Evangelical Lutheran Church, Arlington, New Jersey, 1932; the Church of the Most Precious Blood, Astoria, New York, 1936; St. Joseph's Church, Wilmette, Illinois, 1938; and the Madonna della Strada Chapel, Chicago, Illinois, 1939. This last chapel was designed by Andrew N. Rebori; it is sited right beside Lake Michigan, and the stylized Art Moderne shapes relate to the image of progress favored by the city. The tall bell tower is like a mini skyscraper.

The 1925 Exposition Internationale des Arts Décoratif et Industriels Modernes in Paris introduced the world to the Art Deco style and gave it its name. Art Deco was a modernist style that tried to capture the dynamism of the new electric and radio age with angular shapes and modern materials such as nickel and aluminum. Churches in the Art Deco style transformed the spiky Gothic pinnacles and towers to more geometric shapes and repeated them

Above: Rush, Endacott & Rush; Bruce Goff; and Adah Robinson: Boston Avenue United Methodist Church, 1300 South Boston Avenue, Tulsa, OK, 1927–29.

Above: Ebbets & Frid, Porteus & Walker: Emanuel Synagogue, 246 Greenfield Street, Hartford, CT, 1927. The building is now used as Faith Seventh-day Adventist Church.

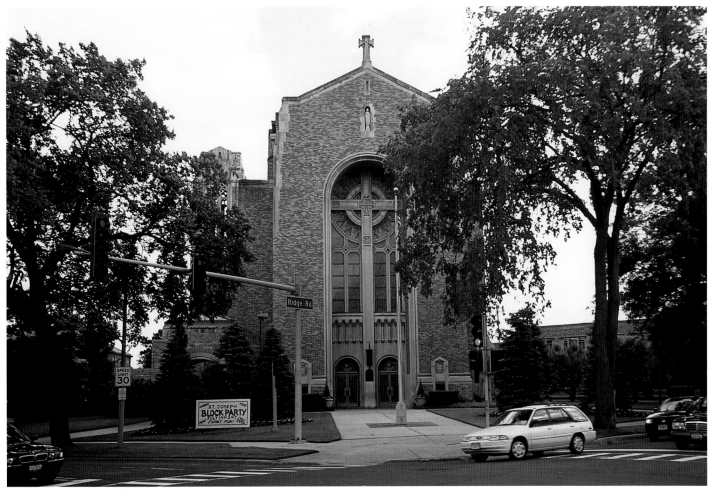

Above: St. Joseph's Church, 1747 Lake Avenue, Wilmette, IL, 1938.

Right: Rush, Endacott & Rush; Bruce Goff; and Adah Robinson: Boston Avenue United Methodist Church, 1300 South Boston Avenue, Tulsa, OK, 1927–29. Elevation. A rare and lavish example of Art Deco church architecture.

Right: Boston Avenue United Methodist Church, Tulsa, OK, 1927–29. Plan.

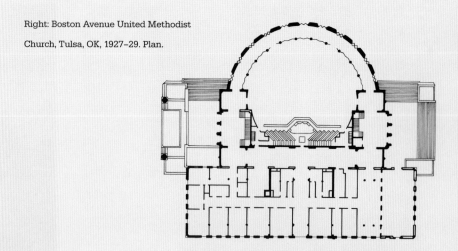

Above: A. Epifano: Jehovah's Witness Kingdom Hall, 1672 Washington Street, West Newton, MA, 1953.

Right: Andrew N. Rebori:
Madonna della Strada
Chapel, 6525 North
Sheridan Road, Chicago, IL,
1939.

in jazzy rhythms. One of the best examples in America is the Boston Avenue United Methodist Church in Tulsa, Oklahoma, built between 1927 and 1929. The architectural firm that designed it was Rush, Endacott & Rush, but the young architect Bruce Goff (1904–82) was largely responsible for the design, along with Adah Robinson,

Above: Andrew N. Rebori: Madonna della Strada Chapel, Chicago, IL, 1939. Interior.

an art professor in Tulsa. It is a large auditorium church, with a 280-foot, steel-framed tower, which can hold 1,800 people. The tower includes eight floors of office space. The cladding of the building is limestone.

A simplified Art Deco design was created by the architects Ebbets & Frid, Porteus & Walker for the Emanuel Synagogue in Hartford in 1927. It is now the home of the Faith Seventh-day Adventist Church.

In Chicago, the First Church of Deliverance was built in 1939 by Walter T. Bailey; Kocher, Buss & DeKlerk. Walter Bailey was Chicago's first African American architect. Twin towers were added to the terra-cotta façade in 1946 by a different architect. The futuristic Art Moderne style of the building reflects the innovative character of the congregation that built it. Founded by the Reverend Clarence H. Cobbs, the church was a leader in the history of Christian radio broadcasting and in the development of gospel music.

As late as 1953, the modernistic Art Deco style was still in use. The Jehovah's Witness Kingdom Hall in West Newton, Massachusetts, was designed by A. Epifano in 1953. The horizontal composition echoes the Streamline Modern style in its curving façade.

Above: Church, Brownsville, TX, from a 1912 photograph. A casual mix of simplified Gothic and classical forms.

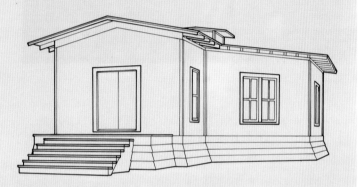

Above: South Texas border Church, Donna, TX. A simplified Arts and Crafts style, marked by the rafter tails.

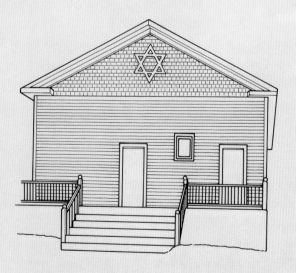

Above: Jewish Synagogue in the Huntington District near Newtown, Connecticut.

Vernacular, or Folk, Churches

In contrast to all the high-style churches that were built in this era, there was an enormous number of vernacular-style, or folk-style, examples built as well. Some of these were simply adapted residential designs, while others borrowed certain aspects from the historical styles. Historic photographs show a casual mix of simplified Gothic and classical forms in churches such as the one in Brownsville, Texas, from about 1912. A simplified Arts and Crafts style, marked by the rafter tails, can be seen in a south Texas border church near Donna, Texas. Similar trends are found across the country. One can find examples such as the Jewish Synagogue in the Huntington District near Newtown, Connecticut, that served fifteen families. It was basically a small domestic structure adapted to a religious purpose.

Notes

1. Ralph Adams Cram, "The Philosophy of the Gothic Restoration," in *The Meaning of Art*, Boston, 1914, quoted in Leland M. Roth, ed., *America Builds. Source Documents in American Architecture and Planning*, New York: Harper & Row, 1983, p. 461.

2. Frank Lloyd Wright, *An Autobiography* (1932), New York: Horizon Press, 1977, p. 184.

3. Frank Lloyd Wright, quoted in Roger G. Kennedy, *American Churches*, New York: Stewart, Tabori & Chang, 1982, p. 32.

4. Frank Lloyd Wright, *An Autobiography* (1932), p. 179.

5. Frank Lloyd Wright, "Architecture and Modern Life: Dialogue" [with Baker Brownell] 1939, *Frank Lloyd Wright Collected Writings, vol. 3, 1931–39*, Bruce Brooks Pfeiffer, ed., New York: Rizzoli and the Frank Lloyd Wright Foundation, 1994, p. 324.

6. Quoted from "The Unitarian Principle as Architecture," in *Genius and Mobocracy* by Frank Lloyd Wright. New York: Horizon Books, 1971.

7. Frank Lloyd Wright, "Starched Churches," in *Frank Lloyd Wright Collected Writings*, vol. 4, p. 298.

8. Frank Lloyd Wright, "Why I Believe in Advancing Unitarianism," *Frank Lloyd Wright Collected Writings*, vol. 4, 296–97.

9. Letter of March 15, 1954, quoted in Patricia Talbot Davis, *Together They Built a Mountain*, Lititz, PA: Sutter House, 1974, p. 45.

10. Frank Lloyd Wright, "Is it Good-bye to Gothic?" in *Frank Lloyd Wright Collected Writings*, vol. 5, p. 231.

Chapter 6

The Modern Age

A church is the symbol of the Divine presence, a prophecy of a better future for this crazy world, and a proclamation of pardon and life for all. Its presence is a perpetual sermon, its steeple a finger pointing earth's weary and heavy laden ones to the heavenly rest, and its ringing bell is a sweet gospel call to worship, to a feast, to a fountain, to highest fellowship on earth, to rest, to comfort, and to the Cross.[1]

—Randolf Rock, 1894

Ornament is crime.

—Adolph Loos, 1908

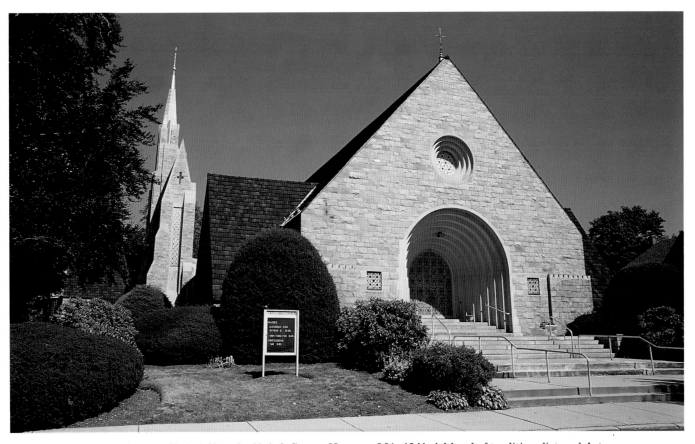

Above: Corpus Christi Church, 41 Ash Street, Newton, MA, 1941. A blend of traditionalist and Art Deco stylistic features.

The modern age brought the tensions between the traditionalists in church design and the inventiveness of modern architects to the fore. Following the shocks to traditional faith posed by the Holocaust and the revolutions of modern science and technology, some churches and temples tried to find a new symbolic form language appropriate to the new conditions of the world.

Modernist/Traditionalist

The conflicting demands of modernism and tradition are manifest in a fairly widespread group of Catholic churches at mid-century. In part they might be considered an updated form of the Art Deco of the 1920s and 1930s. One simple yet elegant example is Corpus Christi Church in Newton, Massachusetts, of 1941. The tall, faceted spire and geometric superimposed arches of the entrance reveal the desire to update the traditional forms.

The challenge was to find forms that expressed the religious identity of the church but were still modern. The former Prairie School architect Barry Byrne created a number of interesting modernist churches in the Midwest. His church of St. Francis Xavier in Kansas City, Missouri (1949), is built of poured concrete. Seen from the air, it has a distinct fishlike shape, symbolizing its Christian identity. Byrne's church of St. Columba in St. Paul, Minnesota (also 1949), has a similar iconographic form.

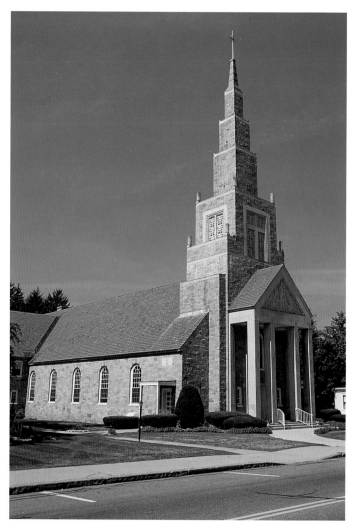

Above: St. Joseph's Church, 150 Central Avenue, Dover, NH, 1946.

Above: Barry Byrne: St. Francis Xavier, Kansas City, MO, 1949. This church is built of poured concrete.

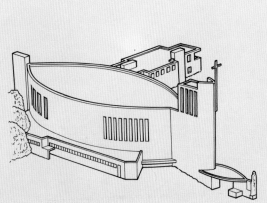

Above: Barry Byrne: St. Francis Xavier, Kansas City, MO, 1949. The fish shape of the plan is evident from above.

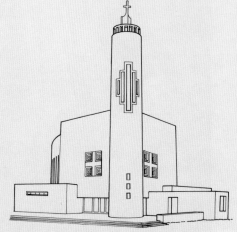

Above: Barry Byrne: St. Columba, 1305 Lafond Avenue, St. Paul, MN, 1949. The plan also has a fish-like shape.

International Style

Architects of the International Style tried to completely break with the past, rejecting historical ornament and traditional forms as wasteful and even immoral. The International Style was named for a 1932 exhibition of the works of architects such as Le Corbusier, Mies van der Rohe, and Walter Gropius at the Museum of Modern Art in New York. The exhibition was curated by Henry Russell Hitchcock and the young Philip Johnson (b. 1904). They stated that the goal of this new style was to go beyond the superficial revivals of the previous architecture, "to emulate the great styles of the past in their essence without imitating their surface" and to establish a new dominant style based on functionalism and structural truth. In practice, this meant flat roofs and glass or brick curtain walls without ornament.

The reductionist quality of this style has made it unpopular for churches, although Mies created a starkly elegant chapel at the Illinois Institute of Technology campus in Chicago in 1952. The St. Saviour's Chapel at IIT is a perfect manifestation of Mies's goal of creating a universal space, an uninterrupted volume that is infinitely adaptable. The steel frame and curtain walls of brick and glass form a self-contained box; it could be located anywhere. There are no external symbols of religion, and only at night does the glass curtain wall reveal the interior, where a large cross on the rear wall indicates the purpose of the building. In a

Above: Ludwig Mies van der Rohe: St. Saviour's Chapel, Illinois Institute of Technology, Chicago, IL, 1952.

1950 address at IIT, Mies proclaimed his faith in technology:

> It is a real historical movement—one of the great movements, which shape and represent their epoch.
>
> It can be compared only with the Classic discovery of man as a person, the Roman will to power, and the religious movement of the Middle Ages.
>
> *
>
> Technology is far more than a method, it is a world in itself.

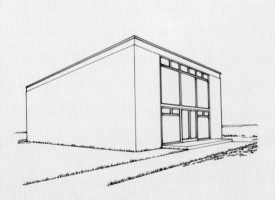

Above: Ludwig Mies van der Rohe: St. Saviour's Chapel, Illinois Institute of Technology, Chicago, IL, 1952.

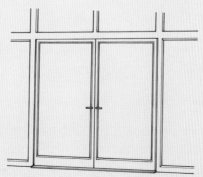

Above: International Style doorway: Chapel, Illinois Institute of Technology, Chicago, IL, 1952.

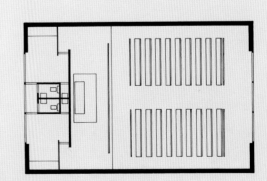

Above: Plan of Chapel, Illinois Institute of Technology, Chicago, IL, 1952.

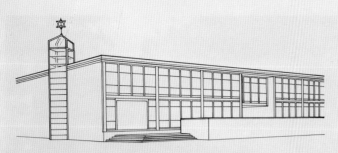

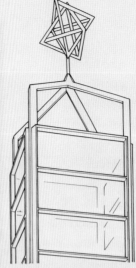

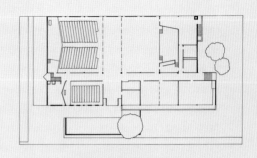

Above: Percival Goodman: Temple Beth El, Gary, IN. A pure example of the International Style, strongly influenced by Mies van der Rohe.

Right: Percival Goodman: Temple Beth El, Gary, IN. Detail of steeple.

Above: Percival Goodman: Temple Beth El, Gary, IN. Plan.

Left: Eliel and Eero Saarinen: First Christian Church, 531 Fifth Street, Columbus, IN, 1942.

Despite his praise of technology, Mies insisted that architecture was primarily an expressive art: "Its real field of activity is in the realm of significance." Almost echoing Ruskin, Mies argued that architecture was the true symbol of a period's cultural values: "Architecture is the real battleground of the spirit…. Architecture depends on its time. It is the crystallization of its inner structure, the slow unfolding of its form."[2] Unlike Mies's office buildings and apartment towers, this particular box has seldom been copied, however. Percival Goodman's Temple Beth El (1952–54) in Gary, Indiana, is a rare example. In commercial and private building, the International Style flourished from 1925 to 1940, with a second phase after World War II until about 1980. It has, in fact, become a kind of modern vernacular and has never really gone away.

Although the stark beauty of modernism was attractive to many in America, particularly those who associated spirituality with a purified, almost ascetic mode of life, most people wanted their churches and temples to be more expressive. The Scandinavian modern style of the Finnish-born architect Eliel Saarinen and his son, Eero, was more successful. The Saarinens were pioneers in creating a new simplified style of church design, which was modern, yet satisfied a sense of spiritual drama. Excellent examples are found in the First Christian Church of 1942 in Columbus, Indiana, and Christ Church Lutheran in Minneapolis, Minnesota (1949). Eliel Saarinen convinced the building committee of the Columbus, Indiana, church that just as

Above: Eliel and Eero Saarinen: Christ Church Lutheran, 3244 Thirty-fourth Street South, Minneapolis, MN, 1949.

Above: First Christian Church, 2201 Stevens Street, Minneapolis, MN. Strongly inspired by the Saarinen's church of 1949.

Above: St. Joseph's Church, 135 Lafayette Street, Salem, MA, 1949. A smaller version of this design can be found in St. Paul's Church, Franklin, NH, 1951.

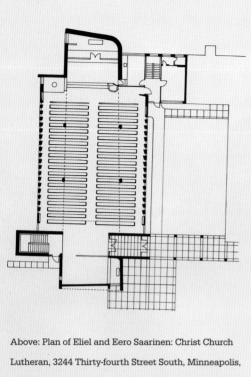

Above: Plan of Eliel and Eero Saarinen: Christ Church Lutheran, 3244 Thirty-fourth Street South, Minneapolis, MN, 1949.

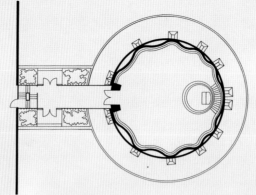

Above: Eero Saarinen: Plan of Interdenominational Chapel, Massachusetts Institute of Technology, Cambridge, MA, 1954. The circular plan of this chapel stood out in the context of the glass boxes of the International Style, which was then dominant.

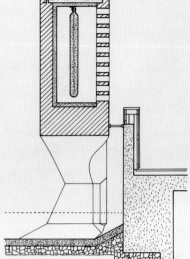

Above: Interdenominational Chapel, Massachusetts Institute of Technology, Cambridge, MA, 1954. Section of wall.

Left: Interdenominational Chapel, Massachusetts Institute of Technology, Cambridge, MA, 1954. Steeple.

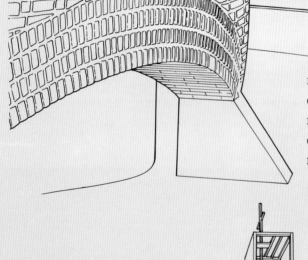

Left: Interdenominational Chapel, Massachusetts Institute of Technology, Cambridge, MA, 1954. Detail of moat.

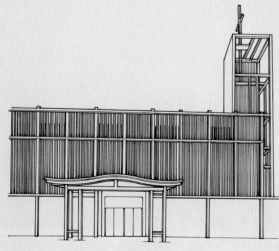

Above: Pietro Belluschi: Central Lutheran Church, 2104 Northeast Hancock Street, Portland, OR, 1948–50.

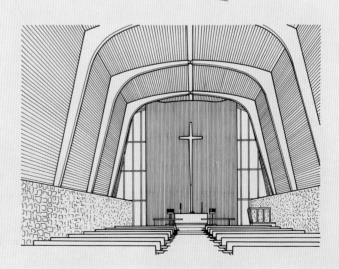

Above: Pietro Belluschi and Skidmore, Owings & Merrill: Trinity Lutheran Church, 2317 Buena Vista Avenue, Walnut Creek, CA, 1956.

JEWISH, PROTESTANT, AND CATHOLIC CHAPELS, BRANDEIS UNIVERSITY

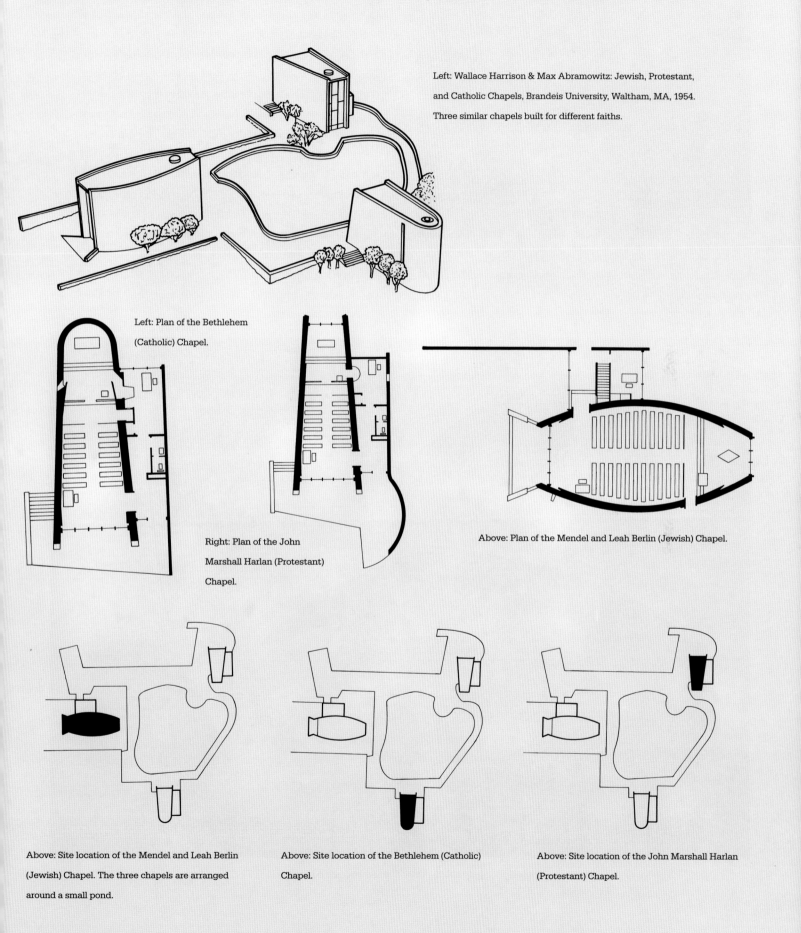

Left: Wallace Harrison & Max Abramowitz: Jewish, Protestant, and Catholic Chapels, Brandeis University, Waltham, MA, 1954. Three similar chapels built for different faiths.

Left: Plan of the Bethlehem (Catholic) Chapel.

Right: Plan of the John Marshall Harlan (Protestant) Chapel.

Above: Plan of the Mendel and Leah Berlin (Jewish) Chapel.

Above: Site location of the Mendel and Leah Berlin (Jewish) Chapel. The three chapels are arranged around a small pond.

Above: Site location of the Bethlehem (Catholic) Chapel.

Above: Site location of the John Marshall Harlan (Protestant) Chapel.

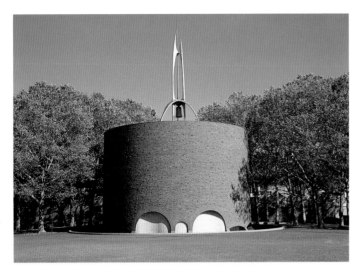

Above: Eero Saarinen: Interdenominational Chapel, Massachusetts Institute of Technology, Cambridge, MA, 1954. Front view.

their church was based on the fundamentals of Christianity, this should be reflected in a design based on the fundamental principles of architecture, not the stylistic patterns of the past. The austerity here is tempered with richly textured light, warm brickwork, and wood paneling. Although the geometric forms are somewhat austere, they are derived from traditional nave and bell tower shapes. The Saarinens' churches were copied many times across the Midwest.

Eero Saarinen (1910–61) went on to create the Kresge Memorial Chapel at the Massachusetts Institute of Technology in 1954, which could be considered a rejoinder to Mies's chapel at the IIT campus. Also designed for a technical university, Saarinen's chapel deliberately avoids the box shape and is instead a fifty-foot-wide cylinder with an abstract sculptural spire by the sculptor Theodore Roszak, which announces its purpose as a church. There is

Above: Eero Saarinen: Interdenominational Chapel, Massachusetts Institute of Technology, Cambridge, MA, 1954. Detail of moat.

a reflecting moat around it, which sets it off from the rest of the campus environment. This moat has a double purpose, in that it also reflects light upward into the church. Light enters through concealed bands of Plexiglas windows in the lower register of the interior walls, so that one sees rippling patterns of light without directly seeing their source. The most dramatic light effect is over the altar, which uses light from a skylight to enhance the effect of a shimmering screen of bronze sculpture by Harry Bertoia. No matter what the season or weather, this creates the effect of frozen light over the altar. Eero Saarinen also influenced the use of A-frame structures in modern church design with his Kramer Chapel at Concordia Theological Seminary (originally Concordia Senior College) in Fort Wayne, Indiana (1953–58). These simple but expressive forms provided an attractive alternative to the International Style.

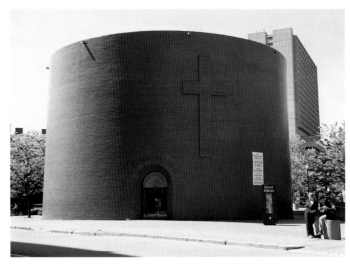

Above: Comparison: Church of All Nations (Methodist), 333 Tremont Street, Boston, MA. A circular church directly copying Saarinen's design.

Above: Eero Saarinen: North Christian Church, 850 Tipton Lane, Columbus, IN, 1964.

Above: Eero Saarinen: Kramer Chapel, Concordia Theological Seminary (originally Concordia Senior College), 6600 North Unton Street, Fort Wayne, IN, 1953–58. Chapel is a large A-frame structure.

At Brandeis University in Waltham, Massachusetts, Wallace Harrison and Max Abramowitz designed a complex of three chapels in 1954: the Bethlehem Chapel (Catholic), John Marshall Harlan Chapel (Protestant), and Mendel and Leah Berlin (Jewish) Chapel. Grouped around a central pond, these similar, but not identical, chapels are clearly modernist with their curtain walls of glass and universal spaces inside. The architects softened the modernist idiom with slightly curving walls and, above all, the relationship to the environment.

The German-born Eric Mendelsohn (he changed his first name from Erich after he was naturalized in 1946), who was one of the pioneering Expressionist architects of the 1920s, designed some intriguing and powerful synagogues in America after WWII. In 1947, Mendelsohn wrote:

Above: Presbyterian Church, 335 Cambridge Street, Burlington, MA, after 1962. An A-frame structure much like Saarinen's.

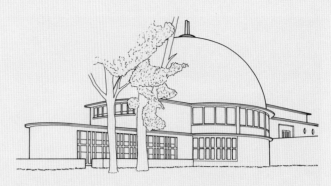

Above: Eric Mendelsohn: B'nai Amoona Synagogue and Community Center, St. Louis, MO, 1946–50.

Above: Eric Mendelsohn: Mount Zion Temple; 1300 Summit Avenue, St. Paul, MN, 1951, altered in 1967. Front view.

It has been said that religious structures must be "traditional" in order to impart a sense of the sacred, that the dignity and emotional significance of such buildings can only be expressed through historical associations. To admit this is to deny that religion is an important part of our contemporary society.[3]

Immediately after the war, he built the B'nai Amoona Synagogue and Community Center in St. Louis, Missouri (1946–50). This was his first religious commission and featured an unusual set of curving steel trusses to define and support the building. Like a folded hand, these trusses curve up and over the ark. The interior layout was innovative also, featuring one of the first large-scale uses of the flexible plan made possible by folding walls that allowed the seating to be doubled on High Holy Days.

In Saint Paul, Minnesota, Mendelsohn built the Mount Zion Temple on Summit Avenue in 1951 (it was expanded and altered in 1967). A severe mountain of a building, it has an unusually monumental presence. The complex consists of the sanctuary, school wing, and offices arranged around a central court.

Pietro Belluschi was a leading figure in postwar design for Lutheran and other protestant churches. One of his earliest designs was the Central Lutheran Church in Portland, Oregon (1948–50). He also built important churches in California and Boston.

American Catholic churches sought an updated look as well; the Cathedral of St. Joseph in Hartford, Connecticut,

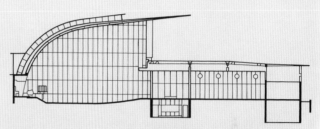

Above: B'nai Amoona Synagogue and Community Center, St. Louis, MO, 1946–50. Section.

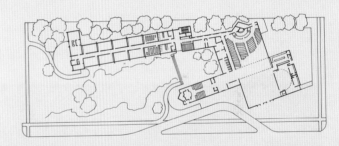

Above: Synagogue and Community Center, Cleveland, OH, 1946–52.

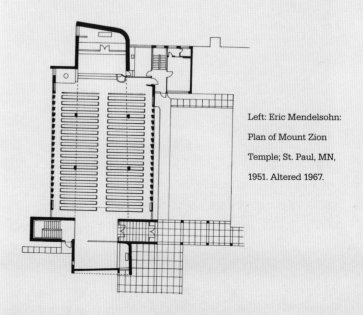

Left: Eric Mendelsohn: Plan of Mount Zion Temple; St. Paul, MN, 1951. Altered 1967.

Above: Wallace Harrison & Max Abramowitz: John Marshall Harlan (Protestant) Chapel, Brandeis University, Waltham, MA, 1954.

Above: Wallace Harrison & Max Abramowitz: Bethlehem (Catholic) Chapel, Brandeis University, Waltham, MA, 1954.

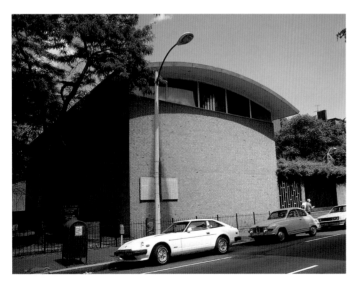

Above: Pietro Belluschi: First Lutheran Church, 299 Berkeley Street, Boston, MA, 1957–59.

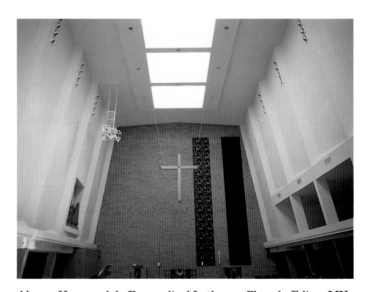

Above: Normandale Evangelical Lutheran Church, Edina, MN, 1959/88. Interior.

Above: Normandale
Evangelical Lutheran
Church, Edina, MN,
1959/88. End view.

Right: Normandale
Evangelical Lutheran
Church, Edina, MN,
1959/88. Very like
Belluschi's Trinity Lutheran
Church of 1956. Front view.

Above: "Speaking architecture"—the Big Duck, Flanders, Long Island, NY, 1931. Modernist architecture downplayed the communicative role of architecture, although it persisted in folk building.

Above: Russell Gibson von Dohlen, Inc.: Blessed Sacrament Roman Catholic Church, East Hartford, CT, 1973. The ceiling displays the structure of the exposed truss.

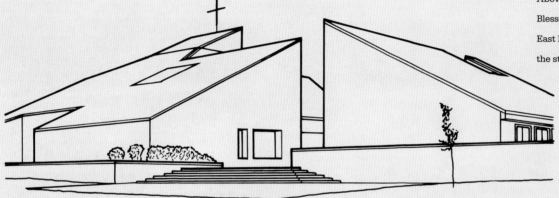

Above: Progressive Design Associates; George E. Rafferty, partner-in-charge; Frank Kacmarcik, consultant: St. John the Evangelist, Hopkins, MN, c. 1970. A late modernist church with multiple shed roofs.

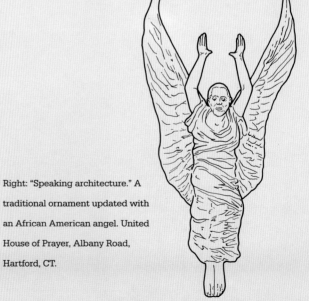

Right: "Speaking architecture." A traditional ornament updated with an African American angel. United House of Prayer, Albany Road, Hartford, CT.

Above: "Speaking architecture"—Edward Slater: Trinity Church ("Fish Church"), Rocky Point, NY, 1964.

of 1960, was designed by the New York architects Otto R. Eggers and Daniel Paul Higgins to replace an earlier church that had been destroyed by a fire. The imposing size and gleaming whiteness of the church spoke of confident new beginnings, and the interior was richly ornamented with colorful modern stained glass set directly in concrete panels.

The Catholic Church, with its tradition of rich imagery and decoration has found the new language of modernism particularly challenging. The enthusiasm for large domed spaces has sometimes found uneasy coexistence with the traditional imagery. The large parabolic dome of steel-reinforced concrete at the Church of Our Lady in Waltham, Massachusetts (1959), is only one of many experiments with modern industrial techniques, which sometimes resemble athletic arenas more than traditional churches. The unresolved conflict between modernism and symbolism is equally stark at the Blessed Sacrament Roman Catholic

Above: St. Helen's Roman Catholic Church, 2315 West. Augusta Boulevard, Chicago, IL.

Above: St. Luke's Lutheran Church, Forty-first Street and Vernon, Edina, MN, 1965. Similar to Frank Lloyd Wright's Unitarian Church in Madison, WI.

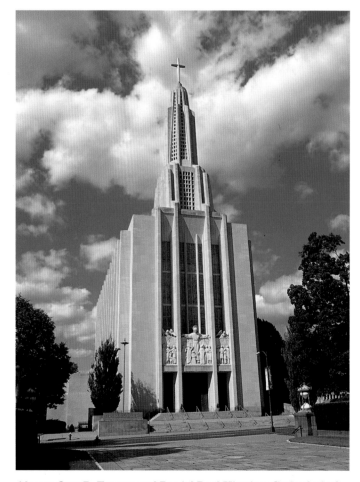

Above: Otto R. Eggers and Daniel Paul Higgins: Cathedral of St. Joseph, 140 Farmington Avenue, Hartford, CT, 1960.

Left: Otto R. Eggers and Daniel Paul Higgins: Holy Trinity Chapel, Washington Square South, New York City, NY, 1964.

Above: Otto R. Eggers and Daniel Paul Higgins: Cathedral of St. Joseph, 140 Farmington Avenue, Hartford, CT, 1960. Interior.

Church in East Hartford, Connecticut (1973), by Russell Gibson von Dohlen, Inc. To soften the blank whiteness of the modernist box, the congregation has installed a lifelike statue of Christ and plastic palms and other accessories to identify and celebrate their central devotion.

Architectural symbolism had been the defining factor in almost all the styles associated with the eclectic revivals of the late nineteenth and early twentieth centuries. The modernist movement had suddenly discarded nearly all of this traditional symbolism. The chapel Mies van der Rohe designed for the Illinois Institute of Technology was deliberately stark and unexpressive, leaving the general public dissatisfied. The chapel is still poorly attended. At the same time, increasing attention was being paid to the theoretical structure of communication and architectural symbolism. Theoreticians such as Charles Jencks applied modern theories of semiotics (the study of signs and symbols) to architecture. Sign theory recognized the importance of the role of the viewer in the structure of meaning; it was not

just the architect's intentions that mattered, nor could the building be said to simply "speak for itself." There is a dynamic relationship between the architect/author, the building (the signifier), and the interpretation.

Learning from Las Vegas (1972) was a seminal text in the development of postmodernism. In this book, Robert Venturi, Denise Scott Brown, and Steven Izenour introduced an important discussion of historical symbolism and modern architecture. They noted that the modernist obsession with space as the fundamental quality of architecture led to the discounting of symbolic features and to the treatment of architecture as another form of abstract expressionism. Even past ages, such as the Gothic era or Renaissance, were forced into this pattern, with the symbolic details considered as superficial in contrast with the space. The modern urban architectural landscape had developed a new communication system based on large signs plastered up in front of very ordinary buildings, which they called the "decorated shed." Even churches were

Above: Joseph Kane: Beth El Temple, 2626 Albany Road, West Hartford, CT, 1963. Circular plan, with twelve radiating vaults symbolizing the twelve tribes of Israel.

Left: Russell Gibson von Dohlen, Inc.: Blessed Sacrament Roman Catholic Church, 15 Millbrook Drive, East Hartford, CT, 1973.

Above: Russell Gibson von Dohlen, Inc.: Blessed Sacrament Roman Catholic Church, 15 Millbrook Drive, East Hartford, CT, 1973. Detail of display window near the entrance; the lifelike statue and accessories contrast with the stark minimalism of the modernist architecture.

treated in this way, with vernacular structures that aspired to no intrinsic meaning fronted by large signs labeling them as houses of worship. Some buildings used their shape to signify their identity, by copying natural forms or creating abstract expressive forms. The authors used a duck store in the shape of a duck as the key example of a shape as both functional and expressive of its purpose. Such vernacular examples highlighted the essential sign theory of architecture, where buildings could be either "ducks" or "decorated sheds." The Gothic cathedral of the Middle Ages, with its sculpted west front with tall steeples, with a barnlike nave behind, could be considered to be both a duck and a shed. Amiens Cathedral, they noted, was a "billboard with a building behind it."

*

Finding the correct match between form and content was challenging to American architects. The Victorian architect Leopold Eidlitz was quoted as saying that "American architecture was the art of covering one thing with another thing to imitate a third thing, which, if genuine, would not be desirable."[4] Modernism sought to express the purpose of the building directly through symbolism or abstract expression. Metaphors based on structure or visual form became more important. In Sedona, Arizona, a small Chapel of the Holy Cross in the remote landscape used the shape of the crucifix as the defining element of the structure of the façade; the key symbol of Christianity was literally incorporated into the form of the chapel. This chapel was designed by the artist Marguerite Brunswig Staude in 1956. In Venturi's terms, this church is definitely a "duck."

Formalist—1954–80

Precisely because the International Style was perceived as lacking in emotional and spiritual expression, many modernist architects experimented with more expressionist shapes in their designs for churches and temples.

Frank Lloyd Wright and Le Corbusier were the leaders in this. Other fine examples include the Air Force Academy Chapel at Colorado Springs, 1956–62; Wallace Harrison's "Fish Church" at Stamford, Connecticut, of 1958; and Marcel Breuer's designs for St. John's Abbey at Collegeville, Minnesota, of 1961. Philip Johnson remarked about his

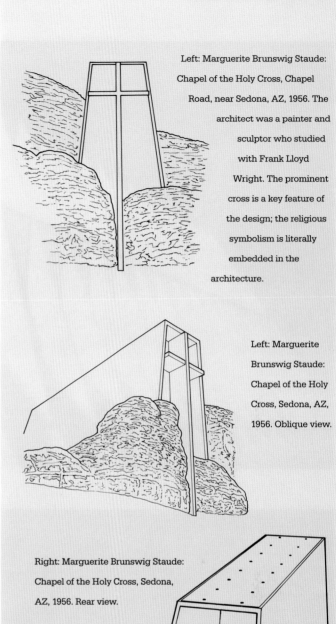

Left: Marguerite Brunswig Staude: Chapel of the Holy Cross, Chapel Road, near Sedona, AZ, 1956. The architect was a painter and sculptor who studied with Frank Lloyd Wright. The prominent cross is a key feature of the design; the religious symbolism is literally embedded in the architecture.

Left: Marguerite Brunswig Staude: Chapel of the Holy Cross, Sedona, AZ, 1956. Oblique view.

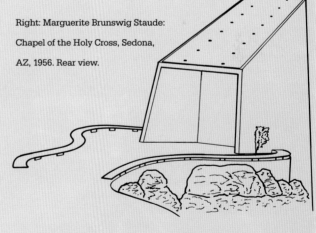

Right: Marguerite Brunswig Staude: Chapel of the Holy Cross, Sedona, AZ, 1956. Rear view.

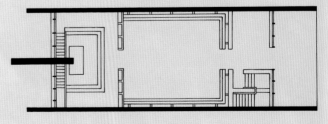

Above: Marguerite Brunswig Staude: Chapel of the Holy Cross, Sedona, AZ, 1956. Plan.

Left: Skidmore, Owings and Merrill (Walter Netsch): Air Force Academy Chapel, Colorado Springs, CO, 1956–62. An abstract construction of tetrahedrons, which is modern and yet echoes tradition.

Below: Air Force Academy Chapel, Colorado Springs, CO, 1956–62. Interior.

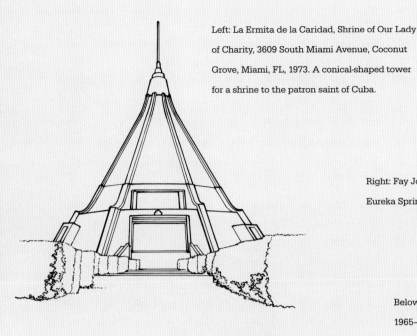

Left: La Ermita de la Caridad, Shrine of Our Lady of Charity, 3609 South Miami Avenue, Coconut Grove, Miami, FL, 1973. A conical-shaped tower for a shrine to the patron saint of Cuba.

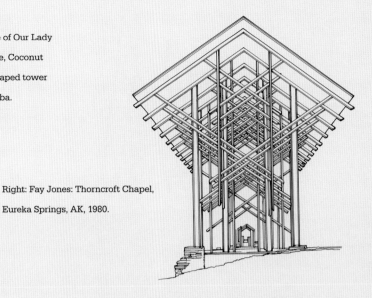

Right: Fay Jones: Thorncroft Chapel, Eureka Springs, AK, 1980.

Below: comparison: Fritz Wotruba: Holy Trinity Church, Georgenberg, near Vienna, 1965–75. A jumble of abstract forms designed by a noted sculptor.

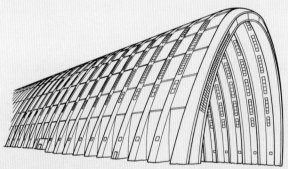

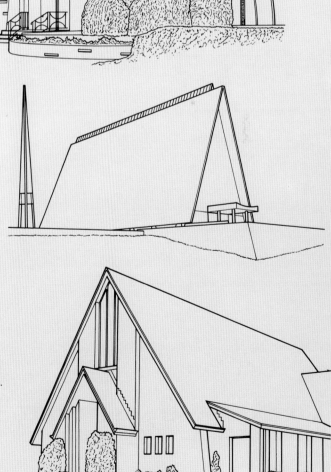

Above: Parabolic airport hangar of reinforced concrete, Orly, France, 1916. This parabolic arch form has been used for a number of modernist churches.

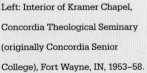

Right: A-frame church; Eero Saarinen: Kramer Chapel, Concordia Theological Seminary (originally Concordia Senior College), Fort Wayne, IN, 1953–58.

Left: Interior of Kramer Chapel, Concordia Theological Seminary (originally Concordia Senior College), Fort Wayne, IN, 1953–58.

Right: First Methodist Church, Navasota, TX, 1959. An A-frame structure in brick.

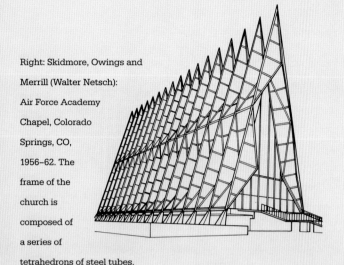

Right: Skidmore, Owings and Merrill (Walter Netsch): Air Force Academy Chapel, Colorado Springs, CO, 1956–62. The frame of the church is composed of a series of tetrahedrons of steel tubes.

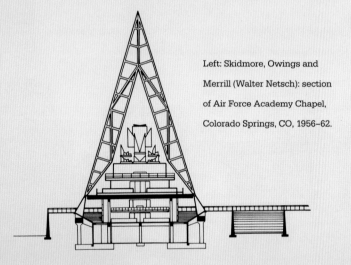

Left: Skidmore, Owings and Merrill (Walter Netsch): section of Air Force Academy Chapel, Colorado Springs, CO, 1956–62.

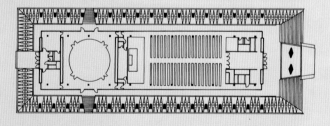

Above: Skidmore, Owings and Merrill (Walter Netsch): Plan of Air Force Academy Chapel, Colorado Springs, CO, 1956–62.

Above: Minoru Yamasaki: North Shore Congregation, Glencoe, IL, 1964.

own Roofless Church, built for the Blaffer Foundation in New Harmony, Indiana, in 1960 that it was "pure form—ugly or beautiful—but pure form."[5]

The United States Air Force Academy at Colorado Springs was designed by Skidmore, Owings and Merrill in the 1950s in a purely Miesian International Style. The two-dimensional grid of the campus plaza is echoed in the rectangular steel-frame classroom buildings, even more strictly constructed than Mies's IIT campus. The only structure to escape the uniformity of the plan was the chapel, which was designed by Walter Netsch, Jr. The chapel comprises three separate worship areas on two floors, one each for Protestant, Catholic, and Jewish cadets, plus two additional interdenominational spaces. The Protestant chapel is the largest and seats 1,200 people on the main floor. The two-floor arrangement was inspired by the Church of St. Francis of Assisi, which Netsch visited on a trip to Europe while working on the designs for the Air Force Academy Chapel. Visits to the French Gothic Cathedral of Chartres and especially the Chapel of Ste. Chapelle in Paris also had an effect, but the design is purely modern. The unconventional church is built of a succession of seventeen triangular tetrahedrons stacked in a row, which caused a senator from North Dakota to disparage it as a "bunch of tepees." The 150-foot-tall exterior is sheathed in aluminum. The silhouette of the chapel derives partly from A-frame structures and partly from the construction of airplane hangars, for which the tubular metal frames had been designed. The space between the tetrahedrons is filled with stained glass, giving an almost Gothic effect to the interior, although the colors and materials are clearly from the jet age.

The Benedictine Abbey of St. John at Collegeville is one of the most successful examples of modernist religious architecture. The college and preparatory school are located in rural central Minnesota in a pastoral setting. The large abbey church is the centerpiece of the complex and is highlighted by an enormous abstract sculpture of a bell tower, the so-called banner tower, of steel-reinforced concrete. Marcel Breuer had been a leading teacher at the Bauhaus in Germany, the architecture school headed by Walter Gropius and Mies van der Rohe. Here, however, he has created a sense of drama and spirituality far removed from the machinelike functionalism associated with the International Style. There are no frills here, but the raw power of the majestic forms is balanced with a sense of shelter. The church creates both the effect of awe as well as a sense of intimacy and meditative peace. The dual aspect of Christianity is well evoked here. The monks follow the Rule of the Order of St. Benedict, a code for monastic behavior that dates back to the sixth century. This age-old tradition did constrain the architect, however; the abbot explained to Breuer that:

> The Benedictine tradition at its best challenges us to think boldly and to cast our ideals in forms that will be valid for centuries to come, shaping them with all the genius of present-day materials and techniques.[6]

The plain materials of the church are primarily concrete and granite and recall the simplicity of early monastic churches. Pier Luigi Nervi supervised the structural design. The use of concrete recalls Frank Lloyd Wright's Unity Temple and the concrete churches of Auguste Perret and especially Le Corbusier in France, but is nonetheless original. In addition to the abbey church, Breuer designed eight other buildings at this site.

The cavernous interior is enriched with light manipulated by stained glass, indirect sources, and ribbons of plate glass. A cantilevered balcony projects over the interior. The acoustics at both levels are excellent.

The possibilities of modern, steel-reinforced concrete made possible the modernist design of the Beth El Temple in West Hartford, Connecticut. It was built by Joseph Kane in 1963. The temple has a circular plan and resembles a large tent, with twelve radiating concrete vaults symbolizing the twelve tribes of Israel. Echoes of the ancient desert tents used by the Israelites before the building of the temple are seen here.

Round, or central, plan churches have long had a resonant image in church building as an image of perfection. Tall spires likewise entered into the vocabulary of religious architecture. The futuristic spire of the Oral Roberts Prayer Tower combines both the circular plan and the soaring spire. The Prayer Tower dominates the campus at Oral Roberts University in Tulsa, Oklahoma. Built in 1967, this 200-foot-tall tower is reminiscent of Seattle's Space Needle of 1962. As simple as it is, the Prayer Tower is replete with suggestive religious symbolism. First of all, it is a beacon, or lighthouse, which is also meant to suggest the shape of the cross when seen in silhouette. An oil flame burns perpetually at the very top, signifying devotion and the tongues of fire associated with the appearance of the Holy Spirit at

Above: Wallace K. Harrison: First Presbyterian Church, "Fish Church," 1101 Bedford Street, Stamford, CT, 1958. Detail.

Above: First Presbyterian Church, "Fish Church," 1101 Bedford Street, Stamford, CT, 1958.

Pentecost. The observation deck is meant to suggest Christ's Crown of Thorns, with a circlet of radiating metal spikes. The red color is symbolic of Christ's blood. Volunteers pray in the upper chambers twenty-four hours a day, seven days a week, answering the telephone calls of the faithful. Oral Roberts began as a tent evangelist before he became a pioneering televangelist.

*

Another round church is found at the shrine of La Virgen de la Caridad del Cobre in Miami. The Virgin of Charity is an important part of Cuban American culture and her shrine in Miami provides an important link to their traditional faith and identity. She is the patron saint of Cuba, inspired by a legendary appearance of the Madonna to a Cuban boy in 1606. The Cuban exile community constructed the conical tower of the Shrine of Our Lady of Charity (La Ermita de la Caridad) in Coconut Grove, Miami, in 1973.

*

The expressive potential of concrete, which can accommodate a wide range of fluid forms, has been explored by a number of leading modernists. These new forms are juxtaposed with historic traditions at the Christian Science Center in Boston, where several new buildings and the redesigned plaza were constructed by the firm of I. M. Pei in 1968–73. The large and confident designs of these buildings, including one skyscraper beside the reflecting pool, create an effective sense of grandeur.

The juxtaposition of old and new is also seen in the First Church in the Back Bay district of Boston. Originally built in the High Victorian Gothic style by William Ware and Henry Van Brunt in 1868, the church burned in 1969. Rather than try to re-create the original style, it was decided

Above: Edward Slater: Trinity Church ("Fish Church"), 716 Route 25A, Rocky Point, NY, 1964. Front view. This church plays on visual semblances to make its point.

to preserve the fragmentary façade—after reinforcing it with concrete and steel beams—and build a new modern church behind it. The new steel-and-concrete church by Paul Rudolph was built in 1971, and the two buildings are definitely juxtaposed rather than blended or integrated. Rudolph favored a rough-textured treatment for the external walls, created by using rough lumber for the concrete forms, occasionally supplemented with hammering to further roughen the surface. Harry Weese used a similar abstract vocabulary of expressive forms and rough, concrete surfaces for the seventeenth Church of Christ, Scientist, built in Chicago in 1968.

The influence of Frank Lloyd Wright's Beth Shalom Synagogue in Elkins Park, Pennsylvania, is evident in the powerful forms of the Beth El Synagogue in St. Louis Park, near Minneapolis, Minnesota. This synagogue, built in 1968, has a powerfully expressive, sweeping form of concrete and glass on the façade.

The sharp angles of Gothic are given an almost expressionistic shape in Hugh Stubbins's modernist design for St. Peter's Lutheran Church at the Citicorp Center, New York City, of 1977. This church is built on the corner of the site of the towering Citicorp Center. The congregation, which was located in a nineteenth-century Gothic Revival church on the site, refused to sell unless their church was to be rebuilt in the same location. The architect of the skyscraper, which is noted for its individualistic shed roof at the top, created this modern abstract shape with sharp angled forms. The church seems to nestle near the skyscraper, on a corner of the plaza. The Chapel of the Good Shepherd here was created by the sculptor Louise Nevelson, who created a mysterious environment with her wall-mounted relief sculptures, monochromatic assemblages of white-painted, wooden shapes that interplay with shadows.

Above: Trinity Church ("Fish Church"), 716 Route 25A, Rocky Point, NY, 1964. Side view.

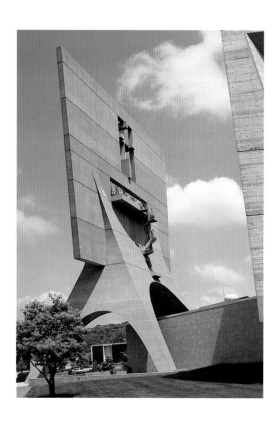

Left: Marcel Breuer: St. John's Abbey, Collegeville, MN, 1961. Detail.

Right: Philip Johnson: Roofless Church, New Harmony, IN, 1960.

Above: Marcel Breuer: St. John's Abbey, Collegeville, MN, 1961. Front view, "banner" bell tower.

The comparison of modern sculpture to these churches is apt, for they seem to derive as much from the tradition of modern art as from architecture. The architects have been freed by the potentials of the modern materials. A European comparison that highlights this point is the Holy Trinity Church in Georgenberg, near Vienna, designed by the sculptor Fritz Wotruba. Built between 1965 and 1975 from Wotruba's models, this church is an abstract composition of tumbling building blocks, which coalesces into an almost medieval interior.

The expressive potential of new materials of steel and glass are realized in the Garden Grove Church, also known as the Crystal Cathedral, in Garden Grove, California. Built by Philip Johnson and John Burgee in 1977–80 for Dr. Robert Schuller of the Reformed Church denomination, the building interior is an enormous open space, covered with a space frame sheathed with 10,000 large panes of mirrored glass. The plan is shaped like a diamond, or four-pointed star. The church is 415 feet long by 207 feet wide, with a height of 128 feet. The exterior angles are acute; from the outside, it gleams like a piece of rare crystal. From the inside, the walls shimmer with translucent views of the sky seen through the rhythmic pattern of the steel trusses. The dissolution of the wall recalls the Crystal Palace Exhibition Hall of 1851, the diaphanous walls of stained glass in Gothic chapels, and the tent revivals of earlier America. The open space and transparent walls and ceiling correspond to the message of infinite possibilities that is associated with this ministry. This is very much an up-to-date church, designed for the electronic age. The church holds 2,890 people, plus a choir of 1,000, but is seen by millions more via the televised program *Hour of Power*, which features the televangelist Robert Schuller. As in a sports arena, the service can be watched on a giant Sony Jumbotron television screen. Schuller preached at a drive-in movie in the early 1950s, and he has been very successful at delivering his message through modern media. The church is, in a sense, a large television studio for his program.

Above: Marcel Breuer: St. John's Abbey, Collegeville, MN, 1961. Detail.

Left: Marcel Breuer:
St. John's Abbey,
Collegeville, MN, 1961.
Interior.

Below: St. John's Abbey,
Collegeville, MN, 1961.
Interior.

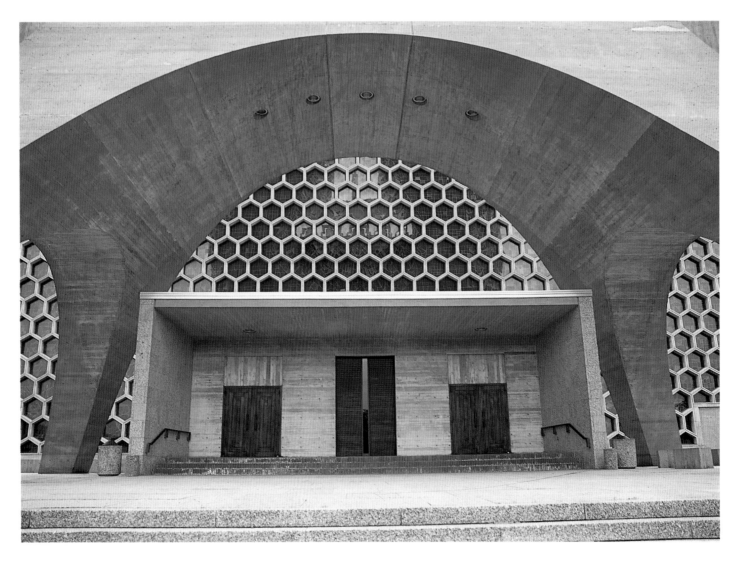

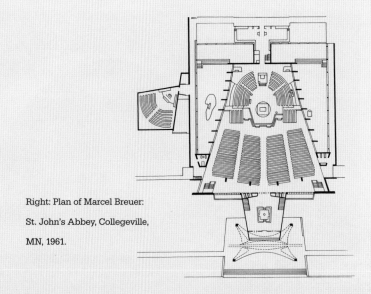

Above: Minoru Yamasaki: North Shore Congregation, Glencoe, IL, 1964. Oblique view.

Right: Plan of Marcel Breuer: St. John's Abbey, Collegeville, MN, 1961.

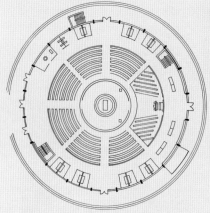

Left: Plan of Hellmuth, Osaba and Kassabaum: Saint Louis Priory, Saint Louis, MO, 1962.

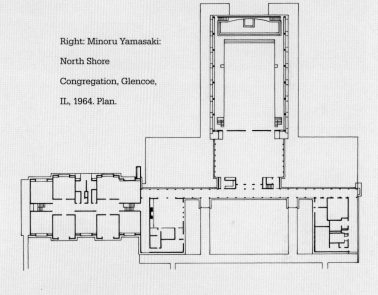

Right: Minoru Yamasaki: North Shore Congregation, Glencoe, IL, 1964. Plan.

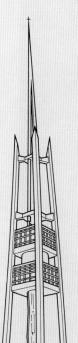

Left: Modernist bell tower; Wallace K. Harrison: First Presbyterian Church, "Fish Church," Stamford, CT, 1958.

Left: Modernist steeple; Otto R. Eggers and Daniel Paul Higgins: Cathedral of St. Joseph, Hartford, CT, 1960.

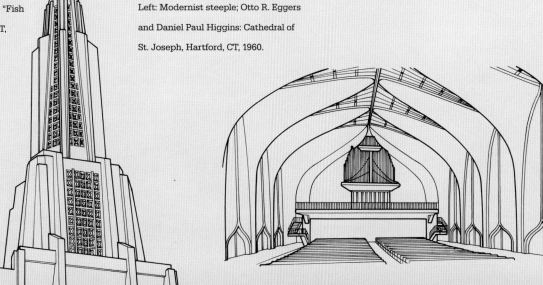

Above: Minoru Yamasaki: North Shore Congregation, Glencoe, IL, 1964. Interior.

Left: Church of Our Lady, River Street, Waltham, MA, 1959. Parabolic dome; front view.

Below: St. John Lutheran Church, 445 Providence Road, Brooklyn, CT, *c.* 1970. Wrightian.

Right: Paul Rudolph: Tuskegee Chapel, Tuskegee Institute, AL, 1969.

Below: Pietro Belluschi and Pier Luigi Nervi: Saint Mary's Cathedral, 1111 Gough Street, San Francisco, CA, 1971.

Above: I. M. Pei: Christian Science Center, Boston, MA, 1968–73.

Left: Hellmuth, Osaba and Kassabaum: Saint Louis Priory, 500 South Mason Road, Saint Louis, MO, 1962.

Above: I. M. Pei: Christian Science Center, Boston, MA, 1968–73.

Above right: First Church, 66 Marlborough Street, Boston, MA, 1868. Originally by William Ware and Henry Van Brunt, architects. New building by Paul Rudolph, 1971.

Right: Harry Weese: 17th Church of Christ (Christian Science), 55 East Wacker Drive, Chicago, IL, 1968.

Above: Beth El Synagogue, 5224 West Twenty-sixth Street, St. Louis Park, MN, 1968. Front view.

Above: Hugh Stubbins: St. Peter's Church, Citicorp Center, New York, NY, 1977.

There is also an outdoor screen for those who prefer to remain in their cars and listen via the car radio.

Two ninety-foot doors can be opened for ventilation and to provide a view; the technology to open them is adapted from the NASA space shuttle launch center in Florida. The wide open space of the interior, which can thus be opened to the infinity of the sky, speaks of the limitless possibilities of the spirit. A tall bell tower—made of highly polished stainless steel prisms and containing a carillon—was added ten years after the church was completed.

An unusual pilgrimage chapel nestles in the forest of Arkansas, near Eureka Springs. The Thorncrown Chapel (1980) was designed by E. Fay Jones (b. 1921), who had worked with Frank Lloyd Wright. As with Wright's Organic architecture, there is a profound sense of the structural and expressive potential of materials and an almost Romantic appreciation for nature and the harmony of the site. Like a balloon frame, the church is built of thin pieces of southern pine; the delicacy of the frame is revealed by the transparent, glass-curtain wall. The repeated patterns of the

Left: Philip Johnson & John Burgee: Garden Grove Church, "the Crystal Cathedral," Los Angeles, California, 1978–80. Interior.

Above: Philip Johnson & John Burgee: Garden Grove Church, "the Crystal Cathedral," Los Angeles, CA, 1978–80. A large modernist church and studio set for one of the most successful televangelists.

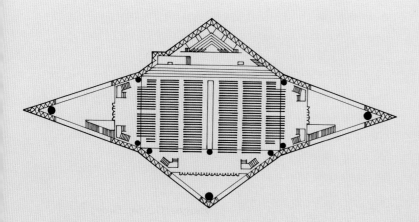

Above: Philip Johnson & John Burgee: Plan of the Garden Grove Church, "the Crystal Cathedral," Los Angeles, CA, 1978–80. It is based on a four-pointed star.

Right: Marcel Breuer: "Banner" steeple, St. John's Abbey, Collegeville, MN, 1961.

Below: Burk, Lebreton & Lamantia: Immaculate Conception Church, 515 Bryan Street Jennings, LA, 1964. The church is supported by large, external trusses, similar to those used by Mies van der Rohe at the Illinois Institute of Technology.

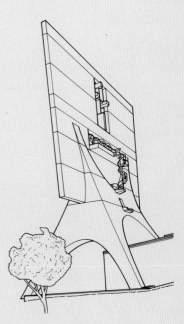

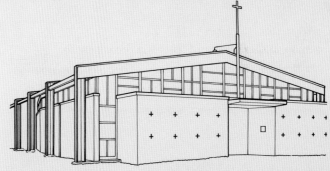

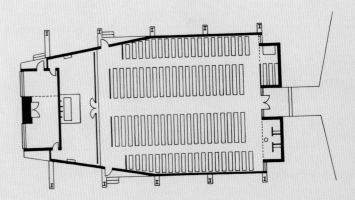

Above: Immaculate Conception Church, Jennings, LA, 1964. Plan.

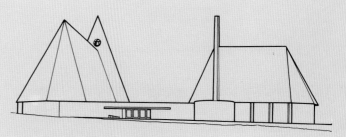

Above: Harry Weese & Associates: First Baptist Church, Columbus, IN, 1965.

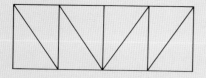

Left: Flat pratt truss. A truss design often used in modern architecture.

Right: Flat warren truss. A variant design.

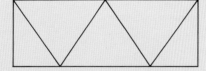

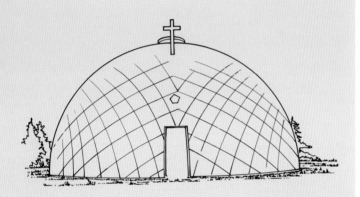

Above: R. Buckminster Fuller: St. Michael's Chapel, St. Columbans, NE, c. 1957.

Above: Geodesic dome, invented by R. Buckminster Fuller.

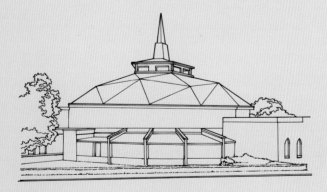

Above: Geodesic church; the "Olympiad" model, 2002. Fuller's design has recently been revived for prefabricated church designs.

latticelike trusses creates a repetitive rhythm that makes the building seem larger than it is—it measures only twenty-four feet wide by sixty feet long by forty-eight feet high. In the terms of nineteenth-century Romanticism, this is called the "artificial infinite," and the chapel does a wonderful job of intimating the infinite spirit of nature and God. Tall and narrow, the chapel evokes the spirit of Gothic architecture in the forest. The apparent simplicity of this chapel is striking, and deceptive—this truly is a case where "less is more."

Modern Vernacular/Contemporary Folk

Inexpensive churches in the period of 1940 to the present include mass-produced modular structures and even Quonset huts, which were used during and immediately after World War II. Other experimental religious structures of this period include very geometric geodesic domes and A-frames. R. Buckminster Fuller is the inventor of the geodesic dome, and in 1957 he designed St. Michael's Chapel, St. Columbans, Nebraska, for a Catholic missionary order. Built as a test for missions in the Far East, this geodesic dome chapel accommodated 400 people. Recently, geodesic dome churches have been put into mass production.

During World War II, the architect Bruce Goff served with the Seabees ("CB" stood for construction brigade). While in the service, he designed the Camp Parks Seabee Chapel (1944–45), using the framework of a Quonset hut. Quonset huts were inexpensive, prefabricated housing based on a series of semicircular arch forms produced in vast quantities during the war. They are named for the naval base in Quonset, Rhode Island, where they were made. After the war, this church was moved off the base and is now used as the San Lorenzo Community Church, San Lorenzo, California.

Quonset huts were sold for very low cost after the war, and anonymous builders have also transformed these prefabricated buildings into churches. There is a Quonset hut church, Barrow, Alaska, as well as examples in the Klondike. With the wide dispersion of these structures, there is even a Quonset hut church in Trinity, Florida.

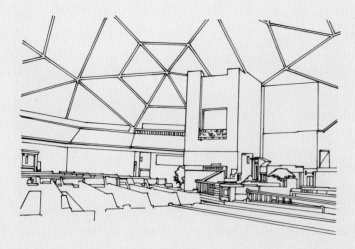

Above: Geodesic church interior; the "Omni" model, 2002.

Above: Bruce Goff: Camp Parks Seabee Chapel, now San Lorenzo Community Church, 945 Paseo Grande, San Lorenzo, CA, 1944–45.

Above: Quonset hut church, Trinity, FL, mid-twentieth century.

Above: Quonset hut church, Barrow, Alaska, mid-twentieth century. Anonymous builders have also transformed these prefabricated buildings into churches.

Below: Our Lady of the Way, Quonset hut church, Haines Junction, the Klondike, mid-twentieth century.

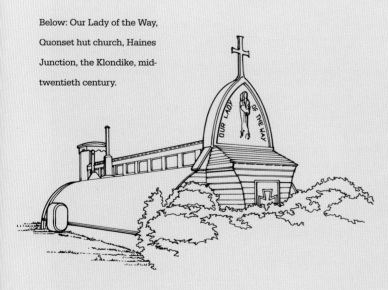

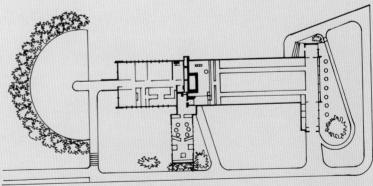

Above: Bruce Goff: Plan of Camp Parks Seabee Chapel, now San Lorenzo Community Church, San Lorenzo, CA, 1944–45.

Recycled Structures—Adaptive Reuse

In recent decades, the conversion of older building types into churches has been a growing trend. Motivated by reasons of economy, as much as a sense of historic preservation, urban churches have successfully converted storefronts, theaters, and even drive-through banks and auto repair centers into houses of worship. It is said that faith can find sacred meaning in all things, and this trend of adaptive reuse certainly proves it. Evangelistic churches have sprung up in many depressed urban centers; Chicago, Bridgeport, and New York City have many former commercial buildings now occupied by Missionary Baptist groups, among others. The abandonment of old movie palaces has led to the conversion of some of them into auditorium-style churches. The spectacularly ornate Tabernacle of Prayer in Queens, New York, was originally built as Loews Valencia Theater in 1929 by the theater architect John Eberson. The exterior façade has the profuse ornament and sinuous scroll gables of Spanish Baroque architecture. The interior is equally lavish, with decoration inspired by Spanish Moorish architecture, creating an elaborate fantasy stage set for the audience. Trimmed with red and gold leaf, the illusion of a rich courtyard is created, with ornamental balconies, stairs, gables, and even fake cypress trees. The movie theater was donated to the church in 1977 and beau-

Above: Holy Word Foundation, 105 Derby Avenue, New Haven, CT.

tifully renovated. The auditorium seating and stage work well for the church sermons and the elaborate setting adds to the feeling of being transported to a transcendent setting outside everyday life, a heavenly mansion, which was one goal of Gothic churches.

The Lighthouse Christian Church in Naugatuck, Connecticut, is a smaller and simpler example of the same trend. Every sort of building can be converted to religious use, it seems. There is even a drive-through bank that has been converted to a center for the Holy Word Foundation in New Haven, Connecticut.

Above: Union Star M.B. Church, 3915 West Chicago Avenue, Chicago, IL. A converted storefront.

Above: New Covenant Church of God, 2010 Boston Avenue, Bridgeport, CT. A converted auto-repair shop has become a church.

Above: Missionary Church, 1853 Barnum Avenue, Bridgeport, CT. A converted storefront.

Above: John Eberson: Tabernacle of Prayer (originally Loew's Valencia Theater), 165-11 Jamaica Avenue, Queens, NY, 1929. This spectacular movie palace of the jazz age has been converted to a large auditorium church.

Right: Lighthouse Christian Church, 173 Church Street, Naugatuck, CT. Converted movie theater.

Mobile Houses of Worship

While much critical attention is normally focused on high-style, architect-designed churches and temples, the modern era has also seen a creative counterculture of houses of worship established in a wide variety of ordinary structures.

Tent revivals, which were popular in the late nineteenth and early twentieth centuries, never disappeared and have continued to thrive in both rural and large urban areas. Across the South and the West, tent revivals flourish in rural areas. They are also popular in industrial areas of the North, typically addressing the spiritual needs of lower-income groups. The urban missionary revival meetings of the Ghetto Missionaries in Chicago and the Revival Tent Crusade in Bridgeport, Connecticut, carry on

Above: Revival meeting, Middletown, CT, 2002. Reverend Lawrence uses a truck as a movable stage.

Above: Ghetto Missionaries revival tent, 3915 West Chicago Avenue, Chicago, IL, 2002. Tent revivals have a long history in American religion and are still going strong.

a century-old tradition of populist evangelism. Both were photographed in the summer of 2002. Reverend Douglas E. Lawrence, a.k.a. "the Preacher on the Move," has updated this tradition with a mobile stage built in a trailer truck where the entire long side falls away. This revival meeting was held in a town park near Wesleyan University. The setting encapsulates the American experience; behind the park is the synagogue of one of the first Jewish communities in Connecticut and directly opposite the preacher is a statue of a Civil War veteran.

The tradition of the wandering evangelist is deeply rooted in Christianity, but the trucking industry has replaced the caravans of old. To serve this new nomadic population, enterprising evangelists have sought new ways to bring their chapels to the congregation, no matter where they might be found. Don Young's Mobile Chapel is designed for interstate truckers and is a trailer truck container converted to a transportable chapel.

These mobile chapels are nearly prefabricated and require only minimal adaptation for use as a church. One of the most pervasive forces in modern building has been the growth of modular construction, and there are companies that specialize in prefabricated, low-cost church designs as well.

Above right: Wedding chapel, Las Vegas, NV.

Right: United House of Prayer, 940 Albany Road, Hartford, CT.

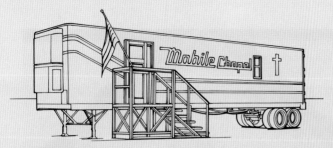

Above: Don Young's Mobile Chapel, a converted truck trailer parked at a truck stop, 2002. In a case of form following function, this is a mobile chapel for truckers.

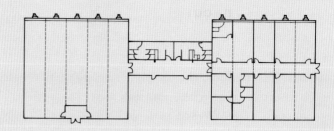

Above: Modular construction sample church plan. Reminiscent of Frank Lloyd Wright's Unity Temple in Oak Park, IL.

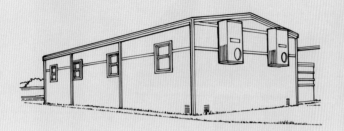

Above: Grace Assembly modular construction church, Flower Mound, TX, 2002. Modular construction is a major factor in modern building.

Above: Drive-in church, Michigan, late twentieth century. Parishioners can remain in the comfort of their cars while attending services.

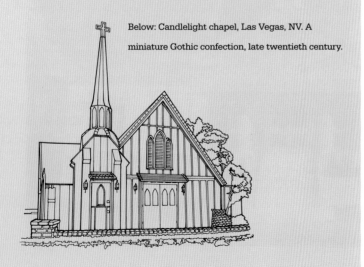

Below: Candlelight chapel, Las Vegas, NV. A miniature Gothic confection, late twentieth century.

The automobile is an inescapable fact of modern American life, and there has been a long trend toward drive-in churches, where the congregation can remain in their cars while attending services. Sometimes the sermon may be heard on the car radio, in the manner of drive-in movies. Such drive-in churches have been popular in summer resort areas, such as Michigan. The church is freed from the burden of building a large structure, and the congregation can remain in their vacation clothing while still filling their spiritual needs.

Las Vegas has always catered to the desires of its public, and there are drive-through wedding chapels where one can arrange a spectacular theme wedding in a 1950s Cadillac convertible that would make Elvis blush. The appeal of Las Vegas is rooted in the gratification not only of the senses, but of sentimentality. Encouraged by liberal legal matrimonial requirements, the city has long been famous for its many wedding chapels. These are designed to appeal to the broadest instincts of the heart, and the Candlelight Chapel and others echo the iconography of rural Gothic chapels. The austere and serious Richard Upjohn would perhaps be shocked to see this incarnation of his designs, but like country music, these chapels solemnly repeat the conventional values of American culture. Robert Venturi found this quintessentially American city to have important lessons for modern architecture, lessons that had been ignored by the purists of the modernist movement. People want, and may even need, imagery in their visual environment. The persistence of folk art in the contemporary world demonstrates this. For every sleek, unadorned, modernist church, there is an equal number of highly ornate popular churches. Some of these, such as the United House of Prayer in Hartford, Connecticut, which features large-scale carvings of African American angels and polychromy, are quite impressive.

Modern Vernacular

The angelic carvings of the United House of Prayer can be described as folk art, although of a high order. The ordinariness of the church building itself, however, identifies it as a kind of vernacular architecture, the architecture of everyday life that has been transformed into a religious function. One important source for vernacular architecture is housing, and there are many cases of domestic structures being converted or even built specially for meetinghouses. This also connects back to the colonial tradition of plain meetinghouses. The Onset Foursquare Church in Onset, Massachusetts, is a two-story house converted to a church.

Commercial building is another important font of vernacular design, and many churches, temples, meetinghouses and schools have clearly been designed or built by developers more familiar with suburban commercial developments than with the great cathedrals of Europe. The dominance of the shopping mall in American culture is also reflected here. On the other hand, such unpretentious design may often be a deliberate choice to avoid the self-aggrandizement of monumental churches. A variety of

Above: Summit Avenue Assembly of God, 845 Summit Avenue, St. Paul, MN, 1953; expanded 1965, 1983, and 1986.

churches for the Jehovah's Witnesses in Rhode Island and Massachusetts illustrate this trend; many other examples could be found across the country. Some of these use the long shed roofs popular in 1970s housing and commercial developments, while others use the vernacular forms of small suburban office blocks.

Above: Church of St. Augustine, 443 Southeast Second Avenue, St. Cloud, MN, 1960.

Left: St. Mary's Church, Tarkiln Hill Road, New Bedford, MA, 1980s.

Below: Jehovah's Witnesses Exeter Congregation, 742 Ten Rod Road, Exeter, RI.

Homeschooling has been a growing trend in the last three decades; there has also been a similar growth in independent-minded people turning to worship in their homes. The Home Church movement is still somewhat underground, but there is a network of websites and publications devoted to the trend. The parallels to the early Puritan meetings held in congregants' homes are deliberate.

Exceptional Cases

Some churches are hard to classify, except as exceptional cases. Bruce Goff was a famously individualistic architect, and his Tipi Church (1948), Oklahoma City, Oklahoma, used a modernistic external steel frame to support a large

Above: Natick Assembly Hall, Jehovah's Witnesses, 85 Bacon Street, Natick, MA, 1973; expanded 1998.

Above: First Church of the Nazarene, 175 Mulbury Street, Claremont, NH. A residential building used as a church.

Above: New London Spiritualist Church, 2 Moore Court, New London, CT.

Above: Onset Foursquare Church, 301 Onset Avenue, Onset, MA. A residential building used as a church.

tepee structure for a new church. A pair of Canadian churches make interesting comparisons with Goff's church. There is another Tipi Church in Alberta, Canada, dating from the late twentieth century; this one is built of logs in a

tepee shape. Another re-creation of Native American shapes is found at the so-called Igloo Church, or Our Lady of Victory Catholic Church, in Inuvik in the Northwest Territories, Canada.

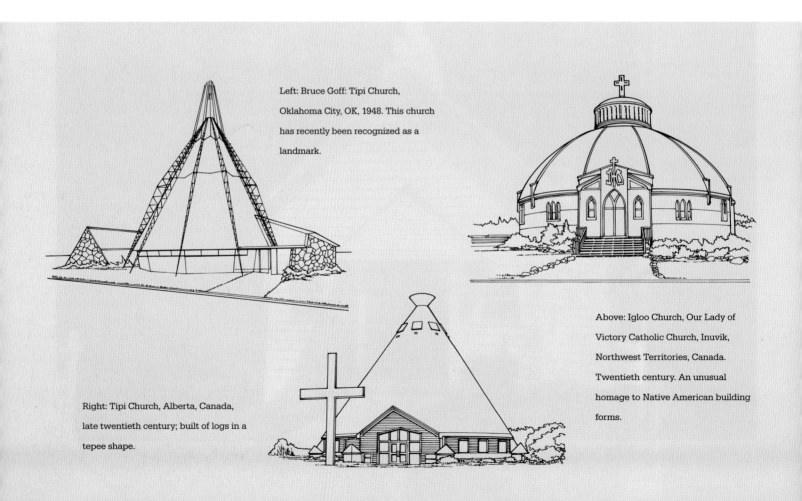

Left: Bruce Goff: Tipi Church, Oklahoma City, OK, 1948. This church has recently been recognized as a landmark.

Above: Igloo Church, Our Lady of Victory Catholic Church, Inuvik, Northwest Territories, Canada. Twentieth century. An unusual homage to Native American building forms.

Right: Tipi Church, Alberta, Canada, late twentieth century; built of logs in a tepee shape.

Latter-day Saints

Although the Church of the Latter-day Saints—frequently called the Mormon Church in the past—is typically associated with its center in Utah, its followers can be found across America. Originating in the nineteenth century with the visionary leaders Joseph Smith and Brigham Young, the first Mormon temple was built in Nauvoo, Illinois, in 1847, but destroyed shortly after its completion. A historically based reconstruction of this temple was just completed in 2002. Twentieth century temples for the Church of Latter-day Saints have followed an interesting, and too little studied, path of modernist explorations. Throughout the century, Mormon churches were built in most of the modern styles, including Frank Lloyd Wright's Prairie Style, Art Deco, and the International Style.

The expressive forms of late modernism and postmodernism have also been employed. The large Chicago Illinois Temple in Glenview, Illinois (1985), is a striking modernist building. The tall towers with the angel Moroni on top are a constant in Mormon design. Nearly identical temples are found in Dallas, Texas; Boise, Idaho; and Buenos Aires, Argentina. The recent Boston Temple in Belmont, Massachusetts (1997–2000), is a similarly austere modernist building with a tall spire with an angel atop it.

The Temple of the Reorganized Church of Latter-day Saints in Independence, Missouri, was designed by Gyo Obata of Hellmuth Obata & Kassabaum. It was built between 1990 and 1994. The spiral form of the temple is 300 feet high; a separate horizontal L-shaped wing of offices and educational facilities adjoins it. The spiral path

Above: Los Angeles Temple, 10777 West Santa Monica Boulevard, Los Angeles, CA, 1951–55.

Above: Oakland California Temple, 4770 Lincoln Avenue, Oakland, CA, 1962–64.

ascending into the heavens is a visual metaphor for the soul's pilgrimage, as well as the reciprocal flow of spirit from heaven. The logarithmic spiral form has links to mathematics, natural growth patterns, ancient Near Eastern ziggurats, Wright's Guggenheim museum, and labyrinths. The tower is built of steel, not concrete. The central sanctuary holds 1,800 people seated in a circle.

Above: Young & Hansen: Church of Jesus Christ of Latter-day Saints, Sixteenth and Harvard Streets, NW, Washington, D.C., 1933.

Above: Nauvoo Temple, 50 Wells Street, Nauvoo, IL, 2002. A re-creation of the first Mormon temple, destroyed 150 years earlier.

Above: Church of Jesus Christ of Latter-day Saints, 2701 Lake Avenue, Wilmette, IL.

Right: Chicago Illinois
Temple, Glenview, IL, 1985.
Detail.

Below: Tsoi/Kobus &
Associates: Boston Temple,
86 Frontage Road, Belmont,
MA, 1997–2000. Front view.

Eastern Religions

The religious diversity of America has been enriched by a wide range of faiths from India and the Far East. A fanciful Hindu temple for the Vedanta Society was built in San Francisco as early as 1905. It is more Victorian than Eastern in its forms, however. More authentic is the Hindu Temple of Greater Chicago, in Lemont, Illinois, in 1985. It is an accurate version of a southern Indian temple built by Indian craftsmen with some modifications for the harsher Midwestern climate. The temple is fully enclosed and heated to compensate for the Illinois winters. Hindu temples are often constructed to resemble a mountain or mountain range. The complex is actually comprised of two temples: the Rama temple and the Ganesha-Shiva-Durga temple. They were constructed by sculptors and builders from India. The Rama temple is built in the style of tenth-century southern Indian temples. The keynote of this temple is the eighty-foot-high tower, which is richly carved with sacred images. The smaller Ganesha-Shiva-Durga temple, to the right of the Rama temple, is built in the style of the first century B.C.

Various Buddhist groups have built temples in New York's Chinatown, sometimes reusing commercial buildings. A special case is the New England Peace Pagoda, Nipponzan Myohoji Sangha, in Leverett, Massachusetts (1985), which is a large Buddhist *stupa*, with four sculptures of the Buddha, a raised walkway for counterclockwise circulation of pilgrims, and a steeplelike *chattravali* at the top. Built of concrete entirely by volunteers, it is a monument dedicated to peace. The stupa is a memorial whose domed form recalls aspects of cosmic symbolism and is based on raised mounds originally built over graves.

The Baha'i House of Worship in Wilmette, Illinois (1920–53), is the national center for that religion, which came to the United States in 1893. This faith is based on the teachings of Bahaullah (1817–92), who was born in Persia and followed a reformer known as the Bab. The

Above: Baryn Basu Associates: Hindu Temple Society of North America, 45-57 Bowne Street, Queens, New York, 1977.

Right: Hindu Temple Society of North America, 45-57 Bowne Street, Queens, New York, 1977.

Below: Hindu Temple Society of North America, Queens, New York, 1977. Detail of sculpture of deity on façade.

Above: Hindu Temple of Chicago, Lemont, IL, 1985. Side view.

Left: Hindu Temple of Chicago, Lemont, IL, 1985. Detail.

Left: Minaret, at the al-Azhar Mosque Cairo, Egypt, after 970. The minaret is the tall tower used for the call to prayer.

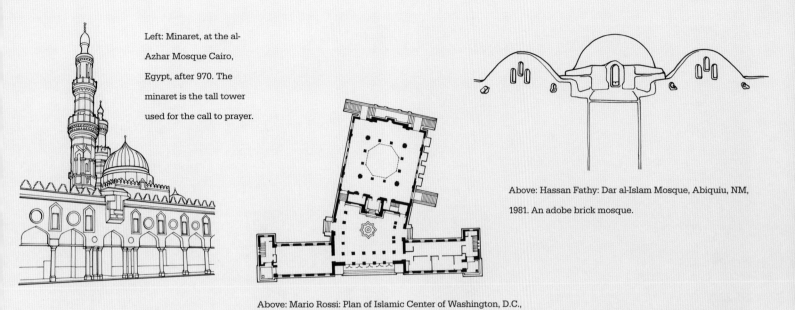

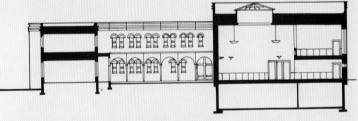

Above: Hassan Fathy: Dar al-Islam Mosque, Abiquiu, NM, 1981. An adobe brick mosque.

Above: Mario Rossi: Plan of Islamic Center of Washington, D.C., 1947–55.

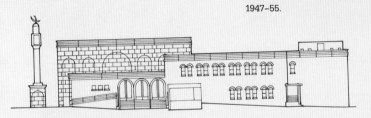

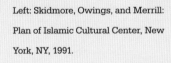

Above: Brown Marazzi and Sanderson-Baoldemas: Dar al-Hijrah, Falls Church, VA, 1991. Elevation of contemporary mosque.

Above: Brown Marazzi and Sanderson-Baoldemas: Dar al-Hijrah, Falls Church, VA, 1991. Section of contemporary mosque.

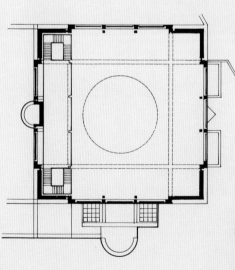

Left: Skidmore, Owings, and Merrill: Plan of Islamic Cultural Center, New York, NY, 1991.

Below: Masjid Hazrat-i-abu Bakr, Queens, NY, 2000.

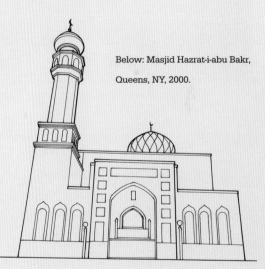

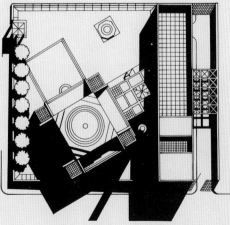

Right: Skidmore, Owings, and Merrill: Aerial perspective of Islamic Cultural Center, New York, NY, 1991.

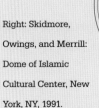

Right: Skidmore, Owings, and Merrill: Dome of Islamic Cultural Center, New York, NY, 1991.

359

Above: Hindu Temple of Chicago, Lemont, IL, 1985. Detail.

Above: Trans World Buddhist Association, 7 East Broadway, New York, NY.

name of the Baha'i Temple is Mashriqu'l-Adhkar, which means "the dawning place of God." It was designed by Jean-Baptiste Louis Bourgeois (1856–1930), a French-Canadian architect. The shape of the dome is loosely inspired by the octagonal Tomb of Uljaytu at Sultaniyya in Iran, which dates from the Ilkhanid era, about 1307–13. It is an enormous nine-sided temple surmounted by a high dome. Nine is the largest single number and it stands for unity and comprehensiveness. Originating in Iran, the Baha'i believe in the unity of religions, and the domed form and prolific carvings are meant to remind one of the oneness of the spirit and to be a temple of light. The temple is built of concrete, steel, and glass, but the structural elements were deliberately concealed with precast screens of cement decoration to make it seem more like a vision. The white cement

was mixed with ground quartz to increase the brilliance. The interior of the temple is essentially one large domed room that can seat up to 1,200 people. The style of the temple, sometimes called "Chicago's Taj Mahal" is purely eclectic, a twentieth-century Orientalist fantasy.

Although Islam came to the United States as early as the eighteenth century, it has become prominent only in the last century. Islam experienced rapid growth in America in the late twentieth century through both immigration and conversions. There are over one hundred mosques in New York City alone. The most prominent early center was the Islamic Center of Washington, D.C. (1947–55). It was designed by Mario Rossi, a convert to Islam. An interesting adaptation of local adobe architecture is found at the Dar al-Islam mosque in Abiquiu, New

Right: Mahayana Buddhist
Temple, 133 Canal Street,
New York City.

Above: New England Peace Pagoda, Nipponzan Myohoji Sangha, 100 Cave Hill Road, Leverett, MA,
1985.

Above: Ashihara Associates: Nichiren Shoshu Temple, 42-32 Parsons Boulevard, Queens, NY, 1984. Japanese Zen Buddhist Temple.

Mexico (1981), designed by Hassan Fathy. The New York Islamic Cultural Center (1991) is a modernistic complex of mosque and study center designed by Michael McCarthy and Mustafa Abadan of the architectural firm of Skidmore, Owings, and Merrill. The tall minaret was designed by the firm of Swanke Hayden Connell. The mosque is oriented so that it faces Mecca. Many other more modest religious and cultural centers have been created in former commercial centers or more plain, vernacular-style buildings with varying degrees of Arabic ornament to distinguish them. Islam has few specific requirements for mosques; many of the most famous features, including minarets, are not required. The few required features are the separation of the sexes during prayer, the avoidance of images of living beings within the mosque, and the orientation toward Mecca.

Above: Jean-Baptiste Louis Bourgeois: Baha'i House of Worship, Wilmette, IL, 1920–53. Overall view. Detail.

Above: Jean-Baptiste Louis Bourgeois: Baha'i House of Worship, 112 Linden Avenue, Wilmette, IL, 1920–53. Overall view; a tall, nine-sided domed temple for the Baha'i faith.

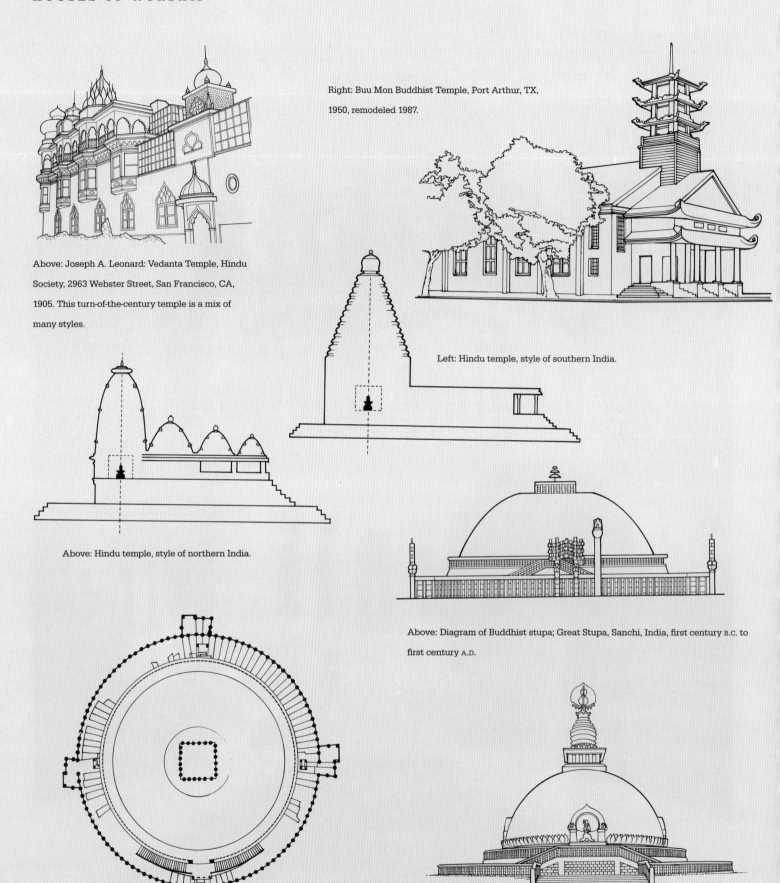

Above: Joseph A. Leonard: Vedanta Temple, Hindu Society, 2963 Webster Street, San Francisco, CA, 1905. This turn-of-the-century temple is a mix of many styles.

Right: Buu Mon Buddhist Temple, Port Arthur, TX, 1950, remodeled 1987.

Left: Hindu temple, style of southern India.

Above: Hindu temple, style of northern India.

Above: Diagram of Buddhist stupa; Great Stupa, Sanchi, India, first century B.C. to first century A.D.

Above: Worshipers circulate around a Buddhist stupa in a clockwise direction; Great Stupa, Sanchi, India, first century B.C. to first century A.D.

Above: Stupa, a sacred mountain shape from Buddhist architecture. New England Peace Pagoda, Nipponzan Myohoji Sangha, Leverett, MA, 1985.

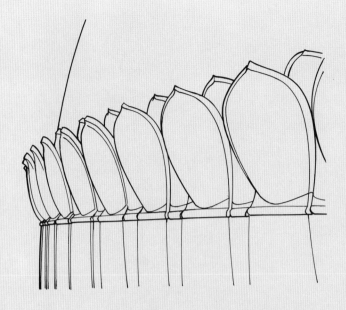

Left: Lotus petals on stupa, sacred mountain shape from Buddhist architecture. New England Peace Pagoda, Nipponzan Myohoji Sangha, Leverett, MA, 1985.

Above: Religious symbolism—the lotus flower, a Buddhist symbol.

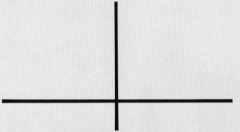

Above: Evolution of the stupa form from a simple burial marker spike; first stage.

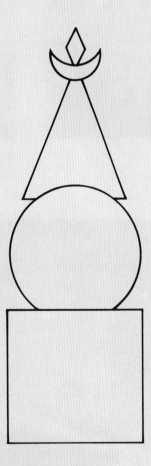

Left: The symbolism of the forms of a stupa—the sphere, cone, and cube—correspond to the five elements (including the mystical ether) and the five senses.

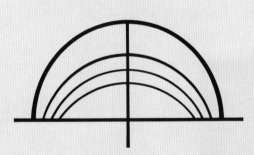

Above: Evolution of the stupa form from a simple burial marker spike; the spike was covered with earth.

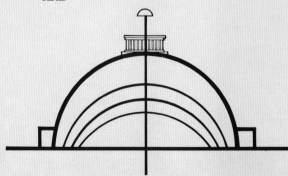

Above: Evolution of the stupa form from a simple burial marker spike; additional features added.

Right: Buddhist stupa with chattravali, the umbrella-like structure at the top.

Above: Mario Rossi: Islamic Center of Washington, D.C., 2551 Massachusetts Avenue, Washington D.C., 1947–55.

Above: Skidmore, Owings, and Merrill: Islamic Cultural Center, New York, NY, 1991. Minaret by Swanke Hayden Connell, 1991.

Left: Mario Rossi: Islamic Center of Washington, D.C., 2551 Massachusetts Avenue, Washington D.C., 1947–55.

Right: Imam Al-Khoei
Islamic Center, 89-89 Van
Wyck Expressway, Queens,
NY, 1989.

Below: Skidmore, Owings,
and Merrill: Islamic Cultural
Center, 1711 Third Avenue,
New York, NY, 1991.

Left: Islamic Society of Boston, 204 Prospect Street, Cambridge, MA, 1990s.

Below: Omar ibn Al-Khattab Mosque, 1025 Exposition Boulevard, Los Angeles, CA, 1994.

New Age Churches

America has been the birthplace of several large denominations: the Church of Latter-day Saints, Seventh-Day Adventism, Jehovah's Witnesses, and Pentecostalism are now well established. More recently, the religion of Eckankar has emerged. The primary Temple of Eck is located in Chanhassen, Minnesota, and was built in 1990. The distinguishing external feature is what is described as a "golden ziggurat" in the group's literature. This form is more like a generic pyramid than an actual ziggurat, but it carries the same symbolism of ascension, or heavenly aspirations. To establish a "brand identity," similar smaller centers have been built in other towns, including one in Middlefield, Connecticut.

The spiral has long been a visual metaphor for the pilgrim's path on the journey of life and also a symbol of the sun. Some of the world's oldest religious carvings and dance circles are based on spiral labyrinths; carvings and coins found at Crete are thought to depict the mythic labyrinth of King Minos. These ancient symbols have been re-created by New Age Americans interested in the roots of tradition. Cretan labyrinths have been constructed of stone, hedges, or earthen mounds in the Southwest and West Coast in recent years. Mainstream Christian churches have also found inspiration in the meditative ritual of following the labyrinth. The famous medieval labyrinth at Chartres Cathedral in France has been re-created dozens of times for people to walk as they pray or meditate.

Above: Temple of Eck, 7450 Powers Boulevard, Chanhassen, MN, 1990.

*

Mathematics is an indispensable tool for architects and has been used as a metaphor for perfection for centuries. Gothic masons closely guarded the secrets of their trade, which included the rules of proportion for their splendid cathedrals. In the Renaissance, theorists such as Alberti searched the writings of Aristotle and Vitruvius to find the secret of classical perfection. Parallels between the mathematical basis of musical harmonies and natural phenomena suggested that mathematical ratios were also the key to perfect beauty and reflected the design principle of God, which could be found in the "music of the spheres," as the cosmos was ordered by divine harmony.

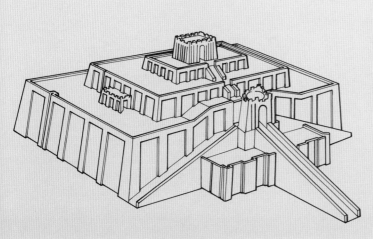

Above: Reconstruction of Ziggurat at Ur, Iraq, *c.* 2500 B.C.

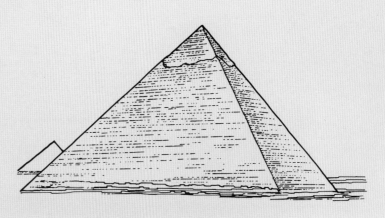

Above: Great Pyramid, Old Kingdom, Egypt.

THE GOLDEN SECTION AND GEOMETRY IN MODERN ARCHITECTURE

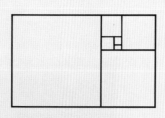

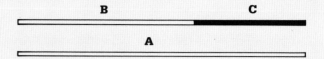

B   C

A

Above: The golden proportion is a ratio where if a line is divided into two parts, the ratio of the whole (A) divided by the length of the longer section (B) equals the ratio of B divided by the length of the shorter section (C), or A/B = B/C. This ratio is approximately 1:1.618.

Above: The golden section is an ideal proportion found in many ancient monuments, including the Parthenon in Athens.

Above: Smaller sections of the Parthenon are also based on the golden section.

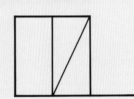

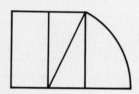

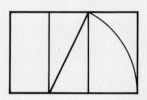

Above: The golden section can be derived geometrically from a square.

Above: Step two is to bisect the square.

Above: Step three is to draw the diagonal between the corners of one of the sections.

Above: Step four is to use the diagonal line to inscribe an arc to the baseline.

Above: Step five is to use the diagonal line to inscribe an arc to the baseline. This gives the length of the golden section.

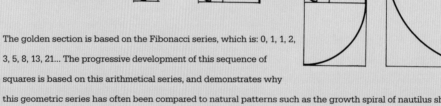

Above: The ratio of the sides of the golden section is approximately 1:1.618... .

The golden section is based on the Fibonacci series, which is: 0, 1, 1, 2, 3, 5, 8, 13, 21... The progressive development of this sequence of squares is based on this arithmetical series, and demonstrates why this geometric series has often been compared to natural patterns such as the growth spiral of nautilus shells and sunflowers. Architects and mathematicians have been fascinated by this supposed visual and structural parallel.

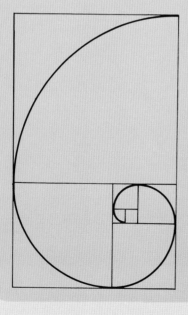

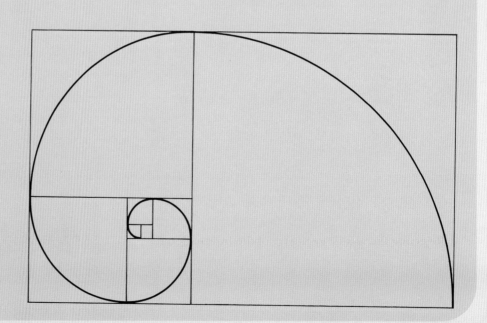

Right: Connecticut Temple of Eck, Route 66 and Harvest Wood Road, Middlefield, CT.

One ratio in particular was the focus of much attention in the Renaissance and still fascinates architects and mathematicians: the so-called golden section. The golden section is an ideal proportion found in many ancient monuments, including the Parthenon in Athens. It can be found in the overall proportion of the façade of the Parthenon, and smaller sections of the Parthenon are also based on the golden section. The golden proportion is a ratio where if a line is divided into two parts, the ratio of the whole (A) divided by the length of the longer section (B) equals the ratio of B divided by the length of the shorter section (C), or A/B = B/C. This ratio is approximately 1:1.618. The golden section can be derived geometrically from a square by extending successive lines from the first square according to the golden ratio. A similar transformation creates a logarithmic spiral generated by the ratio of the golden section. The seeming parallels of this spiral to natural growth patterns in sunflowers and nautilus shells increases the attraction of the ratio for designers and researchers.

Postmodernism (*c.* 1963—present)

Rejecting the ascetic geometry of the International Style, Robert Venturi and other architects sought to reintroduce complexity and rich human experience into their architecture. Historical ornament and contextual

Above: Philip Johnson: Chapel of St. Basil, University of St. Thomas, Houston, TX, 1996–97.

Above: James T. Hubbell: Sea Ranch Chapel, Sea Ranch, CA, 1984. A small, free-form abstract chapel.

Above: Philip Johnson: Chapel of Thanksgiving, Thanksgiving Square, Dallas, TX, 1976. This chapel is based on an Islamic minaret. It is one of Johnson's earliest postmodern works.

Right: The Malwiya minaret of the mosque at Samarra, Iraq, 848–52.

Left: Section of Chapel of Thanksgiving, Thanksgiving Square, Dallas, TX, 1976.

Above: Plan of Chapel of Thanksgiving, Thanksgiving Square, Dallas, TX, 1976. The spiral plan is mirrored in stained glass in the ceiling.

Right: Hellmuth, Obata & Kassabaum (HOK): Reorganized Church of Jesus Christ of Latter-day Saints Temple, Independence, MO, 1994. A spiral ziggurat.

Above: Steven Holl: St. Ignatius Chapel, Seattle, WA, 1995–97. Interior.

allusions were no longer taboo, although frequently used with irony.

Philip Johnson also lost faith in the Miesian style and has designed several postmodern churches. These are first seen in several examples that return to historical precedents. One of his earliest churches was the Thanksgiving Chapel in Dallas, Texas (1976), which adapted the spiral form of the Malwiya minaret of the mosque at Samarra, Iraq (848–52), one of the earliest Islamic minarets. This unusual project was for a nondenominational chapel dedicated to the concept of giving thanks. The spiral form of the tower is inscribed in the floor plan, which unfolds in a logarithmic spiral, and this is mirrored in the spiral patterns of stained glass in the skylights. The spiral is a traditional symbol of a pilgrim's path and also correlates to the unfolding of grace and the outflowing of gratitude in thanksgiving.

A spiral ziggurat similar to Johnson & Burgee's Thanksgiving Chapel can also be seen at the Reorganized Church of Jesus Christ of Latter-day Saints Temple (1994) in Independence, Missouri, designed by Hellmuth, Obata & Kassabaum (HOK).

Twenty years later, Johnson's Chapel of St. Basil at the University of St. Thomas, Houston, Texas (1996–97), derives from Eastern Orthodox forms. The traditional dome, however, is bisected by an abstract sculptural form, a granite plane.

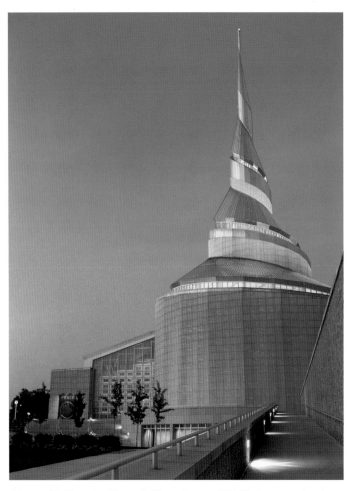

Above: Hellmuth, Obata & Kassabaum (HOK): Reorganized Church of Jesus Christ of Latter-day Saints Temple, Independence, MO, 1994. Spiral ziggurat.

Above: Rafferty, Rafferty & Tollefson: Sexton Commons, St. John's Abbey, Collegeville, MN, 1993. Houses the campus bookstore, cafeteria, pub, and offices. Modeled on the medieval abbey church at Cluny, France.

Above: Suzane Reatig: Metropolitan Community Church, 474 Ridge Street NW, Washington, D.C., 1993.

Above: Thompson Vaivoda & Associates: Marilyn Moyer Meditation Chapel, Portland, OR, 1991. The chapel is dedicated to motherhood.

Philip Johnson's most recent church design is for the Cathedral of Hope, currently underway in Dallas, Texas (scheduled for completion in 2004). Plans and models show it to be a free exercise in abstract form. This is a large cathedral for a gay congregation that has been so challenged by the plague of AIDS in the modern world. It will be a memorial and a testament of faith.

As Johnson's Cathedral of Hope shows, not all postmodernism is based on reworking historical models. There is a rich current of designs that use the abstract language of modernism to create complex visual environments. In a sense, these designers are extending the principles of Le Corbusier, rather than totally rejecting them. One of the most noted designs of recent years was Steven Holl's St. Ignatius Chapel in Seattle, Washington (1995–97), which uses the structures of modernism to shape the church building into a series of "tubes of light" that create a powerful and contemplative mood. The chapel was built for Seattle University, a Jesuit university of about 6,000 students.

The drama of light is used to create a series of spaces and a sense of progression inspired by "The Spiritual Exercises" of St. Ignatius, the founder of the Jesuit order. The artistic vocabulary owes much to Le Corbusier's church at Ronchamp and his abbey church at La Tourette, but the scale and effect here are more intimate and hospitable. The meditations suggested by St. Ignatius are encouraged by the reflecting pool and grass lawn; the mystery and beauty of

Above: Marilyn Moyer Meditation Chapel, Portland, OR, 1991.

Above: Marilyn Moyer Meditation Chapel, Portland, OR, 1991. Interior.

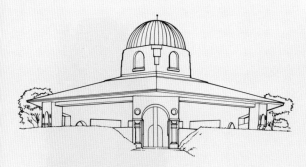

Above: Clovis Heimsath Associates: Kagan-Rudy Chapel, Houston, TX, 1983.

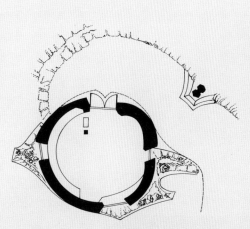

Above: James T. Hubbell: Plan of Sea Ranch Chapel, Sea Ranch, CA, 1984.

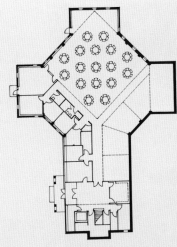

Above: Donham & Sweeney: Plan of Christ Congregational Church, Brockton, MA, 1995.

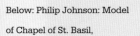

Below: Philip Johnson: Model of Chapel of St. Basil, University of St. Thomas, Houston, TX, 1996–97.

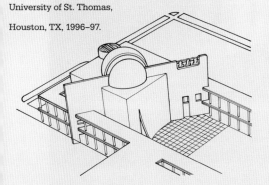

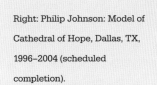

Right: Philip Johnson: Model of Cathedral of Hope, Dallas, TX, 1996–2004 (scheduled completion).

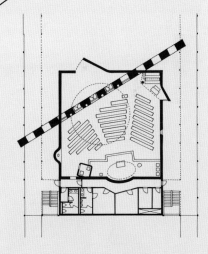

Right: Philip Johnson: Plan of Chapel of St. Basil, University of St. Thomas, Houston, TX, 1996–97.

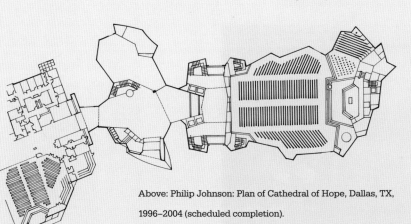

Above: Philip Johnson: Plan of Cathedral of Hope, Dallas, TX, 1996–2004 (scheduled completion).

Below: Steven Holl: Section of St. Ignatius Chapel, Seattle University, Seattle, WA, 1998.

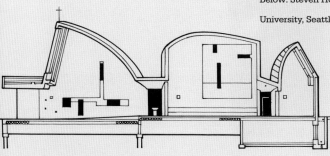

Right: William Rawn Association: Plan of Glavin Family Chapel, Babson College, Wellesley, MA, 1997–2000.

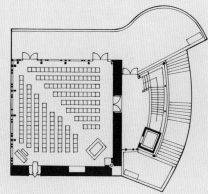

Above: Donham
& Sweeney: Christ
Congregational Church,
1350 Pleasant Street,
Brockton, MA, 1995.

Left: Graham Gund: Young
Israel of Brookline,
62 Green Street, Brookline,
MA, 1996.

Above: Arbonies King Vlock Architects: Kol Haverim Synagogue, 1079 Hebron Avenue, Glastonbury, CT, 1997.

other walls of the cubic structure are of light gray stone.

In Chicago, the recent Chicago Sinai Congregation (1997) is a synagogue that includes an octagonal sanctuary and balcony capable of seating approximately 500 worshipers, as well as a smaller chapel, social hall, classrooms, library, nursery school facilities, and offices. It is the only permanent Reform temple in downtown Chicago. The architects were Lohan & Associates, who also designed the Shedd Aquarium in Chicago. The three-story building is made of a tawny stone and the façade is punctuated by a crisp rhythm of rectangular windows of different sizes. A triangular bay window projects from the right side of the composition. A flowing staircase with square openings in the balustrade adds suppleness to the design.

nature is conducive to the Jesuit directive to "find God in all things."

Another interesting example of a postmodern church that uses all the technology of modernism to great effect is the Glavin Family Chapel (1997–2000) at Babson College in Wellesley, Massachusetts. It was designed by William Rawn Associates. One whole wall is a curtain wall of glass, which looks out onto a peaceful garden and woods. The contemplation of nature is united with meditation and prayer. The

The first Catholic cathedral built in America in over twenty-five years was recently (1998–2002) erected in Los Angeles. The Spanish architect José Rafael Moneo designed the Cathedral of Our Lady of the Angels in Los Angeles to accommodate the desire of the cardinal who wanted it to evoke California's Spanish missionary past and also speak a modern language—to follow the directives of the Second Vatican Council to speak to parishioners in their own language. The cardinal said he wanted a space "like a town meeting," and the interior gives a sense of an

Left: Lohan & Associates: Chicago Sinai Congregation, 15 West Delaware, Chicago, IL, 1997.

Above: St. Ignatius Chapel, Seattle University, Seattle, WA, 1995–97.

informal gathering. The architect avoided the axial focus and instead one can approach the altar from three sides. It is built of concrete, stained with subtle but rich color. The forms are cubic and abstract. Although rooted in the past, it is very much a building of the present. It is located beside the main freeways of Los Angeles, which keeps the church in the eyes of the passersby.

The Marilyn Moyer Meditation Chapel is much smaller and located in a completely different kind of site. It is perched dramatically on the edge of a 130-foot cliff overlooking Portland, Oregon. Nature and architecture work together to create a sense of drama and mystery. The chapel was designed by Thompson Vaivoda & Associates and built in 1991. A pronounced axial path draws one to the chapel on the threshold of the cliff, passing over a

Above: Steven Holl: St. Ignatius Chapel, Seattle, WA, 1995–97. Detail.

Right: McGuire Courteau Lucke: Church of St. Henry, 1001 East Seventh Street, Monticello, MN, 1999. Front view.

reflecting moat that surrounds it. On the interior, the far wall is a glass curtain wall that seemingly dissolves the barrier between viewer and nature, while still offering protection and shelter. The chapel is dedicated to motherhood.

In the postmodern era, a new appreciation of ancient religious practices has developed. This is especially meaningful in churches designed for Native American Christians. This trend began in the 1960s, coinciding with the renewed interest in Native American cultural identity. Christian churches now display a greater sensitivity to local tribal traditions. In the Southwest, the traditional log hogan form has been adapted for Christian churches. On the Navajo reservation in Chinle, Arizona, the Church of Our Lady of Fatima was designed by Edward Preston and Father Blane Grein as a modern wooden hogan, with a seventy-foot-diameter octagon. Round forms are widespread in Native American traditional building, and other round shapes have also been adapted. The tepee plan has been adapted for the Church of God at Wounded Knee in South Dakota.

Right: McGuire Courteau Lucke: Church of St. Henry, 1001 East Seventh Street, Monticello, MN, 1999. Interior.

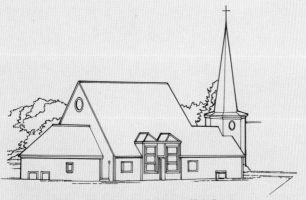

Above: Bahr Vermeer Haecker Architects: Holy Rosary Catholic Church, Pine Ridge, SD, 2001. The simple exterior reflects the desire to keep costs down.

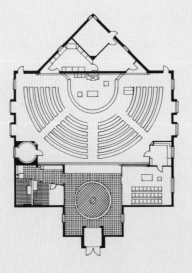

Above: Holy Rosary Catholic Church, Pine Ridge, SD, 2001. The plan draws on the symbolic traditions of the Lakota Medicine Wheel and the Celtic Cross of the Catholic tradition.

Above: Cretan labyrinth, Northern California, c. 2000. In recent years, New Age groups have revived various ritual forms, such as the labyrinth, from past civilizations. The spiral progress is a metaphor for the progress of the human soul.

Above left: William Rawn Association: Glavin Family Chapel, Babson College, Wellesley, MA, 1997–2000.

Above: Prisco Serena Sturm: St. Mary's Church, 1500 South Michigan Avenue, Chicago, IL, 2002.

Although necessity required that the church be built as inexpensively as possible, the plan of the Holy Rosary Catholic Church in Pine Ridge, South Dakota, draws on the symbolic traditions of the Lakota Medicine Wheel and the Celtic Cross of the Catholic tradition. The church was designed by the firm of Bahr Vermeer Haecker Architects and built in 2001.

New Age groups have revived various ritual forms from past civilizations, such as the labyrinth. The spiral form is a metaphor for the progress of the human soul. Cretan labyrinths have been constructed in recent years in several locations in California, Arizona, and New Mexico.

Right: José Rafael Moneo: Cathedral of Our Lady of the Angels, 555 West Temple Street, Los Angeles, CA, 1998–2002.

Notes

1. Randolf Rock, "Our Church-Erection Interests," *United Brethren Review* 5:2 (April 1894), 79–180.
2. Ludwig Mies van der Rohe, "Address to the Illinois Institute of Technology (1950)," quoted in Leland M. Roth, *America Builds* (New York: Harper & Row, 1983), 508.
3. Erich Mendelsohn, "In the Spirit of Our Age," *Commentary* (June 1947), 542.
4. Leopold Eidlitz, quoted by Montgomery Schuyler in *American Architecture and Other Writings*, William H. Jordy and Ralph Coe, eds. (New York: Atheneum, 1964), 57.
5. Philip Johnson, "Letter to Dr. Juergen Joedicke, 1961," in Roth, *America Builds*, 586.
6. Quoted in Roger G. Kennedy, *American Churches*, (New York: Stewart, Tabori & Chang, 1982), 19.

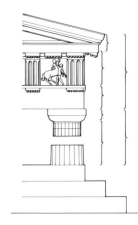

Above: Abacus—Doric order

Above: San Miguel Chapel, Santa Fe, NM, 1709.

A

abacus On a classical column, the flat section at the top of the capital, a square block that divides the column from its entablature.

adobe Architecture built of sun-dried bricks found in the American Southwest in both Spanish colonial and Native American traditions. The Spanish word *adobe* refers both to the mud bricks and, by extension, to the buildings made of them.

altar A structure on which to place or sacrifice offerings to a deity. In Greece and Rome, altars took many different forms. The Christian altar is a table or slab on supports consecrated for celebration of the sacrament; originally usually of stone. In the Middle Ages portable altars could be of metal. After the Reformation, communion tables of wood replaced altars in England, and these are most commonly found in American churches.

apse Roman in origin (found in both religious and secular contexts), an apse is a usually semicircular extension to, or ending of, another structure, with a rounded vault. In Early Christian basilicas, the place of the clergy (Presbytery) and bishop was here.

Above: Arcade—Church of the Sacred Heart, 1321 Centre Street, Newton, MA, 1891–99.

arcade   A line of repeated arches supported by columns; they may be freestanding or attached to a building. The term also applies to a commercial gallery of shops, which may be fronted by an arcade or have an interior atrium lined with arches.

arch   A key element of architecture used to span the distance between columns or walls. It can be either semicircular or pointed. A true arch is self-supporting.

architrave   The lowest portion of a classical entablature, this is the horizontal beam or lintel that spans the distance between columns. It is located directly below the frieze.

ashlar masonry   Masonry of regularly cut stones laid in horizontal courses with vertical joints.

Above: Arch—Louis Sullivan and Dankmar Adler: Pilgrim Baptist Church, originally built as Kehilath Anshe Ma'ariv Synagogue, Chicago, IL, 1891. Detail.

Above: Architrave—Minard Lafever (?): St. James Church (Roman Catholic), 32 James Street, New York, NY, 1835–37.

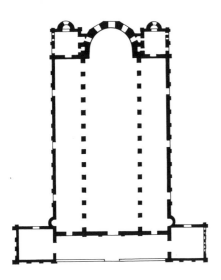

Above: Basilica—S. Apollinare in Classe, Ravenna, Italy, A.D. 533–49.

B

bargeboard   Decorative boards, also called vergeboards, on the edge of gables in Gothic Revival churches; these are often elaborately carved.

basilica   A church divided into a nave and two or more aisles, the former higher and wider than the latter, lit by the windows of a clerestory, and with or without a gallery. In Roman architecture, a basilica was a large meeting hall, as used in a public administration. The term originally indicated function and not form, but Roman basilicas were often oblong buildings with aisles and galleries, with an apse opposite the entrance that might be through one of the longer, or one of the shorter, sides. Early Christian churches evolved from Roman basilicas of this type (not from pagan religious architecture). By the fourth century, the Christian basilica had acquired its essential characteristics: oblong plan; longitudinal axis; a timber roof, either open or concealed by a flat ceiling; and a termination, either rectangular or in the form of an apse.

battlement   A parapet with alternating cutout and raised portions; this is derived from medieval fortifications; also called crenellation or castellation.

bell tower   A tower in which a bell or a set of bells is hung, usually attached to or near a church.

belt course   A horizontal course of masonry that marks the division between floors; the raised profile of the course also helps divert rainwater. Also called a string course.

bimah (or bema)   The Greek word for platform. The term has several meanings, but is most commonly used in Judaism for the platform from which services are

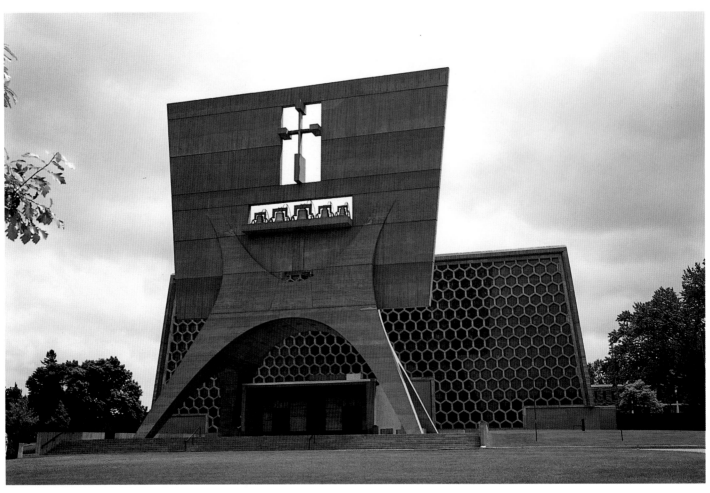

Above: Bell tower—Marcel Breuer: St. John's Abbey, Collegeville, MN, 1961. Front view, "banner" bell tower.

Above: Battlements—A. J. Davis: First Unitarian Church, 71 Eighth Street, New Bedford, MA, 1845.

conducted in a synagogue. In the Eastern Orthodox Church, the term refers to the area of a church in which the altar is located, or the sanctuary. The term was also used for that part of an early Christian church that was reserved for the higher clergy; the inner or eastern part of the chancel.

board and batten A form of vertical siding comprised of boards laid side by side, with the joints covered with narrow battens for weatherproofing. Most commonly found in Gothic Revival architecture.

bracket A projecting support found under eaves, windows, or cornices. These may be used for structural purposes but are often merely decorative. They are especially prominent in the Italianate style of the mid-nineteenth century.

C

capital The top element of a column.

Carpenter's Gothic Carpenter's Gothic refers to Gothic churches and houses built of wood during the mid-nineteenth century. The strong carpentry tradition in America, the demand for quickly constructed buildings, and the abundance of fine

Right: Board and batten—Little Brown Church, Route 32, Round Pond, ME, 1853.

timber combined to make wooden Gothic a natural development. Carpenter's Gothic is distinguished chiefly by its profusion of sawn details. The fact that most of these details were originally designed to be executed in stone did not deter American architects and carpenters from doing them in wood, greatly facilitated by the introduction of the steam-powered scroll saw, which could cut from thin boards the scrolled ornament so often associated with the style.

castellated A parapet decorated with battlements or crenellations.

chancel That part of the east end of a church in which the main altar is placed; reserved for clergy and choir. From the Latin word *cancellus*, which refers to the screen that often separated it from the body of the church.

choir The part of the church where the liturgy is sung, generally located in the rear of the church, behind the transepts.

clerestory The upper stage of the main walls of a church above the aisle roofs, pierced by windows; the same term is applicable in domestic building. In Romanesque architecture it often has a narrow wall passage on the inside.

cloister A quadrangle surrounded by roofed or vaulted passages connecting the monastic church with the domestic parts of the monastery; usually south of the nave and west of the transept.

colonnade A row of columns carrying an entablature.

column A vertical, round structural post. In classical architecture, the column usually consists of a base, shaft, and capital.

corbel A projecting stone that carries a weight above it. It may be decorated. A series of progressively projecting stones may form a corbelled arch, or even a corbelled dome, as is found in Navajo hogans.

Corinthian order The most slender and ornate of the classical orders; Corinthian columns have an

Above: Clerestory—H. H. Hartwell & W. C. Richardson: First Baptist Church, 5 Magazine Street, Cambridge, MA, 1881. Side view, showing clerestory.

Above: Colonnade—Jack Liebenberg: Temple Israel, 2324 Emerson Avenue South, Minneapolis, MN, 1928.

Above: Corinthian order

elaborate base and a tall capital that resembles a basket with acanthus leaves growing through it. The height to width ratio of the column is about 101, and the entablature is about one-fifth the height of the column.

cornice A projecting molding along the top of a building, wall, or arch that caps it off. In classical architecture, the crowning feature of the entablature.

crenellation *See* battlement.

crocket An ornamental feature of Gothic architecture, this is a small leaf-shaped projection found at regular intervals on the angled sides of spires, pinnacles, and gables.

crossing The space at the intersection of the nave, chancel, and transepts of a church; often surmounted by a crossing tower.

crowstep A stepped gable built in front of a pitched roof. Originating in northern Europe, this is commonly called a Dutch (or Flemish) gable, or stepped gable.

cupola A miniature domed shape that rises from a roof like a small tower, usually containing windows to let in light or for ventilation.

D

dentil A small square block used in groups (like rows of teeth) for decoration in classical architecture, typically under a cornice.

Doric order The oldest and heaviest of the classical orders. Doric columns have no base, and the capital is composed of a simple abacus and echinus. The height to width ratio of the column is about 4 or 6 to 1, and the entablature is about the height of the column.

drip molding A molded shape designed to keep rainwater from running down wall

Above: Crowstep—Robert W. Gibson: West End Collegiate Church and School, West End Avenue and West Seventy-seventh Street, New York, NY, 1891–93.

Above: Cupola—Charles Bulfinch: Meeting House, Lancaster, MA, 1815–17. Detail of portico.

surfaces; the projecting form breaks the flow of water, so that drips fall away from the wall.

E

echinus   The cushionlike molding under the abacus of a capital of the Doric order.

egg and dart   An ornamental pattern found in classical architecture, comprised of alternating ovoid (egg) and arrow shapes (darts).

elevation   A two-dimensional drawing made to show one face (or elevation) of a building.

engaged column   A half-column that is set against or into the wall surface.

entablature   The upper part of a classical order, consisting of the architrave, frieze, and cornice.

F

fan light   A semicircular or elliptical window over a door; frequently found in eighteenth- and early-nineteenth-century houses and also in meetinghouses of the same period.

fascia   A flat horizontal band or surface; in classical architecture, these are found in the architrave.

fenestration   From the Latin word for window, this generally refers to the use of windows in a wall.

finial   An ornamental form found on the top of gables, pinnacles, and canopies in Gothic architecture. The most common shape is a fleur-de-lis formed of leaves.

Above: Doric order—Volney Pierce First Congregational Church, Madison, CT, 1838. Detail of portico.

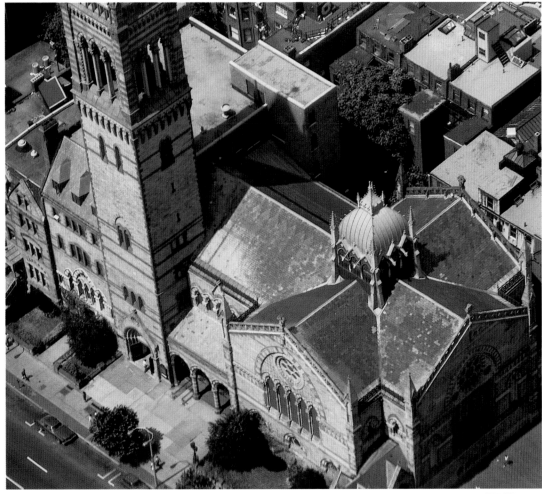

Above: Crossing—Charles A. Cummings and Willard T. Sears: New Old South Church, Copley Square, Boston, MA, 1874–75.

Above: Gable—Walpole Meetinghouse, South Bristol Road, Route 129, Bristol, ME, 1772.

flêche A slender spire, usually of wood, although occasionally made of iron during the nineteenth century, rising from a ridge of a roof; also called a spirelet. Derived from the French word for arrow, *flêche*.

flute The vertical, grooved channel found on classical columns. The concave grooves are separated by an arris, a thin raised strip.

frieze The middle division of a classical entablature, a horizontal band between the architrave and the cornice. This may be decorated with sculpture.

G

gable The triangular end of a wall below a pitched roof and above the level of the eaves.

gambrel A gable roof with two angles of pitch on each side.

geodesic dome An innovative geometric design for domed houses patented by Buckminster Fuller in 1954.

gingerbread A term for the ornate scroll-sawn wooden ornaments, like decorated bargeboards, on Gothic Revival houses and churches.

Greek orders The term "order" refers to the various types of classical columns when combined with their respective pedestal bases and entablatures. These include

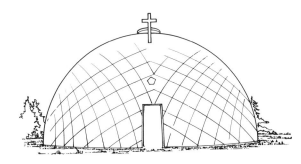

Above: Geodesic dome—R. Buckminster Fuller: St. Michael's Chapel, St. Columbans, NE, *c.* 1957.

Above: Gambrel—Moses Johnson, master builder: Shaker Meetinghouse, Canterbury Shaker Village, 288 Shaker Road, Canterbury, NH, 1792.

Doric, Ionic, and Corinthian; the combination of elements and proportions within these orders was governed by strict rules.

H

half timbering A construction technique where the house is built with a timber frame (post-and-beam construction), with the spaces between the timbers filled in with plaster or brickwork.

hipped roof A roof that slopes upward from all four sides of the house, rather than ending in a gable.

I

iconostasis A screen in Byzantine churches separating the sanctuary from the nave, pierced by three doors and covered with icons.

Ionic order A more slender and ornate order, Ionic columns have a base and a capital composed of scroll volutes emerging from a cushion. The height to width ratio of the column is about 9:1, and the entablature is about one-fifth the height of the column.

Above: Half-timbering—St. Lawrence Roman Catholic Church, 774 Boylston Street (Route 9), Brookline, MA.

Left: Hipped roof—Old Ship Meeting House, 107 Main Street, Hingham, MA, 1681; with additions in 1731, 1755.

Above: Iconostasis—St. Peter and St. Paul Russian Orthodox Church, Bramble, MN, 1915–18.

Right: Ionic order—First Church of Christ Scientist, 190 Court Street, Middletown, CT.

Above: Kiva—Pueblo Bonito (Anasazi), Chaco Canyon, NM, A.D. 900—1300.

J

jamb figures The straight side of an archway, doorway, or window; the part of the jamb that lies between the glass or door and the outer wall surface is called a reveal.

K

keystone The central stone of an arch or vault; *see also* voussoir.

kiva Circular underground chamber used for worship in Native America pueblos.

L

lancet window A tall, narrow window that ends with an acutely pointed arch.

lintel The horizontal beam that spans the distance between two columns or posts or the opening of a window or doorway.

louver In American architecture, this is one of a series of overlapping boards or narrow panes of glass used to fill a window opening, keeping out rain while allowing ventilation.

M

mansard roof A characteristic roof form invented by François Mansart in France in the seventeenth century.

menorah A ceremonial seven-branched candelabra found in Jewish temples; it is associated with the Jewish temple in Jerusalem. The number seven symbolizes the seven days of Creation.

Above: Mansard roof—Frank W. Sandford: Shiloh Temple, Durham, ME, 1896–97.

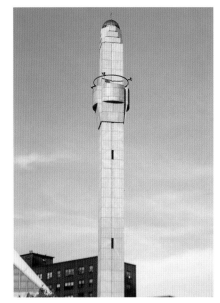

Above: Minaret—Skidmore, Owings, and Merrill: Islamic Cultural Center, 1711 Third Avenue and Ninety-sixth Street, New York, NY, 1991. Minaret by Swanke Hayden Connell, 1991.

metope The square space between two triglyphs in the frieze of a Doric order. Usually left blank in houses, it may contain sculpture.

mihrab A niche cut into the wall of a mosque, facing Mecca and indicating the direction of prayer.

minaret A high tower attached to a mosque and used for the call to prayer.

minbar The pulpit from which the sermon is preached during the Friday prayers in a mosque. It stands to the right of the mihrab.

molding A carved or shaped band projecting from a wall or attached to it.

mosque The principal religious building of Islam and the place for communal prayer. There is an important distinction between the cathedral, or Friday mosque—which serves to hold the entire adult community assembled to perform the ritual Friday prayers and to hear the preacher's sermon—and the simple oratory *(masjid)*, which suffices for daily prayer.

N

nave The main hall area of the typical Christian church. It precedes the altar and transepts, if any, and is often flanked by aisles. From the same etymological root as *naval,* or ship.

O

oculus A round window.

Above: Mosque—Mario Rossi: Islamic Center of Washington, D.C., 2551 Massachusetts Avenue, Washington D.C., 1947–55.

Right: Nave—Patrick C. Keely: St. Bridget's
Roman Catholic Church, Pleasant and Church
Streets, Rutland, VT, 1860–61. Interior.

Above: Palladian window.

P

Palladian window   A three-part window construction associated with the sixteenth-century Italian Renaissance architect Andrea Palladio; a taller central window with arched top is flanked by smaller rectangular windows. The vertical elements are frequently treated like classical columns or pilasters.

parapet   A low wall placed at the edge of a sudden drop, like the edge of a roof.

pattern book   A book containing sample plans, ornamental details, and construction diagrams; popular in the eighteenth and nineteenth centuries.

pediment   In classical architecture, the triangular termination at the ends of buildings or over porticos, corresponding to a gable in medieval architecture, but framed with an enclosing cornice. In later usage, the term is used for any similar feature found above doors or windows; these may be round, segmental, or broken (open at the top).

pendentive A concave span leading from the angle of two walls to the base of a circular dome. It is one of the means by which a circular dome is supported over a square or polygonal compartment, and is used in Byzantine (Hagia Sophia, Istanbul) and occasionally Romanesque (Perigueux) architecture, and often in Renaissance, Baroque, and later architecture. In America, pendentives are found in some Spanish colonial churches and Byzantine Revival churches and temples.

pier A freestanding solid masonry support, usually thicker than a column.

pilaster A flat column, projecting slightly, attached to a wall. This can be of any classical order.

pinnacle A small turret or tall ornament that crowns spires, the peaks of gables, or the corners of parapets.

plinth A square or rectangular base for a column or pilaster.

portico A porch with a roof supported by columns attached to the main entrance of a church.

pulpit An elevated stand of stone or wood for a preacher or reader, which first became common in the later Middle Ages. Very important in American Protestant churches, which emphasize the importance of the sermon. Often elaborately carved, and sometimes with a acoustic canopy above the preacher called a sounding board or tester.

pylon In ancient Egyptian architecture, the rectangular, truncated, pyramidal towers flanking the gateway

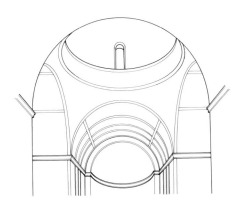

Above: Pendentives—curved triangular transitions between a round dome and square plan of a Byzantine church.

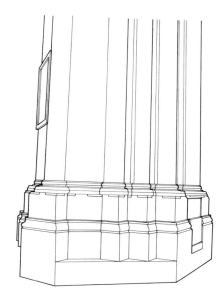

Above: Gothic pier—Ralph Adams Cram: Cathedral Church of St. John the Divine, New York, NY, begun 1893.

Above: Pinnacle—Charles Brigham: Unitarian Memorial Church, Fairhaven, MA, 1901–2. Twentieth Century Gothic pinnacle encrusted with crockets.

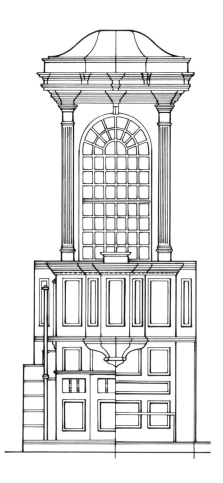

Above: Pulpit—Rockingham Meeting House, Rockingham, VT, *c.* 1787–1800.

of a temple; also, more loosely, any high isolated structure used decoratively or to mark a boundary.

Q

quatrefoil   Literally, "four leaves"; an ornamental pattern comprised of four circular or pointed lobes. Frequently found in Medieval Revival styles. *See also* trefoil.

quoin   The larger dressed stones found at the corners of stone or brick buildings, typically laid in an alternating pattern. Originally used as structural reinforcements, quoins were also used as decorative elements.

quonset hut   Inexpensive prefabricated houses with semicircular vaulted interiors, first built at the Quonset, RI, naval base during World War II. After the war, some of these were converted for use as churches.

R

ribbon window   A continuous band of windows, made possible by modern framing techniques, which emphasizes the transparency and open plans of modernist architecture. A hallmark of the International Style.

rose window   A circular window with foils or patterned tracery arranged like the spokes of a wheel.

S

segmental arch   A shallow arch based on a segment of a circle smaller than a semicircle.

side aisle   Aisle to the side of the nave (central aisle).

soffit   The exposed flat surface on the underside of any overhead building component such as an eave, cornice, arch, or balcony.

spire   A tall pyramidal, polygonal, or conical structure rising from a tower, turret, or roof (usually of a church) and terminating in a point. It can be of stone or of timber covered with shingles.

squinch   An arch or system of concentrically wider and gradually projecting arches, placed diagonally at the internal angles of towers to fit a polygonal or round superstructure on to a square plan.

Below: Pylon—Temple of Horus, Edfu, *c.* 237 B.C.

Above: Quonset hut—Bruce Goff: Camp Parks
Seabee Chapel (San Lorenzo Community Church),
945 Paseo Grande, San Lorenzo, CA, 1944–45.

steeple The tower and spire of a church taken together.

string course *See* belt course.

stupa The simplest form of Buddhist religious monument, often designed to receive relics. Originally, the stupa was a hallowed sepulchral mound. Buddha instructed his disciples to raise such mounds of earth symbolically at crossroads. In India the stupa took the form of a hemisphere reinforced by gateways at the four points of the compass. Later, in Southeast Asia, stupas were often bell-shaped. They are built of stone on a terraced base and crowned with a square top supporting a *chattravali,* the umbrella-like structure at the top. The stupa is often surrounded by a fence or row of columns with imposing gates.

T

tipi A lightweight, portable shelter used by Native American Plains tribes. It is comprised of poles arranged in a conical shape and covered with bark or animal hides.

Torah scroll The five books of Moses (the Pentateuch) written in Hebrew on a scroll kept in the Torah shrine in a synagogue.

Torah shrine An enclosed niche or cupboard for storing the Torah scroll in a synagogue.

tracery In Medieval Revival architecture, the ornamental intersecting work in the upper part of a window, screen, or panel, or used decoratively in blank arches and vaults. Typical forms include a circle, a quatrefoil, or other simple form. More complex, flowing tracery is made up of compound or ogee curves, with an uninterrupted flow from curve to curve; this is

Right: Squinch—Bertram Grosvenor
Goodhue: St. Bartholomew's, New
York, NY, 1919.

Right: Steeple—David Hoadley, builder/
architect: Congregational Church, 6 West Main
Street, Avon, CT, 1818–19.

also called curvilinear or undulating tracery. Later, even more elaborate tracery is known as flamboyant, for the resemblance of the intricate stonework to flames.

transept The transverse arms of a cross-shaped church, usually between nave and chancel, but also occasionally at the west end of the nave as well, and also doubled, with the eastern arms farther east than the junction of nave and chancel. The latter form is usual in English Gothic cathedrals.

trefoil Literally, "three leaves"; an ornamental pattern comprised of three circular or pointed lobes. Frequently found in Medieval Revival styles. *See also* quatrefoil.

triglyph Blocks separating the metopes in a frieze of the Doric order. These blocks usually have three grooves.

triumphal arch A freestanding monumental gateway that originated in Rome in the second century B.C. These were originally temporary structures erected by Roman magistrates for such festive occasions as the triumphs decreed to victorious generals. They were later frequently built of stone. There are two main types: those with a single archway and those with a large archway flanked by two small archways. The form was revived in the Middle Ages and adapted to use as the entrance to a church, with its meaning now changed to signify the triumph over death of the Christian. The triple arch form also symbolized the trinity.

Above: Stupa—New England Peace Pagoda, Nipponzan Myohoji Sangha, 100 Cave Hill Road, Leverett, MA, 1985.

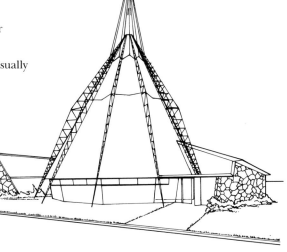

Above: Tipi Church, Oklahoma City, OK, 1948.

Above: Tracery—John T. Comes: Church of
St. Luke, Summit Avenue, St. Paul, MN, 1924.
Detail of rose window.

truss   A framing element composed of several members joined together to make a rigid structure.

V

vergeboard   *See* bargeboard.

vernacular   Meaning "common speech," this word is used to denote folk-style architecture, based on the common practices of building at the time.

viga   The stout horizontal beams used for support in the roofs of adobe structures; the projecting ends are frequently left exposed.

volute   The spiral scroll in a capital of the Corinthian order.

voussoir   The wedge-shaped blocks used to form an arch; the central, uppermost one is called the keystone.

W

water table   A molded course of masonry that bridges the transition between the

foundation wall and the thinner wall above it. The sloping form is sometimes enhanced with a drip mold at the lower edge to divert water from running down the foundation.

Z

ziggurat   An Assyrian or Babylonian temple tower in the form of a truncated pyramid built in diminishing stages, each stage being reached by ramps.

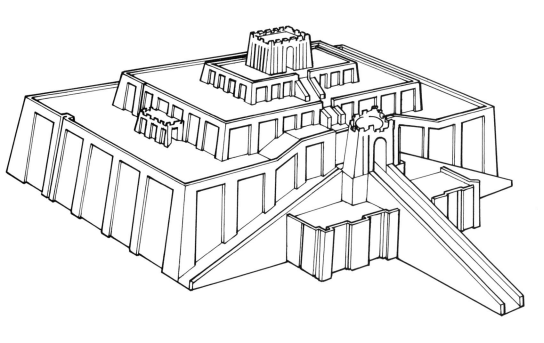

Left: Ziggurat—Reconstruction of ziggurat at Ur,

Iraq, *c.* 2500 B.C.

The Architects

The following is a listing of a number of the most influential architects who have helped shape American religious architecture. Each entry contains a thumbnail biography that gives relevant biographical details and the type of architecture practiced. Some of these people had only short architectural careers; indeed many of the earliest American architects were amateur designers who earned their living from other spheres, Thomas Jefferson being, of course, the most notable example.

Until the late eighteenth century, the most accomplished architects were either immigrants or trained abroad. The nineteenth century brought an increasing professionalism to architecture. Charles Bulfinch and Asher Benjamin made significant contributions through their buildings and writings. The American Institute of Architects was founded in 1857; Richard Upjohn was the first president. In 1868, the first architecture program was established at the Massachusetts Institute of Technology by William Ware. The prestige of European programs was still strong, however; the first Americans to attend the French Ecole des Beaux-Arts were Richard Morris Hunt, Henry Hobson Richardson, and Charles F. McKim.

The twentieth century brought new confidence to American architects. Frank Lloyd Wright founded his own architecture school, the Taliesin Fellowship, in 1932. New technologies and new theories of history and meaning now shape the training of architects at many universities and technical schools.

Adler, Dankmar (1844–1900)

Born in Stadtlengsfeld, Prussia, Adler emigrated to
the United States with his father in 1854 and studied
architecture in Detroit and Chicago. He designed
the Central Music Hall in Chicago and in 1881
entered into partnership with Louis Sullivan. Their
firm, Adler & Sullivan, would be one of the most
influential practices of the late nineteenth century.
Adler provided the engineering skills and Sullivan
provided the aesthetics. Their work served as a
bridge between the eclectic revivals of the
nineteenth century and the simple functionality of
modern architecture. Their work together was
profoundly influential on twentieth-century
architecture. Among their buildings were the
Auditorium Theater in Chicago (1887–89) and the
Wainwright Building in St. Louis (1890), admired
by many as the perfect expression of the first
skyscraper style. Their most important religious
edifice was the Kehilath Anshe Ma'ariv synagogue in
Chicago (1891), now the Pilgrim Baptist Church.
Another important building was the Transportation
Building for the World's Columbian Exposition in
Chicago in 1893. Their partnership dissolved in 1895.

Above: Louis Sullivan and Dankmar Adler: Pilgrim Baptist Church, originally built as Kehilath
Anshe Ma'ariv synagogue, 3235 East Ninety-first Street, Chicago, IL, 1891.

Angell, Truman O. (1810–87)

Truman Osborn Angell was born in North Providence, Rhode Island. After training in
carpentry in his hometown, he moved to upstate New York around 1833. One of his most
notable works is the first temple at Nauvoo in Illinois, where he developed Mormon orders
and forms. This has recently (2002) been reconstructed. He was later recognized as Utah's
most important architect of the mid-century.

Austin, Henry (1804–91)

Best known for his work in New Haven, Connecticut, where he lived and practiced for over
fifty years, this innovative architect started his career working for Ithiel Town as a builder.
He went on to produce numerous public, private, and commercial buildings and works
such as New Haven's City Hall and Railroad Station, the John P. Norton House, and the
monumental Egyptian Revival gateway at the Grove Street Cemetery in 1845. Austin's
abilities also took him further afield: he worked in other parts of New England and the mid-
Atlantic states. His forte was the Italian villa style for which he was much in demand. The
most notable example of this is Victoria Mansion (built as the Morse-Libby House) in
Portland, Maine.

Belluschi, Pietro (1899–1994)

Italian-American civil engineer, designer, and architect. Belluschi served as dean and professor at the Massachusetts Institute of Technology's school of architecture and planning (1951–65). He introduced an innovative series of Protestant church designs in the 1950s in Portland, Oregon, and Boston that strongly influenced postwar architecture.

Benjamin, Asher (1773–1845)

Above: Asher Benjamin: Old West Church, 131 Cambridge Street, Boston, MA, 1806.

Born in Hartland, Connecticut, Benjamin went on to create the first builder's guide written and published in America (1797). This guide consists of seven books that include designs for Georgian, Federal, and Greek Revival styles of architecture. These designs were modeled after architects such as Charles Bulfinch and Robert Adam.

Boyington, William W. (1818–98)

A leading practitioner of the Gothic Revival in the second half of the nineteenth century in the Midwest. Chiefly known for his medieval Water Tower in Chicago (1871), one of the few structures to survive the great fire there, Boyington also built large stone churches in Chicago and Minnesota, including the First Baptist Church of St. Paul in Minnesota.

Breuer, Marcel Lajos (1902–81)

A leading member of the modern movement, Breuer was born in Pécs, Hungary, where he started his studies. In 1920 he went to the Bauhaus in Weimar and was attracted by Walter Gropius's approach to art and architecture. Graduating in 1924, he was given charge of the furniture workshop where he designed the first tubular steel chair, the Wassily (1925). He taught at the Bauhaus in Dessau until 1928, when he moved into private practice in Berlin. After an unsuccessful period when he built only one private house (in Wiesbaden, 1932), he worked for a short time in Switzerland and London before emigrating to the United

States in 1937 following an invitation from his old mentor, Walter Gropius. He joined Gropius as Associate Professor of Architecture at Harvard University, a position he held until 1946. Together they designed several outstanding houses and Breuer developed a bold sculptural use of poured concrete. From 1946 until his retirement in 1976, he ran a New York practice whose early work was largely for domestic buildings. In 1952 he worked as part of a team on the UNESCO headquarters in Paris (completed 1958), and his later work included major public designs such as St. John's Abbey, Collegeville, Minnesota (1953–61), and the Whitney Museum of American Art, New York City (1966).

Brigham, Charles (*c.* 1841–1925)

Born in Watertown, Massachusetts, to an old New England family, Brigham enlisted in the army in September 1862; after hostilities ceased he started practicing. At the end of the decade he joined John Hubbard Sturgis to form the firm Sturgis & Brigham. Until the untimely death of his partner some twenty years later, the firm proved very successful; they designed the Boston Museum of Fine Arts (1870–76), the Church of the Advent, and many fine private mansions. After Sturgis died, Brigham designed alone and was responsible for a wide variety of styles across America, from Redlands, California, to the First Church of Christ, Scientist, Boston (1906). He also designed a major additional wing to the Massachusetts State House, the Maine State House, St. Mark's Catholic Church (Dorchester, Massachusetts), and Foxboro (Massachusetts) State Hospital, plus many other churches and libraries. Eventually Brigham moved to Shelter Island, New York, to live out his last years with his sister.

Below: Charles Brigham & S. Beman; with Brigham Coveney & Bisbee: Mother Church, Christian Science Center, Boston, MA, (chapel by Franklin Welch, 1894), 1906.

Above: Joseph Brown: First Baptist Church, 75 North Main Street, Providence, RI, 1771–75.

Brown, Joseph (1733–85)

Brown created the designs for the oldest Baptist church in America—the First Baptist Church, Providence, Rhode Island (1774–75). In style, the meetinghouse is a combination of classic English Georgian and New England meetinghouse. It was built to Brown's design by unemployed ship carpenters and shipwrights at a time when there was little or no other work. Brown was not a trained architect but an astronomer and mathematician.

Butterfield, William (1814–1900)

Butterfield was born to a successful London chemist in 1814. His most notable work was for the Cambridge Camden Society, where he developed High Church Ritualism in England. Influenced by both A. W. N. Pugin and John Ruskin, Butterfield exemplified the new movement of "constructional polychromy" as shown in the completion of All Saints Margaret Street in London (1850–63), one of the first examples of High Victorian Gothic.

Bulfinch, Charles (1763–1844)

Born into a wealthy Boston family in 1763, Bulfinch studied at Harvard before traveling in Europe between 1785 and 1787. While in Paris he met Thomas Jefferson, who suggested that he concentrate his studies on classical architecture. Enthused with what he saw, he returned to Boston heavily influenced by the churches of Sir Christopher Wren in London and determined to improve his home city's architecture. He was responsible for many fine neoclassical buildings, such as the Massachusetts State House (1798), St. Stephen's Church (built as the New North Church in 1802–4), and Massachusetts General Hospital (1820). He also worked successfully in other states, most notably with the Connecticut State House (1796) and the Maine State Capitol (1831). With such experience behind him he was chosen to succeed Benjamin Latrobe as the architect of the U.S. Capitol in Washington, D.C. He held the position from 1817 to 1830. Many consider his Meetinghouse in Lancaster, Massachusetts (1815), to be his masterpiece.

Burling, Edward (1819–92)

Burling was the second architect to practice in Chicago. Most of his buildings were destroyed in the fire of 1871. His Episcopal Cathedral of St. James (Anglican) in Chicago (1857) was rebuilt in 1875, after Burling had formed a partnership with Dankmar Adler. Their partnership lasted from 1871 to 1879, when Adler joined with Louis Sullivan.

Byrne, Francis Barry (1883–1967)

Born in Chicago, Byrne had no architectural training when he wrote to Frank Lloyd Wright in 1902 asking for an interview. Wright was impressed with his desire to become an architect and hired him as an apprentice. Byrne worked for Wright until 1908 and assisted with houses and the Unity Temple in Oak Park. In 1922, Byrne built his first church, and for the next forty years, he tended to specialize in religious buildings. His designs moved away from the Prairie Style toward a more expressionistic modern version of Gothic design. His Church of Christ the King in Tulsa, Oklahoma, was a major success, and in 1928 he was asked to design a church in Cork, Ireland, which has been described as the first European Catholic church built by an American architect.

Carter, Elias (1781–1864)

The son of an English carpenter, Carter was born in Auburn, Massachusetts. He built many houses and at least a dozen churches. His design for the church at Templeton, Massachusetts, of 1811, was much copied in New England.

Cram, Ralph Adams (1863–1942)

An ardent exponent of Gothic architecture, Cram produced many collegiate and ecclesiastical works in a neo-Gothic style. Among these are part of the Cathedral of St. John the Divine in New York City (1911–42); the graduate school and chapel at Princeton; and buildings at Williams College, Phillips Exeter Academy, Rice University, and the U.S. Military Academy at West Point. He was a successful author of twenty-four books and a founder of the Medieval Academy in America. His first Gothic church was All Saints Ashmont, in Dorchester, a suburb of Boston (1891). The great urban church of St. Thomas in New York City (1906–14) is perhaps his masterpiece. He also designed a charming chapel on his own property in Sudbury, Massachusetts (1914).

Davis, Alexander Jackson (1803–92)

One of the nineteenth century's most prominent architects, Davis was born in New York City and spent

Above: Charles Bulfinch: Meeting House, Town Common, Lancaster, MA, 1815–17.

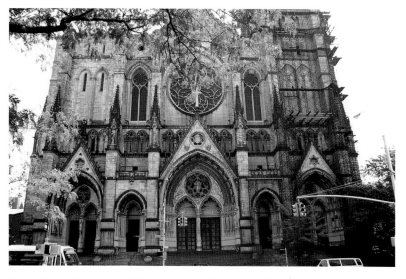

Above: Ralph Adams Cram: Cathedral Church of St. John the Divine, 1047 Amsterdam Avenue, New York, NY, begun 1893.

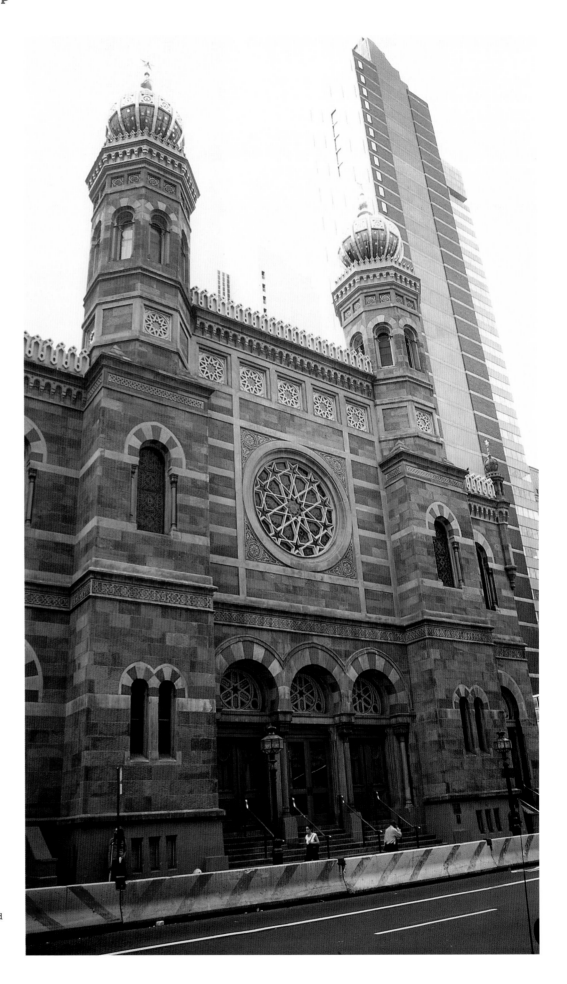

Right: Henry Fernbach: Central
Synagogue, 652 Lexington Avenue and
Fifty-fifth Street, New York, NY, 1872.
Moorish/Islamic Revival.

most of his childhood in New Jersey. He began working as a typesetter in Virginia in 1818 but returned to New York to take up drawing and architecture. He formed a partnership with prominent architect Ithiel Town, designing largely in the Greek Revival style. In 1835, he struck out on his own, drawing upon a number of styles, particularly Gothic Revival. His First Unitarian Church in New Bedford, Massachusetts (1845), is a powerful example of a crenellated Gothic tower. A proponent of the Picturesque movement, integrating rural homes into the landscape, Davis created unusual and asymmetric villas, such as his masterpiece, Lyndhurst (1838/65), in Tarrytown, New York. He collaborated with horticulturist Andrew Jackson Downing (1815–52) in popularizing the Picturesque and became its most prominent proponent. Davis designed not only buildings but furniture and interiors as well. He remained active until the 1870s, though his influence waned as a younger generation of architects emerged.

Downing, Andrew Jackson (1815–52)

Downing is known to have raised the level of building in rural America through his three major books, as well as his writings in *The Horticulturist*. As seen in his examples of Gothic and Italianate designs, Downing successfully provided middle-class America with tasteful designs of simple cottages, therefore raising the aesthetic appeal of the cottage. His early death in a steamboat accident cut short a major career.

Eidlitz, Leopold (1823–1908)

Born in Prague in 1823, Eidlitz was educated in Vienna. He emigrated in 1843 to the United States where he first worked for Richard Upjohn as a draftsman. He built several notable Gothic church designs, including Saint George's in New York City (1846–48), the Second Congregational Church in Greenwich, Connecticut (1856–59), and the Church of the Holy Trinity, New York City (1873). His Temple Emanu-El (1866–68, designed with Henry Fernbach) was a key example of Victorian synagogue architecture. He was a founding member of the American Institute of Architects.

Fernbach, Henry (1829–83)

Born in Loewenberg in Prussian Silesia (now Iwowek, Poland), Fernbach studied at the Berlin Building Academy. He emigrated to New York in 1855, where he built a number of important synagogues, including the Bn'ai Jeshurun Synagogue (1865–66) and the Temple Emanu-El (1866–68), with Leopold Eidlitz.

Fillmore, Lavius (1767–1805)

A resident of Middlebury, Vermont, Fillmore was the architect of numerous Federalist and some early Gothic Revival churches. His works include the First Church (Congregational) in Bennington, Vermont (1805–6), and the Congregational Church of Middlebury, Vermont (1806). He was the cousin of President Millard Fillmore.

Fuller, (Richard) Buckminster (1895–1983)

Born in Milton, Massachusetts, Fuller studied first at Harvard and then at the U.S. Naval Academy, Annapolis, Maryland. In 1917 he developed energetic/synergetic geometry, which some years later led him to devise a structural system that he termed "Tensegrity Structures." He experimented with structural design following the machine aesthetic with the intention of devising an efficient, practical, economic, and trouble-free mass production building system. For this he particularly looked at the way aircraft chassis were produced and put together. His ideas culminated in the design for Dymaxion House in 1927, but it was in the post–World War II years that he gained renown and his geodesic domes won international acclaim. Huge polyhedral frame enclosures, the largest of these domes, were built for the Union Tank Car Repair Shop, Louisiana (1958), but it was as part of the U.S. Pavilion at Expo '67—the Montreal World's Fair —that the geodesic dome was brought to public attention. An experimental mission church with a geodesic dome was built for St. Michael's Chapel, St. Columbans, Nebraska (*c.* 1957). In 1970 Fuller was awarded the Gold Medal of the American Institute of Architects. His designs have recently been revived and used for a number of churches built in the 1990s.

Furness, Frank (1839–1912)

Furness was a major force in shaping Victorian Philadelphia. He created an extremely original and powerful version of the High Victorian Gothic style, which can be seen in the notable Pennsylvania Academy of Art in Philadelphia of 1876. He studied with Richard Morris Hunt from 1859 to 1861, and was influenced by the writings of John Ruskin and Viollet-le-Duc. Rodef Shalom Synagogue (1869–71) in Philadelphia was one of his major religious commissions.

Gibbs, James (1682–1754)

Gibbs was born in Fittysmire, Scotland, and later moved to London, where he practiced architecture. His book entitled *A Book of Architecture* (1728) is one of the most influential sources of Protestant church design in England and America. The style that he promoted in his book can be seen in his works such as the Oxford Chapel in London (1721–25) and St. Martin-in-the-Fields in London (1720–26).

Godefroy, Maximilian (1765–1840?)

Born in Paris in 1765, Godefroy lived in America from 1805 to 1819, while exiled by the Napoleonic regime in France. He became the first professor of architecture in America, at St. Mary's College in Baltimore. While in America, Godefroy designed

Above: Maximilian Godefroy: Unitarian Church, Charles and Franklin Streets, Baltimore, MD, 1817–18.

the Gothic Saint Mary's Chapel (1806–8) and the classical Unitarian Church in Baltimore (1817–18). One year after completing the Unitarian Church, Godefroy and his wife moved to Europe to continue his architectural career.

Above: Bertram Grosvenor Goodhue: St. Bartholomew's, Park Avenue at East Fifty-first Street, New York, NY, 1919.

Goff, Bruce (1904–82)

An extremely inventive and idiosyncratic architect, Goff was born in Kansas and worked mostly in Oklahoma and Chicago. He was also an accomplished artist and composer. While still in his early twenties, he made a major contribution to the Boston Avenue United Methodist Church in Tulsa, Oklahoma (1927–29). During World War II, he served as a Seabee and designed a church from a standard Quonset hut design. Interested in Native American traditions, he designed the Tipi church in Oklahoma City, Oklahoma (1948), a steel frame church inspired by Plains dwellings.

Goodhue, Bertram Grosvenor (1869–1924)

Raised in Pomfret, Connecticut, Goodhue moved to New York City, where he worked in the office of James Renwick. His firm, Cram, Goodhue, and Ferguson, is best known for the design of the U.S. Military Academy at West Point (1903–10). He designed many important Gothic buildings in partnership with Cram; his most important independent church is perhaps St. Bartholomew's on Park Avenue in New York City (1919).

Above: John Holden Green: St. John's Church (now St. John's Cathedral), 271 North Main Street, Providence, RI, 1810. Episcopal.

Goodman, Percival (1904–89)

One of the most prolific Jewish architects of synagogues, Goodman built more than fifty synagogues in his career. Born in New York City, he began designing temples following World War II, after the shock of the Holocaust made him reconsider his origins and faith. With his brother Paul Goodman, he published a book on urban planning, *Communitas* (1947).

Greene, John Holden (1777–1850)

Born in Warwick, Rhode Island, in 1777, Greene worked in Providence, where he designed more than fifty buildings for the capital city. Saint John's Cathedral (1810) and the Sullivan-Dorr House (1809–10) are two of his most notable works in Providence. St. John's Cathedral is an important early example of the Gothic Revival in America.

Gropius, Walter Adolph (1883–1969)

One of the most important architects of the twentieth century, Gropius was the founder of the Bauhaus, probably the most influential design and architectural school of the twentieth century. Born in Berlin, Germany, he studied in Munich and then worked for Peter Behrens in Berlin. His first major commission was the design of the Fagus shoe factory at Alfeld in 1911. In 1918 he was appointed director of the Grand Ducal group of schools of art in Weimar: He amalgamated them and formed them into the Bauhaus. A revolutionary concept, the Bauhaus art schools aimed at a new functional interpretation of the applied arts, utilizing glass, metals, and textiles. But the bold use of unusual building materials was condemned as "architectural socialism" in Weimar, and as a consequence, in 1925 the Bauhaus was transferred to Dessau and a new functionalist building by Gropius. His reputation grew to such an extent that he was even asked to design car bodies (by Adler, 1929–33). When the Nazis came to power, the Bauhaus was closed, and in 1934 Gropius felt it expedient to escape to London. There he worked on factory designs and housing, including a revolutionary adjunct to Christ Church, Oxford, which was never built. In 1937 he emigrated to the United States where he became Professor of Architecture at Harvard (1938–52). While there he designed the Harvard Graduate Center (1949). Later work included the American embassy in Athens (1960).

Harrison, Peter (1716–75)

Above: Peter Harrison: Touro Synagogue, 85
Touro Street, Newport, RI, 1759.

One of the most accomplished gentlemen architects in eighteenth-century America,
Harrison was born in England and worked at first as a sea captain until he emigrated
permanently to the New World in 1740. He married an American heiress and they settled in
Newport, Rhode Island, where he worked in shipping. Like many wealthy gentlemen with
leisure time, he took to architecture and studied books to learn the necessary skills. From
1748 until 1764 he designed a number of austerely classical buildings based on his book
learning, the most notable being Redwood Library, Newport (1748–50). The success of this
got him his next commission, the King's Chapel in Boston (1749–54), and other work
followed, including Christ Church, Cambridge, Massachusetts (1759–61); a synagogue for
Sephardic Jews in Newport (1759–63); and the Brick Market, Newport (1761–62).

Holl, Steven (b. 1947)

Celebrated for his creative use of space and light, Holl was born in Bremerton, Washington,
and then graduated from the University of Washington architecture school. He spent a year
in Rome and then did postgraduate work at the Architectural Association, London. In 1976
he established Steven Holl Architects in New York. His first professional commission was a
sculpture studio and pool house in New York in 1980. Holl has developed a signature style

based on his use of space and light. Among his important works are the Kiasma Museum of Contemporary Art in Helsinki, Finland (1998), the Bellevue Art Museum, Washington (2000), and the Chapel of St. Ignatius, Seattle, Washington (dedicated 1997). In 1989 he became a tenured professor at Columbia University and has also taught at other higher education institutions. He has won many awards for his architectural achievement: the Arnold W. Brunner Prize for Achievement in Architecture as an Art (1990), New York AIA Medal of Honor (1997), National AIA Design Award (for Chapel of St. Ignatius, 1998), Alvar Aalto Medal (1998), Chrysler Award for Innovation in Design (1998), and the National AIA Design Award (for Kiasma, 1998).

Johnson, Philip (b. 1906)

Best known for his Glass House in New Canaan, Connecticut (1949), Johnson was born in Cleveland, Ohio, and graduated from Harvard University. In 1932 he co-curated the exhibition at the Museum of Modern Art titled "The International Style," which gave the modern movement its name. Other notable works include the New York State Theatre at

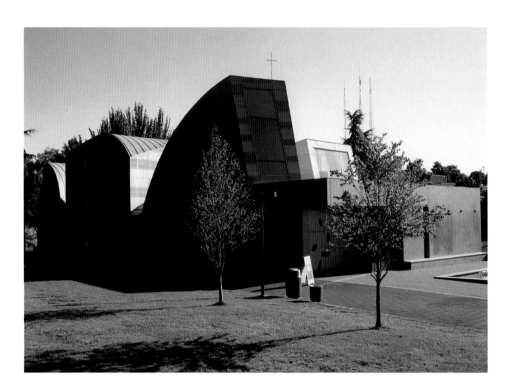

Right: Steven Holl: St. Ignatius Chapel, Seattle University, Seattle, WA, 1995–97.

Lincoln Center (1964) and the AT&T Headquarters in New York (1980). Johnson was awarded the Gold Medal of the American Institute of Architects in 1978. His religious buildings include the innovative Roofless Church at New Harmony, Indiana (1960), the Thanksgiving Chapel in Dallas, Texas (1976), the Garden Grove Church, also known as the Crystal Cathedral (designed with John Burgee), in Los Angeles (1978–80). His most recent church design is for the Cathedral of Hope in Dallas, to be completed in 2004.

Jones, E. Fay (b. 1921)

Born in 1921, Jones studied at the University of Arkansas in Fayetteville and at Rice University in Houston, Texas. He later apprenticed with Frank Lloyd Wright. His

Left: Philip Johnson:
Roofless Church, Blaffer
Foundation, between
Main and West Streets,
New Harmony, IN, 1960.

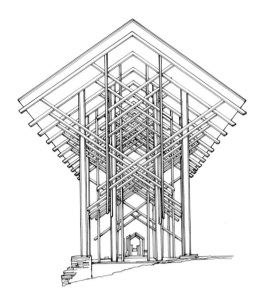

Above: Fay Jones: Thorncroft Chapel, Eureka Springs, AK, 1980.

Thorncrown Chapel in Eureka Springs, Arkansas (1980), is his most famous work. In 1990, he was awarded a gold medal from the American Institute of Architects.

Kahn, Louis Isadore (1901–74)

Born in Ösel (now Saaremaa), Estonia, Kahn and his family emigrated to the United States in 1905 and Kahn became a naturalized citizen in 1917. He graduated from the University of Pennsylvania, taught at Yale from 1947 until 1957, and then taught at the University of Pennsylvania from 1957 until 1974. He was a pioneer of functionalist architecture labeled "New Brutalism," as exemplified by the Richards Medical Research Building, Philadelphia, Pennsylvania (1957–61). Further works include the Yale University Art Gallery (with Douglas Orr, 1953), the Salk Institute in La Jolla, California (1959–65), the Indian Institute of Management, Ahmedabad (with Balkrishna Doshi, 1962–74), and the Paul Mellon Center, Yale (1969–72).

Kearsley, Dr. John (1684–1772)

A physician and amateur architect, Kearsley followed the example of Christopher Wren in his urban churches. One of the most prominent is Christ Church in Philadelphia (1727–44).

Keely, Patrick C. (1816–96)

Born in County Tipperary in Ireland, Keely came to America in 1842, where he became one of the most prolific architects of Catholic churches. More than 600 churches and twenty-one cathedrals have been attributed to him between 1846 and 1896. In Boston, his works include the Cathedral of the Holy Cross (1867–75) and the Church of the Immaculate Conception. He also built the Cathedral of the Holy Name in Chicago (1874–75) and the Cathedral of Saints Peter and Paul in Providence, Rhode Island (1878–89).

Above: Dr. John Kearsley: Christ Church, Second and Market Streets, Philadelphia, PA, 1727–44. Spire by Robert Smith, 1750–54.

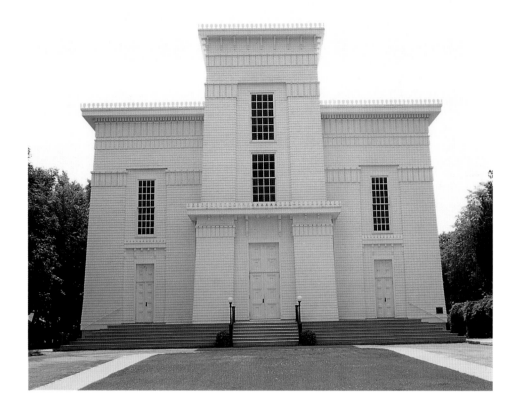

Left: Minard Lafever: First Presbyterian Church (Old Whaler's Church), 44 Union Street, Sag Harbor, NY, 1842–43. Front view.

Lafever, Minard (1798–1854)

Lafever was an important architect and author of pattern books such as *The Modern Builders Guide* and *The Beauties of Modern Architecture*. Most of his designs were classical, but his First Presbyterian Church (Old Whaler's Church) in Sag Harbor, New York (1842–43), is a fine example of an Egyptian Revival church.

Latrobe, Benjamin (1764–1820)

Born in England, where he trained with A. P. Cockerell, Latrobe arrived in America in 1796. He was the architect of many public buildings and banks in Philadelphia and Washington, D.C., including the national Capitol, and brought a new degree of professionalism to American building. His most important church is the Baltimore Cathedral (1804–18), a large classical building with a Roman-style dome, which is vaulted in stone. Latrobe was also versed in the Gothic style, and offered the Bishop of Baltimore plans for a Gothic edifice as well; the Bishop chose the Roman Revival style.

Above: Benjamin Latrobe: Minor Basilica of the Assumption of the Blessed Virgin Mary, Cathedral and Mulberry Streets, Baltimore, MD, 1804–18. Roman revival. Front view.

Long, Robert Cary, Jr. (1810–49)

Long was a leading architect in Baltimore, Maryland. He designed churches and temples in the Greek Revival style, including the Lloyd Street Synagogue in Baltimore, 1841–45. He also designed churches and houses in the Gothic Revival style. His father, Robert Cary Long, Sr. (1770–1833), had also been an architect.

McBean, Thomas

McBean was a Scotsman who had studied with James Gibbs in London. His design for St. Paul's Chapel (1764–66) in New York City is the closest adaptation in America of Gibbs's London church of St. Martin-in-the-Fields (1722–26).

Above: Robert Cary Long, Jr.: Lloyd Street Synagogue, 11 Lloyd Street, Baltimore, MD, 1845.

McKim, Charles Follen (1847–1909)

Born in Chester County, Pennsylvania, McKim studied architecture at the Ecole des Beaux-Arts in Paris. He returned to the United States in 1872 and worked in the office of H. H. Richardson in New York and assisted with the building of Trinity Church, Boston. In 1877 he joined up with William Rutherford Mead, then two years later with Stanford White, to found the architectural firm of McKim, Mead & White. They became the leading architectural practice in the United States, a position they held for many decades. The principals worked together to design classical- and Renaissance-influenced buildings and were instrumental in the Neoclassical Revival in the U.S. at the time. The firm designed a number of notable buildings, including the Judson Memorial Church in New York City (1888–93); Boston Public Library (1887–95); the Rhode Island State House in Providence; Madison Square Garden (1891), the Morgan Library (1903), and Pennsylvania Station (1904–10), all in New York; and the Agricultural Building at the World's Columbian Exposition, Chicago (1893). McKim also took on special projects such as the restoration of the White House and the revival in 1901 of Pierre l'Enfant's 1791 grand plan for Washington, D.C. Personally convinced that aspiring young American architects needed training in the European tradition, he was instrumental in founding the American Academy in Rome, which he supervised from 1894. The American Institute of Architects awarded him its gold medal in 1909. He was elected an associate of the American Institute of Architects in 1875, a fellow in 1877, and its president 1902–03. He died in September 1909 at his summer home in St. James, Long Island, New York.

Maginnis, Charles Donagh (1867–1955)

Born in Derry, Northern Ireland, Maginnis came to America at age eighteen. In Boston, he apprenticed with Edmund Wheelwright as a draftsman. Inspired by the Gothic Revival churches of Ralph Adams Cram, Maginnis became one the leading figures in ecclesiastic design and the collegiate Gothic. He built many churches in the Boston area and won the commission for the Boston College campus in 1909. His most notable commission was the National Shrine of the Immaculate Conception, Washington, D.C., 1920.

Left: Maginnis, Walsh & Sullivan: St. Catherine of Genoa, Catholic Church, 170 Summer Street, Somerville, MA, *c.* 1915. Front view.

Masqueray, Emmanuel (1861–1917)

Masqueray was born in Dieppe, France, and trained at the Ecole des Beaux-Arts in Paris. He emigrated to the U.S. in 1887. He worked for Richard Morris Hunt and assisted in the design of the Breakers Mansion in Newport, Rhode Island, in 1895. In 1904, he served as the chief architect for the World's Fair in St. Louis. This led to the commission for the Cathedral of St. Paul in Minnesota, built between 1907 and 1915 in the Beaux-Arts style. Masqueray built more than two dozen churches and cathedrals in the Midwest.

Maybeck, Bernard Ralph (1862–1957)

The son of a wood carver, Maybeck loved elaborate decoration and idiosyncratic architectural details. His father sent him to Paris to learn to become a wood carver, too, but Maybeck enrolled in the Ecole des Beaux-Arts instead. After graduating he returned to the United States and worked with Carrère & Hastings. Maybeck revered Greek and Romanesque buildings and based his own work on their principles while extravagantly embellishing them, as well as building with a wide variety of apparently disparate materials. He settled in Berkeley, California, where he remained for most of his life, designing private homes and larger public commissions, such as the First Church of Christ, Scientist, Berkeley (1909–11), and the Palace of Fine Arts at the Panama-Pacific Exposition, San Francisco (1915).

Right: Bernard Maybeck: First Church of Christ, Scientist, Berkeley, CA, 1910.

Mead, William Rutherford (1846–1928)

Born in Brattleboro, Vermont, in August 1846, Mead went to Norwich University and graduated from Amherst College in 1867. He began studying architecture in New York and then spent some time in Florence, Italy. On returning to New York, he struck up a professional partnership with Charles F. McKim. Two years later, in 1879, they were joined by Stanford White and named the firm McKim, Mead & White. Together they comprised the leading architectural practice in the United States. Even after the death of the other two principals, Mead continued to head the firm, which worked on many prestigious projects. In 1913, Mead became the first architect to be awarded the gold medal from the Academy of Arts and Letters. Among many other honors, he became a fellow of the American Institute of Architects and president of the New York Chapter (1907–08). King Victor Emmanuel made him a Knight Commander of the Crown of Italy in 1922 for his contribution to the introduction of Roman and Italian Renaissance architectural styles to America. He died in Paris in June 1928.

Mendelsohn, Eric (1887–1953)

German architect, pioneer of expressionism. Born in Germany, Mendelsohn moved to Israel in 1934 and then to the United States in 1941. He is best known for his exuberant, sculptural design for the Einstein Tower in Potsdam (1919–21). In America he designed a number of strikingly modern synagogues, including the B'nai Amoona Synagogue and Community Center, St. Louis, Missouri (1946–50), and the Mount Zion Temple in St. Paul, Minnesota (1951).

Mies van der Rohe, Ludwig (1886–1969)

The founder of the modern style was born in Aachen, Germany, the son of a mason. He studied design under Peter Behrens and became a pioneer of glass skyscrapers. In Berlin he designed high-rise flats for the Weissenhof Exhibition (1927) and the German Pavilion for the Barcelona International Exposition (1929). He also designed tubular steel furniture, most notably the Barcelona chair. He became director of the Bauhaus in Dessau between 1930 and 1933 and emigrated to the United States in 1937. He became Professor of Architecture at the Armour (now Illinois) Institute of Technology in Chicago. Among his works in the United States are two glass apartment towers on Lake Shore Drive in Chicago. He also collaborated with Philip Johnson on the Seagram Building in New York (1956–58). Other works include the Public Library in Washington, D.C. (1967), and two art galleries in Berlin.

Above: Ludwig Mies van der Rohe: St. Saviour Chapel, Illinois Institute of Technology, Chicago, IL, 1952.

Moneo, José Rafael (b. 1937)

Born in Spain, Moneo studied at the Madrid School of Architecture and then worked with the Danish architect Jorn Utzon. In the U.S. he has designed several leading museums in Wellesley, Massachusetts, and Houston, Texas. From 1986 to 1990 he was chairman of the Architecture Department of the Harvard University Graduate School of Design. In 2002, his new Catholic Cathedral, Our Lady of the Angels, in Los Angeles was the first to be built in the U.S. in more than a quarter century.

Mould, Jacob Wrey (1825–86)

Born in Chiselhurst, England, Mould was educated at King's College in London. He worked for the eminent British architect Owen Jones from 1840 to 1848, while Jones was preparing his highly influential book on architectural design, *The Grammar of Ornament*. In 1853 Mould emigrated to New York City, where he worked as an architect designing churches, schools, and residences. His All Souls Unitarian Church, New York City, of 1853–55, was one of the first buildings to manifest the new High Victorian polychromy. Mould also worked with Calvert Vaux on the first Metropolitan Museum of Art (1874-80) and the American Museum of Natural History (1874–77) in New York.

Palladio, Andrea (1508–80)

Andrea di Pietro della Gondola, one of the most important architects of all time, was born in Vicenza and initially trained as a stonemason. He developed a modern Italian architectural style based on classical Roman principles, which moved away from the prevalent heavily ornamented and embellished Renaissance style. The "Palladian" style was widely followed all over Europe, most notably by Christopher Wren and Inigo Jones. Palladio remodeled the basilica in his hometown of Vicenza and then extended his style to villas, palaces, and churches. One outstanding work was San Giorgio Maggiore in Venice. His *Quattro Libri dell'Architetura* (1570) greatly influenced his successors, including many American architects during the eighteenth century.

Parris, Alexander (1780–1852)

A leading figure in the Greek Revival that dominated American architecture in the 1830s and 1840s, Parris was born in Halifax, Nova Scotia. He moved with his family to Maine while a child, then to North Pembroke, Massachusetts. In the 1790s he worked as a carpenter in North Pembroke, but was already fascinated with building design. By the time he was twenty he had already designed and built houses locally. He soon married and moved to Portland, Maine, a lively port in the midst of a building boom. One of his first jobs was to design and build a Navy commodore's house. So successful was this that the Navy engaged him to redesign and rebuild the harbor forts. When work dried up he moved to Boston, and during the War of 1812, he served as a captain in the Army Corps of Engineers. After the war, he became apprenticed to Charles Bulfinch and was given full responsibility for the design of Quincy Market (1825) in Boston. Together they worked on Massachusetts General Hospital, Charlestown Navy Yard, the Watertown Arsenal, and many other important buildings in Boston. As an architect he designed and built grand houses and buildings such as the Pilgrim Hall Museum (Plymouth, Massachusetts) across New England. His work with the Greek Revival style won him national and international acclaim.

Peabody, Robert Swain (1845–1917)

Born in New Bedford, Massachusetts, Robert Swain Peabody was educated at Harvard and the Ecole des Beaux-Arts in Paris, from which he graduated in 1868. He started practicing in Boston in the architectural firm Peabody and Stearns, a firm that won a silver medal at the Paris Exposition of 1900. He received many awards and honors during his lifetime and was president of the American Institute of Architects (1900–1901).

Pei, Ieoh Ming (b. 1917)

Pei was born in China and trained at MIT and Harvard. In 1955, Pei formed I. M. Pei and Partners. In addition to many public buildings, his firm was responsible for the design of the Christian Science Center in Boston (1968–73).

Pugin, Augustus Welby Northmore (1812–52)

Pugin was born in London, the son of French draftsman Augustus Charles Pugin (1762–1832). He was a convert to Roman Catholicism and designed a number of Catholic churches. It was his firm belief that the only appropriate architectural style for a Christian nation was Gothic, and his publications *Contrasts, or a Parallel between the Noble Edifices of the Fourteenth and Fifteenth Centuries and Similar Buildings of the Present Day* (1836) and *True Principles of Pointed or Christian Architecture* (1841) won many enthusiastic converts in England and America. His most prominent commission was for the Houses of Parliament, which he designed with Charles Barry.

Purcell, William Gray (1880–1965)

A Prairie School architect, Purcell was born in Wilmette, Illinois, and raised by his grandfather in Oak Park on the same street where Frank Lloyd Wright would build his first home. Purcell graduated from Cornell University in 1903 and set up a partnership in Minneapolis with George Feick, Jr., in 1907. George Grant Elmslie joined the company in 1909, and over the next decade Purcell and Elmslie (Feick left in 1913) became increasingly productive. Purcell was particularly interested in open-plan living and flexible space. His work included his own house, the William G. Purcell House (1913), Lake Place, Minneapolis, a true example of open-plan living. Other work included the Purcell-Cutts House (1913) in Minneapolis. In 1920 Purcell went into semiretirement because of failing health and moved to Portland, Oregon, where he began writing; from there he moved to Pasadena, California, where he died.

Above: William Gray Purcell and George Feick, Jr.: Stewart Memorial Presbyterian Church, now the Redeemer Missionary Baptist Church, 116 East Thirty-second Street, Minneapolis, MN, 1909–10.

Renwick, James (1818–95)

Born in New York City into a wealthy and well-educated family, Renwick initially studied engineering—following his father and two brothers—at Columbia University. When he graduated in 1836, he was already interested in architecture but had no formal training. His first major commission came in 1843—to design Grace Church in New York City. Three years later he was working on Romanesque designs for Robert Dale Owen, director of the Smithsonian Institution in Washington, D.C. Renwick designed a Norman castle (built 1846–49) of red sandstone—a welcome distinction among Washington's otherwise classical buildings. Other work was for Vassar College's main hall (1860) in Poughkeepsie, New York, and several churches, banks, hospitals, and asylums. He also designed a number of private houses for wealthy New Yorkers. Already known as a designer of churches, Renwick was asked in 1853 by Archbishop Hughes to design St. Patrick's Cathedral in New York, a job that turned out to be a long and much-delayed project. In 1855 Renwick journeyed to Europe where he particularly studied the great French Gothic cathedrals. His original design for St. Patrick's was a grandiose Gothic scheme, which was not fully realized. He and fellow architect William Rodrique were given the contract in March 1859. The church was dedicated in 1879, and completed in 1888.

Right: Richard Upjohn's Trinity Church, New York, NY, 1839–46.

Richardson, Henry Hobson (1838–86)

Born in Priestley Plantation, Louisiana, Richardson was educated at Harvard and then studied architecture in Paris at the Ecole des Beaux-Arts (1859–62). While in Europe he worked under Henri Labrouste and Jakob Ignaz Hittorf. He initiated the Romanesque Revival in the United States, which led to a distinctive homegrown style of architecture called Richardsonian Romanesque, which can be dated 1870–95. The style recalls Spanish and French eleventh-century Romanesque with massive stone walls, large interior spaces, and semicircular arches interacting together in a continuous architectural flow. He specialized in churches, the most famous of which is Trinity Church, Boston (1872–77), but

Left: Henry Hobson Richardson: Trinity Church, Boston, MA, 1872–77. Front view.

also designed other well-known buildings such as the Allegheny County Buildings in Pittsburgh and halls of residence at Harvard. He also designed a number of private houses, railroad stations, and wholesale stores.

Ruskin, John (1819–1900)

The leading British art critic of the nineteenth century, Ruskin helped popularize a modern form of Gothic inspired by Venetian and French precedents through his books *The Seven Lamps of Architecture* (1849) and *The Stones of Venice* (1859). This High Victorian Gothic style is even sometimes called "Ruskinian Gothic."

Saarinen, Eero (1910–61)

Born in Kirkkonummi, Finland, Saarinen was thirteen when he emigrated to the United States with his father, Eliel, the leading Finnish architect (he designed the Helsinki railroad station). Eero came back to Europe to study sculpture in Paris (1929–30) but then returned to America to study architecture at Yale University (1931–34). After a time spent in Finland, he went into partnership with his father and Charles Eames. Their intention was to pioneer a new approach to architecture and furniture design—examples of their work include the Christ Lutheran Church, Minneapolis, Minnesota (1948), and the General Motors

Above: Eero Saarinen: Interdenominational Chapel, Massachusetts Institute of Technology, Cambridge, MA, 1954. Front view.

Technical Institute, Warren, Michigan (1955), completed five years after Eliel died. Saarinen designed many public buildings in both the United States and Europe, including the chapel at MIT (1954–55); the Ezra Stiles and Samuel F. B. Morse College, New Haven, Connecticut (1960–62); the U.S. embassies in London and Oslo; the TWA terminal at John F. Kennedy Airport, New York (1956–62); and Washington's Dulles International Airport (1958–63). His round Kresge Chapel at the Massachusetts Institute of Technology in Cambridge (1954) was an influential alternative to the boxy International Style.

Saarinen, Eliel (1873–1950)

Finnish-American architect and city planner, resident of the United States after 1923. He took second prize in the Chicago Tribune Tower competition in 1922. After moving to the U.S., he designed several buildings at the Cranbrook Foundation in Bloomfield Hills, Michigan, and also headed the Academy of Art. His other major works include two churches in Columbus, Indiana (1941–42), and Minneapolis (1949). His later designs were made in collaboration with his son, Eero Saarinen.

Skidmore, Owings, & Merrill

American architectural firm founded in 1936 in New York City by Louis Skidmore (1897–1962), Nathaniel A. Owings (1903–84), and John O. Merrill (1896–1975). The firm helped to popularize the International Style during the postwar period. Their designs for the modernist campus of the U.S. Air Force Academy in Colorado Springs, Colorado, included an innovative chapel designed by Walter Netsch (1956–62).

Strickland, William (1788–1854)

An influential architect of the American Classical Revival, Strickland was born in Navesink, New Jersey, and studied architecture under B. H. Latrobe. He did most of his work in Philadelphia and continually attempted to reconcile the proportions of classical architecture with the demands of modern living and work. In 1818 he won the Philadelphia competition to design the Second Bank of the United States in Philadelphia (1818–24). It became his masterpiece, with Doric porticoes and elegant rooms. Other major Strickland buildings in Philadelphia are St. Stephen's Episcopal Church (1822–23), with twin octagonal towers; Temple Mikvah Israel (1818); and the Philadelphia Merchant's Exchange (1832–34), on a tricky triangular site that would have presented problems to a lesser architect.

Sturgis, John Hubbard (1834–88)

An Aristocratic sophisticate who won well-paying commissions from wealthy clients, Sturgis traveled extensively in England picking up the latest architectural ideas. He had a twenty-year partnership with Charles Brigham as the firm Sturgis & Brigham. The firm concentrated on fine domestic architecture, with most of the houses being in the Back Bay quarter of Boston and in Newport. However, they did produce fine public commissions such as the Boston Museum of Fine Arts (1872) and the Boston Young Men's Christian Association Building.

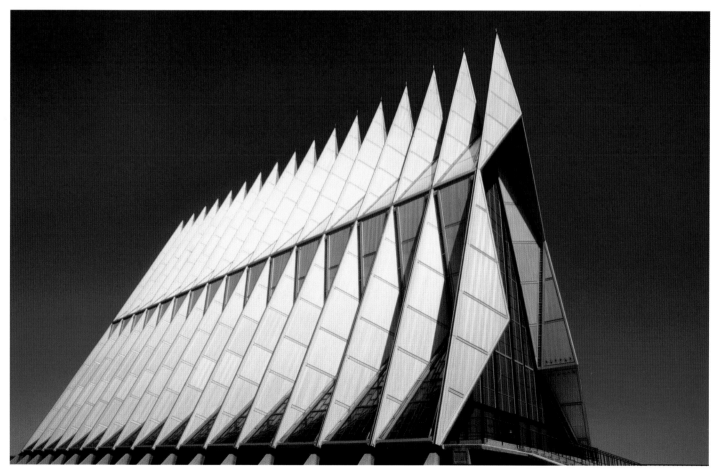

Above: Skidmore, Owings & Merrill (Walter Netsch): Air Force Academy Chapel, Colorado Springs, CO, 1956–62.

Sullivan, Louis Henri (1856–1924)

Above: Louis Sullivan: Holy Trinity Russian Orthodox Cathedral & Rectory, 1121 North Leavitt Street, Chicago, IL, 1899–1903. Front view.

Born in Boston, Sullivan studied for a short time at Massachusetts Institute of Technology and at the influential Paris atelier of Joseph Auguste-Emile Vaudremer. On his return to the United States he worked for Frank Furness in Philadelphia and then in 1873 moved to Chicago (which was being rebuilt after the great fire of 1871) to work in the studio of William Lebaron Jenney. He then returned to Paris to the Ecole des Beaux-Arts to finish his training. He joined the office of a German engineer, Dankmar Adler, and in 1881 they established what was to become one of the most influential of U.S. architectural practices, Adler & Sullivan. Together they were leaders of the Chicago School of architecture and were responsible for a string of successful designs, their hallmark being the rich detailing and ornamentation such as that seen in the Auditorium Building (1887–89). Sullivan became a prolific architect designing, among many others, the Transportation Building for the Chicago World's Fair (1893), the Bayard-Condict Building in New York, and the Guaranty Building in Buffalo, New York. He is widely credited as the designer of the first true skyscraper, the Wainwright Building in St. Louis (1890–91). His experimental skeletal constructions of skyscrapers and office blocks, particularly the Stock Exchange (1893–94), the Gage Building (1898–99), and the Carson, Pirie Scott Department Store (1899–1901) in Chicago earned him the title "Father of Modernism." The author of many architectural articles for technical journals, he is credited with coining the adage "form follows function." After 1900 he and the Chicago School lost out to the resurgence of neoclassicism. The partnership with Adler ended in 1895 and Sullivan turned to designing much smaller scale buildings, such as the Merchants' National Bank in Grinnell, Iowa (1914), and the National Farmer's Bank (1907–8) in Owatonna, Minnesota. Sullivan died in poverty in a Chicago hotel room in April 1924.

Town, Ithiel (1784–1844)

Born in Thompson, Connecticut, Town was an important local architect who wrote and practiced mainly on the East Coast. He started working with Alexander J. Davis in 1829, and together they opened an office in New York. Their contracts included important commissions for the North Carolina State Capitol at Raleigh, North Carolina (1833–40), and the U.S. Custom House in New York (1833–42). One of his best individual works is the Bowers House (1825–26) in Northampton, Massachusetts. Town was also a bridge builder and gave his name to the Town lattice truss design of bridge construction (patented in 1820). It is said that 140 of the original covered bridges in existence in the United States use Town's lattice construction, which he reportedly licensed at a dollar per foot. Town was also a significant author, and among his writings are *Description of his Improvements in the Construction of Bridges* (1821) and *School-House Architecture.*

Upjohn, Richard (1802–78)

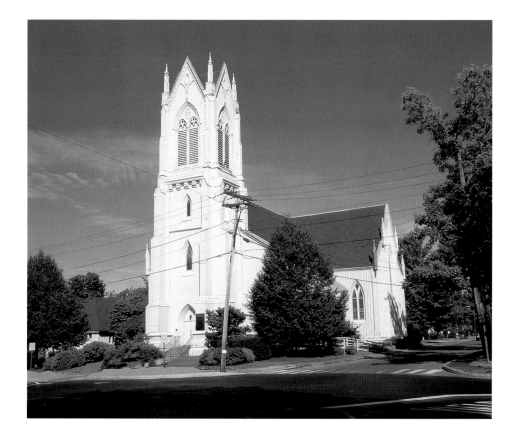

Renowned for church architecture, Upjohn was influential in the spread of Gothic Revival in America. Born in Shaftesbury, in Dorset, England, he initially trained as a cabinet maker. In 1829 he made the long Atlantic crossing to the New World and settled in Boston, where he started to work as an architect under Alexander Parris. By 1834 he was able to start his own firm, making his name by designing Gothic churches, the most notable of which is the brownstone Gothic Revival Trinity Church in New York (completed 1846). In 1852, he published a book of his designs, *Upjohn's Rural Architecture*. Other works include the Isaac Farrar House and St. John's Church in Bangor, Maine (1837–39); City Hall, Utica, New York (1852–53); St Luke's Episcopal Church, Ascension, Brooklyn, New York (1867–71); St. Mary's, Burlington, New Jersey (1846–54); Bowdoin College Chapel, Brunswick, Maine (1844–55); and Trinity Chapel, New York (1853). He was instrumental in founding the American Institute of Architects and was its first president.

Van Brunt, Henry (1832–1903)

In the 1880s, van Brunt was one of the very few professionally trained architects working west of the Mississippi. Born in Boston and educated at Harvard, he practiced architecture in his hometown with William Ware for twenty years before moving to Kansas City in 1887 to join his partner Frank M. Howe. They had opened their office in 1885, and their main client was the Union Pacific Railroad. Van Brunt, now aged fifty, moved to Kansas City to take personal advantage of the building boom the frontier town was enjoying. Together, he and Howe built many of the most important buildings in Kansas City using their progressive

Above: William Ware & Henry Van Brunt: St. Stephen's Episcopal Church, 74 South Common Street, Lynn, MA, 1881.

East Coast ideas combined with detailing from various historic styles. Van Brunt also worked on railroad stations. The firm designed the Electricity Building for the Chicago World's Columbia Exposition of 1893. He retired to Massachusetts in 1899 and died there four years later.

Vaughan, Henry (1845–1917)

Vaughan was born in England and came to the United States in 1881, where he became a leading figure in the late Gothic Revival. His ecclesiastical designs inspired Ralph Adams Cram and others. With George Frederick Bodley, he laid the plans for the Cathedral Church of St. Peter and St. Paul (Washington Cathedral) in Washington, D.C., which was begun in 1907.

Vitruvius Pollio, Marcus (First century B.C.)

Vitruvius was a northern Italian in the service of Emperor Augustus for whom he worked as an architect, engineer, and writer. He wrote the only surviving Roman treatise on architecture, *De Architectura* (*c.* 27 B.C.); his other works have not survived. *De Architectura* was rediscovered during the Renaissance and was eagerly read by the great Renaissance artists and architects whom it undoubtedly inspired. The humanist Poggio Bracciolini rediscovered a Vitruvius manuscript in the Swiss monastery of St. Gall early in the fifteenth century, and from then on Vitruvius was studied carefully. Vitruvius defined architecture as consisting of "order…and of arrangement…and of proportion and symmetry and décor and distribution."

Walter, Thomas Ustick (1804–87)

Walter's claim to fame is that he designed and built the wings and enormous cast-iron dome of the Capitol in Washington, D.C., adding them to the original building of Bulfinch's design. Work on the wings started in 1851 and the dome was constructed between 1855 and 1865; work continued through the war years at President Lincoln's behest. Walter was assisted from 1855 by the French-trained Richard M. Hunt. The family architectural tradition was continued by Walter's grandson who studied architecture at his grandfather's office and went on to practice extensively throughout the South.

Ware, William (1832–1915)

Born in Cambridge, Massachusetts, in May 1832, Ware graduated from Harvard University in 1852. He studied at the Lawrence Scientific School before moving to New York to become a draftsman in the architectural offices of Richard Morris Hunt. Eight years later he moved to Boston to start his own firm in partnership with Henry van Brunt. However, Ware's architectural reputation rests not so much on his designs as on his gifts as an educator. In 1868 he was responsible for organizing the first school of architecture in the United States at MIT in Boston. Then, in 1881, he set up the School of Architecture at Columbia University in New York. He remained head of the school until 1903 when he was made Professor Emeritus. In 1901 Ware belonged to the commission that designed the buildings for the Pan-American Exposition in Buffalo, New York. He was awarded many architectural honors and plaudits and was the author of many technical books, including the definitive *Modern Perspective*. He died at his home in Milton, Massachusetts, in June 1915.

White, Stanford (1853–1906)

Born in New York City, White learned architecture under H. H. Richardson, later moving to Paris where he lived with the family of the sculptor Augustus Saint-Gaudens. In 1872 he joined the office of Gambrill and Richardson in Boston and worked on the design for Trinity Church, Boston. In 1879, along with two old architect friends, he formed the influential practice of McKim, Mead & White. He was a man of enormous creative energy with truly eclectic tastes. In New York his two surviving works—the Washington Square Arch and the Century Club—both display marvelous Renaissance ornamentation. He designed the old Madison Square Garden in 1889; for the cupola of this building, he commissioned a statue of a nude Diana that scandalized New York. In the tower itself he built an opulent private apartment and roof garden that became notorious for his romantic rendezvous—he was finally shot and killed there by the jealous husband of his lover, Evelyn Nesbit Thaw. His religious architecture includes the Renaissance Revival Judson Memorial Church in Washington Square in New York City (1888–93) and the Colonial Revival Congregational Church in Naugatuck, Connecticut (1901–3).

Wren, Christopher (1632–1723)

Now known as the greatest architect of the English Baroque style, his most important church designs include St. Paul's Cathedral in London (1675–1711) and the designs for fifty-one city churches to replace those destroyed in the Great Fire of London in 1666. These smaller church designs were highly influential in shaping the typical American colonial church in the eighteenth century.

Above: Stanford White: Lovely Lane United Methodist Church, 2700 St. Paul Street, Baltimore, MD, 1882–87.

Wright, Frank Lloyd (1867–1959)

The most famous of all American architects was born in Richland Center, Wisconsin. He studied engineering at Wisconsin University but resolved to become an architect, and he set up practice in Chicago after working for a period for Adler & Sullivan, during which time he designed private homes for the firm and his "Bootleg" houses for private clients. He developed his own unique style with his Prairie houses, long low buildings that merged with the landscape, such as the Robie House, Chicago (1908–10). Always interested in the latest technology, he explored more daring and controversial designs that exploited modern technology and Cubist spatial concepts, developing this into his Usonian houses, such as the Herbert Jacobs House, Wisconsin (1936). He experimented continuously on his own homes—the first at Oak Park near Chicago, then Taliesin at Spring Green, Wisconsin (1911), and a third home in 1938 with a connecting studio and school, named Taliesin West, near Phoenix, Arizona. His buildings are largely confined to the Midwest, especially the Chicago area, and California, where he constructed a series of textile-block houses such as the "Hollyhock" House in Los Angeles (1920) and the Mrs. G. M. Millard House in Pasadena (1923). One of his few foreign commissions was the earthquake-proof Imperial Hotel in Tokyo (1916–20). Public commissions include the Johnson Wax office block in Racine, Wisconsin (1936), the Florida Southern College (1940), and the spiral Guggenheim Museum of Art in New York City (1959). The Kaufmann House, "Fallingwater," in Connellsville, Pennsylvania (1934–37), is generally regarded as his masterpiece. His architectural ideas were internationally influential, especially his explorations of open plan living. Wright also designed glass, furniture, and textiles for his buildings. He was a prolific writer of his thoughts and ideas on architecture and design. He died in New York after a long and successful career and is widely acclaimed as the greatest American architect of the twentieth century.

Below: Frank Lloyd Wright: Annunciation Greek Orthodox Church, 9400 West Congress Street, Wauwatosa, WI, 1956. Front view.

Bibliography

BOOKS AND PERIODICALS

General

Ahlstrom, Sydney E. *A Religious History of the American People*. New Haven, CT: Yale University Press, 1972.

Gausted, Edwin Scott, and Philip L. Barlow. *New Historical Atlas of Religion in America*. New York: Oxford University Press, 2001.

Olsen, Brad. *Sacred Places North America: 108 Destinations*. Santa Cruz, CA: Consortium of Collective Consciousness, 2003.

Taylor, Alan. *American Colonies*. New York: Viking, 2001.

American Architecture—General

Andrews, Wayne. *Architecture, Ambition and Americans*. New York: Harper Brothers, 1955.

Burchard, John, and Albert Bush-Brown. *The Architecture of America: A Social and Cultural History*. Boston: Little, Brown, 1961.

Cole, Doris. *From Tipi to Skyscraper: A History of Women in Architecture*. New York: G. Braziller, 1973.

Condit, Carl W. *American Building: Materials and Techniques from the First Colonial Settlements to the Present*, 2nd ed. Chicago: University of Chicago Press, 1982.

Curtis, William J. R. *Modern Architecture Since 1900*, 3rd ed. London: Phaidon Press Prentice Hall, 1996.

De Long, David G., Helen Searing, Robert A. M. Stern, eds. *American Architecture: Innovation and Tradition*. New York: Rizzoli, 1986.

Drexler, Arthur. *The Architecture of the Ecole des Beaux-Arts*. New York: Museum of Modern Art, 1977.

Fitch, James Marston. *American Building: The Historical Forces that Shaped It*, 2nd ed., New York: Schocken Books, 1973.

———. *American Building 2: The Environmental Forces that Shaped It*, Boston: Houghton Mifflin, 1972.

Gelernter, Mark. *A History of American Architecture: Buildings in Their Cultural and Technological Context*. Hanover, NH: University Press of New England, 1999.

Gifford, Don, ed., *The Literature of Architecture: The Evolution of Architectural Theory and Practice in Nineteenth Century America*. New York: E. P. Dutton, 1966.

Gowans, Alan. *Styles and Types of North American Architecture: Social Function and Cultural Expression*. New York: Harper Collins, 1992.

Hafertepe, Kenneth, and James O'Gorman, eds. *American Architects and their Books to 1848*. Amherst, MA: University of Amherst Press, 2001.

Handlin, David. *American Architecture*. London: Thames and Hudson, 1985.

Jencks, Charles. *The Language of Post-Modern Architecture*. New York: Rizzoli, 1977.

Jordan, Terry G. *American Log Buildings: An Old World Heritage*. Chapel Hill, NC: University of North Carolina Press, 1985.

Jordy, William. *American Buildings and Their Architects: Progressive and Academic Ideals at the Turn of the Twentieth Century*, vol. IV. Garden City, NY: Doubleday, 1972.

———. *American Buildings and Their Architects: The Impact of European Modernism in the mid-Twentieth Century*, vol. V. Garden City, NY: Doubleday, 1972.

Kaplan, Wendy. *"The Art that Is Life": The Arts & Crafts Movement in America, 1875–1920.* Boston: Little, Brown and the Museum of Fine Arts, Boston, 1987.

Kaufmann, Edgar W., ed. *The Rise of an American Architecture.* New York: Praeger Publishers, 1970.

Kidney, Walter C. *The Architecture of Choice: Eclecticism in America, 1880–1930.* New York: Braziller, 1974.

Matheson, Susan B., and Derek D.Churchill. *Modern Gothic: The Revival of Medieval Art.* New Haven, CT: Yale University Art Gallery, 2000.

Morrison, Hugh. *Early American Architecture from the First Colonial Settlements to the National Period.* New York: Dover Publications, 1987.

Mumford, Lewis. *Roots of Contemporary American Architecture.* New York: Dover Publications, 1972.

Noffsinger, James P. *Influence of the Ecole des Beaux-Arts on the Architecture of the United States.* Washington, D.C.: Catholic University of America Press, 1955.

O'Gorman, James. *H. H. Richardson, Architectural Forms for an American Society.* Chicago: University of Chicago Press, 1987.

Pierson, William H., Jr. *American Buildings and Their Architects: The Colonial and Neoclassic Styles*, vol. 1. Garden City, NY: Doubleday, 1970.

———. *American Buildings and Their Architects: Technology and the Picturesque—The Corporate and Early Gothic Styles*, vol. 2. Garden City, NY: Doubleday, 1978.

Reiff, Daniel D. *Houses from Books: Treatises, Pattern Books, and Catalogs in American Architecture, 1738–1950: A History and Guide.* University Park: Pennsylvania State University Press, 2000.

Roth, Leland M. *American Architecture: A History.* Boulder, CO: Westview Press, 2001.

Roth, Leland, M., ed. *America Builds: Source Documents in American Architecture and Planning.* New York: Harper & Row, 1983.

Whiffen, Marcus, and Frederick Koeper. *American Architecture 1607–1976.* Cambridge, MA: MIT Press, 1981.

Whittaker, Craig. *Architecture and the American Dream.* New York: Clarkson N. Potter, 1996.

Wilson, Richard Guy. *The American Renaissance.* Brooklyn, NY: Brooklyn Museum, 1979.

———. "Architecture and the Reinterpretation of the Past in the American Renaissance," *Winterthur Portfolio* 18 (Spring 1983), 69–97.

Reference Books

Avery Index to Architectural Periodicals, 2nd ed. Boston: G. K. Hall, 1973.

Avery Obituary Index of Architects and Artists. 1963. Reprinted 1980.

Biographical Dictionary of American Architects (Deceased). Los Angeles: Hennessey & Ingalls, 1970.

Burden, Ernest. *Illustrated Dictionary of Architecture.* New York: McGraw-Hill, 1998.

Catalog of the Avery Memorial Architectural Library of Columbia University, 2nd ed. (19 vols. and 5 supplements to 1982). Boston: G. K. Hall, 1968.

Hunt, William Dudly, Jr. *Encyclopedia of American Architecture.* New York: McGraw-Hill, 1980.

Nash, Judy. *Thatchers and Thatching.* London: B. T. Batsford, 1991.

Packard, Robert T. *Encyclopedia of American Architecture.* New York: McGraw-Hill, 1995.

Pevsner, Nikolaus, John Fleming, and Hugh Honour. *A Dictionary of Architecture.* Woodstock, NY: Overlook Press, 1976.

Phillips, Steven J. *Old-House Dictionary: An Illustrated Guide to American Domestic Architecture (1600–1940).* Lakewood, CO: American Source Books, 1989.

Placzek, Adolf K., ed. *MacMillan Encyclopedia of Architects.* New York: Free Press, 1982.

Saylor, Henry H. *Dictionary of Architecture*. New York: John Wiley & Sons, 1952.

Sharp, Dennis, ed. *Illustrated Encyclopedia of Architects and Architecture*. New York: Whitney Library of Design, 1991.

Sobon, Jack A. *Timber Frame Construction: All About Post and Beam Construction*. Pownal, VT: Garden Way, 1984.

Turner, Jane, ed. *Grove Dictionary of Art* (34 vols.). London: Macmillan Reference, 1996.

Style Guides

Andrews, Wayne. *American Gothic: Its Origins, Its Trials, Its Triumphs*. New York: Random House, 1975.

Bayer, Patricia. *Art Deco Architecture*, London: Thames & Hudson, 1992.

Blumenson, John J.-G. *Identifying American Architecture: A Pictorial Guide to Styles and Terms, 1600–1945*. New York: W. W. Norton, 1981.

Eberlein, Harold, and Cortland Hubbard. *American Georgian Architecture*. Bloomington: Indiana University Press, 1952.

Lewis, Michael A. *The Gothic Revival*. London: Thames and Hudson, 2002.

Lowe, David G. *Beaux Arts New York*. New York: Whitney Library of Design, 1998.

Matheson, Susan B., and Derek D. Churchill. *Modern Gothic: The Revival of Medieval Art*. New Haven, CT: Yale University Art Gallery, 2000.

Poppeliers, John C., S. Allen Chambers, Jr., and Nancy B. Schwartz. *What Style Is It? A Guide to American Architecture*. New York: Preservation Press, 1983.

Rifkind, Carole. *A Field Guide to American Architecture*. New York: New American Library, 1980.

Whiffen, Marcus. *American Architecture Since 1780: A Guide to the Styles*. Cambridge, MA: MIT Press, 1981.

Pattern Books

Benjamin, Asher. *The Country Builder's Assistant*, Greenfield, MA, 1797.

———. *The American Builder's Companion, or, a New System of Architecture Particularly Adapted to the Present Style of Building in the United States of America*. Boston, 1806.

———. *The Rudiments of Architecture*. 1814.

———. *The Practice of Architecture*. 1830.

———. *The Practical House Carpenter*. 1830.

———. *The Builder's Guide*. 1830.

———. *The Beauties of Modern Architecture*. 1835.

———. *Elements of Architecture*. 1843.

Haviland, John. *The Builder's Assistant*, 3 vols. 1818.

Lafever, Minard. *The Modern Builder's Guide*. New York: W. D. Smith, 1841.

Moxon, Joseph. *Mechanick Exercises* (1703). New York: Praeger, 1970.

Upjohn, Richard. *Rural Architecture*. 1852.

Theoretical Issues

Barrie, Thomas. *Spiritual Path, Scared Place: Myth, Ritual and Meaning in Architecture*. Boston: Shambala, 1996.

Chidester, David, and Edward Tabor Linenthal. *American Sacred Space*. Bloomington: Indiana University Press, 1995.

Eliade, Mircea. *Encyclopedia of Religion*. New York: Macmillan, 1987.

Humphrey, Caroline, and Piers Vitebsky. *Sacred Architecture*. Boston: Little, Brown, 1997.

Jarves, James Jackson. *The Art-Idea: Sculpture, Painting and Architecture*. New York: Hurd and Houghton, 1864. Reprinted 1960 (Cambridge, MA: Belknap Press).

Lawlor, Anthony. *The Temple in the House: Finding the Sacred in Everyday Architecture*. New York: G. P. Putnam, 1994.

Niebuhr, Reinhold. "The Weakness of Common Worship in American Protestantism." *Christianity and Crisis* 9, no. 9 (May 28, 1951): 68–70.

Rock, Randolf. "Our Church-Erection Interests." *United Brethren Review* 5, no. 2 (April 1894): 179–80.

Smith, Jonathan Z., and William Scott Green. *HarperCollins Dictionary of Religion*. San Francisco: Harper San Francisco, 1995.

Turner, Harold W. *From Temple to Meeting House: The Phenomenology and Theology of Places of Worship*. The Hague: Mouton, 1979.

Upton, Dell, ed. *America's Architectural Roots: Ethnic Groups that Built America*. New York: Preservation Press, 1986.

Venturi, Robert, Denise Scott Brown, and Steven Izenour. *Learning from Las Vegas*. Cambridge, MA: MIT Press, 1997.

White, James F. *Protestant Worship and Church Architecture*. New York: Oxford University Press, 1964.

Winckelmann, Johann Joachim. "On the Imitation of the Painting and Sculpture of the Greeks," translated by Henry Fuseli (1755), in David Irwin, ed., *Writings on Art* (London: Phaidon, 1972).

Surveys of American Religious Architecture

Broderick, Robert C. *Historic Churches of the United States*. New York: Wilfred Funk, 1958.

Chiat, Marilyn. *America's Religious Architecture: Sacred Places for Every Community*. Washington, D.C.: Preservation Press, 1997.

Dupré, Judith. *Churches*. New York: HarperCollins, 2001.

Egbert, Donald Drew. "Religious Expression in American Architecture." Quoted in W. Eugene Kleinbauer, ed., *Modern Perspectives in Western Art History* (New York: Holt, Rinehart Winston, 1971), 312–338.

Kennedy, Roger. *American Churches*. New York: Crossroad, 1982.

Pierson, William H., Jr. *American Buildings and Their Architects* (2 vols.). Garden City, NY: Doubleday, 1978.

Williams, Peter W. "Religious Architecture and Landscape," in Charles H. Lippy and Peter W. Williams, eds., *Encyclopedia of the American Religious Experience* (New York: Scribners, 1988), 1325–1340.

———. *Houses of God: Region, Religion and Architecture in the United States*. Urbana: University of Illinois Press, 1997.

Period/Regional Studies

New England

Benes, Peter, ed. *New England Meeting House and Church*. Boston: Boston University, 1979.

Donnelly, Marian Card. *The New England Meeting Houses of the Seventeenth Century*. Middletown, CT: Wesleyan University Press, 1968.

Greenagel, Frank L. *The New Jersey Churchscape. Encountering Eighteenth- and Nineteenth-Century Churches*. New Brunswick, NJ: Rutgers University Press, 2001.

Riess, Jana. *The Spiritual Traveler, Boston and New England: A Guide to Sacred Sites and Peaceful Places*. Mahwah, NJ: Hidden Spring, 2002.

Rose, Harold Wickliffe. *The Colonial Houses of Worship in America*. New York: Hastings House, 1963.

Shivell, Kirk. *The Steeples of Old New England*. Marina del Rey, CA: Lighthouse Press, 1998.

Sinnott, Edward W. *Meetinghouse and Church in Early New England*. New York: McGraw Hill, 1963.

Smith, G. E. Kidder. *The Beacon Guide to New England Houses of Worship*. Boston: Beacon, 1989.

Tucci, Douglass Shand. *Church Building in Boston 1720–1970: With an Introduction to the Work of Ralph Adams Cram and the Boston Gothicists*. Concord, MA: Rumford Press, 1976.

———. *Built in Boston: City and Suburb, 1800–1950*, Boston: New York Graphic Society, 1978.

Weeks, Silas B. *New England Quaker Meetinghouses*. Richmond, IN: Friends United Press, 2001.

The South

Heck, Robert W. *Religious Architecture in Louisiana*. Baton Rouge: Louisiana State University Press, 1995.

Lane, Mills. *Architecture of the Old South; Greek Revival and Romantic*. Savannah, GA: Beehive Press, 1996.

Upton, Dell. *Holy Things and Profane: Anglican Parish Churches in Colonial Virginia* . New York: Architectural History Foundation, 1986.

Southwest

Kennedy, Roger G. *This History and Architecture of the Missions of North America*. Boston: Houghton Mifflin, 1993.

Kubler, George. *The Religious Architecture of New Mexico in the Colonial Period and Since the American Occupation*, 4th ed. Albuquerque: University of New Mexico Press, 1972.

Quirarte, Jacinto. *The Art and Architecture of the Texas Missions*. Austin: University of Texas Press, 2002.

Robinson, Willard B., and Jean M. Robinson. *Reflections of Faith: Houses of Worship in the Lone Star State*. Waco, TX: Baylor University Press, 1994.

Treib, Marc. *Sanctuaries of Spanish New Mexico*. Berkeley: University of California Press, 1993.

Midwest

Armstrong, Foster, et al. *A Guide to Cleveland's Sacred Landmarks*. Kent, OH: Kent State University Press, 1992.

Lane, George A. *Chicago Churches and Synagogues*. Chicago: Loyola University Press, 1981.

West

Willard, Ruth Hendricks. *Sacred Places of San Francisco*. Novato, CA: Presidio Press, 1985.

AIA Guides

Gournay, Isabelle. *AIA Guide to the Architecture of Atlanta*. Athens: University of Georgia Press, 1993.

Sinkevitch, Alice, ed. *AIA Guide to Chicago*. San Diego, CA: Harcourt Brace, 1993.

Southworth, Susan, and Michael Southworth. *The Boston Society of Architects' AIA Guide to Boston*, 2nd ed. Chester, CT: Globe Pequot Press, 1992.

Weeks, Christopher. *AIA Guide to the Architecture of Washington, D.C.* Baltimore, MD: Johns Hopkins University Press, 1994.

Willensky, Elliot, and Norval White, eds. *AIA Guide to New York City*, 3rd ed. San Diego, CA: Harcourt, Brace, Jovanovich, 1988.

Nineteenth Century

Blau, Eva. *Ruskinian Gothic: The Architecture of Deane and Woodward, 1845–1861*. Princeton, NJ: Princeton University Press, 1982.

Clark, Kenneth. *The Gothic Revival: An Episode in the History of Taste*. 1950. Reprint, New York: Harper and Row, 1973.

Crinson, Mark. *Empire Building: Orientalism and Victorian Architecture*. New York: Routledge, 1996.

Early, James. *Romanticism and American Architecture*. New York: A. S. Barnes, 1965.

Germann, Georg. *Gothic Revival in Europe and Britain: Sources, Influences and Ideas.* Cambridge, MA: MIT Press, 1972.

Hayden, Dolores. *Seven American Utopias.* Cambridge, MA: MIT Press, 1976.

Kilde, Jeanne Halgren. *Spiritual Armories: A Social and Architectural History of Neo-Medieval Auditorium Churches in the U.S., 1869–1910.* Minneapolis: University of Minnesota, 1991.

Richardson, Henry Hobson. "A Description of Trinity Church, by the Architect." Pamphlet, n.d.

Stanton, Phoebe. *The Gothic Revival and American Church Architecture.* Baltimore, MD: Johns Hopkins Press, 1968.

Visser, John De, and Harold Kalman. *Pioneer Churches.* New York: Norton, 1976.

Modern

Brooks, H. Allen. *The Prairie School. Frank Lloyd Wright and His Midwest Contemporaries.* New York: W. W. Norton, 1972.

Christ-Janer, Albert, and Mary Mix Foley. *Modern Church Architecture.* New York: McGraw-Hill, 1962.

Crosbie, Michael J. *Architecture for the Gods.* Victoria, Australia: Images Publishing Group, 1999.

Davis, Patricia Talbot. *Together They Built a Mountain.* Lititz, PA: Sutter House, 1974.

Hayes, Bartlett H. *Tradition Becomes Innovation.* New York: Pilgrim, 1983.

Shear, John Knox, ed. *Architectural Record: Religious Buildings for Today.* New York: F. W. Dodge, 1957.

Wright, Frank Lloyd. *An Autobiography* (1932). Reprinted 1977 (New York: Horizon Press).

Individual Traditions

African American

Rankin, Tom. *Sacred Space: Photographs from the Mississippi Delta.* Jackson: University Press of Mississippi, 1993.

Smith, Edward D. *Climbing Jacob's Ladder: The Rise of Black Churches in Eastern American Cities, 1740–1877.* Washington, D.C.: Smithsonian Institution Press, 1988.

Catholicism

Brannach, Frank. *Church Architecture: Building for a Living Faith.* Milwaukee, WI: Bruce Publishing Company, 1932.

Kane, Paula. *Separatism and Subculture.* Chapel Hill: University of North Carolina Press, 1994.

U.S. Catholic Historian 15, no. 1 (Winter 1997), special issue.

Christian Science

Ivey, Paul Eli. *Prayers in Stone.* Urbana: University of Illinois Press, 1999.

Episcopalian

Shinn, Rev. George Wolfe. *King's Handbook of Notable Episcopal Churches in the United States.* Boston: Moses King Corporation, 1889.

Islamic

Blair, Sheila S., and Jonathan M. Bloom. *The Art and Architecture of Islam 1250–1800.* New Haven, CT: Yale University Press, 1995.

Dodds, Jerrilyn, and Edward Grazda. *New York Masjid: The Mosques of New York City.* New York: Powerhouse Books, 2001.

Holod, Renata, and Hasan-Uddin Khan. *The Contemporary Mosque: Architects, Clients and Designs Since the 1950s.* New York: Rizzoli, 1997.

Serageldin, Ismail, and James Steele, eds. *Architecture of the Contemporary Mosque*. London: Academy Editions, 1996.

Judaism

Fine, Renee, and Gerald R. Wolfe. *The Synagogues of New York's Lower East Side*. New York: New York University Press, 1978.

Israelowitz, Oscar. *Synagogues of the United States*. Brooklyn, NY: Israelowitz Publishing, 1992.

Two Hundred Years of American Synagogue Architecture. Catalog of exhibition. Waltham, MA: Rose Art Museum, Brandeis University, 1976.

Wischnitzer, Rachael. *Synagogue Architecture in the United States*. Philadelphia: Jewish Publication Society of America, 1955.

Methodism

Rowe, Kenneth. "Redesigning Methodist Churches: Auditorium-Style Sanctuaries and Akron Plan Sunday Schools in Romanesque Costume 1875–1925." Quoted in Russell Richey, ed., *Connectionalism* (Abingdon, November 1997).

Mormon

Andrew, Laurel B. *The Early Temples of the Mormons*. Albany: State University of New York Press, 1978.

Francaviglia, Richard V. *The Mormon Landscape*. New York: AMS Press, 1978.

Hamilton, Charles Mark. *Nineteenth-Century Mormon Architecture*. New York: Oxford University Press, 1995.

Native American

Ballantine, Betty, and Ian Ballantine, eds. *The Native Americans: An Illustrated History*. Atlanta, GA: Turner Publishing, 1993.

Bullock, Alice. *Mountain Villages*. Santa Fe, NM: Sunstone Press, 1991.

Bunting, Bainbridge. *John Gaw Meem: Southwestern Architect*. Albuquerque: University of New Mexico Press, 1983.

Cole, Doris. *From Tipi to Skyscraper: A History of Women in Architecture*. New York: G. Braziller, 1973.

Iowa, Jerome. *Ageless Adobe: History and Preservation in Southwestern Architecture*. Santa Fe, NM: Sunstone Press, 1985.

Jett, Stephen, and Virginia E. Spencer. *Navajo Architecture: Forms, History, Distribution*. Tucson: University of Arizona Press, 1981.

Krinsky, Carol Herselle. *Contemporary Native American Architecture: Cultural Regeneration and Creativity*. New York: Oxford University Press, 1986.

Laubin, Reginald, and Gladys Laubin. *The Indian Tipi: Its History, Construction & Use*. Norman: University of Oklahoma Press. 1977.

Lekson, Stephen H. *Great Pueblo Architecture of Chaco Canyon, New Mexico*. Albuquerque: University of New Mexico Press, 1986.

Mays, Buddy. *Ancient Cities of the Southwest*. San Francisco: Chronicle Books, 1990.

McHenry, Paul Graham, Jr. *Adobe: Build It Yourself*. Tucson: University of Arizona Press, 1985.

Nabokov, Peter. *Architecture of Acoma Pueblo: The 1934 Historic American Buildings Survey Project*. Santa Fe, NM: Ancient City Press, 1986.

Nabokov, Peter, and Robert Easton. *Native American Architecture*. New York: Oxford University Press, 1989.

O'Connor, John F. *The Adobe Book*. Santa Fe, NM: Ancient City Press, 1973.

Orthodox

Mathew, Gervase. *Byzantine Aesthetics.* New York: Harper and Row, 1971.

Rice, David Talbot. *Byzantine Art.* Harmondsworth, England: Penguin Books, 1968.

Stokoe, Mark, with Leonid Kishkovsky. *Orthodox Christians in North America, 1794–1994.* Wayne, NJ: Orthodox Christian Publications Center (OCPC), 1995.

Shaker

Schiffer, Herbert. *Shaker Architecture.* Atglen, PA: Schiffer Publishing Ltd., 1979.

Individual Architects

Elman, Kimberly J., and Angela Giral, eds. *Percival Goodman: Architect, Planner, Teacher, Painter.* Catalog of exhibition. New York: Columbia University, 2001.

Hitchcock, Henry Russell. *The Architecture of H. H. Richardson and His Times.* Cambridge, MA: MIT Press, 1970.

Kirker, Harold. *The Architecture of Charles Bulfinch.* Cambridge, MA: Harvard University Press, 1969.

Landy, Jacob. *Architecture of Minard Lafever.* New York: Columbia University Press, 1970.

Levine, Neil. *The Architecture of Frank Lloyd Wright.* Princeton University Press, 1994.

Morgan, William. *The Almighty Wall: The Architecture of Henry Vaughan.* New York: Architectural History Foundation, 1983.

Muccigrosso, Robert. *American Gothic: The Mind and Art of Ralph Adams Cram.* Washington, D.C.: University Press of America, 1980.

Ochsner, Jeffrey K. *H. H. Richardson: Complete Architectural Works.* Cambridge, MA: MIT Press, 1982.

O'Gorman, James F. *The Architecture of Frank Furness.* Philadelphia: Philadelphia Museum Press, 1973.

———. *H. H. Richardson: Architectural Forms for an American Society.* Chicago: University of Chicago Press, 1987.

Oliver, Richard. *Bertram Grosvenor Goodhue.* New York: Architectural History Foundation, 1983.

Scully, Vincent. *Frank Lloyd Wright.* New York: Braziller, 1960.

Shand-Tucci, Douglass. *Ralph Adams Cram: Life and Architecture.* Amherst: University of Massachusetts Press, 1994.

Siry, Joseph. *Unity Temple: Frank Lloyd Wright and Architecture for Liberal Religion.* New York: Cambridge University Press, 1996.

Smith, Christine. *Saint Bartholomew's Church in the City of New York.* New York: Oxford University Press, 1988.

Thomas, George E., Jeffrey A. Cohen, and Michael J. Lewis. *Frank Furness: The Complete Works.* New York: Princeton Architectural Press, 1991.

Upjohn, Everard Miller. *Richard Upjohn: Architect and Churchman.* New York: Columbia University Press, 1939.

van Rensselaer, Mariana Griswold. *Henry Hobson Richardson and His Works.* 1888. Reprint, New York: Dover Publications, 1969.

Woodbridge, Sally. *Bernard Maybeck: Visionary Architect.* New York: Abbeville Press, 1992.

Wright, Frank Lloyd. *Collected Writings,* 5 vols. New York: Rizzoli Publications, 1992–95.

Cemeteries

Jackson, Kenneth. *Silent Cities: The Evolution of the American Cemetery.* Princeton, NJ: Princeton University Press, 1990.

Linden-Ward, Blanche. *Silent City on a Hill: Landscapes of Memory and Boston's Mount Auburn Cemetery.* Columbus: Ohio State University Press, 1989.

McDowell, Peggy. *The Revival Styles in American Memorial Art*. New York: Popular Press, 1994.

WEBSITES

This is just a brief selection of some of the many useful websites currently available. Many individual churches and temples have their own sites, which can be located by using one of the major search engines, such as Google, and entering the name of the church.

General

American Memory All Collections Search; Library of Congress
http://rs6.loc.gov/ammem/mdbquery.html

Home Church Movement
http://homechurch.org

Library of Congress Historic American Buildings Survey / Historic American Engineering Record
http://lcweb2.loc.gov/ammem/hhquery.html

Material History of American Religion Project—The Built Environment of American Religion
http://www.materialreligion.org/journal/archbiblio.html

Nexus Network Journal: Architecture and Mathematics Online
http://www.nexusjournal.com/

Partners for Sacred Places
http://www.sacredplaces.org/

Religion and the American Revolution (Religion and the Founding of the American Republic, Library of Congress Exhibition)
http://www.loc.gov/exhibits/religion/rel03.html

Native American

Native American Sacred Sites and the Department of Defense, Table of Contents
https://osiris.cso.uiuc.edu/denix/Public/ES-Programs/Conservation/Legacy/Sacred/toc2.html

Native Americans and the Environment: Sacred Lands and Graves
http://www.cnie.org/nae/sacred.html

Architects

Patrick C. Keely
http://www.irishheritagetrail.com/pkeely.htm

Charles D. Maginnis
http://e-views.net/StAidans/CharlesMaginnis.html

Picture Credits

The publisher wishes to thank all of the photographers, libraries and places of worship that kindly supplied images for this book. Thanks to Mark Franklin and John Lucas, who provided all the illustrations for this book (illustrations © PRC Publishing). Thanks to Jeffery Howe for providing all the photographs, including the photographs on the front and back cover, with the following exceptions :

© Chrysalis Images (photographer: Simon Clay) for pages 2 (bottom left), 119 (top), 199 (top right), 200 (top left), 297 (top and bottom) and 298 (bottom);
© Gail Mooney/CORBIS for pages 8 and 120 (top left);
Photograph on page 14 supplied by kind courtesy of Historic St Luke's Church (photographer: Fran Olsen);
© Hulton Archive for pages 19 and 21 (top);
© Buddy Mays/CORBIS for pages 21 (bottom), 119 (bottom) and 155 (bottom right);
© David Muench/CORBIS for pages 65, 96 (top), 98 (top) and 393;
© Scott T. Smith/CORBIS for pages 66 (top), 226 and 228 (top);
© Bettmann/CORBIS for page 66 (bottom);
© Bill Ross/CORBIS for page 67;
© Michael S. Lewis/CORBIS for page 68;
© Richard A. Cooke/CORBIS for page 69;
© Marilyn Bridges/CORBIS for page 73;
© Canadian Museum of Civilization/CORBIS for page 74;
© Gunter Marx Photography/CORBIS for pages 75 and 337 (top);
Photographs on pages 84 (all) and 85 (left) supplied by kind courtesy of © Bing Owens;
© Kevin Fleming/CORBIS for pages 88 (left) and 189 (top);
© Lee Snider; Lee Snider/CORBIS for pages 88 (right), 93 (left), 153 (bottom), 232 (bottom right) and 382 (left);
© Phil Schermeister/CORBIS for page 89 (top);
© Wolfgang Kaehler/CORBIS for pages 89 (middle) and 98 (bottom left);
© Jan Butchofsky-Houser/CORBIS for pages 89 (bottom) and 100 (bottom right);
© Bo Zaunders/CORBIS for page 92 (top left);
© Richard Cummins/CORBIS for pages 92 (top right), 92 (bottom) and 98 (bottom right);
© Mark E. Gibson/CORBIS for page 93 (right);
© Michael Freeman/CORBIS for page 96 (bottom);
© Tom Bean/CORBIS for page 97 (left);
© Chris Rogers/CORBIS for page 97 (right);
© G.E. Kidder Smith/CORBIS for pages 109 (top left), 136, 142 (bottom right), 155 (top), 156 (left), 178 (bottom), 193 (top left), 193 (bottom left), 229 (bottom), 255 (middle), 285, 299, 303 (top left), 310 (bottom), 315 (bottom), 316 (top), 337 (bottom left) and 338 (bottom);
© Kelly-Mooney Photography/CORBIS for pages 118 (top right) and 282 (top right);
© Medford Historical Society Collection/CORBIS for page 142 (bottom left);
© Joseph Sohm; ChromoSohm Inc./CORBIS for pages 227 and 368 (bottom);
© CORBIS for page 228 (bottom);
© Chase Swift/CORBIS for page 236 (bottom);
David H. Wells/CORBIS for page 273 (top right);
© Vince Streano/CORBIS for pages 326 (top) and 429;
© Tim Thompson/CORBIS for page 326 (bottom);
© Layne Kennedy/CORBIS for pages 332 (top right) and 417;
© Annie Griffiths Belt/CORBIS for page 337 (bottom right);
Photograph on page 347 (top) supplied by kind courtesy of A Special Memory Wedding Chapel;
© Dave G. Houser/CORBIS for page 353;
© Ted Streshinsky/CORBIS for page 354 (top left);
© Bob Rowan; Progressive Image/CORBIS for pages 366 (top left) and 395;
Photograph on page 367 (top) supplied by kind permission of Imam Al-Khoei Islamic Center;
© John McAnulty/CORBIS for page 373 (top);
Photographs on pages 374 (top, bottom left and bottom right) supplied by kind permission of Marilyn Moyer Meditation Chapel, Portland, OR;

Final thanks to Brother Gregory Atherton, OSM, Robert F. Casper/Sarbo®, Patricia B. Lopez and Santa Maria de la Paz, Joni Moss, Bing Owens, Meesam Razvi and Joe Sevenz for their help with this book.